IS ANYTHING HAPPENING?

IS ANYTHING HAPPENING?

MY LIFE AS A NEWSMAN

ROBIN LUSTIG

\Bᵇ\
Biteback Publishing

First published in Great Britain in 2017 by
Biteback Publishing Ltd
Westminster Tower
3 Albert Embankment
London SE1 7SP
Copyright © Robin Lustig 2017

ISBN 978-1-78590-103-4

10 9 8 7 6 5 4 3 2 1

A CIP catalogue record for this book is available from the British Library.

Set in Adobe Garamond Pro

Printed and bound in Great Britain by
CPI Group (UK) Ltd, Croydon CR0 4YY

MIX
Paper from
responsible sources
FSC
www.fsc.org   FSC® C020471

For Ruth, Josh and Hannah

CONTENTS

Who feared us?

People in positions of power who abused that power.

Do-nothing officeholders and bureaucrats. Politicians with dirty money and conflicts of interest. Businesses that violated regulation and operated counter to the public's safety and welfare.

Those who would harm the helpless and the voiceless.

Grifters, grafters, cheats, scammers, influence-peddlers, abusive cops, bad doctors, bent lawyers, look-the-other-way inspectors, under-the-table lobbyists, polluters, fakes, frauds, flim-flammers and fly-by-nights.

They feared us for good reason.

THE LAST PRINT EDITION OF
THE *SEATTLE POST-INTELLIGENCER*,
17 MARCH 2009

ACKNOWLEDGEMENTS

JOURNALISTS' MEMORIES ARE NOTORIOUSLY unreliable, so I have tried wherever I could while writing this book to check my recollections of long-ago events with people who were with me at the time. I am immensely grateful to them all, although, as most of them are also journalists, it may well be that their memories are no better than mine.

I cannot name them all, but I would particularly like to thank Deb Amos, Shyam Bhatia, David Boddy, Margaret Budy, Alice Cairns, Gillian Dear, David Edmonds, Linda Grant, Duncan Greenland, Peter Griffiths, Richard House, Nikki Johnson, Paul Lashmar, David Leigh, Magnus Linklater, Bob Low, Heather Maclean, Philippa Mole at the Guardian and Observer archives, Kylie Morris, Jeremy Mortimer, Anne Sebba and Vicky Taylor. I am especially grateful to my old friend Professor Ivor Gaber for his invaluable comments on an early draft of my final chapter. None of the above-named, of course, is in any way to be held responsible for any errors that are contained in the text that follows.

I also want to thank my former BBC colleague Dan Isaacs, who allowed me access to his extensive collection of photographs of me doing improbable things in improbable places.

Wherever possible, I have provided references for articles or broadcasts referred to, to enable sceptical readers, if they are so minded, to double-check that I have not made it all up. I owe a special debt of gratitude to my father, whose pathological inability to throw anything away meant that I had invaluable access to all of the letters that I wrote to my parents while I was living overseas in the 1960s and '70s.

I am also deeply indebted to Iain Dale of Biteback, who first suggested that I should write a book, and to my editor Olivia Beattie, for her meticulous professionalism, enthusiasm and support.

INTRODUCTION

News is what a chap who doesn't care much about anything wants to read. And it's only news until he's read it. After that it's dead.
SCOOP, EVELYN WAUGH

IN THE DAYS BEFORE the internet, mobile phones, Twitter and 24-hour news channels – in other words, in the days just after dinosaurs roamed the earth – there was only one way for British foreign correspondents to find out what was happening on their patch.

The procedure was to phone the local office of Reuters news agency – after a boozy long lunch or a weekend on the beach – and ask the poor bastard who was on shift: 'Is anything happening, old boy?' That is how I started: as the poor bastard answering the phone in the Reuters office. Decades later, I had the dubious pleasure of being able to turn the tables: as a BBC radio presenter on an evening news programme, I developed a new way of asking the same question when I phoned in to the office every lunchtime: 'What's going on in the world?'

Different words, same question. And it pretty much defines the essence of journalism, or at least of what my journalism has been for more than four decades: a quest to find out what is happening, and then to tell everyone else. This book is an attempt to describe how I did it, why I did it, and what happened to me while I was doing it. I am the son of refugees from Nazi Germany, I did not go to a private school, or to Oxford or Cambridge, yet somehow I still managed to carve out a modestly successful career, usually surrounded by those who were both far better educated and much better connected than I was. (Spoiler alert: it was mainly luck.)

I find it hard to believe that when I started in 1970, reporters out in the field still had to use coin-operated public telephones to make contact with their offices. (Finding a phone that worked was an absolutely essential journalistic skill.) Even in the 1980s, when I was based in the Middle East, I often had to make a booking for an overseas phone call, and it could take several hours for the connection to be made. Writing about it now, in the age of instant information, always makes me feel as if I am writing about Noah assembling his ark.

My journalistic role models were William Boot, the hero of Evelyn Waugh's novel *Scoop*, who was sent overseas by mistake to report on a war he knew nothing about, and Charles Wheeler, the craggy-faced, white-haired BBC correspondent who carried on working until well into his eighties and whose integrity and professionalism exemplified all that is good about journalism. I have to admit, though, that on the Boot–Wheeler spectrum, I have usually been a lot closer to the former than to the latter.

I have always thought of myself first and foremost as a reporter, even if during my twenty-three years at the BBC my main job was sitting in a studio in London asking questions. I would always leap at the chance to fly off somewhere, preferably somewhere off the beaten track, the further away the better. And if it was somewhere I had never been before, that was always a bonus.

There are plenty of faraway places in this book, and plenty of stories about what can go wrong when the demands of editors in London clash head-on with the technological and logistical challenges of reporting from some of the world's poorest countries. But the book starts in a BBC studio, because there is often plenty of drama in a studio too. The main difference between the life of a presenter and the life of a reporter is that presenters can be relatively confident of going home to sleep in their own beds when the day is done. Believe me, it is no small thing.

In the UK, I became mainly known for my work presenting *The World Tonight* on Radio 4, which I used to describe as a broadsheet programme for broadsheet listeners. (Now that there are hardly any broadsheet newspapers left, I am somewhat stuck. But if I tell you that in the days when we shared an office, Jeremy Paxman used to call us the 'senior common room' – it was not meant as a compliment – you will get the general idea.)

Outside the UK, however, I was best known for my work on the BBC World Service. For more than two decades, I was one of the regular presenters on the flagship news programme *Newshour*, and I also presented a global phone-in programme called *Talking Point*, which for a while was broadcast simultaneously on radio, TV and the internet. The potential audience could be measured in the tens of millions, and when I presented the World Service's UK election night broadcasts, I liked to claim – I hope accurately – that I had a bigger audience than all the Dimblebys put together.

Throughout my career, I have suspected that someone, somewhere had made a terrible mistake, and that it was not really me who was meant to be having so much fun. So far, no one has owned up to having made that mistake, even though they know perfectly well who they are. I hope that even if they read this book, they will still have the decency to keep quiet.

CHAPTER 1

THE DAY THE WORLD
CHANGED

To the journalist, every country is rich.
SCOOP, EVELYN WAUGH

I DO NOT DO jetlag. Or, rather, I have always claimed that I do not do jetlag, mainly because if you are flying round the world chasing news stories, there simply is no time for such indulgences. Editors do not, in my experience, take kindly to the notion that just because you have been awake for thirty-six hours, you have had nothing to eat, and your brain is refusing to function, you would rather not wait up till 4.30 a.m. to do yet another two-way conversation with Radio Ulster. (Please note: I have nothing against Radio Ulster.)

Never has my foolish boast been more sorely tested than in September 2001. I had flown overnight from London to Johannesburg to record an hour-long programme with Nelson Mandela. From there, I had flown to Tokyo, via Taipei, to produce a series of reports about the Japanese economy. I had arrived back in London, still claiming – absurdly – not to suffer from jetlag, on the evening of 10 September.

The following afternoon, as I was stumbling about in the kitchen at home trying to find something to eat, the phone rang. It was a colleague at the BBC World Service, sounding seriously stressed. 'Robin, a plane has just flown into the World Trade Center in New York. How soon can you get to Bush House?' Less than forty-five minutes later, just as the first of the Twin Towers crumpled to the ground, I was on air at the start of what was to become several days of round-the-clock live coverage. It was 3 p.m. in London, 10 a.m. in New York.

I remember asking, as I rushed into the studio, if someone could find out how many people were likely to have been working in the two towers. When I got the answer, my blood ran cold. I was told it could be as many as fifty thousand – and I knew that I could not, must not, say that on air. Not until we knew for sure. (My caution was justified; the figure I had been given was a huge exaggeration.)

Live broadcasting often teeters on the edge of either absurdity or disaster. Sometimes both. Everyone involved – producers, sound engineers and, yes, even presenters – put themselves through ridiculous bouts of adrenalin-fuelled stress, often for no better reason than to make sure that the last item in the show will end at precisely the right second. On the BBC World Service, there are 'hard posts' that need to be observed – moments in the programme, accurate to the precise second, when the presenter has to stop talking so that radio stations around the world can opt in to, or out of, the BBC output to make way for their own commercial breaks or news headlines. It is fiendishly complicated, causes immense headaches for all concerned, and the listeners – if it is done properly – are blissfully unaware.

But there was nothing absurd about what happened on 11 September 2001. If your reason for being in journalism is that you want to tell people things that they would not otherwise know, then an event on the scale of what happened that day is about as big as it gets. And I am well aware of the danger of sounding horribly crass when I talk about broadcasters' stress in the context of what so many thousands of families went through that day. The truth is that, just as is the case for emergency workers and medical teams, journalists' professionalism and skill are tested to the full when disaster strikes – and it would be dishonest to pretend that we do not relish the challenge. It is not necessarily a pretty sight, and it is not easy to admit, but journalists get a particular professional satisfaction from doing a job well in the midst of turmoil.

Something very strange happens when you are broadcasting live about a major, unexpected news event – your brain discards all extraneous information and processes only what it needs for the business in hand. With my eyes glued simultaneously to the television screen on the studio wall and the mass of information scrolling across my computer screen, I could not have told you what day of the week it was (I have just looked it up: it was a Tuesday), or even which city I was in. All I knew was that I was broadcasting to millions of people and something truly dreadful had happened.

Try to imagine what it is like to be an editor in charge of a live news programme on the day of a major disaster. It could be an earthquake, a tsunami or a plane crash – the challenges are exactly the same. Which correspondent is closest to the scene? Who else is there? Do we have their phone number? How soon can we put them on air? What can we do while we are trying to find them? Is there anyone in the building who might know something – anything – about what has happened? What is our Plan B? Do we have one? Why the hell not?

You probably get the picture. Now try to imagine being the presenter, sitting in the studio on the other side of the glass window that separates you from the control room. Every time you look up, you see scenes of panic through the glass. Stay calm, you tell yourself, stay calm. Through your headphones comes a constant babble of information and instructions. Rarely does it make much sense.

'We've got Pete. He's next. Go to him now. No. Wait. We've lost him. Read the headlines. No, hang on. He's back. Go to him now. Now! Two minutes with him because tele need him. Oh, shit, they've grabbed him. Sorry.' (At no point, you will have noticed, have you been told who, or where, Pete is.) Now imagine listening to all that while you are interviewing someone else, on a terrible phone line, who has only a rudimentary grasp of the English language.[*]

The events of 9/11 have been told and retold so often that it is not easy now to imagine a time when they had not already happened. For the first few hours after the planes hit the World Trade Center in New York and the Pentagon in Washington, we had no idea if there

---

[*] I once got hold of a copy of the guidelines issued to new BBC radio news producers. One line in particular has remained in my memory: 'Don't pass on too much information to presenters; it only confuses them.'

were more hijacked planes heading for more targets. At one point, the White House, the US Capitol and the State Department were also thought to be under attack – and it was to be several days before the final, terrible death toll could be calculated. Nor did we know whether other, similar attacks were imminent in other cities in other countries – I remember feeling grateful not to be working that day in one of the high-rise office buildings in Canary Wharf.

Working for the BBC on such a day is an awesome responsibility. Both in the UK and around the world, it has a well-deserved reputation for being a reliable source of news. But no organisation is better than the people who work for it, and people working under pressure can sometimes make mistakes. One of the jobs of the news presenters is to try to catch those mistakes – and not to make too many of their own.

Bush House was the internationally known home of the BBC World Service for seventy years, from 1941 until the end of the midday news bulletin on 12 July 2012. ('This is the BBC World Service, broadcasting from Bush House in London.') It was built by, and named after, an American industrialist, Irving T. Bush, who was also responsible for the building of the Bush Terminal (now Industry City) in Brooklyn, New York. Originally designed as a trade centre, when Bush House opened in 1925, it was said to be the most expensive building in the world.

It is certainly an impressive edifice, not unlike a Greek temple on the outside, with its colonnaded portico and imposing main doorway. Inside, though, the BBC, which never actually owned the building, had not been kind to it: decades of refurbishments and changes had turned it into a muddled warren of identical corridors and boxy offices and studios. Only the marble staircase, the bronze-doored lifts and the chutes that in years gone by had taken letters down to the mailroom in the basement (one chute for 'London and Abroad', the other for 'Country Letters') served as reminders of its past splendour.

I grew immensely fond of Bush House, much as one might grow fond of an old piece of furniture, and, like all World Service veterans, I was sad when we had to move out to join the rest of the BBC at the newly extended Broadcasting House, just up the road from Oxford Circus. To me, Bush House represented the home of more knowledge and expertise about more places than anywhere else on earth. In its heyday, more than forty different language services were broadcast from its studios, ranging alphabetically from Albanian to Vietnamese – and each one was staffed by journalists from the country to which they were broadcasting. If there was anything you needed to know about the remotest, tiniest pinprick of a place on the map, you would almost always be able to find someone in Bush House who had at least visited it, and quite possibly had been born and brought up there.

So where better to be on 11 September 2001? Through the third-floor studio, as the hours turned into days, came a procession of BBC experts on Afghanistan, Saudi Arabia, al-Qaeda and Osama bin Laden. It was like being in a seminar in the best university in the world, and, of course, this being the BBC, there was also a correspondent right there on the scene, at the World Trade Center, as the planes struck. (To his immense good fortune, he was on the ground floor, so he was able to get out well before the towers collapsed.)

At some point during the afternoon, a message flashed across the top of my computer screen. It was from a very senior BBC executive, and it said: 'Don't forget this is the biggest story you will ever cover.' Thanks, I thought, I needed that. No pressure. Then I was told that an increasing number of US radio stations were picking up our output, at least in part, apparently, because the National Public Radio network, on which they would normally have relied, had lost their transmitters when the Twin Towers came down.

All the more reason, I realised, to get it right. There could well be people listening to my words who feared that their own relatives were among the victims. To them, this wasn't just a news story; this was intensely, searingly personal. A few days after the attacks, on a BBC phone-in programme, I found myself talking to a teenage boy whose father had been in one of the WTC towers when the planes hit. Nothing had been heard of him since, and the boy was desperate to hear from anyone who might have seen his father that day. It was heartbreaking.

Was 9/11 the biggest story I would ever cover? Without a shadow of a doubt. Did it change the world? It did. At the time, I was reluctant to slip into the easy journalist clichés – our temptation is always to reach for the dictionary of superlatives, as if calling an event 'the biggest ever' or 'the worst ever' will somehow make us sound more important. But, by the time President Bush addressed the American people that night – 'We will make no distinction between the terrorists who committed these acts and those who harbor them' – it was clear that the global repercussions would be both profound and long-lasting.

When I finally handed over the reins of the BBC World Service's continuous programming that evening, I switched on my mobile phone and found a text message from my daughter, Hannah. She was fifteen and had come home from school to find that her usual TV programmes had been replaced by continuous news coverage of the day's events. Her message to me read: 'Dad, what's going on? Are we all going to die?'

CHAPTER 2

FROM SCUD FM TO WILLS AND KATE

The rules are self-imposed ... Not to underestimate the intelligence of the audience, and not to overestimate its information.
ERIC SEVAREID, CBS NEWS

ANY REPORTER'S FIRST INSTINCT when a major story breaks is to get to the scene as quickly as possible. But, by 2001, I had learned that sometimes it can be more rewarding – and certainly less frustrating – to stay put and take a bird's-eye view of what is going on. So I was not one of the thousands of newsmen and women who desperately tried to get to New York within hours of the 9/11 attacks. With the airspace shut and all flights cancelled, the city was virtually sealed off, much to their fury.

It did not take them long to work out that flying into Canada and then driving south across the border was the answer, and that is what they did. I suspect there were soon more reporters in New York City than had ever before been assembled in one place. It was as if the biggest and strongest beast on the planet had been attacked by an unexpectedly fearsome wasp – everyone wanted to see how the wounded beast would react.

This is not the place for a potted history of the first decade of the twenty-first century. I doubt that you need to be reminded that the invasions of Afghanistan and Iraq, the horrors of Guantanamo and Abu Ghraib, the introduction of anti-terrorism legislation and mass surveillance programmes, all flowed from that one cataclysmic event.

If somewhere in the most remote mountains or deserts of Pakistan, Somalia, Yemen or Libya there is a University for the Training of Terrorists, the lessons of 9/11 will surely be a compulsory element on the syllabus. Strike hard, kill hundreds, make sure the TV cameras can get there. They are, unfortunately, lessons that have been learned too well: in the years that followed 9/11, there were attacks in Bali in 2002 (more than two hundred dead); Madrid in 2004 (nearly two hundred dead); London in 2005 (fifty-two dead); and Mumbai in 2008 (a hundred and sixty dead). And that was all before the emergence of the group that chose to call itself Islamic State.

I did get to New York, eventually: on the first anniversary of the attacks, I anchored an entire day of non-stop BBC news coverage from a vantage point in a hotel room high above Ground Zero. It was, of course, unbearably poignant: the day-long roll call of the names of the 2,974 victims, the haunting solo cello of Yo-Yo Ma, the accompanying ceremonies at the Pentagon in Washington and Somerset County, Pennsylvania. I also co-hosted a two-hour global phone-in with one of my oldest friends, Deborah Amos of US National Public Radio. To our regret, it was the only time we were allowed to work together. We thought we made a pretty good team.

It has become commonplace these days to talk of how the revolution in digital communications technology has created a space for a permanent global conversation. Anyone can talk to anyone, wherever they are, whenever they like, often at no cost, thanks to mobile phone and online messaging apps and live streaming technology. In 2002, though, the idea of a global conversation was still new and exciting, and when the BBC linked up with NPR and the American Forces Network, broadcasting simultaneously on all three networks, we did bring people together from right across the globe. So successful were we that an estimated 50,000 people tried to phone in, and I was told later that two of the BBC's three switchboards had crashed while we were on air. Our colleagues in the newsroom were not best pleased when they discovered they could make no outgoing calls.

It took quite a long time for the world to understand the true significance of 9/11 – and it is salutary for those of us in the instant analysis business to look back sometimes on how wrong we often are. One highly respected BBC correspondent – I shall spare his blushes by not naming him – wrote on the first anniversary of the attacks: 'A year later, the world does not seem to have changed so very much after all. The attacks on New York and Washington were not followed up.' I doubt that he would say the same thing now.

I readily admit that I have said, and written, a great deal over the years that turned out to be nonsense. Happily, radio is an ethereal medium: most people only half-hear what you say anyway and, even if they are listening attentively, they will have forgotten your pearls of wisdom within minutes. The important thing for the listener to bear in mind is that reporters rarely know as much as they would like you to think – they hate the idea of having to answer a question with the words 'I don't know', even if that would be by far the most accurate response.

There was, though, one BBC correspondent who ignored all the conventions. His name was Alex Brodie, and he was based in Jerusalem during the first Gulf War in 1991, when Iraq was firing Scud missiles into Israel. More than once I found myself asking him from a studio in London: 'So, Alex, what's been happening?', only to hear a weary, somewhat irritated voice echoing down the line from Jerusalem: 'I … don't … know.' It was not what any presenter wants to hear.

Alex was a first-rate journalist, and he later joined the team of *Newshour* presenters on the World Service. I never discovered if any correspondent had the courage to do to him what he had so enjoyed doing to us when he was in their shoes.[*]

By the time of the 9/11 attacks, I already had quite a bit of experience of what is officially called 'rolling news' but is often known to its practitioners as 'rolling bollocks'. The rationale for non-stop, real-time news is that listeners (or viewers) want to be sure that they are being kept informed of all the latest news as it happens, at any hour of the day or night. Waiting patiently for the next scheduled news bulletin is no longer acceptable. But since the development of news on social media

---

* Alex later left the BBC and founded the highly successful Hawkshead micro-brewery in the Lake District. I have sampled his produce – and very good it is too.

sites, and mobile and online news alerts, it is an open question whether there is still the same appetite or need for continuous news channels on radio and television. In the words of two former BBC news executives, Richard Sambrook and Sean McGuire: 'Cable news established the 24-hour news habit, but today social media and mobile phones fulfil the instant news needs of consumers better than any TV channel can.'[1]

The virus that is rolling news can be traced back to Saddam Hussein. When he invaded Kuwait in 1990, and an international US-led coalition went to war to force him out again, the rolling news channels had a field day. Peter Arnett of CNN, which had until then been derisively known in the trade as the Chicken Noodle Network, became an international celebrity as a result of his dramatic live reports from Baghdad. The BBC had nothing like it, but soon invented a back-of-the-envelope radio equivalent. Its official title was Radio 4 News FM, but it became far better, and more accurately, known as Scud FM.

I shall have more to say about Scud FM, for which I retain enormous affection, in Chapter 12 – I became one of its core team of presenters and quickly learned how to fill several hours of airtime with little or nothing new to report. I had become a novice broadcaster barely a year earlier, but I told my bosses (the 'suits', in BBC-speak) that, unlike my much more experienced colleagues, at least I had the advantage of having reported in my newspaper days from both Iraq and Kuwait, so I did know what they looked like.

And so it was that I joined such established BBC stars as Brian Redhead, John Humphrys, Nick Clarke and Nick Ross. From the beginning of the *Today* programme until the end of *The World Tonight*, if you were listening to Radio 4 on its FM frequency, you were fed a diet consisting only of war news. Plenty of people, including many of the BBC's most senior executives, thought it would be an unmitigated disaster. In fact, it was a huge success and led directly to the launch three years later of Radio 5 Live as an all-news and sports network, and in 1997 of the BBC's all-news TV channel, News 24, later renamed the News Channel.

In the ten years between Scud FM and 9/11, there was at least one other global news event that ate up countless hours of airtime, not only at the BBC but around the world. It was what the police call an RTA, a road traffic accident, as mundane a story as you could imagine. Except that one of the three people who died was Diana, Princess of Wales, probably the best-known – certainly the most photographed – woman on the planet.

Six a.m., Sunday 31 August 1997. The phone rings, my wife answers it and immediately hands it to me. I recognise the voice on the other end: it is Keith Somerville, one of the most experienced and respected editors at the BBC World Service. He uses the minimum number of words to convey the maximum amount of information. 'Robin? Keith. Di and Dodi are dead. Can you come in?'

It was the start of one of the weirdest weeks in my professional life – and, I think, one of the weirdest weeks in modern British history. At one point, we seriously began to wonder whether the British royal family could survive what seemed like a vast wave of public hostility, sweeping tsunami-like towards Buckingham Palace. I began to ask myself if I understood anything at all about the country I lived in.

But first things first. What happened in that Paris underpass? Tell us again. What happened? Hour after hour, with only the skimpiest details of the car crash to go on, we could do little else but repeat the headline, over and over again. 'For those of you just joining us, we have suspended normal programming to bring you continuous news coverage following the death of Princess Diana in a car accident in Paris.' I can still say it in my sleep, nearly twenty years later.

The second question was the obvious one: what does it mean for the future of the royal family? Diana was a superstar, and her story – the child of a broken marriage, an unhappy young princess in a loveless marriage to an unfaithful husband – was the stuff of fairy tales. And then that stupid, unnecessary death that could so easily have been avoided if their driver had not been drinking and if they had all been wearing seatbelts.*

It is rare for me to remember what anyone has said to me in an

---

* Diana's bodyguard, Trevor Rees-Jones, the only person in the car who survived the crash, was the only one who had been wearing a seatbelt.

interview – I have done far too many of them over the years. The truth is that although every interview is of vital importance, and often of real interest, at least to me, at the moment it takes place, I have usually forgotten everything about it within an hour or two. For the same reason, I am too often embarrassed when I meet someone whose opening words after we are introduced are: 'We've already met. You interviewed me once many years ago.'

However, I do remember three remarks made to me about Diana's death by three different interviewees in the hours and days that followed. The first was the journalist and political historian Anthony Howard. At some point on that Sunday morning, I asked him what he thought her death would mean for the royal family. 'I know this might not be a popular thing to say,' he replied, 'but it's the best thing that could have happened for them. She represented a huge problem following her divorce from Prince Charles, and now she's gone.'

The second was the novelist Linda Grant, when I asked her to explain why Diana had attained such an extraordinary level of adulation. She replied:

> Even though she was a princess, she represented something that every woman in Britain could identify with. She was a mother of young children who had struggled with bulimia and post-natal depression. She had been trapped in an unhappy marriage. Her husband had been unfaithful to her. She didn't get on with her in-laws, and she fell in love with someone she shouldn't have. So she became a clothes horse on which a great many women could pin their own unhappiness.

The third was the Scottish political theorist and republican Tom Nairn, who said in response to the public reaction to Diana's death: 'The people of Britain have this week elected their first president. The trouble is she's already dead.'

Two other people whom I interviewed on that Sunday in August 1997 were the actor and comedian Billy Connolly and his wife Pamela Stephenson, who had been friends of Diana's. I had been warned that Pamela Stephenson, who has a PhD and is a licensed clinical psychologist in the US, was very particular about how she was to be addressed. So, before the pre-recorded interview on the line to their home in California, I checked with her: 'I understand you prefer to be addressed as Dr Pamela Connolly.' Quick as a flash, back came the unmistakable gravelly, Glaswegian tones of her husband: 'Yeah, and I prefer to be addressed as Captain Fantastic.' It was a welcome moment of relief at the end of a very long day.

There has been a great deal of debate over the years about whether the media over-reported – and misrepresented – the public reaction to Diana's death. My own belief, in retrospect, is that we did, but for understandable reasons. It was not because somehow the media were in awe of royalty (although large sections of them were certainly in awe of Diana), but because they were genuinely taken aback by the vast piles of flowers that were left outside Kensington Palace and the rising tide of anger among some exceedingly vociferous Di-admirers and Charles-haters.

On the Tuesday after her death, I went to Kensington Palace myself to talk to some of the people who had gathered there. I was so shocked by the vehemence of the anti-royal family sentiments that I advised my editors not to broadcast them. They were unlikely to be typical, I said; I was worried that I may have just found the angriest and most vocal people in the crowd, attracted by the sight of a BBC microphone.

But by the following day, those same sentiments that I had heard, but not broadcast, were on several newspapers' front pages. Not for the first time, or the last, my judgement had been less than perfect. By the following Friday, Scotland Yard were warning that they were expecting up to two million people to line the streets of the funeral procession, and the route was doubled in length to accommodate the anticipated crowds.

It was as if some hitherto undiagnosed form of mass hysteria had taken hold – but it was officialdom and the media that had succumbed. I was one of the BBC's team of commentators who would line the funeral procession route, and I had been allocated a position in Whitehall, just across from the archway into Horse Guards Parade, from which the procession would emerge before turning right down

Whitehall to make its way towards Parliament Square and Westminster Abbey.

We had had less than a week to prepare for the occasion, but the BBC has a well-oiled royal funeral machine permanently on standby, so it managed to get itself into shape in good time. As I sat in my commentary box, perched precariously fifteen feet above street level, I reflected that I would probably have at most sixty seconds on air as the *cortège* passed in front of me. It was my first experience of live commentary and I did not want to mess it up.

Next to me in the commentary box was an experienced outside broadcast producer, and on a makeshift desk in front of us was a tiny TV screen on which we could watch the progress of the funeral procession as it made its way through central London from Kensington Palace. After a long, long wait, it reached us, and only at the very last moment did I remember to look up from the TV screen and focus directly on the scene in front of us.

Immediately, my eye was caught by the simple wreath of white roses on the gun carriage bearing Diana's coffin, and a white card with just a single word on it: 'Mummy'. As I described the scene, I looked at her two sons, William, then just fifteen, and Harry, aged twelve, walking stiffly behind the coffin in their immaculate dark suits, white shirts and black ties. I have a tendency to cry at the least provocation, much to my family's embarrassment, and it was all I could do to keep my voice steady.

Because of the fears of unprecedented crowds, all BBC personnel involved in coverage of the funeral had been booked into central London hotels so that we could walk to our allocated positions before dawn and be ready in good time. No one was going to risk relying on public transport or taxis. I set three alarms for 4 a.m., and I did not oversleep.

But the sight that greeted me as I left the hotel and set out on my pre-dawn walk through central London was not at all what I had expected. Yes, there were people who had spent the night on the pavements, huddled in their silver-foil thermal blankets, shimmering in the reflected glow of the London street lights, but there were nothing like the numbers that we had been led to expect. The numbers swelled, of course, as the morning wore on, but the estimates had been wildly exaggerated.

I think I know why. First, the media had been madly in love with Diana, and the reason was obvious: she was the best guarantee of reader interest in decades. Put a picture of Di on the front page and you sold more papers. It was as simple as that. (The *Daily Express* thinks it is still true, twenty years later.) So there was a natural tendency to exaggerate the reaction to her death, which in turn fed back into public sentiment. It was a perfect emotional feedback loop, increasing in intensity with every passing day.

Second, TV cameras love crowds, again for a very simple reason: you can see them and film them, and they look suitably dramatic. What the cameras don't see, and therefore don't show, is all the people who have stayed at home and gone about their everyday business dry-eyed. It is the same with mass demonstrations: no matter how big the crowd – for example, the estimated 750,000 to a million people who protested against the imminent invasion of Iraq in February 2003 – there will always be many more people who did not bother to leave home. But you will not see them on the TV news.

So yes, I do think we got it wrong at the time of Diana's death, but I do not think it was a deliberate conspiracy. I know there were anxious debates, especially at the BBC World Service, about how much time to devote to the story. I argued, and I still think I was right, that there was immense international interest both in her and in the British royal family and it would have been crazy not to have reflected that. The same applied when Michael Jackson died in 2009 – some public figures really do have a global reach, even if they are not world leaders or Nobel Prize-winners.

I finally realised that we had probably overdone the Diana story on the first anniversary of her death. It passed virtually unnoticed. *Sic transit gloria mundi*.

I would never describe myself as a royalist, or as a traditionalist – I am, after all, a child of the '60s – but I do have a soft spot for a nice bit of pageantry. Military bands, colourful costumes and meticulously choreographed ceremonial can always be guaranteed to bring a tear to my eye. To me, it is like theatre, and I felt much the same when I attended Midnight Mass one Christmas Eve in St Peter's Basilica in Rome – I do not have a religious bone in my body, but I did love the sheer theatricality of it all.

In November 1999, I was asked to be Radio 4's commentator on Remembrance Sunday. I knew I had been called up from the subs' bench: the Queen and Duke of Edinburgh were both away at a Commonwealth conference in South Africa, and the BBC's royal correspondent, Nick Witchell, who is as much part of the traditional Remembrance Sunday proceedings as the two-minute silence, had gone with them, leaving Radio 4 scrabbling around to find someone to fill the gap.

I felt the full weight of the responsibility upon my shoulders. This was not like presenting any old news programme; this was being the voice of BBC radio on the most solemn day of the ceremonial calendar. So I read all the briefing notes and tried to memorise the wealth of information on the file cards. They looked as if they had been passed down by successive generations of commentators over the decades, and I was surprised to discover that they had not been written on vellum and kept tightly rolled in an airtight box.

As it was the last Remembrance Sunday of the century, I decided to add a *fin de siècle* flourish to my script. 'This twentieth century has been a century of war,' I intoned. 'And as we look back and remember, perhaps also, at the century's end, we look forward too, and hope for a more peaceful century to come.' What a forlorn hope that turned out to be.

There is one moment above all on Remembrance Sunday when you do not want to make a mistake. As Big Ben strikes 11 a.m., the moment the First World War armistice was signed on 11 November 1918, silence descends on Whitehall – and the commentator must not, repeat *not*, break that silence. I had decided, stupidly, that just before Big Ben's bongs, I would recite a few lines from the Ode of Remembrance by Laurence Binyon, and I worked out the timings to the last second, so that I would get to the end of the last line just as the clock whirred into action.

I was one second out. The military bands fell silent, and in my best Richard Dimbleby commentator voice, I read the poem's best-known lines: 'They shall grow not old, as we that are left grow old: Age shall not weary them, nor the years condemn. At the going down of the sun and in the morning…' Which is when, to my horror, Big Ben started chiming. The final four words – 'We will remember them' – were drowned out.

I was never asked to do the Remembrance Sunday commentary again.

Fortunately, BBC bosses can be a forgiving lot when they are so minded and, as time passed, my faux pas, which contrary to my fears did not result in a major constitutional crisis, was forgotten. Even so, I was quietly relieved to be called back into action for the funeral of the Queen Mother, whose death in 2002, at the remarkable age of 101, put an end to one of the longest waits in British journalism. It is well known by now, so I am not giving away any state secrets, that the BBC, like other major broadcasters, holds regular rehearsals for what are known diplomatically as 'Category A' deaths, and generations of BBC journalists had got into the habit of praying every night that the death of the Queen Mother would not be announced on their watch.

I got away somehow with attending only one of these death rehearsals; it was so long ago that we were still using spools of magnetic tape, and the one – admittedly rather important – lesson that was learned was that no one could remember where the tape of the national anthem was kept. Fortunately, it all became a lot less fraught after the dawning of the digital revolution, when all the senior editors who needed to know what to do could access special computer files with everything already prepared and ready for broadcast.

For the Queen Mother's funeral, I was again allocated a commentary position in Whitehall, and, as for the funeral of Princess Diana, the BBC's royal funeral machine functioned flawlessly. It helped, of course, that the BBC has an extensive network of underground cables permanently in place in some of the key locations – in front of Buckingham Palace and in and around Westminster Abbey, for example, so that when the need arises, they simply have to plug in the cameras and microphones and they are ready to roll. (Some of the network is shared with other broadcasters like ITN and Sky.)

I had learned by now, having already been the BBC World Service commentator for the funeral of King Hussein of Jordan in 1999, that when commentating at funerals, the usual rules of broadcasting do not always apply. 'Dead air', for example, that awful, embarrassing silence when something technical has gone wrong or a broadcaster's brain has frozen, is not a problem at a funeral: after all, silence equals respect, as do long pauses. And if you really do not have anything to say, you simply describe what you can see in front of your eyes, very … very … slowly.

Perhaps I sound as if I am mocking when I refer to the 'BBC's royal funeral machine'. Nothing could be further from the truth, because when I was first introduced to its inner workings, I was awestruck by the precision of its engineering and the care with which it is built and maintained. To be a BBC royal event commentator is to be a tiny cog in an immensely complex piece of machinery; all that is required is that you mesh perfectly with the other cogs.

Fortunately, not every major royal event is a funeral, so the mood was very different on 29 April 2011, when Prince William, second in line to the throne, married Kate Middleton, a – shock! – commoner, who seemed to have a much better idea of what she was getting into than poor Princess Di had done thirty years earlier. The BBC's briefing notes for the occasion ran to more than 100 pages, and they were worth reading with care. This time, I had been allocated a position actually on Horse Guards Parade, rather than outside it, and I had been provided with plenty of facts and figures about all the historic buildings that flank the parade ground.

To the north, the Old Admiralty building, completed in 1726 and described, somewhat unflatteringly, as Britain's first purpose-built office block. To the south, the Foreign and Commonwealth Office, designed in the Italianate style by George Gilbert Scott and completed in 1868. To the west, the green open spaces of St James's Park, and to the east, the archway leading into Whitehall, through which the royal couple would ride on their way to Westminster Abbey. I even managed to squeeze in a disrespectful fact of my own: that beach volleyball would be played on the parade ground when the Olympic Games came to town the following year.

About two-thirds of the way through the royal wedding briefing pack was a section entitled 'The bride's hair', which contained invaluable information about her favourite stylists and the advance speculation about how she would wear her hair on the big day. The next section was entitled 'The groom's hair' and was much shorter, as indeed was his hair. It consisted of a single sentence and I remember the words exactly: 'Don't be silly.'

I was, therefore, perfectly prepared when the happy couple's open carriage passed in front of my commentary box and I was able to announce to a waiting world, with all the authority of which I was capable: 'I can confirm that the bride is wearing her hair down.' I acknowledge that it was perhaps not a scoop that added greatly to the sum of human knowledge. Even so, I have never fully understood why some of my more serious-minded colleagues at *The World Tonight* claimed to be shocked and horrified that I would stoop so low as to comment on royal hairstyles.

CHAPTER 3

THE GOOD, THE BAD...

No matter how imperfect things are, if you've got a free press everything is correctable, and without it everything is concealable.
NIGHT AND DAY, TOM STOPPARD

THERE ARE BROADLY THREE types of people that a journalist encounters professionally: they can be categorised as players, pundits or 'real people'. Players are the people who have the power to change things or who are themselves in the news: political leaders, businesspeople, sportsmen and women. Pundits are the ones who have specialist knowledge and who are able to explain the significance of a newsworthy development: academics, commentators or other journalists. Real people? The rest of the world.

Some of them are interesting, some are boring; some stay in the memory for ever. Like Pepile, who was seven years old when I met her in her bare, stone-built home at the end of a dusty hillside track in the rolling countryside of KwaZulu-Natal in South Africa. She was desperately ill with Aids, having been infected by a neighbour who had raped her in the belief that having sex with a virgin would cure him of the disease. She sang for us and showed off the few words of English she had learned before becoming too ill to go to school. She was one of the saddest, and sweetest, children I had ever met, and when I got back to London a few days later, I emailed the health workers who were caring for her and asked if there was anything I could do to help.

Their reply broke my heart. 'You're too late. She died.'

It was more than fifteen years ago and I remember her to this day.

At the other extreme was Radovan Karadžić, the leader of the Bosnian Serbs known as the 'Butcher of Bosnia', who was indicted for war crimes in 1995 and eventually captured in 2008. I met him when he came to London in 1992 for so-called peace talks, at a time when his forces were laying siege to the Bosnian capital, Sarajevo, and firing mortar and artillery shells into the city at a huge cost to human life.

I told my colleagues that I did not relish the prospect of interviewing a man whom I regarded even then as a war criminal. But they were insistent, so we reached a deal that would enable me to live with my conscience while still doing the job for which I was being paid.

'Show him into the studio and then call me,' I said. 'I won't shake his hand, and I won't make small talk. I'll go into the studio, I'll do the interview and then I'll say, "Thank you" and walk out.'

That is what we did. I challenged him as hard as I could when he denied that his forces were firing indiscriminately into a heavily populated city and I hoped that listeners would understand that he was lying. I was persuaded, reluctantly, that they deserved a chance to be able to make up their own minds, but I hated doing it.

Karadžić had an extravagant head of flowing silver hair, of which he seemed inordinately proud. He also had what I can only describe as 'dead eyes', and not an ounce of charm. He had studied psychiatry, including for a time at Columbia University in New York, and spoke reasonable, if heavily accented, English. In the 1980s, he had been convicted of embezzlement and fraud in connection with a property deal; there were also reports that he had been suspected of signing fake medical certificates while he was employed at a hospital in Sarajevo.

Four years after I interviewed him in London, following the signing of the Dayton peace agreement that ended the Bosnian War, I travelled to Sarajevo to report on the aftermath of what had been the bloodiest conflict in Europe since the end of the Second World War. An estimated 100,000 people had been killed during five years of conflict. Karadžić was now in hiding, having been indicted by a specially constituted war crimes tribunal in The Hague. But I soon discovered that just about everyone in Sarajevo seemed to know where he was, so I got someone to draw me a map, showing exactly where he was believed to be living.

Together with *World Tonight* producer Craig Swan, with whom I was to make many more overseas trips over the next few years, I set out to find him. Along the way, on the road to Pale, in the mountains outside Sarajevo, we encountered a UN checkpoint, manned by Ghanaian soldiers.

'Excuse me, we're looking for Dr Karadžić's house. We've been told he lives along this road and wondered if you had seen him.'

They laughed heartily. In theory, they should have been keeping a careful lookout for him, but they could not have been less interested in our information as to his likely whereabouts.

'Who is this guy?' one of them asked with a grin. 'We've never seen him.'

'But this is the right road?'

'Yes. This is the road. You can drive maybe two kilometres and then you will see the house on the right-hand side.'

They were right. At the end of the driveway were two Serb police officers. I told them we hoped to be able to interview Dr Karadžić and asked them to convey a message to him that we were waiting outside. There was something utterly surreal about standing outside the home of an indicted, supposedly fugitive, war criminal, while armed police passed on a request for an interview.

The answer, when it came, was no. 'Dr Karadžić is not at home, so now we would like you to leave.' We saw little point in arguing.

Perhaps I should have been disappointed, but I was not. We had surreptitiously recorded all our conversations along the way, so we had a wonderfully dramatic piece of radio, proving that the alleged war criminal's whereabouts were perfectly well known, even to the UN, and that he was being deliberately allowed to evade capture.

He was finally arrested twelve years later, after apparently having lived under an assumed identity in Belgrade since 1999. He had grown a huge white beard, had a long mane of white hair and wore a giant pair of glasses. He called himself Dr Dragan Dabić and had set himself up as a practitioner of alternative medicine. In March 2016, the international war crimes tribunal in The Hague found him guilty of genocide, war crimes and crimes against humanity, and he was sentenced to forty years in jail.

I have not deliberately gone out of my way to cross paths with people accused of war crimes, but Karadžić is not the only one I have encountered. During my time based in Jerusalem as the Middle East correspondent for *The Observer*, I reported on the trial of a man known as Ivan the Terrible, John Demjanjuk, a Ukrainian-American who was alleged to have been a brutally sadistic guard at the Treblinka death camp in Nazi-occupied Poland in 1942 and 1943.

He had been deported from the US to stand trial in Israel, and his family had come with him. One weekend, when we were relaxing at the American Colony Hotel, the favoured hang-out for all correspondents in Jerusalem, I noticed that my then five-year-old son was in the hotel garden, playing with Demjanjuk's grandchildren. My immediate instinct was to snatch him away, but then I paused. Even if Demjanjuk was guilty of the appalling crimes that he was alleged to have committed, his grandchildren were guilty of nothing at all. So why should I mind if my son played with them? The truth is that I did mind, but I did not stop him.

Demjanjuk was found guilty in 1988 and sentenced to death. But the conviction was overturned on appeal after serious doubts emerged that he had ever been at Treblinka. He returned to the US but was then deported again, many years later, to face trial in Germany, where he was accused of having been a guard at a different Nazi camp, Sobibór. Again, there were serious doubts about his true identity, but again he was convicted, this time of being an accessory to the murder of some 28,000 Jews. He died at the age of ninety-one before his appeal against the German conviction could be heard, and the conviction was therefore invalidated.

Was Demjanjuk a war criminal? Because the trials took place so long after the events in which he was alleged to have participated – and because the identity documents on which the prosecutors relied could so easily have been forged – my own conclusion is that his guilt was never satisfactorily proved. But even if it had been, I think I would still have been right to allow my son to play with his grandchildren.

The first time I interviewed Henry Kissinger, the former US Secretary of State under Presidents Richard Nixon and Gerald Ford, was in

1993 for a BBC television film about the role of NATO following the end of the Cold War. We flew to New York, set up the cameras and lights in a book-lined room in his suite of offices – and waited.

When the great man entered, he took one look at the lighting rig, which had been set up so that some of the light would bounce off the bookcases and cast him partly in shadow, and growled. 'Huh,' he said in that unmistakable, heavy German accent. 'You vant to make me look like a var criminal.' He then sat down without further comment and indicated that he was ready to begin the interview.

I have never been quite sure what to make of a man who has no apparent objection to being made to look like a war criminal. He was well aware that many believed he was guilty of war crimes for his role in the US bombing of Cambodia during the Vietnam War, but he was also the recipient of a Nobel Peace Prize, so perhaps that meant more to him than the lighting for a BBC television interview.

Editors love it when they land an interview with a major world figure. With luck, it will get the name of their programme in the newspapers, and clips from their interview will feature on the news bulletins. Immense effort goes into arranging these interviews, although, if truth be told, they do not often yield genuinely interesting insights. I would not want to pretend that I did not enjoy meeting world-famous politicians, but I was not so keen on the enormous stress that accompanied the entire interview process, and the absurd and unnecessary hoops that we had to jump through before getting to see the object of our desires.

Political leaders lead busy lives, with every minute of their day controlled by all-powerful diary secretaries. When unexpected events disrupt their schedule, interviews with BBC broadcasters can often be the first casualty, no matter how many months in advance the arrangements were made, or how many phone calls and emails have confirmed that the interview will take place.

So my default position before every major interview was: 'It probably won't happen.' I am not a natural pessimist, but I prefer to be proved right than to be disappointed. I once spent an entire day in Kiev sitting outside the office of the then Ukrainian Prime Minister

Yulia Tymoshenko waiting for a promised interview. Every time her office door opened, she would see us sitting there and smile apologetically. At the end of the day, we were told, 'Sorry, there just wasn't time.'

In the Cambodian capital, Phnom Penh, we had been promised an interview with the country's strongman Prime Minister Hun Sen, a man who was notoriously unwilling to be interviewed. I was more than usually sceptical, but his office repeatedly confirmed the arrangements. It was only as we were getting into a taxi to drive to his office at the appointed hour that they called to cancel. 'So sorry, the Prime Minister is unwell.'

'Will he be better tomorrow?'

'No. We don't know when he will be better. So sorry.'

In Abuja, the capital of Nigeria, we were promised an interview with the then President, Olusegun Obasanjo. Again, I was sceptical, but at exactly the appointed hour, he swept into the room where we had been waiting and did the interview.

I interviewed him a second time some years later, just after a deeply flawed election during which everything that could go wrong did go wrong. Ballot papers were not ready in time, and those that had been printed by polling day often failed to get to the polling stations. Lines of voters were turned away when officials ran out of ballot papers, and there were – as always in Nigeria – widespread allegations of fraud.

The President readily acknowledged that it had been an imperfect process but was still in ebullient form. He was, I think, one of Africa's more impressive leaders – far from perfect, to be sure – and it is arguable that he failed to deliver what so many Nigerians still hope for: an end to corruption and a reliable electricity supply. In what should be one of the continent's wealthiest countries, it really ought not to be too much to ask for.

On the other side of Africa, in Uganda, one of the world's longest-serving leaders, President Yoweri Museveni, first elected in 1986, also promised us an interview. There was one condition: it would have to be conducted at his ranch, about a five-hour drive from the capital, Kampala, and we would have to be there by 10 a.m. Setting out before dawn for an interview I never expected would take place was not my idea of the glamorous life that foreign correspondents are supposed to live – but we made the journey, and, to my surprise, we got the interview.

There had been an earlier condition that needed to be met as well: the President's foreign media adviser, a former international cricketer called John Nagenda, had challenged my producer colleague, David Edmonds, to a tennis match. The deal was that the loser would buy dinner at a restaurant to be chosen by the winner. Mr Nagenda (always Mr Nagenda, never John) was by then in his late sixties but still prided himself on his physical fitness. I suggested to Dave that perhaps this was one tennis match it might be politic to lose.

In the spirit of comradeship, I should not have been as relieved as I was when Dave pulled a muscle in his leg in the second set and had to retire hurt. We duly bought Mr Nagenda dinner in a fancy Chinese restaurant and in return he invited us to a traditional open-air Ugandan feast a few days later. He also generously provided a picnic lunch for us while we waited patiently on the lawns of President Museveni's ranch. It included ham sandwiches, which Dave politely declined. 'I'm afraid I'm a vegetarian, Mr Nagenda. And I'm also Jewish.'

Our host professed himself shocked. 'Are you a homosexual as well?' We decided without exchanging a word that this was neither the time nor the place to be offended, so we let it go.

Unlike Obasanjo, Museveni did not enjoy being interviewed and had little charm. He did not like being pressed on why he kept standing for re-election, especially when I ventured to compare him to Nelson Mandela, who had stood down after just five years in office. Museveni's response was: 'You do not change your doctor when you are in the middle of treatment for cancer.' In his eyes, he was the doctor, and Uganda was the patient. Next question.

I have tried over the years to work out what, if anything, all these powerful men have in common. Admittedly, my assessments are based on only fleeting impressions, half an hour, maybe an hour, in their presence, always in the semi-formal setting of an interview for broadcast. Nevertheless, I have reached some conclusions.

With rare exceptions (Museveni being one of them), they have an element of magnetism in their character. It is a form of charisma, an ability to appear interested – and interesting, at the same time, so that whoever they are with wants to hear what they think. Most of them, even those with a reputation for political ruthlessness, also have a degree of charm that can be disarming.

When I met President Hugo Chávez of Venezuela, I described him as 'a charming provocateur'. To his critics, he was one of the most dangerous politicians in Latin America – he was close to Cuba, Libya and Iran, and an implacable enemy of the United States. But to this BBC interviewer, he was a pussy cat, having carefully read his briefing notes ahead of time so that he could demonstrate his impressive familiarity with my CV.

His security people, on the other hand, were not so charming. After we had set up our makeshift TV studio in his Paris hotel suite, they peremptorily threw us out so that they could sweep and swab every last bit of our equipment to ensure that there were no concealed explosives. Even the earpieces – one for me, and one for the President so that he could hear his simultaneous interpreter translating my questions – had to be checked. Charm and paranoia are not always mutually exclusive.

Another unlikely charmer was the Palestinian leader Yasser Arafat. The first time I met him was at an Islamic conference in Kuwait in 1987, when, true to his reputation as a night animal, he summoned a select band of Western correspondents for an impromptu post-midnight press conference.

'Why don't you all introduce yourselves?' he suggested, as we sat round a giant oval-shaped table. 'Tell me where you are from.' I described what happened next in a piece I wrote after his death in 2004.

In turn, we each named our home town and the publication or broadcast organisation we represented. 'No, no,' he grinned. 'Where in Jerusalem do you all live?' This was guaranteed to make us feel distinctly queasy. It was true that many of us were indeed based in Jerusalem, but it was not something we were keen to admit to, as no Arab state other than Egypt in the 1980s would accept travellers from Israel – hence, frequent overnight stops in Cyprus and hasty swapping of passports. Score one to the Chairman.[2]

Perhaps it was just my imagination, but I often sensed a degree of semi-concealed menace when I encountered world leaders. Behind the eyes, there seemed to be an unspoken warning: 'Don't forget who I am. Don't mess with me.' The trick was to remember the advice supposedly given to a newly elected MP, terrified at the prospect of facing the baying mob on the other side of the House of Commons: 'Imagine them in their pyjamas.'

And, of course, as a journalist with a job to do, remember what that job is: to ask the questions that need to be asked, and insist, where possible, on a proper answer.

Even Nelson Mandela conveyed some of that 'Don't mess with me' aura. Yes, he had charm by the bucket-load, but he knew who he was, and what he represented, and he certainly did not like being messed around or kept waiting. Which, unfortunately, was exactly what happened when I flew to Johannesburg in August 2001 to record an hour-long programme with him and his wife, Graça Machel.

For some reason, it had been decided to record the programme in London rather than in Johannesburg. That meant establishing a satellite link – and satellite links are notoriously unreliable. Mandela's time was precious – he was already eighty-three years old and in poor health – and for an hour-long programme we had been allocated … one hour.

He and his wife arrived precisely on time, introductions were made, they sat down, microphones were attached, and: 'Shall we start?' 'Not yet,' came the voice in my earpiece. 'We haven't got the link yet.'

Believe me, making small talk with the most admired man on the planet is seriously nerve-racking. Fortunately, I had recently met his former comrade-in-arms Denis Goldberg, who had been one of his co-defendants at the Rivonia trial in 1964. (Goldberg was the only white defendant in the trial and had been the first to be released from jail, in 1985.) I was therefore able to tell Mandela a bit about Goldberg's life in London, where we were near neighbours. He was gracious and understanding, but I knew that the minutes were ticking by, and I dreaded him getting up at the end of our allotted slot, leaving us with an embarrassing hole to fill. When we finally got going, I decided to plough on regardless, blithely ignoring our supposed stop time, until his much-feared personal assistant Zelda la Grange stepped in to make clear that our luck had run out.

We were still several minutes short, and I never found out how the BBC managed to fill the resulting hole in the schedule. In my experience, there are some questions that it is better not to ask.

Was I nervous when I met these global titans? Of course I was. Was I intimidated or cowed? No, because I believe that interviewers are automatically equipped with a special suit of protective armour. It is invisible externally, but it exists inside their heads. This special suit enables the interviewer to break all the usual rules of social intercourse: you are allowed to ask rude questions, you are allowed to interrupt, and you are allowed to be a major pain in the backside. You are invincible in your suit of armour.

If I could choose whom to interview, I would always prefer writers and historians over politicians. The writers are usually articulate and have interesting things to say about the world we live in, and the historians are often able to make sense of it all by referring back to what has happened in the past.

So, for example, the Nigerian writer Chimamanda Ngozi Adichie, the award-winning author of *Half of a Yellow Sun* and *Americanah*. I interviewed her after she had given a lecture in London about the novelist's craft, which she defined as turning facts into truth, so I thought it would be interesting to contrast the way that novelists tell stories with the way journalists do.

'If you and I were to witness the same event,' I asked her, 'and then each of us wrote about it, how would our accounts differ?' She looked across the studio desk and smiled.

'People would be moved by what I wrote; they would be informed by what you wrote.'[3]

I still think a lot about that distinction, and I still envy the novelist's ability to convert facts into truth.

❦

The bread and butter of any BBC news presenter's job is interviewing British politicians. The truth – how can I put this? – is that most of them are not people with whom I would choose to go on holiday. I did not buy them lunches, or drinks – and I don't think I have ever exchanged a Christmas card with anyone who has the letters MP after their name.

Fortunately, there are a handful who come close to being fully functioning human beings. The former Tory Chancellor Ken Clarke has always been a man who clearly enjoys life, both in and out of politics, and he was perfectly happy to be regarded as a normal human being. I once interviewed him immediately after he had been interviewed by a colleague from the BBC Radio 1 news programme *Newsbeat*. 'Ah, *The World Tonight*,' he said as we shook hands. 'I'd better try to get it right this time.' It was certainly less than complimentary about Radio 1's listeners, but at least it seemed to show that he was not taking himself too seriously.

Mo Mowlam, the Labour former Northern Ireland Secretary, was another minister who gave every impression of enjoying life, even though throughout her time in office she was secretly suffering from the brain tumour that eventually killed her, at the age of fifty-five, in 2005.

At one Labour Party conference, when I was due to interview her live some time after 10 p.m., she turned up half an hour early. 'You're rather early,' I remarked. 'I'm also rather drunk,' she replied, 'so you'd better find me some strong coffee.'

I often felt that one reason why politicians sometimes seemed reluctant to appear on the programme was that it meant they would have to go easy on the vino during dinner.

Another possible reason was given, although not to me personally, by another former Labour minister, Peter Mandelson. According to a newspaper colleague, who later gleefully recounted the conversation to me, Mandelson observed that although he enjoyed appearing on *The World Tonight*, 'I always feel as if I am talking to myself.' (The insult was entirely undeserved, as far more people usually tune in to *The World Tonight* than to, for example, *Newsnight* or *Channel 4 News*.)

Some politicians are simply rude. Robin Cook, the Labour Foreign Secretary from 1997 until 2001, was a man for whom I had considerable respect, but he had a notoriously short fuse. Interviewing him once at an EU summit, I was less than thrilled when, after a perfunctory couple of minutes, he turned on his heel and walked off with the words 'I think that's quite enough, don't you?'

The early-twentieth-century American journalist and satirist H. L. Mencken came up with an admirably pithy way to describe how journalists should approach politicians: 'Journalist is to politician as dog is to lamp-post.' I have always found it an extremely useful axiom to keep in mind.

And perhaps this is as good a place as any to put to rest one of the most enduring myths of contemporary British journalism. It was not Jeremy Paxman who pioneered the idea that interviewers encountering a politician should always ask themselves: 'Why is this lying bastard lying to me?' The earliest reference I have come across is in the memoirs[4] of a great former Fleet Street figure, Louis Heren, who rose to become deputy editor of *The Times*. He described how, during the fuel crisis of 1946–47, when he was a young reporter, he asked a colleague from the Communist Party newspaper, the *Daily Worker*, for some advice before interviewing a senior government official. The response was: 'Always ask yourself why these lying bastards are lying to you.' Heren added: 'I still ask myself that question today.'

Heren also spelt out the essential mindset for any decent reporter:

If death is to be the last enemy, for all reporters the enemy on earth is authority. He comes in many guises, benign, authoritarian, democratic, elitist, populist, ideological, stupid or just plain nasty. He can stand at the dispatch box in the House of Commons or above Lenin's tomb in Red Square. He can sit in the Oval Office of the White House in Washington or in the TUC headquarters in London. He is the enemy because he holds, and can seek to deny or falsify, information the reporter wants. What is more, what he says often has to be reported,

including the half-truths and prevarications. To that extent he holds
the high ground and dominates the terrain.

It is as true now as it was when Heren wrote those words. Two examples: the first is from the time in the 1990s when the post-Thatcher
Conservative Party was tearing itself apart over Europe. I was interviewing two Tory MPs from opposite wings of the party, men who
were known to disagree with each other about virtually everything.
As soon as the interview was under way, it became clear that they
had agreed beforehand that they would form a united front – try as I
might, I failed to entice a single murmur of disagreement from either
of them. As they left the studio, I heard them sniggering: 'Well, that
wasn't what he expected, was it?'

On another occasion, we had been tipped off that the former
Conservative Cabinet minister Cecil Parkinson was making himself
available to say some disobliging things about the way a successor
was implementing a particular policy. In the studio, it was a different
story: he lavished his colleague with generous praise and paid tribute
to his skill and sagacity. As he left, he apologised: 'Sorry about that, I
just felt he needed a bit of support.'

Sometimes, the lying bastards lie.

There are a few politicians who seem genuinely to enjoy the cut
and thrust of debate and who are happy to engage with an interviewer
without necessarily sticking to their party's same old talking points.
David Willetts, David Blunkett and Menzies Campbell are just three
whom I would always enjoy talking to, not because I always agreed
with them but because I knew there was a good chance that they
could provide light rather than heat on whatever was the topic under
discussion. (And I hope you noticed how old BBC habits die hard:
without even trying, I have named one figure from each of the three
main UK political parties.)

So what, really, is the point of interviewing politicians, if they either
lie or say nothing of any interest? Hope springs eternal, I suppose,
and there are a few occasions when, either deliberately or by mistake,
politicians actually say something in a broadcast interview that they

have not said before. But that is not the main point: interviews on radio or television are now virtually the only occasions when voters can assess for themselves the claims of those whom they have elected to high office.

If politicians refuse repeatedly to answer a particular question, voters can draw the appropriate conclusion. If they obfuscate and dissemble, voters will notice. If they are honest and upfront, likewise. It would, of course, be better if voters themselves were able to ask the questions – hence the enduring popularity of programmes like *Question Time* and *Any Questions?* – but journalists who are properly briefed and good at their jobs can also have their uses.

Between 2007 and 2010, the British Foreign Secretary was David Miliband, a ferociously clever and hugely ambitious Labour politician who had every reason to suppose that he might one day be Prime Minister. During his time at the Foreign Office, I interviewed him probably more often than any other senior politician before or since, not only because foreign policy was always *The World Tonight*'s main interest but also because he was unusually willing to make himself available. On one occasion, we devoted an entire programme to an in-depth interview with him, interspersed with field reports from the world's main trouble spots. He covered the terrain effortlessly and gave the appearance of having thoroughly enjoyed the experience.

Miliband also had the distinction, as local government minister in 2005, of having made one of the most open confessions ever of a government U-turn. After it was decided to abandon plans to revalue all residential properties for council tax purposes, he said on *Question Time* on BBC television: 'I am happy to come on this programme and say, "Be in no doubt this is a U-turn." No one can accuse us of trying to cover it up – it's a U-turn.' If only more of his colleagues could have been persuaded to be equally forthright.

I was never a disciple of the Rottweiler school of interviewing, even though I enjoyed a good cut-and-thrust as much as the next person. The fact remains, however, that listening to a politician in full drone is rarely big box office, hence the success of the Rottweiler Kings, John Humphrys and Jeremy Paxman. I preferred to probe rather than thump, and my weapon of choice tended to be a scalpel rather than a machete. Alas, elegantly constructed debates in which opposing viewpoints are debated in a calm and rational way will never attract as many punters as a heavyweight boxing match which ends with one of the contestants lying comatose in a pool of blood. Nevertheless, many listeners used to tell us that they appreciated our less gladiatorial approach: given that a large number of them were listening in bed and gently drifting off to sleep, we tried not to leave them with images of bloodied ministerial corpses as they entered the Land of Nod.

I have always had a weakness for interesting academics who can cast new light on whatever the story of the day is. Perhaps because my own academic achievements were so undistinguished, I have always had the greatest respect for scholars who can relate past learning to present crises, especially if they can do so amusingly and in less than four minutes. The late Lisa Jardine for art and culture, Peter Hennessy for political history, Michael Clarke for defence and security – give me my wish for a perfect studio discussion and they are the ones I would invite to the table.

Columnists, critics and commentators are nearly always good value as well, simply because they know how to conjure up an interesting thought or two at a moment's notice. One of the best examples was when it was announced late one evening in 1999 that Cherie and Tony Blair were expecting their fourth child, who would become the first baby to be born to a serving Prime Minister for 150 years. After some frantic phone-bashing, the *World Tonight* production team rustled up a columnist prepared to comment live on air.

'So,' I began. 'What do you make of this news?'

The answer was the quintessential reply of the freelance commentator: 'About 600 words, I hope.'

There is one journalistic activity that I regard as of even less value than the fake jousts with politicians. Vox pops* – the dismal practice of stopping people in the street, supposedly at random, and sticking a microphone under their noses – must surely be every broadcast

---

* *Vox populi*: voice of the people.

journalist's least favourite pastime. They are designed to convince listeners and viewers that broadcasters are canvassing the views of 'real people'; the truth is that they are constructed as carefully as everything else that is broadcast.

In the US, they are known as MoS (man on street) interviews, or, more properly, PoS (person on street) interviews. But whatever you call them, they rarely add much useful new information to a news report. They do, perhaps, serve one useful stylistic purpose, however: they add different voices to a programme that might otherwise consist only of boring politicians or equally boring pundits (aka 'talking heads').

So, on the off-chance that one day you find yourself on a windswept street corner clutching a microphone, here is what you need to know. First, choose your question with care – and make sure you ask exactly the same question of each person you talk to, so that their answers can be edited together and still make sense. Second, try to choose a fair cross-section of passers-by: young and old, male and female. Third, choose a location where you will not encounter a preponderance of one sort of interviewee: not at the gates of a college, where you will meet only students, or at a railway station, where you will meet only commuters. Shopping centres and coffee shops are good, except that increasingly they feature piped music that makes it impossible to edit your material.

Chicago in December is not the best time or place to spend hanging around on street corners asking people damn-fool questions. It is a particularly imbecilic pastime if the question you are asking is 'What do you think about global warming?' as the snowflakes flurry in the biting wind and the air temperature hovers several degrees below freezing. Still, no one ever said that reporters never act like idiots, and it was on that same reporting trip in 2009 that a senior BBC colleague was to be observed dementedly chasing geese across a stretch of lakeside parkland in the hope of being able to record them quacking. Her name is being withheld for her own protection.

The vox pops that I really hate are the ones conducted in countries where you know people do not feel free to speak openly. In pre-invasion

Iraq, with Saddam Hussein still in power, no Iraqis would dare to say what they really thought to a Western reporter, but that never stopped editors in London insisting that they should be asked. And there are many more countries where the same is true.

Just occasionally, though, a vox pop does produce a genuine nugget. In 1998, I was in Washington DC at the height of the Clinton–Lewinsky scandal, when the then President was accused of having had an improper sexual relationship with a young White House intern, Monica Lewinsky. I had been dispatched to a soup kitchen in one of the poorest areas of the city to ask women there what they made of the allegations. An elderly African-American woman looked at my microphone, listened to my question and then looked me straight in the eye.

'What do I think of our President's behaviour? Honey, he's a man, ain't he?'

Eddie Watkins was certainly a real person. But no one would ever have called him an ordinary person. He was a convicted murderer, known to his fellow inmates as 'The Bear', because his car repair business, used as a front for drug-running, was called Edward Bear Motors. He was serving a life sentence in Long Lartin maximum security prison when I first met him, and he made an instant, and lasting, impression. We wrote to each other on and off over the next couple of years, but it was not until two years after he had stopped writing that I discovered why the letters had dried up.

Eddie had killed himself with an overdose of pills. In a note that he left for the woman he loved, he wrote: 'Sorry, the pain is too much. The system kills in so many ways.'

When journalists write about a murderer, they must never forget that, however charming, interesting and intelligent he may seem, that man killed a fellow human being. Eddie had been a professional drug smuggler, with close links to some extremely dangerous London gangs, and when he was caught in a joint police–customs ambush while driving a container lorry laden with cannabis from Pakistan worth an estimated £2.5 million, he tried to shoot his way out of trouble. His victim, Peter Bennett, was the first UK customs officer to have been killed on duty for 182 years.

By the time I met Eddie, at a seminar about prison reform organised by Long Lartin prisoners themselves, held inside the jail, he had already served ten years. He told me that he believed in capital punishment and that he should have been hanged for what he did. I was part of a discussion group that he chaired and, later, in his cell, he showed me some of the poetry he had written.

> I have drunk from the well of bitterness
> Filled with shattered crystal tears
> I have gone beyond the shadows
> And realised my fears.

What I found remarkable was not that he was writing poetry, but that he was prepared to share it with an outsider and give me permission to publish it in *The Observer*. The tough-guy killer, who had been abandoned by his mother as a child, brought up in a Barnado's home because his father, who later committed suicide, could not cope, had become a poetry-writing role model for his fellow prisoners. After his death, an inmate at Long Lartin wrote of Eddie: 'I was never alone, not while I had The Bear to turn to. When I lost him, I lost a dad and a brother too.'

I had, unknowingly, acted as Cupid for Eddie, because when my first article about him was published in 1989, an artist by the name of Holly Spencer-Bourne had been struck by his poems and started writing to him. She then took to visiting him from her home in Surrey, and they fell in love. Neither was in the first flush of youth, but somehow each met a need in the other. Eddie was painting as well as writing, and when I visited Holly in her cottage outside Guildford after his death, she showed me the huge collection of his work that she had acquired over the four years of their relationship.

Why do I still remember Eddie so vividly more than twenty-five years after we met? Perhaps because he personified so much that is wrong with the way we deal with the rehabilitation of offenders. Even a man who has committed murder is capable of changing; as Eddie himself wrote:

> A human being, man or woman, no matter his or her past crime, needs the tiniest hope of release from purgatory, some faint light at the end of the longest imaginable tunnel, if the ever-rising incidents of slashed wrists or knotted bedsheets are not to replace Pierrepoint's gallows as a jaded population's uncaring answer to crime and punishment.

After Eddie died, Holly told me which of his poems had most struck her when she first read it in my magazine article:

> When all is still and the doors shut tight
> And not a sound is heard
> When you're all alone to face an endless night
> That's when you do your bird.
> ... Yes, the days are the time for the tough guy act
> On this I'll stake my word.
> But it's late at night
> When the eyes can't see
> That's when you do your bird.

CHAPTER 4

WAR AND PEACE

A foreign correspondent is someone who lives in foreign parts and corresponds, usually in the form of essays containing no new facts. Otherwise he's someone who flies around from hotel to hotel and thinks that the most interesting thing about any story is the fact that he has arrived to cover it.
NIGHT AND DAY, TOM STOPPARD

MY DEFINITION OF THE best journey in the world is the drive from an airport into town in a country that I have never visited before. There is always a sense of anticipation, sometimes of dread, but the overriding sense is of adventure. What is out there? Whom will I meet? And, most important, will I find the story that I came here for?

The flight has been long and uncomfortable. The in-flight meal has been inedible, and the entertainment system was rubbish. The thick file of background material that I have brought with me seems both inadequate and irrelevant. Passport checks at the airport have taken for ever, I have a tight knot of anxiety in the pit of my stomach, and an essential bit of our kit has gone missing. The good news is that our hotel driver is waiting for us, even though it is three o'clock in the morning. The bad news is that his car has no seat belts and he is a terrible driver.

'Welcome, welcome,' he says. 'David Beckham. Very good. Manchester United. Yes?' My producer and I smile weakly, and hope that every time he turns round to smile at us, as we sit stiffly in the back seat, whichever God he prays to will keep an eye on the road ahead. When we arrive at the hotel, there is no one at the desk. We shout. 'Hello?' A man appears, bleary-eyed, a grubby white shirt hanging loosely over his trousers. We fill in the forms, he takes our passports (will we ever see them again?) and hands us the keys to our rooms.

Only two crucial questions remain. Does the shower work? And is there Wi-Fi in our rooms? If the answer to both questions is yes, nothing else matters. I shall sleep soundly (mattress and mosquitoes permitting). If the bar is still open, perhaps there is time for a cold beer.

The most terrifying country that I have ever visited is a place that you have never heard of and that you will never find on a map. It is called Hostalia, and it exists only in the imagination of the people who provide hostile environment training for journalists heading into war zones. On each occasion that I was there, I was kidnapped, held up at gunpoint and stranded in a minefield. And all that in countryside within fifty miles of London.

'Hostile environment' is a useful euphemism for a place where you might get killed. Once, shortly after hostile environment training was introduced at the BBC, I overheard a discussion about whether a particular reporter, unusually well-spoken and well-bred, might be a suitable candidate to send on a course. 'Her?' someone snorted. 'Her idea of a hostile environment is a boring dinner party.'

By the time I arrived at the BBC, I already had some idea what a hostile environment looked like, having reported extensively from Lebanon during its fifteen-year civil war. But following the death in Croatia of my talented young *World Tonight* colleague John Schofield, I was hardly going to kick up a fuss about being reminded that bullets can be dangerous.

Hostile environment training is specifically designed to be frightening – and it is. I know of one reporter who came back from his course so traumatised that he decided he would never ever volunteer for duty in a war zone. He was worried that it would count against him, and I tried to reassure him that it would not. Not even the BBC expects everyone to be prepared to risk their life in the service of the licence fee-payer.

The trainers on these courses are usually former soldiers, and they do not have a very high opinion of university-educated journalists whom they have probably seen poncing about in body armour in front of the TV cameras. So they enjoy their work and, quite rightly, make no allowances. Nevertheless, I was occasionally left feeling uneasy at what sometimes verged on sadism as they relished their make-believe roles as drunken gunmen at roadblocks. They could be horribly convincing.

So much so that one woman had to be withdrawn from a course that I was on after a 'gunman' had reduced her to tears as he taunted her about the fate of her children. 'What kind of a mother are you? Why did you come here? How will your children cope after we have killed you? Don't you care about them?'

Was it realistic? Unfortunately, it was. Was it necessary? I am not so sure.

I am in the back of a Land Rover with three colleagues, bumping along a mud track somewhere deep in the countryside of Hostalia. Suddenly, a group of masked gunmen appear from the side of the track, blocking our way and shouting angrily. 'Stop. Out. Now.' We scramble out and they push us to the ground.

'Hands behind your heads. No talking.' We do as we are told.

'You. Get up.' They kick at the youngest woman member of our team. 'Over here.' And they shove her roughly to one side.

'Who is the leader?'

We are prepared for this: How to Negotiate Checkpoints, Lesson One, includes a whole section on why you should always designate a team leader. Gunmen can get twitchy if they do not know who is in charge. I am the oldest, and most experienced, member of our group, so I have drawn the short straw. It is the only time that presenters are allowed to think of themselves as team leaders, and I regard it as an honour that I could well do without.

'Why are you here? Who sent you? You are spies. We will shoot you.'

'No,' I say in my best BBC voice. 'We are not spies. We are reporters. Press. And if you do not want us here, we will turn round and go back. I am sorry if we have entered a forbidden area.'

We go on like this for a few minutes, he shouting, and me trying to sound suitably apologetic. There is no point standing on your dignity when you are surrounded by men with guns. So I act humble.

Then the mood changes suddenly.

'You can go. But she stays.'

He points at our colleague, standing to one side. 'She is young. Pretty. She will have a good time with us. Party time.'

I look him in the eye: 'Could we have a word in private?'

We step to one side and I make my pitch. 'I can see that you are an honourable man. A soldier. I know that you would never leave your sister with strangers. I cannot leave my colleague; it is against our honour, too. But I understand that we have inconvenienced you, so we are prepared to compensate you.'

I pull a fat bundle of (fake) dollar bills from my pocket – always carry dollar bills in Hostalia and be ready to give them away – and I thrust them into his hand.

'Here. I know you will not accept it for yourself, but give it to your men. They will thank you.' I calculate that he will, of course, keep the cash for himself, but by suggesting that it is for his men, I avoid the danger (I hope) that he will accuse me of impugning his honour.

'All right. You can go. All of you. Now.'

And so the roleplay ends. Would it have worked for real? Probably not, and thank goodness I never got the chance to find out. But that night, in the bar, I am crowned King of the Checkpoints. And all the ex-soldiers have a good laugh.

The next day, we are out again. This time, we are ambushed by gunmen who shove black sacks over our heads so that we can see nothing. We are marched round in circles, frequently doubling back on ourselves, until we have totally lost any sense of where we are.

'Who are you? What is your name?' The questions come thick and fast.

'How old are you?'

I tell him, and there is a pause.

'Aren't you a bit old for this?'

I tell him that I probably am.

For me, the most valuable part of these training courses was what we learned about First Aid, because what used to keep me awake at night in places where men with guns were on every street corner was the prospect of a colleague being hurt and me not knowing how to help. (Say the words 'sucking chest wound' to anyone who has been on a hostile environment course and see what reaction you get.)

Feeling for a pulse should be pretty basic stuff and, as everyone knows, or should know, you can feel for a pulse in various places on a person's body: the inside of their wrist, at the side of their neck where the carotid artery runs just beneath the surface of the skin, or by finding the femoral artery in their groin.

You get to know your colleagues pretty well on these courses, but sometimes a line has to be drawn. The only woman on our team was Shelagh Fogarty, then one of the biggest stars on BBC Radio 5 Live and now with LBC; and when it came to the feeling-for-the-pulse lesson, she made it absolutely clear where she drew the line. There was an unmistakable growl: 'Don't any of you even think of going for my groin.'

I am ushered into a totally dark room. A colleague comes with me. The noise is deafening: gunfire, explosions, the shouts of injured people. We can see absolutely nothing and have no torches, but we have been told that there are two bodies with serious injuries somewhere in the room: one is a volunteer, the other is a medical dummy.

My colleague and I have to find and identify the bodies, work out which is the volunteer and which is the dummy, find and identify their injuries, and then treat them.

We end up groping and touching not only the supposedly injured bodies but also each other in a manner that would have resulted in instant dismissal back at the office. Thank goodness for the unspoken rule: what happens on a hostile environment course stays on a hostile environment course.

But of course, working in a genuinely hostile environment is no joke, and there is a very good reason why correspondents are sent on these courses. I have lost too many friends and colleagues to take any of this lightly. When I was Middle East correspondent for *The Observer* in the 1980s, my rival on the *Sunday Times* was David Blundy, who was exactly the kind of man you do not want as your rival. He was much taller than I was, much better-looking, a much better reporter and a much better writer. Fortunately, he was also very charming and a great companion. If you walked into any hotel bar in the Middle East in the 1980s and saw Blundy there, you would know that you were in for an enjoyable evening.

He was shot dead by a sniper in El Salvador in 1989 at the age of forty-four. Blundy was not a cowboy, but he was certainly brave. His friend and colleague Anthony Holden put it well:

> Any journalist drawn, like him, to scenes of conflict, to the chronicling of violent death, lives with the permanent knowledge that he could be next. The job, as he would have been the first to agree, does not include some macho brand of courage – in Beirut as in Belfast, he confessed to being 'shit-scared' – so much as a willingness to sublimate fear in pursuit of adventure or a good story, preferably both.[5]

Farzad Bazoft had also been in pursuit of adventure and a good story when he was arrested by Saddam Hussein's security police in Baghdad on 15 September 1989. Farzad, who looked a bit like a young Omar Sharif, had been born in Iran and came to Britain at the age of sixteen. I got to know him when he started freelancing for *The Observer*; always keen, always ambitious, and always in a hurry to make his mark.

During the long Iran–Iraq war, access to the front lines was difficult and dangerous. More than once, Farzad was invited by the Iraqis to participate in closely controlled press trips to the front, presumably because they calculated that to have an Iranian reporting from their side would somehow be to their advantage. On what was to be his last trip, Farzad was more than usually excited, because the Iraqis had promised him an interview with Saddam himself. We warned him of the dangers, and urged him not to go. But he was determined.

On the day he left London, a huge explosion was reported at a military complex outside Baghdad. Once in Iraq, Farzad managed to break free from his official minders and got to the site of the blast, where he took dozens of photographs and collected soil samples that he hoped to have analysed back in London. He also, fatefully, started asking people in his Baghdad hotel if anyone there knew what had happened. The hotel security staff were alerted, tipped off the police, and he was arrested at the airport as he was waiting for his flight back to the UK.

Farzad was accused of being a spy, and was later forced to make a televised 'confession'. He was sentenced to death and hanged on 15 March 1990. His body was returned to the UK, and he was buried in Highgate cemetery in north London.

There was a postscript. After Saddam had been overthrown in 2003, the man who had ordered Farzad's arrest and interrogated him claimed that he never believed that Farzad was a spy but that his execution was on the direct orders of Saddam himself. In an interview with the journalist Ed Vulliamy, Kadem Askar, a former colonel in the Iraqi intelligence service, said: 'Bazoft was obviously innocent. I could tell that he was simply chasing a story. And I submitted my report saying that.'[6]

Farzad was just thirty-one when he was executed; John Schofield was even younger, twenty-nine, when he was killed by a single bullet in Croatia in 1995. He had joined *The World Tonight* from *Channel 4 News* and, because radio people tend to have a chip on their shoulder about TV (is there any worse insult than 'He's got a face for radio'?), he was greeted with some initial suspicion.

It did not last long. John was a first-rate reporter who wrote like a dream. He was reporting from the Krajina region when he was killed, and he had been doing everything right. He was wearing body armour and travelling with colleagues in an armoured vehicle. He died because a Croatian army unit, watching them from a couple of miles' distance, mistook them for Serb forces. A high-velocity bullet hit him in the neck, just above his flak jacket.

As always when a reporter dies on duty, his friends and colleagues agonised: why do we do this job? Is any story worth dying for? Should we stop kidding ourselves and find a more sensible way to earn a living? On my way back from John's funeral, I shared a car with a BBC colleague. We asked ourselves the questions, and came up with an answer. John thought it was worth it, and so do we. What other answer is there?

Marie Colvin said it like this:

> Someone has to go there and see what is happening. You can't get that information without going to places where people are being shot at, and others are shooting at you. The real difficulty is having enough faith in humanity to believe that enough people – be they government, military or the man on the street – will care when your file reaches the printed page, the website or the TV screen. We do have that faith because we believe we do make a difference.[7]

Marie had taken over from David Blundy as Middle East correspondent for the *Sunday Times*. I first met her when she was still with the American news agency UPI and starting to make a name for herself by securing exclusive interviews with the Palestinian leader Yasser Arafat. She became one of the best-known war correspondents of her generation, reporting with great courage from East Timor, Sri Lanka, where she lost an eye after being hit in the face by shrapnel from a grenade, Kosovo, Chechnya and Zimbabwe.

She went to more dangerous places, and stayed there longer, than anyone else I knew. She lived as hard as she worked, and was married at various times to two friends of mine: my *Observer* colleague Patrick Bishop, and the Bolivian journalist Juan Carlos Gumucio, whom I got to know in Beirut and who committed suicide in 2002. The last time I saw Marie was at Heathrow airport, when I found myself, totally by chance, standing behind her in line at the security scanner. We both put our laptops through the machine, then she picked up mine by mistake. Only when she turned round did her instantly recognisable black eyepatch give her away. We laughed and hugged and went our separate ways.

Marie was killed in the Syrian city of Homs on 22 February 2012. The previous night, I had left a note for the editor of the following day's edition of *The World Tonight*: 'If you want a voice out of Homs tomorrow, my old mate Marie Colvin of the *Sunday Times* is there.'

In a tribute published on the day of her death, Lindsey Hilsum of *Channel 4 News* wrote:

> Marie was glamorous. At parties, which she loved, she would wear a tight black cocktail dress and a special eye-patch studded with rhinestones. Parties at her house were full of actors, politicians, writers and journalists. She drank and smoked and had lovers. She liked to take time off in the summer to go sailing. But what absorbed her most was reporting.[8]

Why do I dwell on the deaths of friends and colleagues? Because journalists do not often get a good press these days, so it is important to be reminded that some of them are very fine people who do very fine work. And that some of them pay a very high price.

The first time I was dispatched to what might have become a war zone was in July 1974, after the Turkish army invaded Cyprus. Greek Cypriots who wanted to unite Cyprus with Greece had staged a *coup d'état* and deposed the venerable independence leader Archbishop Makarios. It was a dangerous time: both Greece and Turkey were members of NATO, and there was a real chance that the two countries could end up at war with each other.

I was based in Rome, working for Reuters, and I was ordered to make my way as quickly as I could to the only stretch of land border between Greece and Turkey, east of the town of Alexandroupolis in the far north-eastern corner of Greece, where the river Ebros forms the international frontier. If Turkey was going to invade Greece, this was where the tanks would roll across – and Reuters wanted to make sure that they had a man on the spot.

Alexandroupolis began life as a little Ottoman fishing village called Dedeağaç. It was captured by Russian forces during the Russo-Turkish war of 1877–78, reverted to Ottoman rule in 1878, but was then seized by Bulgaria in 1912. The following year, it was taken by Greek forces, but handed back to Bulgaria under the terms of the Treaty of Bucharest.

The town reverted to Greek rule at the end of the First World War following the collapse of the Ottoman Empire, and was named Alexandroupolis in honour of King Alexander when he paid a visit in 1920. It was occupied again by Bulgarian forces between 1941 and 1944 after the invasion of Greece by Germany and Italy.

And now, in 1974, it was again at risk of being overrun from the east. This was my first time in the Balkans and as I gave myself a crash course in the region's history, I found myself sympathising with Winnie-the-Pooh: 'I am a bear of very little brain and long words bother me.'[9] It was to become an all-too-familiar emotion twenty years later, when the Balkans again slid into war as Yugoslavia disintegrated and I tried to make sense of its swirling conflicts and get my head around its bewilderingly unpronounceable names.

When I got to Alexandroupolis, I checked in to an undistinguished hotel on the edge of town and headed straight for the border. There was little sign of any heightened tension, and no sign of any other reporters, which I found worrying. If I was the only newsman there, there was a strong possibility that I was in the wrong place. Either that or I was about to get a world scoop.

There were a couple of Greek soldiers at the Greek end of the road bridge across the river and, as far as I could see, just a couple of Turkish soldiers at the other end. But the river banks were thickly wooded and I suspected there might well be more military activity out of sight in the undergrowth.

Halfway across the bridge, a line was painted across the road. The border. On one side was a Greek soldier and, less than a yard away, just the other side of the line, standing almost shoulder to shoulder, was a Turkish soldier. I spent several hours observing them, but they showed not the slightest interest in me.

Waiting for war is a very tedious business and tends not to produce dramatic copy for impatient editors back at head office. It is the polar opposite of newsworthy. Understandably enough, Reuters were extremely keen for me to file a story, having gone to the trouble of sending me there, but my difficulty was not only that I did not have a story, but also that I saw little prospect of having one. There was no traffic on the highway, and no one wanted to talk to me. So on Day Three – it might have been Day Four – inspiration struck.

I would try to cross the border myself. On foot. With great care.

'Good morning.' I smile at the Greek soldiers. 'Can I cross?' They speak no English and I speak no Greek, so I make a walking sign with my fingers. They shrug. I cannot be sure whether the shrug indicates total incomprehension or total indifference, but I calculate that if they do not want me to cross, they will soon make it clear enough.

I start walking and hear no shouts of anger from behind me. So I continue, walking as nonchalantly as I can manage towards the two armed men standing on each side of the line in the road, halfway across the bridge. It is 800 yards from one side to the other, so it takes me nearly five minutes to get to the middle.

Again, I smile and greet the soldiers warmly. 'Good morning.' There is no reaction from either of them. I keep walking. I cross the line into Turkey. There is still no reaction. So I keep going until I reach the other side and the Turkish sentry box.

'Good morning.' I smile again. They smile. 'How are you?' Perhaps one of them speaks English. They do not. I wander about for a few minutes but notice nothing of any interest. There is only one thing to do: I walk back across the bridge. Nothing happens. No story.

One of my favourite apocryphal stories from the annals of journalistic myth concerns a telegram allegedly sent by the monstrous American media tycoon William Randolph Hearst to an artist whom he had sent to Cuba in 1897 to cover what he believed was an impending war with Spain. After a few days there, the artist, Frederic Remington, said there was unlikely to be a war and requested permission to return home. The supposed answer from Hearst, which is now a much-loved journalistic legend but almost certainly devoid of historical accuracy, was: 'Please remain. You furnish the pictures, and I'll furnish the war.'

In 1974, Reuters failed to furnish a Turkish invasion of Greece, and I was not sorry to leave Alexandroupolis. The story that I filed was not going to win any journalism prizes.

> On the Greek–Turkish border, 15 Aug 1974, Reuter – The frontier
> between Greece and Turkey was quiet and open to normal traffic today.
> I walked across a bridge into Turkey over the river Ebros which
> forms the border near Ebros town without any difficulty...

My first experience of war reporting had been a big disappointment.

My second experience was not much better. In January 1980, by
which time I had started working for *The Observer*, I was taken deep
into the Western Sahara by fighters belonging to the Polisario Liberation Front. They were fighting for independence from Morocco,
which had seized control of the former Spanish colony in 1976 and
was determined not to give up.

We spent several days driving through the desert in a convoy of
open-topped jeeps, seeing nothing but sand, sand and more sand, and
discovering that if you sleep out in the open in January, even in the
Sahara, temperatures can fall to below freezing and ice will form on
your blanket. My dispatch was somewhat lacking in what war reporters call bang-bang:

> On a journey covering several hundred miles with Polisario guerrillas
> last week, I saw no evidence of a Moroccan military presence other than
> the burnt-out remains of tanks, munition trucks and other vehicles.
> Even when we entered Morocco itself, we encountered no opposition
> ... We travelled without compass, maps or radio. At night we slept
> beneath the stars as temperatures fell to below zero. The guerrillas took
> it for granted that we would not be disturbed by the Moroccans...[10]

It was one of those trips when I could not help but wonder if I was
the victim of a gigantic hoax. Did we really cross into Morocco itself?
Were we really in disputed territory? Perhaps we had done no more
than drive round and round in circles for a week, never leaving Algeria,
which is where I had met up with the Polisario fighters. After all,
one Saharan sand dune looks very much like another. These days,
with global positioning technology available on every mobile
phone, it would be much easier to work out exactly where I was

– but in 1980, I found myself with no option but to believe what I was told.

I have often had cause to remember a line from Evelyn Waugh's comic novel *Scoop*, which offers a glorious satirical depiction of the life of a war correspondent. At one point in the tale, the hapless William Boot, a country life writer mistakenly sent to cover a war in the fictional African state of Ishmaelia, sends a cable to his editor:

THEY HAVE GIVEN US PERMISSION TO GO TO LAKU AND EVERYONE IS GOING BUT THERE IS NO SUCH PLACE AM I TO GO TOO SORRY TO BE A BORE.[11]

Going to a place that does not exist, and then being expected to provide dramatic news stories from there, is only marginally dafter than going to places that do exist but where nothing at all of any interest is happening. Editors sometimes like to challenge keen young reporters by offering them assignments that look exciting on paper but can turn out to be a lot less thrilling on the ground. 'See what you can find, old boy. There's bound to be something going on.'

In April 1982, there was plenty going on in the Falkland Islands, those tiny British colonial outposts in the South Atlantic, more than 11,000 miles from the UK, but only about 300 miles from Argentina, which had long claimed them as its own. When the islands were captured by Argentine forces, Margaret Thatcher dispatched the Royal Navy to seize them back for the British crown, a task that was achieved with the loss of six hundred and forty-nine Argentines, two hundred and fifty-five British military personnel, and three Falkland Islanders. The war lasted seventy-four days from start to finish.

I was dispatched to the Falklands (Malvinas to the Argentines) two years later, when all was quiet. My instructions were to 'see what's going on'. The most accurate answer would have been 'not a lot', but that does not make for great copy.

As it turned out, the long flight south turned out to be a great deal more interesting than the islands themselves. We left from the Royal Air Force base at Brize Norton in Oxfordshire, which is, or was, a major international airport in its own right, complete with a terminal building, flight indicator boards and boarding announcements. From there, we flew to Ascension Island, another British colonial pin-prick stuck in the middle of the ocean, 1,000 miles from the coast of west Africa and 1,400 miles from the coast of Brazil. (It is said that one reporter who asked his newspaper's travel department to book him tickets to Ascension found himself in Paraguay instead. The capital of Paraguay is Asunción – it is an easy mistake to make.)

From Ascension, my journey became much more interesting. In the mid-1980s, there were no planes that could reach the Falklands without refuelling, and there were no suitable countries en route that would grant refuelling rights to British military aircraft. So the only way to get there was on board an RAF C-130 Hercules transport plane, a great lumbering beast of an aircraft that looked as if it would have difficulty making its way to the end of a runway, let alone lifting itself into the air. And then to refuel, twice, in mid-air.

A Hercules is built neither for comfort nor for speed. We sat on simple webbing seats, extending along each side of the fuselage and facing into the body of the plane, which was piled high with military equipment and supplies. The roar of the aircraft's four turbo-prop engines was deafening, and there was little light. Total flying time Ascension–Falklands: thirteen hours. In-flight entertainment: zero.

When it was time for the mid-air refuelling, I was allowed up on the flight deck to watch how it was done. The procedure was not designed for those of a nervous disposition. The tanker plane approached us from behind and then seemed to hover above us, frighteningly close, positioning itself so that an extendable hose could be lowered towards us. The Hercules pilot then had to manoeuvre his plane to within 100 feet of the tanker, enabling the rigid fuel-receiving probe that poked up from above the cockpit to make contact with the end of the tanker's hose. It was like watching two flying elephants trying to have sex.

Sometimes, I was told, if they got it just slightly wrong, the fuel-receiving probe would snap off. I decided not to inquire what would happen next.

But I did get another chance to experience the joy of flying in a Hercules when the RAF offered to take me on one of their aerial patrols over the islands. They flew low over the water, checking that no rogue Argentine warships had been foolish enough to venture back into British territorial waters.

'Come and sit next to me on the flight deck,' said the pilot. 'You'll have a great view.'

Then, with just a hint of a glint in his eye: 'Have you ever flown a plane? Why not have a go?'

I declined with as much grace as I could. Somehow I did not think that my first ever flying lesson should be at the controls of a giant RAF transport plane. But then he took his hands off his control stick and pointed at the one in front of me: 'You're in charge. Grab hold of it.'

Perhaps it was a joke. I never found out. But when I gingerly pushed the stick forward, and then forward a bit more, the plane's nose dipped alarmingly towards the ocean below, and the pilot quickly took control again. When we were back on terra firma, I apologised to the rest of the crew, but they simply grinned broadly. I doubt that it was the first, or the last, time that they enjoyed terrifying a clueless civilian by enticing them onto the flight deck.

The place to stay in the Falklands was the Upland Goose Hotel in Port Stanley. Not because it was the best hotel in town, but because it was the only hotel in town. (It no longer exists, having recently been converted into apartments.) It was comfortable enough and only a short-ish walk along the gale-buffeted main street up to the Cable and Wireless station with its massive satellite dish and the only international telephone connection in the entire territory. (I was taken aback to read recently that one of the Upland Goose's successor hotels now has Wi-Fi. Wi-Fi? In the Falklands?)

They used to say that the Falklands were the ideal place to settle if you were likely to find life in New Zealand too stressful. The islanders were known to the British soldiers stationed there as 'Bennies', after the simple-minded handyman Benny Hawkins, a character in the then-popular ITV soap opera *Crossroads*. The islanders returned the compliment by calling the soldiers 'Wenneyes', because of their habit of starting every conversation with the words 'When I was in Cyprus...' or 'When I was in Belize...'

After a week there, I was close to despair and sorely tempted to send a William Boot-style cable back to London: 'EVERYTHING FINE HERE NO PROBLEMS WEATHER WINDY SHALL I COME HOME?' But I knew that I had to come up with something a bit better. Two thousand words better, in fact. My report began:

> Britain is spending £1 million a day in the Falkland Islands to ensure that time stands still. No one knows which way to move, so no one moves at all. There is no more talk of a new beginning: instead they talk of how to slow a decline which saw the colony's gross domestic product slump by 25 per cent in the years before the Argentine invasion. The Falklands were dying even before that cataclysmic day two years ago – and all the signs are that they are dying still.[12]

Little did I know then – although to be fair, little did anyone know then – that within just a few years, the sale of squid fishing licences to international fisheries companies would give birth to an economic boom. The licences now generate roughly 35 per cent of the islands' annual GDP; sheep-farming, which used to be the islands' main economic activity, accounts for a mere 2 per cent. Income per head of population (admittedly there are still fewer than three thousand people living on the islands) is now higher than in the UK. It just goes to show how accurate is one of my favourite quotations, variously attributed either to the economist Ezra Solomon or to J. K. Galbraith: 'The sole function of economic forecasting is to make astrology look respectable.'

Look up Shangri-La on Wikipedia and you will learn that it is a fictional place, a mystical valley synonymous with paradise on earth, as described in the novel *Lost Horizon* by James Hilton. But I can tell you different, because I have been there. In reality, it is called the Panjshir Valley and it is located in Afghanistan, north of Kabul, just off the main highway that leads to the mountains of the Hindu Kush and the Salang Tunnel.

Turn right off the highway about two hours out of Kabul and soon you enter a narrow gorge, with the river Panjshir flowing at the bottom and jagged cliff faces rising vertically as far as the eye can see. When I drove along it in 2002, just a few months after the US-led invasion that had defeated the Taliban, the road was little more than a deeply rutted dirt track, hugging the cliff face precariously and with vertiginous drops to the valley floor.

But suddenly the gorge opened out into a much wider valley, green and lush, with wheat fields and apple orchards, an exact depiction of what I had always imagined Shangri-La to look like. There was just one sight that I had not expected to see: lines and lines of tanks and other military vehicles, neatly parked in fields along the roadside.

Here, safely out of harm's way, was the bulk of the Afghan army's weaponry. Mohammad Qasim Fahim, the interim defence minister, was also the de facto leader of Afghanistan's Tajiks, who are the dominant ethnic group in the Panjshir region – and he was making sure that he had what he needed to defend the Tajik heartland. Fahim had taken over as the commander of the anti-Taliban Northern Alliance after the assassination of the country's most powerful anti-Taliban resistance leader Ahmad Shah Massoud just two days before the 9/11 attacks in New York and Washington.[*]

Although the Panjshir Valley has a well-deserved reputation as an impregnable redoubt of the Tajiks, having never been occupied either by the Soviet Red Army or by the Taliban, my producer Craig Swan and I were keen to be out of the valley by nightfall. Apart from any other considerations, we were not keen to be driven back along the deeply rutted road through the gorge after dark. Our driver told us not to worry: if we were still in the valley when the sun went down, it would be easy to find a local villager to offer us shelter for the night.

We told him that was good to know, but our firm preference was to be back in Kabul by bedtime. What we should have realised was that he would interpret our wish as a challenge to his driving skills – and

---

[*] Fahim remained a powerful figure in Afghan politics throughout his life. He was the subject of several assassination attempts and died of a heart attack in 2014.

that he would therefore be determined, come what may, to get us out of the valley by sunset. So we raced back down the valley at dizzying speed, negotiating hairpin bends and deep potholes with reckless abandon. The fact that you are reading these words tells you that we made it back in one piece. But our expedition to Shangri-La could have ended rather differently.

So too could our decision to drive through the Salang Tunnel, built by the Soviets in the 1960s and at the time of its construction the highest road tunnel in the world. It had been badly damaged by fighting between the Taliban and rebel fighters after the Soviets withdrew from Afghanistan in 1989, and had been reopened only after the Taliban were overthrown in 2001. When we reached it in June 2002, after several hours of negotiating pot-holed mountain roads, past blown-up bridges and burnt-out Soviet tanks, we discovered that to say it had 'reopened' was perhaps a slight exaggeration.

True, it was now just possible to steer very carefully round the piles of rubble at the southern entrance and drive at snail's pace through the 1.5-mile-long tunnel. There was no lighting, and water was pouring through the tunnel roof. Our driver seemed no happier than we were as we crawled through the blackness; he was even less happy when, on reaching the northern end, we told him that we now wanted to turn round and immediately return whence we had come.

I admit that I have a weakness for exotic-sounding places. I still hope one day to get to Timbuktu and Ouagadougou, if only because of the beauty of their names. So I did not need much persuading when it was suggested by a BBC colleague, Catherine Miller, in 2006 that a reporting assignment to Nepal, where a ten-year-long civil war was just ending, might be combined with a side trip to the neighbouring Himalayan kingdom of Bhutan.

To fly from the Nepalese capital Kathmandu to the Bhutanese airport of Paro is, like mid-air refuelling aboard an RAF Hercules, not for the faint-hearted. The flight itself is breathtaking, as it takes you along the highest ridges of the Himalayan peaks, including Everest. The landing, on the other hand, is seriously scary. (Some sources claim that only eight pilots in the world are qualified to land in Paro.)

The descent starts as the plane threads its way through a gap in the mountains and follows the course of the Paro River in the valley below. But then, moments from touch-down, the plane takes a sharp right as the runway comes into view, followed by a sharp left just 100 feet above the valley floor to line up with the runway itself. (Type the words 'Paro landing' into YouTube to see for yourself.[13]) If the weather is bad, you do not fly to Bhutan – it is as simple as that.

Bhutan has its own claim to be regarded as a real-life Shangri-La; it is the world's only Buddhist kingdom and its Himalayan scenery is truly spectacular. But, for reasons that will become clearer later in this book, I did not fall in love with Bhutan, and I was not sorry to leave.

The Amazonian rainforest of Brazil is another place that has always been high on my list of places that must be visited. It was, therefore, fortunate that my editor at *The World Tonight* for more than a decade, Alistair Burnett, had a deep interest in Brazil and was determined that it should receive far more attention than most of the British media were prepared to allow it. His judgement was spot-on: in the first decade of this century, the Brazilian economy was one of the most vibrant in the world, its charismatic President Luiz Inácio Lula da Silva became a global superstar, and it was awarded in quick succession the rights to stage both the 2014 World Cup and the 2016 Olympics. No one could argue that Brazil did not matter.

But was a rapidly growing economy compatible with guardianship of one of the planet's most important rainforests, uniquely critical as an absorber of carbon dioxide and therefore a crucial component in the fight to contain climate change? Let's send Lustig to find out.

And so it was that in June 2011 I set out with producer-photographer Beth McLeod and sound engineer-videographer Phil Zentner on a road trip deep into the Amazon, and across the mighty Xingu River to meet the indigenous Kayapo people and their leader, Chief Raoni. They had been campaigning for years against plans to build the huge Belo Monte dam upriver, a project that they said would destroy their livelihoods and have a devastating impact on the environment. It was a perfect example of the balancing act that the Brazilian government had to perform: on the one hand to legislate for continued economic growth and to meet a growing global demand for its food and minerals; on the other, to acknowledge the urgent need for effective environmental protection measures.

Raoni certainly qualifies as one of my more memorable interviewees. When he greeted us, he was bare-chested and wearing just a pair of red shorts. His lower lip was distended by the insertion of a wooden disc, perhaps four inches in diameter. Our conversation was conducted with the help of not one but two interpreters, one translating from Kayapo into Portuguese, and the second from Portuguese into English. Despite the difficulties, we got on splendidly.

I was somewhat taken aback, however, when we asked the villagers if there were any musicians among them and whether we could record some Kayapo music. A flute player was duly summoned, but demanded $100 before he would play a note. It quickly became clear that we were not the first media visitors who had found our way to their village, remote as it was. My first reaction was that we were being ripped off, but then I thought again. After all, musicians the world over expect to be paid when they perform, so why should a Kayapo flautist be any different?

CHAPTER 5

DEPARTURES AND ARRIVALS

There are two invaluable rules for a special correspondent
– Travel Light and Be Prepared.
SCOOP, EVELYN WAUGH

MUCH AS I HAVE always loved travelling, I have always hated airports. Unlike railway stations, or docks, which are full of the spirit of adventure, of setting off into the unknown, airports are sterile and characterless. If you were to remove the signage from almost any major international airport, you would have great difficulty identifying which country you were in. It is as if they are all built from the same template. And, for reasons that I have never understood, they all seem to feature an Irish-themed pub.

In my experience, airports equal stress. For a reporter, often travelling at short notice to a place where all hell is breaking loose, not always in possession of the correct documentation (visa, press accreditation etc.) and usually carrying a lot of heavy and deeply suspicious communications equipment, the stressometer can sometimes rise to alarming levels.

Early morning, Stansted airport. I am on my way to The Hague to cover yet another tedious EU summit meeting. I check in, bleary-eyed, semi-comatose.

'I'm sorry, sir. This doesn't seem to be your passport.' Suddenly, I am wide awake. I snatch it back and, sure enough, I have picked up my son's passport by mistake and there is now no time to rush back home to swap it for my own. There is only one possible way for me to get to The Hague: if I can arrange for the Dutch immigration authorities to send a fax to Stansted, guaranteeing that they will not turn me back on arrival, the airline will allow me to board the plane even if I am not in possession of a valid passport.

Somehow (this is before the days of mobile phones), from a public payphone in the Stansted terminal, I get through to the head of immigration at Schiphol airport. He roars with laughter when I recount my tale of woe, promises to send the required fax and tells me to ask for him personally when I land. He meets me at the passport control desk, hands me a wonderfully impressive *laissez-passer* and sends me on my way to the EU summit.

All that remains is to negotiate my way back into the UK at the end of the assignment. The man at UK immigration listens carefully as I tell my unlikely tale. 'You mean to tell me that you got through Schiphol without a passport?' I confirm that this is indeed the case. 'Well done, sir. I congratulate you.' And I am on my way home. But since then, I have always been very careful to check which passport I have with me before I leave home.

In fact, I learned very early in my career how important a passport can be. My first overseas posting was to Madrid in the early 1970s, when the Fascist dictator General Francisco Franco was in charge. Any sign of opposition to his rule was ruthlessly crushed, but that did not stop left-wing students regularly taking to the streets to protest against his regime.

On one occasion, I found myself caught up in the midst of one such demonstration in the company of a splendid old-school BBC correspondent called Gordon Martin, then diplomatic correspondent for the BBC World Service. As the grey-uniformed riot police (known as *los grises*) bore down on us with batons raised, he whipped out his UK passport (then still the dark blue, hard-covered version), held it aloft as if it were a magic talisman and shouted at the top of his voice, in English: 'British citizens!'

The police ranks parted as they reached the spot where we were cowering, swept past us and continued on their way, leaving us untouched. Such was the power of those magisterial words inscribed on the inside of our passports' front cover: 'Her Britannic Majesty's Secretary of State requests and requires in the Name of Her Majesty...' Or perhaps the police simply did not notice us.

Some years later, while I was based in Italy, I had to return to the UK for medical treatment, having contracted a nasty case of hepatitis A. I was severely jaundiced, so to disguise the fact that the whites of my eyes were a deeply unpleasant shade of yellow, I was wearing sunglasses as I made my way through immigration at Heathrow.

I had also grown a beard while languishing in my sick bed, so the photograph in my passport could no longer be described as anything resembling an accurate likeness. The immigration officer took one look at it, then at me, and then at the photo again. 'I'm very sorry, sir,' he said, 'but I shall have to ask you to remove either the beard or the sunglasses.' In the circumstances, I felt I was getting off lightly.

When I was based in the Middle East, I was the proud possessor of no fewer than three UK passports: one for Israeli stamps, one for Arab ones (most Arab countries will not let you in if you have an Israeli stamp in your passport), and a third that was kept in a desk drawer in the office in London for whenever a visa needed to be applied for in a hurry.

Sometimes, out of a spirit of sheer devilment, I would present my Arab-stamped passport to Israeli immigration officials at Ben Gurion airport and, explaining that I was a journalist, ask them very kindly not to stamp it. A red paper marker would be inserted into the passport instead of a stamp and as I made my way through to the baggage area, I would be pulled to one side to answer 'just a few questions'.

Usually, it was little more than routine, but one official was so curious about the bewildering variety of Arab visa stamps that she went through them, page by page, asking me to identify each of them in turn. 'That one is Saudi Arabia,' I told her. 'That one is Syria, that one is Libya.' There were several others as well and, at the end of the process, she handed my passport back. 'I see,' she said with a wry smile. 'You seem to have visited *all* our friends.' I rather admired her sangfroid.

I admit to having a soft spot for all the visa and entry stamps in my passports – they seem to hark back to an era when travel was much more exotic than it is now. If I could, and if I was not convinced that to do so would make me look like an utter prat, I would gladly plaster destination stickers all over my luggage, just as transatlantic steamship passengers did a hundred years ago.

There have been times, though, when I would gladly have swapped my UK passports, with all their echoes of Britain's imperialist past, for a passport from a less – how should I put this? – history-laden nation. Especially in the Middle East, the UK is often blamed for the region's current troubles, having played a less than glorious role in its recent past, and I have often hankered after a Swedish or an Irish passport. No one hates the Swedes or the Irish.

But even a passport from the most blameless of nations – Luxembourg, perhaps? – would offer no protection against the health-endangering frustrations of airport officialdom. I have never understood the sense of the maxim 'To travel hopefully is better than to arrive.' It plainly dates back to long before the days of modern air travel and the hell that is an airport departure lounge.

Rio de Janeiro, checking in for an overnight flight back to London. Lee Chaundy, a BBC sound engineer with whom I frequently travelled to far-flung places, has a lightweight collapsible camera tripod strapped to the outside of his backpack. (The introduction of multi-skilling at the BBC meant that many sound engineers were also trained as photographer-videographers so that they could carry twice as much kit and work twice as hard.) At the security scanner, an official tells him that he will not be allowed to take the tripod on board and will have to return to the check-in desk to have it tagged and put in the hold.

We try to reason with him but, in true jobsworth fashion, he will not be moved. 'Here,' says Lee, as he unstraps the tripod and thrusts it into the official's hands. 'You can have it.' The official walks across to a refuse container and ceremoniously disposes of the tripod. We are not amused.

At some point during the flight, as we are trying without much success to get some sleep (yes, we are flying economy), a member of the BA cabin crew comes down the aisle with a message. The tripod has been retrieved from the airport refuse bin and is in the hold. We will find it on the carousel at Heathrow.

We never discovered exactly how they did it, but I can only imagine that a BA crew member had observed our altercation at security and somehow managed to retrieve the confiscated tripod. Just as had been the case at Schiphol, I was left marvelling at how, just occasionally, officials go out of their way to be helpful.

In 1997, my long-suffering producer colleague Craig Swan and I were dispatched to report on a massive flooding disaster in southern Somalia. The country had already plunged into anarchy following a coup that had dislodged its President Mohamed Siad Barre six years earlier, after more than twenty years in power. There was no central authority and only piecemeal relief efforts to help the hundreds of thousands of people who had had to flee from their homes.

Craig and I flew first to the Kenyan capital, Nairobi, and then to Garissa, in eastern Kenya, about 125 miles from the Somali border. (In April 2015, gunmen from the Somali al-Shabaab group attacked Garissa University College, killed 150 people and took 700 students hostage.) We were reliant on aid flights to get us into Somalia, often travelling there and back on the same day because the relief agencies (or, more likely, their insurers) were not keen to risk having their aircraft parked in Somalia overnight.

On one occasion we hitched a ride on a giant Soviet-made helicopter, piloted by Bulgarians who spoke no English. The chopper was elderly, as were the pilots, but they got us as far as Kismayo, the lawless port city which had become a frequent battleground during Somalia's endless civil war. As Craig and I walked with some trepidation from the runway towards the airport exit, having no idea what to expect, a man approached us with hand outstretched.

'Are you gentlemen from the BBC?' We admitted that we were. 'That is wonderful. I am the stringer here for the BBC Somali service. Can I offer you a lift into town?' We were so pleased to meet a colleague in such a godforsaken place that it occurred to neither of us to ask him for any form of identification. Instead, we clambered eagerly into his Land Rover, grateful to have found a friendly face.

Just as we were setting off, however, four more men climbed on board, and each one of them was carrying a Kalashnikov automatic weapon. Craig and I exchanged glances but said nothing. I noticed Craig discreetly switching on his mini-disc recorder as we bumped our way along a mud track into Kismayo. Just in case.

A man sitting behind me poked me between the shoulder blades with the barrel of his gun. 'Me, immigration officer,' he said with a big grin. 'Visa, hundred dollars.' I told him I would buy his visa when we reached our destination, but when we got there, I managed to lose him and no money changed hands. As far as I know, the man whom we met at the airport was indeed the local BBC stringer, and the gunmen were probably his security detail. But we never saw them again so we were never able to find out for sure.

Arriving in dodgy airports in dodgy countries is one thing; leaving them should be a lot easier, but sometimes can be even more stressful. Arriving in Kinshasa, the capital of the Democratic Republic of Congo, in 2013 was not as bad as it might have been – only one small 'fine' was demanded for some entirely fictitious documentation infraction – leaving, on the other hand, was much more traumatic.

To be fair, the airport's computerised baggage-tagging system had collapsed, something that would put even the best-run airport under strain. (And no one would describe Kinshasa as one of the world's best-run airports, even if it has apparently improved somewhat since I was there.) The check-in staff were refusing to check anyone in, which inevitably caused vast overcrowding and a significant losing of tempers in the departure hall.

Then, under dangerously mounting pressure from mutinous passengers, the harassed staff started to issue handwritten baggage tags – I watched my bag disappear onto a mountainous pile and silently bid it a fond farewell, expecting never to see it again. Seat allocations were also done by hand, with the inevitable result that when my colleague and I finally managed to force our way through security and onto the plane, there were already passengers firmly installed in the seats that theoretically had been allocated to us.

Yet again, officialdom came to the rescue. (Brussels Airlines, take a bow.) A cabin steward took our scribbled boarding passes, told us to wait by the doorway and disappeared towards the front of the plane.

Moments later, he beckoned us towards the expensive seats in business class, sat us down and brought us two glasses of something cold, alcoholic and bubbly. And in case you are thinking that we were offered preferential treatment because of the colour of our skins, I am happy to be able to reassure you that two Congolese passengers who were in similar difficulty were also found seats up front.

Postscript: after the overnight flight to Brussels – unexpectedly comfortable on our business class flat beds – and a quick transfer onto a flight to London, my bag was the first one onto the carousel at Heathrow. Who needs computerised baggage labelling?

There is one airport about which I have more memories, both good and bad, than any other, even though it is now nearly thirty years since I was last there. To land at Beirut airport in the 1980s was to enter a world in which it was always impossible to anticipate what would happen next. The road from the airport into the city was, for a time, one of the most dangerous stretches of road in the world, passing through Beirut's feared southern suburbs where Shia militias, including an early incarnation of Hizbollah, held sway.

In April 1986, the British TV journalist John McCarthy was kidnapped on the airport road, on the same day as the bodies of three other hostages, teachers at the American University of Beirut, were found dumped in the street. Each of them had been shot in the back of the head, apparently in retaliation for US bombing raids on Libya two days earlier.[*]

Travelling to the airport was just as dangerous as travelling from it. Once, waiting to board a flight to Cyprus after having spent a week in Beirut, I was frightened out of my life to hear my name being called on the terminal's PA system. 'Would Mr Robin Lustig please report to

---

[*] McCarthy was held for more than five years and freed in August 1991. The Church of England envoy Terry Waite, who had gone to Beirut to try to negotiate his release, was himself kidnapped in 1987 and held until November 1991.

security?' Convinced that I would find a gang of kidnappers waiting to grab me, I asked a friendly-looking airline pilot to accompany me.

At the security gate, there was indeed someone waiting for me, but it was a journalist colleague, Chris Drake, then working for the US network NBC, who had a small package that he wanted me to take to Cyprus. He was – of course – duly apologetic when he realised how he had terrified me.

On another occasion, again waiting for a flight to take me to safety, I witnessed what may well have been the only occasion in aviation history when a plane was hijacked while still on the ground. I was idly staring out of the terminal window when I saw the emergency escape chutes suddenly deploy from a plane waiting to take off. Moments later, passengers started sliding down the chutes and running in panic towards the terminal.

As if that were not surreal enough, the plane's engines then fired up and it started to taxi towards the end of the runway. To my utter astonishment, it took off, with all its doors open and emergency chutes flapping. Lebanese security forces shot at it as it gained height, which was perhaps not, I thought, the best way to deal with the crisis.

Naturally, I made it my business to find some of the passengers who had managed to escape and get their story. But, before long, word spread that the plane had been denied landing permission in Cyprus – it is only a 45-minute flight to Larnaca – and was heading back to Beirut. Sure enough, it soon reappeared, doors still open and emergency chutes still flapping. It landed safely, and taxied to the far end of the runway, at which point the solitary hijacker vanished. It turned out that he was a Lebanese immigration officer whose demands included a promotion, a pay rise and warmer winter coats for himself and his colleagues.

One passenger died of a heart attack during the hijack but otherwise no one was the worse for their experience. I had a cracking exclusive story for the next day's paper (this was when I was working for *The Observer*) and managed to persuade an official to allow me to use one of the few phones in the airport that had an international connection. I dictated my scoop off the top of my head, full of colour and drama, got on the next plane to Cyprus and headed back to my base in Jerusalem.

The story made one paragraph in the News in Brief column.

At least airport traumas usually last no more than an hour or two. Hotel traumas are a different matter, and all travelling reporters have plenty of horror stories to swap over a beer or three at the end of another frustrating day. In the days before mobile phones, an efficient hotel switchboard, with helpful operators who knew how to place long-distance calls and take messages, was even more important than hot water in the shower and a functioning toilet. (A useful piece of advice from yesteryear: when checking out of a hotel and distributing tips to the staff – reception desk, housekeeping, bellboy – never forget to tip the switchboard operators.)

At the height of the Lebanese civil war, the Commodore Hotel in Beirut was the only place to be. It would never have won prizes for architectural distinctiveness or even for cleanliness, but it knew exactly what journalists needed: a bar that stayed open for as long as there were customers, a telex machine that worked, and a manager who knew enough of the right people (and paid them) to keep his hotel out of trouble.

Its luck finally ran out in early 1987, when it was captured by Druze milltiamen and comprehensively trashed. In an article lamenting its demise, I wrote:

There was always a palpable air of unreality about the Commodore. You could sit in the ground-floor coffee shop, as I once did, calmly eating breakfast, while outside the plate glass windows a nonchalant militiaman equally calmly erected a machine-gun position. Or you could be dictating a dispatch from one of the tiny telephone booths in the lobby and have to break off suddenly when a deafening explosion set the whole edifice rocking on its foundations. 'Sorry,' you would say to your head office. 'That one was a bit close.'[14]

Checking in at the Commodore at the height of the civil war invariably involved a black comedy routine at the front desk. 'Would you prefer a room pool-side or street-side?' you would be asked. You knew – and the check-in clerk knew that you knew – that pool-side meant being more exposed to shell fire from the mountains to the east of the city, whereas street-side meant being at greater risk from car bombs. There was no right answer, and no scientific risk analysis – it was simply down to superstition. So I always went for street-side. Don't ask me why.

Even thirty years later, I remember the dapper hotel manager, Fuad Saleh, always immaculately turned out in a light-grey suit; and Georgette in the coffee shop, always ready with fresh orange juice and strong coffee, until she changed into a bright turquoise silk blouse for the evening shift in the hotel's Chinese restaurant.

And then there was Eddy, in his little bookshop in the lobby, where he sold the customised cigarette lighters that became an essential item of equipment for any self-respecting Middle East correspondent, and who, when he learned that I was working for *The Observer*, smiled warmly and said: 'Ah, *The Observer*. I well remember one of your predecessors, Mr Kim Philby. A wonderful man.'

The least popular resident at the Commodore – and when I say least popular, I mean least popular by a very long way – was the grey parrot that lived in a cage at one end of the dimly lit circular bar, and whose favourite party trick was to imitate the long, slowly descending whistle of an incoming shell. Late at night, we would amuse ourselves by dreaming up a variety of increasingly grisly ends for the wretched bird.

There was also the Commodore cat, Tommy, rather larger than was good for his health, who liked to warm his tum by snoozing for hours on end on top of the Reuters and Associated Press tape machines in the lobby. At least he never whistled.

You could not find a hotel more different from the Commodore than Mrs Bhandari's guesthouse in Amritsar, northern India. Mrs Bhandari was one of those characters whom reporters dream about: full of stories and knowledge, with an opinion about everything, and fabulously rude about nearly everyone.

She was already in her late seventies when I met her, a proud Parsi in a city that, as the site of the Golden Temple, is at the centre of

Sikhism. The Parsis are a Zoroastrian community who originated in Persia but migrated to northern India between the eighth and tenth centuries to escape persecution by Muslim invaders. Mrs Bhandari therefore regarded herself as far superior to the Indians among whom she lived, and she made little secret of it.

When I arrived at her modest guesthouse in April 1984, I was not feeling my best. A couple of days' stay at a five-star hotel in Delhi had left me with a severe bout of food poisoning; Mrs Bhandari took one look at me, ordered me to bed and prescribed a bowl of home-made chicken soup. It was just like going home to Mum.

I discovered later that Mrs Bhandari had a colourful past. Born in 1906, she still remembered the infamous Amritsar massacre of 1919, when British troops under the command of Colonel Reginald Dyer opened fire on Indians who had gathered for a religious festival. According to the British, 379 people were killed and more than 1,000 wounded. Indian sources insisted that more than 1,000 people had died.

Mrs Bhandari was said to have been the first woman in Amritsar to own and drive a car, and the first to run her own business. Her first husband was a Hindu, whom she insisted on marrying against the wishes of her family; one of Amritsar's best-known road bridges, the Bhandari Bridge, is named after him. In her younger days, she was known as the 'spitfire' because of her often abusive language, especially when aimed at young men attracted to her three daughters. By the time of her death in 2007 at the age of 101, she was believed to be the last remaining Parsi living in Amritsar.

During my time as a Middle East correspondent based in Jerusalem, my home from home was the American Colony Hotel, as it was for dozens of foreign correspondents who came to regard it as a blessedly peaceful oasis and an invaluable place to pick up stories and gossip. Its origins were as a community of devout American Christians brought together in the 1880s by the Spafford family of Chicago after their four daughters had drowned in a shipwreck. Their grandson, Horatio, and his English wife Val were still very much around when I first arrived in Jerusalem, and after Horatio's death, Val could be found having breakfast every morning in the hotel restaurant, keeping a motherly eye on any British correspondents whose names she had spotted on the hotel register.

The hotel was originally a rather grand, stone villa built for a nineteenth-century Turkish pasha, and it owes its enduring popularity with journalists, diplomats, businesspeople and spies to the fact that it occupies the closest thing in Jerusalem to a neutral space. It is located in the eastern, Arab part of town that had been ruled by Jordan until 1967 but close to the now invisible line that used to divide the Arab and Jewish sections of this supposedly holy city. It is still owned by the descendants of the Spaffords, although it is managed these days by a Swiss hotel group. Its staff are mainly Palestinians, and in my day we became good friends with George Qumsieh, the Bethlehem-born doorman who had been working there since 1948, knew everything that was worth knowing and was always able to lay his hands on a couple of extra cookies for our young children when we showed up for a couple of hours' lazing by the swimming pool on a Saturday.

On one occasion, after we had moved back to London, I was visiting Jerusalem to make a radio documentary for the BBC, and George had the difficult task of interrupting my lunch to whisper that my rental car had just been firebombed in the hotel car park. I had made the mistake of renting from a Jewish-run agency at Ben Gurion airport rather than from a Palestinian-run agency closer to the hotel, and the local car rental people apparently wanted to let me know of their displeasure. George was hugely embarrassed and apologetic, but he knew I would understand.

As did the staff on the hotel switchboard when I had to ask them not to be too specific about my precise whereabouts when they put calls through to me from the office in London. The words 'One moment, please, he's by the pool' would not, I feared, have conveyed the right impression.

In the dimly lit basement bar, Ibrahim the barman knew every regular's favourite tipple and could always be relied upon to be the soul of discretion. The bar's ill-lit alcoves were ideal for illicit liaisons of all descriptions, both personal and political, and often served as a hidden meeting place for unofficial Israeli and Palestinian negotiators.

(Just round the corner was Orient House, which for many years was the unofficial, and illegal, Jerusalem headquarters of the PLO.) The American Colony was one of the very few places in Jerusalem were both Jews and Palestinians could feel comfortable, although the Israeli security people at the airport were always deeply suspicious of it as a destination address on my landing card.

'Why are you staying in the Arab part of Jerusalem? Why don't you stay in the Jewish part?' I used to tell them the American Colony was by far the best hotel in town, but they were rarely convinced.

Oasis it may have been, but in Jerusalem you are never far from trouble. On a return visit to the city in the late '90s, I was eating lunch in the hotel's beautiful courtyard, sitting at one of the characteristic brightly tiled tables with a young BBC producer, when we heard a huge explosion. It was obviously a bomb, so we set off towards where the blast had come from, weaving our way on foot through the back streets to avoid the inevitable road closures. As we approached the Jewish ultra-religious area of Mea Shearim, I suggested that we should skirt round it, as my female colleague was wearing tight jeans and a sleeveless top, and would certainly be regarded as improperly dressed by the area's ultra-Orthodox Jewish residents.

'Listen,' she said. 'I'm an Australian girl, and I regard being properly dressed as wearing both parts of my bikini.' Her name was Kylie Morris and she went on to become an award-winning TV correspondent, first for the BBC in Gaza, Kabul, Bangkok and Iraq, and later for *Channel 4 News* in Bangkok and Washington DC.

I am not a great fan of international business hotels (is anyone?), even if I recognise that they do usually provide all the services that a hard-pressed reporter is likely to need. So, since the introduction of online hotel booking sites, I regarded it as my task, while a producer was fixing interviews, researching stories and generally committing journalism, to track down a nice-sounding hotel which offered all the basic services (Wi-Fi, shower, food) and then something extra, all at a price that was likely to be acceptable to the people in the BBC expenses department.

In normal times, Dwarika's Hotel in Kathmandu would certainly fail the last of those tests. But, in May 2006, Nepal was in the throes of revolution and visitors were thin on the ground. Dwarika's was more than happy to negotiate a special cut rate for the intrepid BBC team – producer Catherine Miller and myself – who were prepared to risk a few days of revolutionary fervour. It was, and is, a welcome sanctuary amid the unceasing clamour of Nepali life.

Dwarika's is built almost entirely of wood, featuring the intricately carved timbers that are characteristic of the Newar culture of the Kathmandu valley. It was established by the hotel's founder, Dwarika Das Shrestha, after he spotted workmen feeding ancient carvings into a fire as they renovated an old royal palace. He resolved to devote his life to the preservation of the ancient carvings and of the skills that enable modern craftsmen to continue the tradition.

The rooms at Dwarika's are enormous. The bathrooms alone are about three times the size of a New York hotel room. But my favourite memory is the warning sign placed on the desk in my room: 'Please be sure to close all windows before leaving your room. Otherwise monkeys from the temple will enter.'

One of the most shameful episodes in my career of hotel-hopping took place in the Nigerian capital, Abuja, which is one of those fake cities built in the middle of nowhere simply in order to be a national capital. (Brasília and Naypyidaw, in Myanmar/Burma, are two others.) It took over from Lagos as the national capital in 1991, so there has not been much time yet for any traditions to take hold. There is not a lot of ancient carved timber in Abuja.

There are, however, the usual international business hotels, and it was at one of these that I was forced to confront my own prejudices about Nigeria and Nigerians. (As it happens, I am very fond of the country and of its people, who have an infectious can-do energy that always reminds me of New York.)

It was election time, and a sizeable BBC team was in town, because Nigerians are by far the biggest single audience for the BBC World Service, which broadcasts to several million Nigerian listeners in both English and Hausa. When it was time for us all to leave, the senior BBC field producer arranged to pay the entire BBC bill before he checked out, so that those of us who were staying a little longer would simply pay any charges that we had incurred after his departure.

So I was not amused when I was presented with a bill that included everything for my entire stay. 'No,' I protested. 'Most of this has already been paid by my colleague.' The cashiers disagreed and, to my shame, I have to admit that my head filled with tales of Nigerian fraudsters and scammers. But I kept my cool and made no accusations. It was obviously a simple mistake – that, at least, is what I said. It was not what I thought.

Eventually, I phoned my senior colleague who had already returned home. I asked him to confirm to the hotel that he had indeed paid the bulk of the bill. 'God, I'm so sorry,' he said. 'I left in such a rush, I never got round to paying for everyone.' Humble pie? I grovelled. And then I grovelled some more. And I will never ever again even think that I am being defrauded unless I have irrefutable evidence. Let the record show: I was not cheated in Nigeria.

On the contrary. Some of my happiest reporting memories are from Nigeria, a country where everything is possible and nothing ever works. Where else could I have interviewed a self-confessed vote-buyer, a man hired by a major political party to loiter outside polling stations on election day and offer cash bribes to voters in return for their support? He even demonstrated how he could slip a banknote into my hand without anyone noticing. But vote-buying, he told me, was a precarious living: he had to finance the bribes out of his own pocket, and had not been reimbursed because the candidate on whose behalf he was doing the bribing still failed to win.

I also spent an unforgettable couple of hours at The Shrine nightclub in Lagos, home of the leading Nigerian musician Femi Kuti, whose father Fela Kuti had been one of Africa's most revered musical pioneers and human rights activists. When we asked him to play a few notes on his saxophone for the benefit of the BBC's listeners, Femi immediately started an impromptu jam session with a few friends, stripped off his shirt and treated us, especially my female colleague, to an unexpectedly exciting recording experience.

Have I mentioned food yet? I should have done, because one of the first pieces of advice I received as a very young reporter was nothing to do with how to get a story or how to beat the competition. It came from a grizzled old hack who had obviously been around for quite a while. 'Never forget,' he said. 'Eat and pee whenever you have the opportunity. You never know when you'll get another chance.' I took his advice and, for the past forty-five years, I have eaten and peed whenever I had the opportunity.

My BBC sound engineer colleague Lee Chaundy could not have paid me a nicer compliment when I finally hung up my microphone for the last time: 'Your ability always to plan at least two meals ahead will be much missed.' It is true: I have always found that I work much better if I know when and where my next meal is coming from.

So I fondly remember a superb Japanese restaurant in Beirut, as well as a more than adequate spaghetti house in the same city; a very decent Lebanese restaurant in Kano, in northern Nigeria, and an unexpectedly tasty pizza place in Kinshasa. I choose not to remember the countless club sandwiches I have eaten late at night in hotel rooms, washed down either with warm Coca-Cola (you should never add ice to drinks in hot and dusty countries) or truly disgusting coffee. And I definitely choose not to remember the too many occasions when my stomach has violently objected to my choice of career.

Sometimes I have been required to eat a specific food at a specific time solely in the interest of journalistic integrity. Once was in Ukraine, when a very clever BBC producer, David Edmonds, who in his other life is a widely respected philosopher, decided that in order to illustrate some profound truth about the nature of Ukrainian democracy, I was required to eat (noisily) a bowl of Ukrainian borscht, or beetroot soup.

He even found a Ukrainian journalist who was prepared to stand up his thesis. 'There are at least twenty-six recipes for borscht,' he told us. 'Everyone has their own recipe. So it's like democracy. People in Ukraine have one kind of democracy; people in the US have another kind.'[15]

The second occasion was when another bright BBC producer, Leana Hosea, wanted me to cover a report from the UN Food and Agriculture Organization on the subject of entomophagy, or the consumption of insects by humans, which the FAO suggested was to be greatly encouraged. You can imagine my delight when she announced that she had found a restaurant[16] in London where they happily offered insects on the menu – and that the only possible way to report the story adequately was to drag me along and record me feasting on some of their delicacies.

'Yum, yum,' I obediently reported. 'Scorpions dipped in chocolate. And oh look, I must try the love-bug salad with deep-fried locusts and crickets.' (The truth? I quite liked them. Crunchy, slightly salty, not unlike prawns.)

It was not the only occasion when I reflected that BBC licence fee-payers ought to be much more appreciative of the efforts that I made to report world events for their benefit.

CHAPTER 6

A SUBURBAN CHILDHOOD

I am a big boy now, and I want to know everything.
ME, AGED THREE

THERE IS A PARTICULAR type of interview that is often favoured by radio news editors when a new story breaks in an unfamiliar part of the world – it is known as the 'how did we get here?' interview, and its purpose is to fill in some of the background and context to whatever is dominating the headlines. The interviewer's first words are usually along the lines of: 'So, fill in some of the background for us…'

Here is some of the background.

I was born on 30 August 1948, by Caesarean section, at the Bearsted Memorial Hospital in Stoke Newington, north London. My parents were both refugees from Nazi Germany: my father had arrived in the UK in April 1939; my mother in July of the same year. They met during the Second World War, when both were working in a top-secret unit of British military intelligence, and they married in 1945. I was the first of their two sons; my younger brother, Stephen, was born three years later.

We 1948ers are said to have been born in the best year ever. Among our number we count Prince Charles; the former chief rabbi, Jonathan Sacks; the singer Lulu; and the former governor of the Bank of England, Mervyn King. What we have in common is that we have all been able to benefit from the National Health Service, free education up to and including university level, a booming property market and state pensions at a much younger age than our children will enjoy. By the time we reached adolescence, the contraceptive pill had become widely available, which did wonders for our sex lives. (How many of these benefits the Prince of Wales has taken advantage of I cannot say, but the principle holds good even for him.)

My father, Fritz, was the youngest of four children in a typically middle-class Berlin family. They were of Jewish origin, but had abandoned any overt religious identity – his own father had been brought up in a totally non-religious household, and my father, like his three siblings, was baptised in a Lutheran church and attended Christian religious instruction lessons at school. Like many secular German Jews at the time, his parents believed that by adopting a Christian religious identity, they would be more readily accepted as 'real' Germans. It was not, in the circumstances of the time, an unreasonable assumption – until the Nazis came to power in 1933.

Remarkably, given that throughout his entire adult life my father never had any time at all for religion (I often referred to him as a 'fundamentalist secularist'), he never forgot the biblical text that he chose for his confirmation at the age of fourteen. It was Corinthians Chapter 13, the one that ends: 'And now abideth faith, hope, charity, these three; but the greatest of these is charity.'

In his memoirs, my father wrote:

> My confirmation proved to be a milestone, but not in the expected sense. Having got it behind me I found that there was no longer any need to pretend anything, either to myself or to others, and I felt free to admit that in fact I did not 'believe' in anything. I became an agnostic overnight, so to speak, and have never entered a church for worship since – only to admire, or dislike, its architecture, or play music in it; and I have not said a prayer either.

His decision to leave Germany came after the horrors of *Kristallnacht*, the Night of Broken Glass, on 9 November 1938, when thousands of synagogues and other Jewish targets throughout Germany were attacked and set alight and more than thirty thousand Jews were arrested. My father and grandfather both had to go into hiding for a few days to escape arrest, sheltering in the home of a non-Jewish family friend.

In order to get out of Germany, he enlisted the help of an English family with whom he had stayed on a visit as a schoolboy in 1936. Reg and Elsie Francis, of Letchworth, Hertfordshire, helped him to obtain a 'trainee visa' which would allow him into the UK on condition that he learned a trade and then left again within twelve months for either Australia or New Zealand. Relatives in Cambridge arranged for him to be apprenticed to a local builder, but his parents were anxious that, as a gifted young cellist who they hoped might one day become a professional musician, he should not take up work that risked damaging his hands.

The response from the relatives in Cambridge was not sympathetic: what exactly was the priority? To get him safely out of Germany, or to preserve his precious hands?

The answer was obvious, so, on 13 April 1939, two weeks after his twentieth birthday, my father set sail from Hamburg on board the SS *President Roosevelt*. His parents came with him to the quayside, and his mother told him later that, as they waved goodbye, she was convinced that she would never see him again. Two days later, he was in Southampton.

My mother was born Susanne Cohn in what was then the German city of Breslau, and is now the Polish city of Wrocław (pronounced *Vrots-woff*). She had no brothers or sisters; her father had been a cavalry officer in the German army in the First World War and had suffered a shoulder injury that left him without the use of his left arm. Her mother's family had been relatively prosperous – her maternal grandfather had been a successful cattle dealer – but her father was a much less successful businessman.

After his death from a heart attack in April 1938, and then *Kristallnacht* a few months later, she and her mother decided that they would have to try to leave Germany. They both applied for visas to the US, but the waiting list was so long that my mother also applied to come to the UK on her own as a domestic servant. (Their richer friends were buying forged visas for countries in South America, an option that was not available to my cash-strapped mother and grandmother.) A cousin of her father's, who was already living in London, found some friends who said they would be prepared to employ my mother as a domestic, and she duly got her visa.

To pay for her ticket to England, her mother sold a large Persian rug and a set of coffee cups. She also managed to provide my mother with twenty pairs of stockings, ten tubes of toothpaste and ten bars of soap so that she would not have to waste money buying them in England. Passage was booked on the SS *Washington* and, like my father, my mother sailed from Hamburg to Southampton via Le Havre.

Years later, she wrote:

> I was quite looking forward to it; I liked the idea of leaving Germany, I liked adventure, and the whole thing didn't worry me one bit … The first thing I did on the boat was buy some lipstick, because my mother had never allowed me to wear it. It was a wonderful feeling; I felt free.[17]

She was eighteen years old and never saw her mother again.

I think of my parents' stories every time I read of the hundreds of thousands of refugees who have fled from countries like Syria, Iraq, Afghanistan and Eritrea. Each one of them, and each one of their children, will have similar tales to tell, and when I look at their faces on the TV news, it is easy for me to imagine that I am looking at the faces of my own parents.

My father and mother could not have been more different: my father tall and slim, thoughtful, cautious and happiest when either listening to classical music or playing his beloved cello; my mother short and round, cheerful, gregarious and happiest when surrounded by family, friends and food. Yet they were happily married for sixty-seven years, until my mother's death in 2013, just a few weeks before her ninety-second birthday.

They were married in a civil ceremony in Hampstead Town Hall on 6 June 1945, exactly twelve months after the D-Day landings. My father had been reluctant to splash out on a wedding reception, but my mother, typically, had insisted. He also saw no need for anyone to take photographs to mark the occasion ('too bourgeois', apparently), but, again, my mother insisted. She bought a new dress to wear on her wedding day, but my father was still in the army, so he wore his uniform. They invited about thirty friends and relatives to a small party in the house where my mother had lived during the war; the wedding cake was made by my father's eldest sister, using powdered egg and powdered milk, all that was available.

Their army friends had clubbed together to buy them a radio as a wedding present, so perhaps it was then that the seeds of my future career were sown. The honeymoon was a week in Cornwall, where it rained the entire time. Five weeks later, my father was posted to Germany, and my mother was left behind to find their first marital home.

In bomb-shattered London, with just £25 to her name and a weekly wage of £4.50 as an office supervisor, it was a huge challenge. In later life, she recalled: 'For the only time in my life, I really felt suicidal.' Eventually, she found a two-bedroom flat in a mansion block, Elmhurst Mansions, in Edgeley Road, just off Clapham High Street in south London. 'It was filthy dirty, completely unfurnished, and the kitchen was full of mouldy food. There were cockroaches crawling around, and the bath was in an indescribable condition, but despite all that, I felt I could deal with it.'[18]

The rent was £1.25 a week, and under the post-war rationing system then in force, she was allocated coupons that would enable her to buy enough furniture for just one room. She bought two armchairs (they were both still in use seventy years later), a sideboard, also still in use, a table and four chairs. She also found a lodger to help with the rent: a wartime friend, Elizabeth (Beth) Rees-Mogg, elder sister of William, later Lord, Rees-Mogg, who went on to become editor of *The Times*, chairman of the Arts Council and vice-chairman of the BBC.

When my father left the army the following year, he had to find a job. He had no qualifications and no experience that was likely to be of any use to potential employers. My mother was working in what was then the temporary headquarters of the United Nations in London; when it moved to New York, she joined the Inter-Governmental Committee on Refugees, which dealt with the hundreds of thousands of people throughout Europe who had lost their homes in the war and were now on their way to Canada, the US and Australia.

Both my father's parents, Franz and Rose, survived the war: they escaped from Germany to Italy in 1940 and managed to make their way to Portugal, where they lived with one of their daughters and her Portuguese husband. In December 1946, they moved to London, but my grandfather collapsed as soon as he got to my parents' flat and never fully recovered. He died the following May at the age of seventy-four. My grandmother outlived him by thirty-five years and died just nine days after her ninety-eighth birthday.*

Before the First World War, my grandfather Lustig had been a moderately successful businessman, but after the war, during which he served in a field artillery unit, he became a sales representative for bicycle manufacturers, a job that he eventually lost after *Kristallnacht* in 1938. His great passions were music and writing: he enjoyed writing poetry, often humorous ditties for family occasions, and would probably have been amused that both his British grandsons ended up in the words business: my brother in publishing and me in journalism. My father remembers playing piano duets with him as a child, and being taken to concerts; music played an important part in Lustig family life, and my father continues to play the cello even in his nineties.

Among my earliest memories is lying in bed after supper listening to the sound of a string quartet wafting upstairs from the front living room, and when my brother and I were growing up, we were often expected to demonstrate our prowess on the piano or recorder at family parties. If nothing else, the tradition served as an invaluable training in how to put on a show, something that broadcasters need to master even if they are in the news business. By the time I reached my teens, I preferred to perform with words rather than music, so I devised 'comedy' items modelled on whichever comedian was being featured on the radio at the time. One Christmas, I decided to write a parody of a BBC radio news bulletin, in which each news item featured a different member of the family. The shape of things to come...

---

* My wife's maternal grandmother lived to ninety-six, and her mother made it to a hundred, so we have warned our children that they should expect to live for ever.

Bearsted Memorial Hospital, where I was born, had been founded in the late nineteenth century in the East End of London as a place where Orthodox Jewish women could give birth. It was not the obvious place for my mother to choose, because, as she recalled much later: 'I'd become very anti-Jewish because of everything that had happened [in Nazi Germany], so I just wanted to cut myself off from Judaism.'[19]

As I was due to be born by Caesarean section, my mother was told that she could choose, a few days either side of her due date, the exact date of my birth. Although throughout the war she had not known what fate had befallen her own mother, by the time of my birth, she knew that she had perished in the Holocaust. So she chose her mother's date of birth to be mine as well, a decision that was to create an immensely powerful bond across the generations when, more than sixty years later, I stood on the exact spot where my grandmother had been murdered.

Fathers were not expected to play any role during childbirth in the 1940s, so my father went to work as normal on the day that I was due to be delivered, and was informed by phone of my eventual safe arrival. It was only at the end of his working day that he made his way to the hospital to meet me for the first time.

Three days later, my father's older brother, my uncle Ted, wrote to him from the US, where he had settled after leaving Germany. The letter came to light only recently, but it was remarkably prescient. After congratulating my parents on the birth of their first child, he wrote: 'If he grows up to be an asker of questions, he will be, indeed, one of the rare men who may find an answer here and there. Let him be an asker-of-questions. That is my wish for him.'

I had been a journalist for many years when I first saw that letter, and both my uncle and my parents had forgotten all about it. I still think it is extraordinary that, almost like a fairy godfather, he had peered into my future and somehow divined the path that my life would take. Although he and I lived on opposite sides of the Atlantic, I always felt extremely close to him and I am still close to my three

American cousins. And I can think of no better epitaph than 'He was an asker of questions.'

My lifelong obsession with questions seems to have started at a very early age. In a letter written shortly after my third birthday, my mother reported:

> Robin talks such a lot now that it often gets a bit too much for us. And the questions!!! The other day he saw a photo of a candidate in the general election and wanted a full explanation. When I said that there were things he did not understand yet, he said: 'But I am a big boy now, and I want to know everything.'

I still feel the same way.

My first childhood home was in a London suburb so anonymous that I am still not quite sure exactly what to call it. The postal address was Greenford, Middlesex, the telephone exchange was Wembley and the nearest Tube station was Sudbury Town. It was about a fifteen-minute walk from Ruislip Gardens, immortalised by John Betjeman in his poem 'Middlesex': 'Gaily into Ruislip Gardens / Runs the red electric train / With a thousand Ta's and Pardon's / Daintily alights Elaine.'

My parents had paid £2,100 for a three-bedroomed terraced house at 73 Drew Gardens. It was conveniently close to the green open space of Horsenden Hill, which soars to a mighty 280 feet above sea level, and where evidence has been found of Iron Age settlements. Of more interest to me as I grew up was the golf course, and the trees that surrounded it, where lost balls could be retrieved by eagle-eyed young boys and then sold back to golfers in the clubhouse. Our home was also only about a fifteen-minute walk from where my grandmother was living, with her sister and eldest daughter, so it was, for my parents, a very suitable house in which to raise their family.

North Greenford, which is probably the most accurate name for the area, will never win any prizes for architectural distinction. It was developed, like so many London suburbs, between the two world wars, and time has not been kind to it. Gentrification has passed it by, and in the streets around Drew Gardens some houses are now boarded up. Others look as if they have had little care devoted to them since I was growing up there more than fifty years ago. Nearly all the front gardens have been paved over to provide off-street parking.

My father's first job after leaving the army was in the offices of the *Anglo-Palestine Yearbook*, a publication that gathered together all the essential facts and figures that might have been of interest to companies thinking of doing business in Palestine, which was still, until the establishment of the state of Israel in 1948, ruled by Britain under a mandate from the League of Nations. It was a job that was clearly going nowhere, so he started looking around for something more promising.

> Educated, intelligent young man (27), just demobbed, wants progress-
> ive job. 3 years' resp. work Mil. Intelligence. Organ. and admin. ex-
> perience, used working on own initiative and responsibility. Bilingual
> English/German. Good knowledge general office routine and typing.
> Wide interests. Reliable and eager worker. Any offers?

So what exactly had been his 'resp. work Mil. Intelligence'? It was so secret that not until the 1970s did he tell anyone, including his own family, what he had been doing in the British army's Intelligence Corps. (My mother, of course, already knew, because she had worked in the same unit.) My father had been a 'secret listener', eavesdropping on German prisoners of war as they spoke to each other unguardedly in their bugged prison cells. Microphones were concealed in the cells' light fittings, and teams of native German speakers, most of them refugees, worked in shifts to listen to what they told each other and activate recording devices whenever they discussed matters that might be of interest to British military intelligence.

There were three locations where these 'secret listeners' worked: Trent Park, in Enfield, north London; and Latimer House and Wilton Park in Buckinghamshire. The full value of the work that was done there – including some of the earliest intelligence on the Germans' development of the V-1 flying bombs, or doodlebugs, which were an early form of cruise missile, and the V-2 long-range guided missiles – was revealed only when the transcripts of the bugged conversations were declassified in the late 1990s and later written about.[20] My father then found himself very much in demand by television documentary-makers to talk about his work, as one of the very few 'secret listeners' still alive.

His second job once he had left the army was as an invoice clerk at Cahn and Bendit, a company that dealt in accessories for ladies' handbags, at a starting salary of £7 per week. He also went to evening classes at the Regent Street Polytechnic in central London (now the University of Westminster) to gain a qualification that would enable him to work as a company secretary. Having left Germany with just a school-leaving certificate, he knew that he needed some kind of professional qualification, which he duly obtained in 1950.

My father's modest salary was not enough to pay the mortgage, so my mother did typing jobs at home in the evenings, and they took in lodgers who lived in the small bedroom at the top of the stairs. Even fifty years later, my mother remembered each of them by name: Mrs Barnes, who worked in a local bus garage and went to the cinema every evening; Mr Cole, who went ballroom dancing every night and always left his shoes at the bottom of the stairs so as not to disturb the rest of the household when he came home late; and Mr Mirza, from Pakistan, who burnt incense which made the whole house smell.

Money was always tight: my father also went to woodwork evening classes so that he could learn to make some basic furniture for the family home, and in later years he remembered agonising over whether he could afford to buy a new paintbrush when a room needed redecorating. Fortunately, my mother had a well-off cousin who had settled in California and who used to send boxes of hand-me-down children's clothes; her own son was just a few months older than I was, and I still remember the excitement when the boxes were delivered. For some reason I have a particularly vivid memory of a pair of dark blue skiing trousers that I especially treasured, even though I never once went skiing.

These days, we post-war baby boomers are held responsible for most of the world's ills, but my memories of life as a child in post-war

Britain are not of a life of luxury. Some foods were still rationed for several years after I was born, and I remember going to pick up the government-issue concentrated orange juice that was meant to reduce malnutrition among post-war toddlers. I also remember the coal being delivered to our house in huge sacks, and the milk that was delivered in pint bottles by horse-drawn cart (on Saturdays I was sometimes allowed to ride on the horse, Molly, as she made her way down our street). With no central heating, we would often wake up on a bitterly cold winter morning to find our bedroom windows encrusted with ice. On the inside.

None of this is meant to sound as if I endured a Dickensian childhood of misery and deprivation, because nothing could be further from the truth. For my parents, though, those early years were a struggle, as they were for millions of other people in the immediate post-war years. They had few friends and little time for a social life. As refugees, they had only a limited network of friends and relatives to fall back on when help was needed, although both my grandmother and my aunt Eva, who was fifteen years older than my father, were usually on hand for occasional babysitting duties.

My grandmother was sixty-four when I was born, and she told me many years later that her hope had been that she would live long enough to see me go to school. In fact, she saw me go on from school to university, and then get married and have a child. She died just five weeks after my son Josh, her first great-grandchild, was born.

I was, by all accounts, a serious child, never happier than when I had my head buried in a book – or asking questions. My father got into the habit of bringing home library books every week in an attempt to feed my curiosity, and soon every birthday and Christmas would be marked by another volume of the Oxford Children's Encyclopaedia.

My parents did not approve of television, so there was no TV set at home. There was a Grundig radio in the corner of the living room, which would be switched on for the BBC Home Service news at eight o'clock in the morning and six o'clock in the evening.* Comedy shows

---

* The Home Service was replaced by Radio 4 in 1967.

– The Navy Lark, The Clitheroe Kid, The Men from the Ministry – were tolerated if not exactly approved of. Piano practice was compulsory. As we grew older, my brother and I took up the violin and clarinet respectively; he became a professional-standard violinist, while I preferred to nestle unobtrusively in the back of the woodwind section of the local youth orchestra.

My mother had an enormous capacity for fun and liked nothing more than to make her children laugh with silly invented words and stories. One of my earliest memories is of clutching my stomach in pain and complaining: 'You make me laugh too much.' My father was good at making things and had infinite patience. On Saturday mornings, he would cycle to the baker's to buy bread and, until I grew too big, I was allowed to go with him, sitting on a special child's saddle attached to his crossbar, with his chin resting on the top of my head and the wind blowing in my face.

In July 1951, I received a postcard from my mother, who was in hospital. 'Now at last we have got our baby. His name is Stephen and you must try to learn to say "Stephen" before we come home. He is still very small and I still have to stay in hospital to look after him for a few days.' When it was time for them to come home, my father and I went to collect them, and our journey back by taxi is my earliest memory. It was two months before my third birthday.

The overwhelming priority for my parents, after having grown up in the turmoil of Nazi Germany, was to create a safe and secure environment for their family. They could, of course, have chosen to bring up their sons bilingual in English and German if they had spoken to us in German at home. But in 1950s London, only a few years after the end of the Second World War, speaking the language of Britain's wartime enemy was the last thing they wanted their sons to be good at. They even spoke to each other only in English – they had, after all, met while serving in the British army, and to have spoken to each other in German then would have been highly ill-advised.

I did, however, hear German spoken when we visited our elderly relatives – and especially when they visited us at Christmas. There was a Lustig family Christmas tradition, dating back to pre-war Berlin, which my father, probably mainly for the benefit of my grandmother, was determined to observe. A Christmas tree would be bought and decorated, with real candles, not electric lights, and my grandmother, great-aunts Hansi and Ada, and aunt Eva would come to our house on Christmas Eve for the ritual of present-opening and a Christmas meal. When everyone was assembled, fur coats had been taken off, and bags full of presents handed over to my father, we would all be ushered into the back room while my father lit the candles on the tree in the front room and laid out the presents on chairs, a different chair for each member of the family. Then, we would be summoned to make our way into the front room, singing that most German of Christmas carols, 'O Tannenbaum', to the same tune as the Red Flag.

As my brother and I grew up, we began to subvert the ritual by delaying the opening of our own presents until everyone else had opened theirs. It annoyed the elderly relatives, since it somehow destroyed the illusion that we children were overwhelmed with uncontrollable excitement. Excited, us? By the time we reached the age of eleven or twelve, we were far too cool for such nonsense.

I remember two particular German phrases from my childhood: '*Er ist tot müde*' ('He is dead tired'), which is what my mother would say to my father if either my brother or I were misbehaving at bedtime, and '*Wo ist meine Tasche?*' ('Where is my handbag?'), which was the cry of our aunts as they gathered their belongings together at the end of a visit. Unfortunately, neither phrase proved particularly useful during my career as a foreign correspondent. But I did manage to pick up a few more words of German along the way, the most useful of which – '*ein kleines bisschen*' ('a little bit') – became my stock response to the question '*Sprechen Sie Deutsch?*' ('Do you speak German?')

I never had the chance to learn German at school, so I got into the habit, if I wanted to say something in German, of trying to imagine hearing my grandmother say it. It was a technique that worked remarkably well, even though she spoke surprisingly good English. My great-aunt Hansi, a large and somewhat forbidding woman with piercing brown eyes who had been a teacher before she left Germany, did try to teach me German for a while, but it was not a success. I think

I must have subconsciously adopted my parents' view that speaking German was not a particularly valuable skill in 1950s London.

Despite my parents' best efforts, it was obvious when I started going to school that I came from a somewhat different family background than my schoolmates. One boy delighted in calling me a Nazi, which seemed odd to me even then, since I knew that my family had escaped from the Nazis and regarded them as very nasty people. But the fact that my parents spoke English with an accent was probably more than enough to identify me as a suspicious foreigner.

My classmates' favourite pastime in the school playground, when not playing football, was to zoom about, arms outstretched, pretending to be fighter pilots shooting down German warplanes. And their favourite reading material – comics like the *Beano*, *Eagle*, and *Dandy* – often featured wartime storylines in which the Nazi villains were called Fritz, like my father. But even though I was in some senses a child apart, it never bothered me. I was always happier sitting in a classroom with a book than rushing around outside and, as far as I can judge, I suffered no childhood trauma as a result of being the son of refugees.

What was far more difficult to deal with was the lack of a television at home. How could I discuss the previous evening's programmes with my schoolmates in the playground if I had not seen them? What did I know of *Crackerjack*, *The Lone Ranger* or *Robin Hood*, unless I had been invited to a friend's house for tea? The solution I came up with was to develop a skill that proved invaluable in my later career: to be able to talk, apparently knowledgeably, about things that I knew nothing about. I have lost count of the occasions when, as a news broadcaster, I have made use of this skill, perfected in the school playground, to ask questions and participate in conversations from a position of total ignorance.

The first evidence of my journalistic ambitions dates back to 1959, when I was still at primary school and was one of four co-editors of the Horsenden Primary School magazine. We asked our fellow pupils to send in contributions for publication, but our editorial included an unmistakable note of disapproval: 'Some entries, we discovered, were copied and although these were good, we had to reject them as we wanted your own work.' There is clearly nothing new about the curse of journalistic plagiarism, nor indeed of that other curse, nepotism, since the magazine also included two limericks by my brother and a final story written by me, presumably to fill the blank space on the last page.

At home, before my arms were long enough to hold the open pages of a broadsheet newspaper, I would kneel on the floor of the living room, with the *News Chronicle* laid out in front of me, reading the cartoon strips – Colonel Pewter and Tintin – and beginning my descent into a lifelong addiction to news. My parents also bought me a subscription to *The Children's Newspaper*, a weekly publication that had been started after the First World War and which at its peak had sold half a million copies a week. As a result, I was in hopeless thrall to newsprint long before I went to secondary school.

On the first day of the new decade, 1 January 1960, we moved out of London and into a new home in Reading, forty miles to the west. My father had found a new job, working as an accountant for a plastics company, so we upped sticks and settled at 49 Southcote Lane, in a semi-detached house with garage where my parents lived for the next fifty-one years.

Reading in the 1960s was a staid, unremarkable market town, home to Simonds brewery, Sutton Seeds, and Huntley & Palmers biscuit factory. All have long gone now, but for many years Reading was known principally as the town of beer, bulbs and biscuits. These days it is one of the fastest-growing towns in England, thanks to its proximity to Heathrow airport and its good road and rail links to London. It is also, of course, where Oscar Wilde was incarcerated in 1895 for gross indecency, and the site of the remains of Reading Abbey, founded in 1121 by King Henry I, who is buried there.

The oldest example of written English music, the song 'Sumer Is Icumen In', is said to have been composed by a monk in the abbey in or around 1250. It is the earliest known example of both secular and sacred words being used in the same piece of music, but most notable, for those with a taste for vulgarity, is that it contains the earliest documented use of the word 'fart': '*Ewe bleateth after lamb, Calf loweth after cow, Bullock starteth, buck farteth, Merry sing cuckoo!*' Not bad for a thirteenth-century monk.

With the benefit of hindsight, I sometimes wonder whether first the outer London suburbs and then Reading were perfect places for my parents to bring up their family: slightly dull, but, much more importantly, totally safe. After the traumas of growing up in Nazi Germany and then living through the Second World War, who could blame them for opting for a little less excitement? And, who knows, perhaps a childhood spent cocooned in such a safe environment led to my own decision to flee the nest at the earliest opportunity and seek out a career that certainly never lacked for excitement.

My father would have liked me to go to Reading School, a highly selective grammar school with a 900-year history and an enviable academic record. (In 2010, it was named state school of the year by the *Sunday Times*.) But I did not meet its rigorous entry standards, so I went instead to Stoneham School for Boys, which was certainly less prestigious and was in reality two schools under the same roof: a grammar school and a secondary modern school, each of which tried to pretend that the other did not exist. Grammar school boys had to wear uniforms, whereas secondary modern boys did not. We even had separate staircases and different teachers.

It was a truly bizarre arrangement, and the school was finally put out of its misery in 1985, when it merged with the neighbouring girls' school to become Prospect School. Twenty years earlier, I had organised a pupils' petition calling for just such a merger, although that had little to do with the potential educational benefits and much more to do with teenage boys' obsession with girls. The headmaster, Dr Smith, was not amused.

In fact, Stoneham suited me just fine (I was admitted to the grammar school side as I had passed my eleven-plus exam before we moved from London and had already spent one term at Greenford Grammar

School). My best subjects were English and French, I played clarinet in the school orchestra, conducted by the music teacher Eric Few, who always had a cigarette dangling from his lower lip during rehearsals, and I took small parts in school plays under the direction of drama teacher Charles Uzell.

One production daringly included girls from the neighbouring school: it was *Lady Precious Stream*, by the Chinese writer S. I. Hsiung, which had had hugely successful runs in both London and New York in the 1930s and had gained a reputation as one of the most performed plays in the world. The leading role was taken by a girl called Angela Pearson, who later became much better known as the Conservative minister Angela Browning, now Baroness Browning of Whimple. Some years after I had started working for the BBC, and had interviewed her several times, she noticed my name in an old school programme and made the connection. We had a nostalgic lunch to mark the coincidence.

It was while I was at Stoneham School that I first developed a serious interest in politics. It began when I started to sell ladybird lapel pins on behalf of the Pestalozzi Children's Village charity, which helped children who had become orphans or refugees during the Second World War. (It still offers scholarships to young people from some of the world's poorest countries, and its logo is still a ladybird.)

From selling ladybirds, I soon moved on to selling CND badges, as Reading is only ten miles from Aldermaston, where the UK's nuclear warheads were manufactured, and in the 1960s the campaign for nuclear disarmament was a local as well as a national issue. Every Easter, the anti-nuclear Aldermaston protest marchers would pass by the end of our road on their way to or from London, and before long I was joining them.

But, as Isaac Newton discovered, for every action there is an equal and opposite reaction, and soon my CND badges were being challenged in the school playground by badges bearing the symbol of the League of Empire Loyalists, a far-right group that eventually became the National Front. Unsurprisingly, the school quickly banned the wearing of all political symbols on school uniforms; equally unsurprisingly, we found a way to get round the ban by wearing our badges on the insides of our blazer lapels and displaying them surreptitiously when no teacher was in sight.

At the time of the 1964 general election, which came after thirteen years of uninterrupted Conservative rule, the school held a mock election of its own. I stood as a candidate for the Communist Party, much to the disapproval of my father, who assumed, no doubt correctly, that my candidacy would immediately lead to the opening of an MI5 file about me. (Although I did not know it at the time, my father had himself showed an interest in the Communist Party in 1943, which had brought him to the attention of a certain Sergeant Eric Hobsbawm, who was stationed in the same army barracks in Wiltshire.)* I came a respectable third in the school election, behind Labour and the Conservatives but ahead of the Liberals.

Inevitably, I was also a keen member of the school debating society, and I still have my notes from a debate in 1965 in which I spoke in favour of abolishing the death penalty for murder. I ended my speech with the words: 'Every person who votes against the abolition of capital punishment shares part of the responsibility for every subsequent execution – and I will be much happier in the knowledge that I, for one, am without that burden.' I was sixteen years old.

There were several areas of school life for which I was grievously ill-suited. I could neither draw nor paint, nor could I wield a chisel or a saw to create anything recognisable in woodwork. On the sports field, I was a complete disaster and I hated cross-country running more than anything in the world. I was also the school's most un-popular cricketer, as I was a left-handed batsman (I do everything else right-handed), which meant that when it was my turn to bat, the fielders all had to be repositioned accordingly. As I was then usually bowled out with the first ball, they stayed in their new positions for no more than a few seconds before having to return to where they had been just moments before.

---

* Hobsbawm later became Britain's leading Marxist historian. He and my father had been at the same school in Berlin in the 1930s; they rekindled their friendship in later life and remained friends until Hobsbawm's death in 2012.

It is no wonder that I was designated team scorer and, for a time, I became surprisingly proficient in the arcane science of cricket scoring, which consists of a bewildering variety of hieroglyphs entered into a complex series of tables and charts. My preference, though, was to escape to the school library, where I would very happily re-cover damaged books with adhesive plastic, or classify new acquisitions according to the Dewey classification system (100 for philosophy and psychology, 200 for religion, 300 for social sciences…)

For a politically obsessed teenager, which I soon became, the early 1960s were an era dominated by fear of nuclear war. The Cuban Missile Crisis in 1962 brought the world perilously close to the edge, and on the day when a Soviet tanker was due to reach the naval blockade that had been put in place by the US off the Cuban coast, I remember coming out of school at 4 p.m. and looking up into the sky to see if there was any sign of a mushroom cloud signifying a Soviet nuclear strike on Aldermaston. The fear was very real.

My literary influences during my adolescence encouraged a somewhat bleak outlook on life. I read Jean-Paul Sartre (*The Age of Reason*, which portrays the human condition in a deeply unflattering light, was a particular influence) and Albert Camus; I also ploughed my way through Bertrand Russell's *A History of Western Philosophy*. My musical tastes tended towards Joan Baez and protest folk, although I was, of course, as caught up in Beatlemania as everyone else of my generation. (I am happy to admit that meeting and interviewing Paul McCartney thirty-five years later was one of the most rewarding moments of my entire journalistic career, as well as being the only occasion on which my then teenage children were seriously impressed by what I did for a living.) The acquisition of a second-hand transistor radio, complete with earpiece, meant that I could listen in secret to the commercial pop music station Radio Luxembourg late at night, with the radio concealed beneath my bedclothes. (BBC Radio 1 was introduced only in 1967, as a direct response to both Radio Luxembourg and the pirate radio stations that had sprung up, broadcasting from ships moored offshore.)

I had one teacher who was a major influence on my later life: Gwyn Evans, a ruddy-faced Welshman of pronounced left-wing views. He

had twinkly blue eyes and a love of mischief, and although his official job was to teach French, he also taught me a great deal more. I
somehow doubt that he would get away today with the lively political
discussions that he encouraged while supposedly teaching us the finer
points of French grammar. In a letter written in 1965, I described him
as 'a convinced Communist' and said: 'Due to his influence, I fear I
am developing rather extremist views, proof of which is my new nickname among my school-pals: "little red Robin".'

For my last two years at school, Gwyn Evans also taught me Spanish
and, as only one other boy was interested in learning it, we had what
in effect were private lessons that enabled us to reach A-level standard
from scratch in just two years. My fellow pupil, Richard House, went
on to become a teacher of French and Spanish in the United States,
while my first two overseas postings as a foreign correspondent were
to Spain and France. Both of us owed our entire adult careers to this
one, outstanding teacher.

My first unaccompanied foreign trip was in March 1964, when at the
age of fifteen I was dispatched to spend the Easter holiday with a family
in rural France to improve my French. It was an ambitious journey:
first the flight to Le Bourget, then a coach to the main airline terminal
at Les Invalides, a Metro to the Gare de Lyons, and finally a train to
Moulins, about 125 miles north of Lyon. Waiting to meet me at the
station were M. Pisano, who worked at the local Simca tractor factory,
and his son Serge, who was my own age and my designated playmate
for the duration. Mme Pisano was a schoolteacher, and the family was
completed by eighteen-year-old Monique, who took pity on me and
repeated everything that was said to me slowly so that I might have
some chance of understanding, and Daniel, aged eight, with whom I
would spend many happy hours reading *Tintin* comic books.

My letters home suggest that my adventurous spirit was already
well developed. The weather was foul for most of my stay, and Serge
and I had little in common, yet I plainly enjoyed myself thoroughly.
A high point was my introduction to French cuisine: in one letter, I
reported: 'On Easter Sunday, we had a gorgeous lunch with pigeon,
two white wines and one red. There was one white wine for the hors

d'oeuvres, a different one for the salad, red for the pigeon, then white again for the cheese.'

My French improved dramatically – how could it not? – and by the time I returned home, I had fallen hopelessly in love with travel. I still feel the same unique mix of apprehension and anticipation that I felt on that first overseas adventure: apprehension that something will go horribly wrong, and anticipation at venturing into the unknown. No matter how meticulous the preparations – my hosts in France had thoughtfully sent me a copy of the French teen magazine *Salut les copains* to hold under my arm as I got off the train so that they would recognise me – disaster can never be ruled out. The pulse quickens, and the hands go clammy: even after all these years, there is still no agony to compare with the wait at an airport luggage collection carousel or at a passport control booth without a visa.

My next adventure overseas was far less successful, a useful lesson that travel is not always undiluted joy. A year after my visit to France, Gwyn Evans had offered to drive my classmate Richard and me to Spain for the Easter holidays, leaving us to spend a couple of weeks improving our linguistic skills while he and a friend went off camping. Richard stayed with a friend of Gwyn's in Bilbao, while arrangements had been made for me to stay in Madrid at the home of a friend of my aunt Dora, who had lived in Spain in the 1930s. The friend was a single woman of advanced years, and although she had evidently agreed to offer me a bed as a favour to my aunt, she saw no reason to take any further interest in my welfare. So for two weeks, with just two terms of Spanish lessons to my name, I was left entirely to my own devices.

My first letter home reported that I was 'completely miserable and extremely unhappy'. My hostess did not regard it as her responsibility to make sure that I was fed, so for the first couple of days I ate nothing. Eventually, I plucked up courage to go to a restaurant and ordered the only thing that I recognised on the menu: *huevos revueltos* (scrambled eggs). I lived on little else for a fortnight and spent most of my time being a lone tourist, visiting the Prado museum, El Escorial and Toledo, but talking to no one and therefore learning little

Spanish. My main achievement was to spend £5 (equivalent to about £85 now) on a rather bad oil painting of a Madrid street scene from a seller outside the Prado.

It is no bad thing to have learned at the tender age of sixteen that wandering the streets of a strange city on one's own can be a rewarding way to spend some time. I did plenty more of it when I found myself back in Madrid as a foreign correspondent five years later, and it is still one of my favourite pastimes whenever I have an hour or two to myself. So my ideal timetable when arriving in a new city is: first, check in to the hotel, establish that the Wi-Fi connection works and check emails, then venture forth to explore, sniff the air and get a feel for the place (which includes getting an idea of which promising restaurants are in the vicinity). The reality of life as a reporter, alas, is that all too often I would hit the ground running and be hard at work long before I had even found my way to the nearest street corner.

By the time I left school, I realised that the world was a big and fascinating place and that I had a burning desire to see as much of it as I could. Gap years had not yet been invented, but I discovered that it was possible to apply for a university place and then defer it for a year. A teacher told me about an organisation called Voluntary Service Overseas, which sent keen eighteen-year-olds to spend a year in one of the world's poorest countries doing useful work for no pay. It was exactly what I was looking for. Unlike what tends to happen with modern gap year placements, volunteers were not expected to pay their own way – flights were paid for and I even received a small monthly stipend which left me with about £5 a week after paying to rent a room in a student hostel.

First, though, I had to get a university place. Much to the disapproval of my headmaster, I refused even to consider applying to Oxbridge – much too fuddy-duddy for my taste; this was, after all, the 1960s – and I applied only to so-called 'plate-glass universities', the new institutions like Sussex, York, Essex and Kent that were making a name for themselves as go-ahead and unstuffy, more in keeping with the spirit of the age than the boring old Oxbridge. When I told my headmaster that I had made Sussex my first choice, he sniffed: 'From what I hear, the biggest department at Sussex is their public relations department.'

He had a point: Sussex was rarely out of the newspapers, often in the gossip columns, helped by the presence among its first student intake of two highly photogenic and well-connected sisters, the Jay twins. For a time, Helen and Catherine Jay, daughters of the Labour Cabinet minister Douglas Jay and sisters of Peter Jay, later to become British ambassador to the US and economics editor of the BBC, were the faces of the '60s. Photographed by David Bailey and written about in *Tatler*, they were – at least as far as tabloid newspaper editors were concerned – the epitome of what '60s students were all about: Sussex, sociology and sex. But they were not the reason that I wanted to go to Sussex and, even if they had been, they had gone by the time I got there.

What I most liked about Sussex, apart from the fact that it was by the seaside, was that it had done away with traditional faculties and replaced them with multi-disciplinary schools of study. On the humanities side, there was a School of European Studies, a School of English and American Studies, and a School of African and Asian Studies, the idea being that students in each school, even if studying different subjects, would take some courses together and benefit from each other's insights. I thought, and still think, that it was an excellent idea.

I was offered a place at Sussex to read philosophy in the School of English and American Studies (I also got an offer from York to read linguistics), and then immediately told them that I wanted to delay my arrival to enable me to go overseas with VSO. I hoped that I would be sent to Latin America, where I would be able to make use of my modest Spanish language skills. In the event, I was sent to Uganda, to make use of my even more modest musical skills, to work as a music teacher in the capital, Kampala. It was not exactly what I had had in mind – teaching music was not how I had imagined saving some of the world's poorest people from starvation – but signing up with VSO was like joining the army: you went where you were ordered, and you did what you were told.

And so it was that on my eighteenth birthday, my parents drove me to Gatwick airport and waved me goodbye as I headed off for a twelve-month adventure in east Africa. In the days long before emails, Skype and mobile phones, it felt much more than it would today as if I was heading off into the Great Unknown. But I had set myself a challenge, and I was determined to meet it.

If I survived this, I told myself, I could survive anything.

CHAPTER 7

FROM KAMPALA TO CAMPUS

Tomorrow has been cancelled due to lack of interest.
POPULAR 1960S STUDENT SLOGAN

UGANDA IN THE 1960S was known as Africa's Garden of Eden. It had gained its independence from Britain in 1962 with none of the unpleasantness that had accompanied its neighbour Kenya's similar transition from colonial rule, although the seeds of later trouble were already being sown when, just months before my arrival, the then Prime Minister Milton Obote abolished the country's semi-autonomous traditional kingdoms and declared himself President.

The country is green, fertile and hilly, with a climate that avoids the excessive humidity of much of west Africa. Because it was never a British colony (it was one of the last bits of Africa to be reached by Europeans, and Britain designated it only as a 'protectorate' after it took control in 1896), it was never settled by whites, and therefore, unlike Kenya, Zimbabwe (formerly Southern Rhodesia) and South Africa, did not inherit a significant white minority population.

It did, however, have a well-established Indian community, descended from some of the fifteen thousand labourers who had been brought in by the British to build a railway line from the Kenyan port of Mombasa on the Indian Ocean to the shores of Lake Victoria. Other Indians followed to set up shops and other services for the railway workers and, by the time of independence, Asians played a major role in the Ugandan economy, especially the sugar industry. (In 1972, Idi Amin expelled more than seventy thousand Asians from Uganda; nearly thirty thousand of them came to Britain.)

For me, stepping bleary-eyed off the plane after a gruelling, sixteen-hour overnight flight and setting foot in Africa for the first time, it was love at first sight. We were shepherded onto a coach and driven twenty-five miles along a dusty red mud road from Entebbe airport to Kampala. That early-morning drive, the first of dozens such journeys I have made over the decades in many different African countries, remains firmly imprinted in my memory, like a first kiss. There is a special freshness of the air, a crispness of the light, in the first couple of hours after an African dawn, as villagers prepare for a new day and children in bright white shirts with freshly scrubbed faces walk along the side of the road on their way to school.

In my first letter home, I declared myself to be 'very content, but oh so tired'. And I vowed that when the time came to return to the UK at the end of my year-long adventure, I would try to find some alternative way to make the journey. Long-distance air travel, especially on a plane packed to the gills with over-excited teenagers (it had been specially chartered by VSO), was not to my taste. Little did I imagine how many more long, uncomfortable overnight flights I would endure during my adult life, each time vowing never to do it again.

The school where I would be teaching, Makerere College School, was attached to the Department of Education at Makerere College (now Makerere University). It was originally established as a place where education students could do some teaching practice but, by the time I got there, it had become a well-regarded secondary school with a flourishing music department. Hence the request for a volunteer music teacher from the UK to help out.

I have always felt somewhat ambivalent about the work I did in Uganda. No one would argue, then or now, that turning out a handful of young pianists or clarinettists could be regarded as a key priority for a developing country. Yet if young Ugandans wanted to learn to play the piano or clarinet, they surely had the same right to do so as their British or American equivalents. I tried to salve my conscience by learning to play a couple of traditional instruments of the Baganda people among whom I was living; as a result of the disbanding of the court of the King of Buganda,* his official musicians were now out of work and trying to scratch a living by making and selling musical instruments. They were only too happy to teach an ignorant *mzungu* (white man) how to play a simple tune on the *endere*, a traditional flute made of bamboo, and the *endingidi*, a one-string fiddle, with a single string attached to a flexible stick and stretched across a tubular resonator made of goat skin. So I was not, I reasoned, indoctrinating young Ugandans with imperial cultural practices but merely exchanging our respective cultural skills.

The truth, recognised by anyone who has done any gap year voluntary work, whether for a few weeks or for a year or two, is that the volunteers invariably benefit from the experience far more than the people of the country in which they are working. This does not mean that I would discourage young people from volunteering, nor would I argue that the work that they do is worthless. Nevertheless, I seriously doubt that any volunteer agency these days would dispatch an unqualified teenage music teacher to spend twelve months in east Africa.

Since I was totally inexperienced and untrained, but was expected somehow to teach students who were often older than I was, the benefit that I brought to their lives or future prosperity was sometimes hard to discern. Yet there was never any shortage of students who wanted to learn a musical instrument or to play in the school orchestra; my workload included taking eight class lessons per week, nine individual clarinet lessons, and six piano lessons, in addition to conducting the school band and helping out with the orchestra and choir.

The head of music at the school, and therefore my boss, was a formidable Englishwoman called Pat Foster. She was originally from Liverpool and had studied at the Royal Northern College of Music in Manchester. She was in her early forties when I met her, a woman of forthright views and a highly developed talent for falling out with people. At times, I felt as if I had travelled halfway across the world to act as her unpaid personal assistant – she was certainly not always an

---

* Buganda is one of four recognised traditional kingdoms of Uganda, the others being Bunyoro-Kitara, Busoga and Toro.

easy person to work with – but at the age of eighteen, it was probably time for me to learn how to work with difficult people.

During my time at Makerere, I lived in one of the college halls of residence on Makerere Hill, just a short walk from the school. The arrangement should have been ideal for meeting Ugandan students of my own age, but for some reason I made no friends among the other residents and spent what little free time I had in the company of fellow expatriates. Many were themselves teachers, and I think they took pity on the naïve teenager who had turned up in their midst. Some invited me to join them and their families on safari in Kenya and Tanzania, and occasionally, in return, I would babysit for their young children.

My parents, understandably, were anxious for regular reassurance that I had neither been eaten by lions nor starved to death without the benefit of my mother's home cooking. I wrote a weekly letter home, usually typed on flimsy pale blue writing paper, each letter carefully replied to by my parents (and often, separately, by my brother Stephen as well) and then filed away for posterity. My father's refusal over several decades to throw anything away, which greatly exasperated my mother, has been thoroughly vindicated: this book would have been far more difficult, if not impossible, to write without recourse to the contemporary accounts contained in the letters that I wrote not only from Uganda, but from the various other countries where I later lived and worked as a foreign correspondent.

I rarely wrote about politics while I was in Uganda and I seem to have been only dimly aware of the slowly emerging crisis that would eventually erupt in 1971 when the army chief Idi Amin overthrew President Obote and ushered in a rule of terror that plunged Uganda into the abyss. In one letter I commented presciently: 'Obote doesn't seem to have control of his army – they have set up a roadblock on the main Uganda–Kenya road … rumours are everywhere: army coup, assassination attempt, anything or everything. So we're all keeping our ears to the ground and our mouths firmly shut.'

The overall picture that emerges from the Lustig Uganda Letters is of an eighteen-year-old who was first overwhelmed by a sense of adventure and then slowly became worn down by the pressures of working under stress in an environment where forward planning was a rare luxury. What I learned over the months, however, was that I could cope, even if I soon came to the conclusion that whatever else I might do with my life, teaching was not for me. It was no fault of the students, but I realised early on that although I would be able to muddle through for a year, the idea of spending the rest of my life as a teacher filled me with dread.

My life at Makerere was mainly a succession of daily crises and frustrations. Everything had to be improvised at the last minute, which turned out to be an excellent preparation for a life in journalism. We never had enough functioning musical instruments for our needs, so I taught myself to become a useful musical technician, replacing springs and pads on woodwind instruments and oiling sticky valves on trumpets and horns.

By the end of my VSO year, I was not only older and wiser, but had also become deeply attached to the people with whom I had been working. In my last letter home before heading for Nairobi to catch my return flight (my determination to find an alternative way back to the UK had been defeated by both cost and logistics), I wrote: 'I feel very miserable at the thought of saying goodbye to all the people at school – I've been so happy here, despite all the difficulties ... it is so sad that I have to leave.'

So what was my Ugandan legacy? Towards the end of my year there, eight of my music pupils took Associated Board exams on their chosen instruments, assessed by an examiner who had flown out from the UK especially for the purpose. One clarinettist failed his Grade 6 exam, but four other students gained passes, and three, one of them a bassoonist, were awarded merits. One clarinettist even went on to become a music teacher herself. I also entered myself to take Grade 8, the top grade, on the clarinet, and, to my astonishment, was awarded a distinction. It was to be the peak of my somewhat short-lived career as a musician, because by the time I left university three years later, the demands of journalism had consigned my clarinet to near oblivion.

Makerere College School also gathered more than its fair share of awards at the 1967 Uganda Music Festival, where it won a clutch of prizes in several categories and was presented by the First Lady, Miria Obote, with a special shield as 'the organisation which has contributed most to the Festival'. The closest-fought competition was in the category 'European Instrumental Ensemble', in which there were only two entries, both from Makerere: the recorder group, trained and conducted by my boss Pat Foster, and the school band, trained and conducted by me. The experienced professional, with fifteen years' teaching experience under her belt, was up against the bumptious teenager. The adjudicator, a former music education inspector in Kenya, had no inkling how much was riding on his verdict.

It could not have been closer: Pat's recorder group scored 84 points; my school band scored 85 points. I tried not to gloat, but it meant that I could return home with my head held high.

There was just one more mission to accomplish. I had arranged to team up with two young British teachers, both a few years older than I was, to attempt to climb Mount Kilimanjaro in Tanzania, Africa's highest mountain, and, with its peak 19,341 feet above sea level, the highest mountain in the world that can be climbed without the use of additional oxygen. Three-quarters of the climbers who attempt it suffer from altitude sickness, and fewer than two-thirds make it to the summit. I have never been, even at the age of eighteen, much good at physical exertion, so this was a significant gamble. I suppose it was an indication of how my self-confidence had grown during my year away that I felt it was worth trying.

My letter home dated 15 August 1967 tells the story: 'No time for preliminaries – WE DID IT! Yes, all three of us actually did it.' It took us three days of steady climbing to get to the plateau from which the final ascent could be attempted; then...

> Up at 1 a.m., not having slept at all and having had blinding headache all night. Bitterly cold. Was very sick before starting out ... impossible to describe effect of lack of oxygen. Was indescribably ill up to top. Very beautiful views (I think) ... You cannot imagine the agony of the final climb to the top – it is something I never wish to repeat.

I described the ordeal as 'a battle of mind versus body – in the event, the mind won, but not without the body putting up an impressive struggle'. A few years ago, I thought it might be fun to try to do it again, with my son, but having now re-read my contemporaneous account, I am glad I never did. The ascent in 1967 remains the most significant physical achievement of my life, just as getting through my Grade 8 clarinet exam remains my most significant musical achievement.

Two weeks after my triumph on Kilimanjaro, having first spent a few days recovering on the beach at Mombasa, I was on my way back to London. It was my nineteenth birthday, exactly 365 days after my adventure, and my love affair with Africa, had begun.

Uganda remains my favourite country in Africa, my first love, although it was to be nearly forty years before I was able to return and revisit Makerere College School. And I found another love while I was in Uganda: the BBC World Service, on which I relied for daily news of the outside world. What a wonderful job it must be, I thought, to sit in a radio studio and broadcast to people all over the world. One day, perhaps...

The University of Sussex was just six years old when I arrived there in the autumn of 1967. It had been the first of the new wave of '60s universities,* and it was proud of its reputation as an institution at the forefront of all that was exciting in 1960s Britain. It was the time of flowered shirts and long hair (men), and miniskirts and the Pill (women), and the university cultivated a rakish air perfectly suited to the nearest town, Brighton, which had long enjoyed a reputation as a place of dubious pleasures and loose morals. Not at all the sort of town, according to critics like my former headmaster, for a serious place of learning, even if it had already earned itself the nickname

---

* The others were East Anglia, Essex, Kent, Lancaster, Warwick and York.

'Balliol-by-the-sea' because of the number of ex-Oxbridge academics on its payroll.

Its buildings, in pale brick and concrete, had been designed by one of Britain's leading architects, Sir Basil Spence, who had also designed Coventry Cathedral, and its location on the grassy slopes of Stanmer Park, halfway between Brighton and Lewes, enabled it to boast that it was the only university in the UK to be built entirely in an officially designated area of outstanding natural beauty.

It suited me perfectly. My first task when I arrived was to switch courses, because during my year in Uganda my interest in philosophy had waned while my interest in politics had grown. My new chosen course was Politics in the School of African and Asian Studies, but it played a much less important role in my student life than my decision to join the staff of the student newspaper *Wine Press*, to which I devoted far more time than I did to my academic commitments.

My home during my first year at Sussex was a shared room in a guesthouse at 42 Devonshire Place, just a five-minute walk from Brighton Pier. There were only three halls of residence on campus, so most first-year students were accommodated in guesthouses, an arrangement that worked very well for the proprietors, who were delighted to have paying guests during term-time. At the end of term, we had to vacate our rooms to make way for the holidaymakers.

There were eight of us in the guesthouse, all male, and as there was no lounge and no TV, the only opportunity we had to socialise was at breakfast, which is rarely a time when students are at their most interesting. So I spent much more of my time, when I was not in the *Wine Press* office on campus, in a nearby women's guesthouse where there was both a lounge and a colour television.

I cannot think of any time, except perhaps in the 1930s, when it could have been more exciting to be a British student than in the late 1960s. There was a real sense that we were in the vanguard of the deep social changes under way: the liberalisation of the laws on abortion and homosexuality, the introduction of the contraceptive pill, the rise of the feminist movement, the civil rights movement in the US, and the politicisation of a whole generation of students over the war in Vietnam.

But I soon discovered that I preferred to be a chronicler rather than an activist. Then as now, I was happier asking the questions than deciding upon the answers. I did, in fact, put myself forward as a candidate to be president of the students' union – more, I think, because I felt it would be interesting to discover what it was like than because I had any burning wish to hold elected office – but I was beaten into an ignominious third place by both the mainstream Communist Party candidate and by the eventual winner, a 31-year-old former lorry driver who had been regarded by the campus commentators as the 'joke candidate'.

I learned two useful lessons from the experience: first, that running for office is immensely hard and dispiriting work, and second, that suspicion of journalists, even student journalists, runs very deep. On one canvassing call to a guesthouse, I was treated to the sight of my beloved *Wine Press* being ceremoniously burnt in a wastepaper bin. In a letter home, I explained to my disappointed parents that I owed my defeat to an ill-advised reliance on 'floating voters' whose support I did too little to win over, and to the salience of the 'trendy careerist' label that was routinely attached to student journalists by student revolutionaries on the barricades.

1967 was the year of the Six Day War in the Middle East, when Israel pre-empted a feared attack by its Arab neighbours and ended up occupying east Jerusalem, the Golan Heights, West Bank and Gaza Strip. It was the year when a right-wing military junta seized power in Greece, and China exploded its first H-bomb. Race riots erupted in several cities in the US, and in apartheid South Africa, Christiaan Barnard performed the first successful human heart transplant. The US had nearly half a million troops in South Vietnam; 11,000 were killed in action. The following year would be even more momentous.

It is not difficult to explain why I became a journalist. To be a student, and to be a student journalist, while the world was undergoing such fundamental change was bound to have a lasting effect. By January 1968, when I had already seen one of my news stories splashed across the front page of *Wine Press*, I was writing to my parents that the experience 'has made me all the more convinced that journalism or something akin to it is the life for me'.

The following month, Sussex burst into the national and international spotlight when a pot of red paint was thrown at a visiting official from the US embassy, Robert Beers, who was accompanied for some reason by his twenty-year-old daughter Elizabeth. It was, by the standards of the day, a shocking act of political violence, and the university authorities responded by suspending the two students responsible for eight weeks. A vote at an emotional meeting of the students' union on whether to support the two students by going on strike was overwhelmingly defeated, with 1,000 votes against to sixty in favour.

For us student journalists on the ground, of course, it was all wonderfully exciting. Fleet Street's finest descended on the campus and made a beeline for the *Wine Press* offices. We did our best to explain the background, to no obvious effect. An American news agency report set the tone:

> A US embassy official today said police saved his 20-year-old daughter and himself from death at the hands of an anti-Vietnam war crowd hurling paint, eggs and rocks Wednesday night. 'They saved our lives. The students had rocks and were really out to get us,' said press attaché Robert Beers.[21]

It has gone down in the history books as 'the red paint incident', and it taught at least one budding journalist an important lesson: never trust other journalists to get things right. I count myself fortunate that I learned the lesson even before I went into the business.

Not every student, even in the febrile '60s, was obsessed by the war in Vietnam or US military expansionism. Within a couple of weeks of the red paint incident, *Wine Press* reported that the students' union had successfully reduced the fee payable to Jimi Hendrix for his appearance at a union function from £500 to £250 because he had performed for only thirty-eight minutes instead of the hour for which he had been booked, and had spent eight of those minutes replacing a broken string on his guitar.

It also found space to report the view of a leading Brighton councillor, Alderman Gerald FitzGerald, that prescribing the contraceptive pill to unmarried students 'allows students to avoid practising self-discipline, that the free love which it encourages is a prostitution of the marriage vows, that it is against Christian teaching, and that this sort of freedom does not provide a happy foundation for marriage'.

Sex, music and politics: Sussex in the '60s. And in 1968, *Wine Press* was named the best student newspaper in Britain. Bliss was it in that dawn to be alive...

Not so blissful, however, for the management of the *Kent and Sussex Courier* in Tunbridge Wells, where *Wine Press* was printed. As editor, it was my job to drive the thirty miles from Brighton to Tunbridge Wells each week to oversee the production process, a task that often pitted the anarchic, libertarian tendencies of Sussex undergraduates with the very much more traditional approach of the *Courier*. Four-letter words were banned, and satire and personal abuse were frowned upon. Just as unwelcome was our inability to match the number of written words per page with the space available, which frequently meant either the hasty cutting of over-written material, or the equally hasty filling of gaps at the foot of a column.

In the days of hot-metal printing, the art of 'stone-subbing' – the editing of material even after it had been cast in metal and page proofs had been run off – was the most highly prized of all editorial skills. To have an opportunity to learn the rudiments of the art while barely out of short trousers was a rare privilege, and the unforgiving printers of the *Kent and Sussex Courier* were determined that we would never forget it.

Even fifty years ago, I realised that there was more to journalism than ink on paper, and I was part of a team that set up the first on-campus TV network. In my debut as a broadcast interviewer, I subjected the vice-chancellor Asa Briggs to a grilling that was so gentle that a camera operator, dying of boredom, wandered over to me mid-interview – out of shot, fortunately – and whispered in my ear: 'I think you should ask him another question.'

I also did some reporting for BBC Radio Brighton, which went on air in February 1968 as one of the first of the BBC's local radio stations. On one occasion, I was sent to interview Lord Caradon, the British ambassador to the United Nations, who was visiting Brighton.* When I returned to the studios with the tape, shaking with nerves, I discovered that the tape was blank. 'Never mind,' said the station manager. 'You'll just have to go back and interview him again, won't you?'

Which, of course, I did. Just as I did on many other occasions in the decades that followed, when I suffered the embarrassment of having to explain to a variety of eminent interviewees why a technical malfunction (never my own incompetence) meant that we would have to record an interview a second time. I was always pleasantly surprised by how understanding the interviewees were when confronted with a gibbering, grovelling wreck of a radio reporter.

As part of my degree course, I was expected to research and write a final-year dissertation on a subject of my own choosing. Despite the fact that I was attached to the School of African and Asian Studies, I decided to write about the doomed US presidential campaign of the Democratic Party Senator Eugene McCarthy, who in 1968 was challenging his fellow Democrat, and incumbent President, Lyndon Johnson. My dissertation was decidedly thin, little more than an extended piece of journalism, depending largely on the weekly reports that I read in *Newsweek* magazine and containing not a single reference to any recognisable principle of political theory.

It did, however, provide a perfect excuse to spend the summer of 1968 in the US, staying mainly with my American uncle's family just outside Washington DC and sitting up late into the night watching the TV coverage of a chaotic and violent Democratic Party convention in Chicago. The civil rights leader Martin Luther King had been assassinated in April, Robert Kennedy, brother of the assassinated President John F. Kennedy, was shot dead in June, and anti-Vietnam War protests were at their height. This was politics as high-octane

---

* Caradon's younger brother, Michael Foot, became leader of the Labour Party in 1980.

drama, and I was utterly transfixed. The most powerful nation in the world, with a nuclear arsenal big enough to destroy our planet many times over, was on the brink of revolution.

And as if all that was not enough, in August, Soviet-led troops invaded Czechoslovakia to end the 'Prague Spring' experiment, during which the Czech leader Alexander Dubček had tried to introduce a form of liberal Communism, and France exploded its first hydrogen bomb. For me, as a student of politics with dreams of becoming a journalist, 1968 was the year that the die was cast. I had never felt so alive, and my summer in the US marked the start of a lifelong fascination with both the country and its politics.

It was while I was in Washington that I first met the man who was later to become my journalistic mentor and guru. Anthony (Tony) Howard was Washington correspondent for *The Observer* and when I contacted him to seek his advice about the US political scene, he was generous with both his time and his knowledge. Later, when I was looking for a job and he was back in London working for the *New Statesman*, he arranged for me to meet several of his journalist friends and contacts in high places. None of them was able to offer me work, but Tony and I remained friends and, for a time, colleagues – until his death in 2010.*

Wine Press did not long survive my editorship. In June 1969, the students' union, by now firmly in the control of the extreme left, voted to end its annual subsidy. I commented, I suspect disingenuously, in a letter home: 'It's no great tragedy that *Wine Press* is dead, as it was never a very good newspaper.' The minutes of the final meeting of its management board ended with the words: 'The management board committed suicide at 3.58 p.m.'

My personal tutor throughout my time at Sussex, Professor Bruce Graham, was a man of seemingly infinite patience and understanding who had little difficulty in seeing where my loyalties lay. 'You know,'

---

* By pure coincidence, the first home I bought after I got married in 1980 was in the house in Highgate, north London, where Howard had been born and spent his early childhood.

he said to me one day, 'you are going to have to make up your mind soon. Are you going to be a political scientist, or are you going to be a journalist?' I am sure he knew perfectly well what the answer would be, although my determination to land a job in broadcasting was thwarted at every turn.

It was to be nearly twenty years before I was finally able to say: 'I work for the BBC.'

CHAPTER 8

AGENCY MAN

Comfort the afflicted, afflict the comfortable.
AMERICAN HUMORIST FINLEY PETER DUNNE
(1867–1936), DESCRIBING THE ROLE OF
JOURNALISTS

I OWE MY CAREER to a woman called Carolyn Robb. She worked at the Sussex University Careers Advisory Service, and when she heard that I was getting nowhere with any of my multiple applications to join the BBC, she managed to persuade me to look elsewhere. Reuters news agency, one of the most venerable and respected of British journalistic institutions, ran a training scheme aimed specifically at university graduates, and Carolyn had a pile of application forms. With great reluctance, I filled one in and posted it.

On 9 April 1970, after a series of interviews and a written test, and shortly before I sat my final exams at Sussex, I received the letter I had been waiting for:

> Dear Mr Lustig,
>   Following your recent interviews here, we are pleased to offer you an engagement as a trainee journalist with Reuters General News Division … Your starting salary will be £1,190* per annum.

Reuters was founded in 1851 by Paul Julius Reuter, born Israel Josaphat, the son of a rabbi, in Kassel, Germany. He had moved to London in 1845, after establishing a successful news service in Germany using

---

* Equivalent to about £17,500 today.

carrier pigeons to carry stock market prices between Berlin and Paris. (There was no telegraph link between Brussels and Aachen at the time and the pigeons were faster than the trains. Later, Reuter invested in telegraph communications, which were even faster than the pigeons.) According to the official company history, the agency soon earned 'an enviable reputation for speed, accuracy, integrity and impartiality'.

Reuters was famed for going to extraordinary lengths to be first with the news. In 1865, after Abraham Lincoln was shot while in the audience at Ford's Theatre in Washington, the news reached Europe only twelve days later, but it would have taken even longer had Reuters not been able to make use of its own private communications network.

We forget sometimes in this era of instant news how complex and cumbersome news technology used to be, so this is how it was done. First the news flash was transmitted by telegraph from Washington to New York. But the next mail steamer heading for Europe was not due to leave until the following afternoon, so the Reuters man in New York chartered a fast tug boat to chase after a steamer that had left a few hours earlier. It caught up, and a canister containing the Lincoln dispatch was thrown on board.

Once the steamer had crossed the Atlantic, the canister was transferred onto a smaller vessel off the west coast of Ireland, so that the news could then be transmitted onwards via telegraph. And because Julius Reuter had laid his own private telegraph line that reached further west – to Crookhaven – than the commercial line that stopped at Cork, he could get the news onto the telegraph several hours before anyone else.

Right from the start, Reuters' emphasis was on financial news. By the time I joined in 1970, the company had just launched its Videomaster service, an early on-screen display of stock and commodity prices. Even then, we were taught always to be on the lookout for stories that were known as 'market-movers'.

That is probably why, at my job interview, I was asked the following question:

Suppose you were the Reuters correspondent in Havana, and you learned exclusively that the Cuban sugar harvest had failed, but you had also been warned that if you published the information, the Reuters office in Havana would be shut down and you would be arrested and expelled from the country. What would you do?

I replied that I would seek advice from head office in London, which seems to have been the right answer because I was one of only six university graduates who were offered a place as a graduate trainee. It was not the job I had set my heart on, but it was the only one I was offered.

All six of us were men, and two of our number went on to spend their entire careers, more than forty years, in the company's service. Our training was designed largely in accordance with the educational principle known to its practitioners as 'sitting next to Nellie', in other words, watching over the shoulder of someone who knew what they were doing and learning from them. We were, however, taught the rudiments of shorthand and media law, neither of which I made much use of during my nearly seven years with the company.

The Reuters training scheme has gone through many incarnations over the years, but it has a pretty good track record: among its alumni are such former newspaper editors as Jonathan Fenby of *The Observer*, Andrew Gowers of the *Financial Times* and Alexander Chancellor of *The Spectator*. The current editor of *The Times*, John Witherow, is also a former Reuters trainee, as are many of the UK's top foreign correspondents and broadcasters. (In 2012, Reuters was reported to take on fifteen trainees annually from around two thousand applicants around the world.)

We in the 1970 batch were treated in our first week to a welcoming address from the Reuters general manager, Gerald Long, an imposing figure with a luxuriant moustache and a no-nonsense manner. He had a well-earned reputation as a man who was aggressive, short-tempered, arrogant and intolerant of fools.

Long told us two things that have stuck in my mind for nearly half a century. The first, in the context of war reporting, was: 'Just remember – you're no use to me if you're dead.' The second, in the context of competing with rival agencies, was equally useful: 'I'd rather you were second and right than first and wrong.' It is a principle that I have tried to follow ever since, even today with all the temptations of the Send button on a mobile phone. (Sky News, on the other hand, at least in its early days, was said by its critics to operate according to the opposite principle: Never wrong for long.)

Gerald Long was credited with turning Reuters from a loss-making, traditionally minded news organisation into a profitable, forward-looking venture that understood the full potential of computerised financial data provision tailored to the needs of the financial services industry. So successful was he that when the company went public in 1984 (it had previously been owned by a trust made up of British national and regional newspapers), some of its most senior executives ended up with stock options worth several million pounds. Long was not one of them – he had left Reuters in 1981 after accepting an offer from Rupert Murdoch to become managing director of Times Newspapers. The *Daily Mail* described him as 'the man who let £4 million slip through his fingers'.

Gerald Long was never a newspaper proprietor, so his name has never figured alongside such other monstrous Fleet Street legends as Beaverbrook, Northcliffe and Maxwell. It probably deserves to be, even if only for the wonderfully surreal manner of his fall from grace after barely a year as Murdoch's henchman at *The Times*. It was all because of a row over French cheese, about which Long believed himself to be a world expert.

The saga started in November 1981, when Long had a meal at Le Gavroche, a renowned French restaurant in central London which was about to be awarded a third Michelin star, the first restaurant in the UK to be thus honoured. Long was not impressed and wrote to the proprietor, Albert Roux, to tell him so.

Dear Mr Roux,

I dined recently at your restaurant Le Gavroche for the first time. I would like to draw one small matter to your attention.

The large selection of cheeses was presented as specially chosen for Le Gavroche by a French cheese expert, and consisting of only French farmhouse cheeses.

This last expression surprised me, since it would, in my experience, be difficult to make such an absolute claim for any cheese board of such variety, here or in France, if one were to translate the rather vague word 'farmhouse' as 'de fabrication fermière', which has a precise meaning.

The chef replied, as you would expect, with appropriately Gallic elegance. But he stuck to his fromological guns and, after a further exchange of letters, dripping with ill-disguised hostility, M. Roux turned the faux charm-o-meter up to maximum:

> The fact that you have taken so much trouble to write about food leaves me with endless pleasure. So much so, that I would very much like you and your wife to be my guests for lunch or dinner, as I find from your letter that we have a great deal in common – a great love of food.

Only a man of Long's immeasurable arrogance could have replied as he did:

> Thank you for your letter of 23rd November, your kind words, and for your generous invitation; I greatly appreciate it, but I hope you will understand if I do not accept it. In any event, I eat very rarely in restaurants, in this country even less than in France.

The correspondence was published in full in *The Times* of 6 February 1982; the editor, Harold Evans, was engaged in a brutal war of attrition against both Long and Rupert Murdoch at the time, but Long, who approved publication, seems not to have suspected any ulterior motives. Evans later wrote, with what seems like considerable satisfaction: 'Murdoch did not regard the letters as entertaining when he read them in the paper. He regarded them as incendiary.'[22]

The timing, as Evans must have known, could not have been worse. Murdoch was about to tell the print unions that he intended to cut 600 jobs, and to have his managing director publicly engaged in an esoteric dispute about French cheeses in a Michelin three-star restaurant was unlikely to be helpful. Long was kicked upstairs to become deputy chairman of News International and left the company in 1984. He retired to live in France, where he died in 1998.

My first day at Reuters was 21 September 1970, and I was immediately assigned to the agency's London bureau, responsible for reporting the UK to the rest of the world. To emphasise that Reuters regarded its UK output as no different from its output from anywhere else in the world, the bureau was not based in the agency's grand main office, which was shared with the Press Association at 85 Fleet Street, but in much more modest premises tucked away in Gough Square. It did not matter. I still walked up Fleet Street every morning on my way from Blackfriars Tube station, so I had arrived at the centre of British journalism, where the smell of printer's ink, the rumble of the subterranean presses and the endless lines of trucks taking each day's newspapers to every corner of the nation meant that I had arrived in heaven.

Two weeks before I started at Reuters, a hijacked Israeli airliner had landed at Heathrow airport. It was one of several planes that had been hijacked almost simultaneously by members of the Popular Front for the Liberation of Palestine (PFLP); three were forced to land at a former RAF base at Dawson's Field in Jordan, where they were blown up, and the fourth, El Al flight 219 from Amsterdam to New York, ended up in London.

One of the hijackers on board, a Nicaraguan-American called Patrick Argüello, was shot and killed by Israeli security agents on the plane; the other, Leila Khaled, a Palestinian, was captured, handed over to British police and detained at Ealing police station in west London. The PFLP demanded her release in return for the release of the hijacked planes and their passengers, and as the crisis dragged on, young Lustig, one of the new batch of wet-behind-the-ears trainees, was dispatched in the company of a more experienced reporter to await developments outside Ealing police station.

Jordan itself had become engulfed in civil war. The Palestinians, who formed a substantial part of the population, rose up under the leadership of Yasser Arafat to try to seize power from the Hashemite monarch King Hussein. What became known as Black September threatened to tip the Middle East back into the turmoil from which it had only recently recovered following the Six Day War of 1967.

It was a huge story, and Britain was directly involved because of Leila Khaled's presence on British soil. I could not believe my luck: literally days after joining Reuters, I was being asked to help report on a major world news event. Britain was a signatory to the 1963 international convention on hijacking, which committed it not to negotiate with hijackers, but it soon became clear that the UK government led by Edward Heath was doing exactly that. All eyes were on Ealing and, to raise the tension even further, the government was being privately advised by the British ambassador in Jordan that Khaled had become 'a symbol of Palestine resistance and a folk heroine'.[23] She had already hijacked a plane on its way from Italy to Israel the previous year, and had had extensive plastic surgery to disguise her identity. She was, in other words, a female equivalent of the Argentine revolutionary fighter Che Guevara, who had been killed in Bolivia just three years previously.

The Ealing police station experience is deeply embedded in my memory because it taught me, right at the start of my life as a journalist, an important truth: being at the centre of a major global news event is not inevitably exciting. I spent several days standing in the street outside that police station, but the most exciting thing that I was asked to do in all that time was find a nearby public telephone box that worked. In the days before mobile phones, public phone boxes were an essential journalistic resource, and woe betide a reporter who failed to find one in time to file a dispatch.

On 1 October, after twenty-eight days in detention, Leila Khaled was released and driven to Northolt airport, from where she was flown out of the country. But the first any of the reporters gathered outside the police station knew of it was when we heard it on the BBC *Six O'Clock News*.

Lesson One: reporting a major news story can often be very boring.

Lesson Two: being in the right place at the right time is not the same as knowing what is going on, even right under your nose. (Khaled had been smuggled out of the police station in the back of a van. It drove right past us.)

The life of an agency man (we were almost all men in the 1970s) is not a life of unending glamour or glory. News agencies do the journalism donkeywork, churning out stories to fill the gaps between what the newspapers' own correspondents have provided. So the rare moments of glory are moments to be fully savoured, and I got my first, tantalising taste in April 1971, when the Russian composer Igor Stravinsky died in New York at the age of eighty-eight.

'Does anyone know anything about music?' asked the head of Reuters London bureau. 'We need to get some reactions.' I volunteered to see what I could come up with and, with the help of the London telephone directory, I phoned every leading musical figure I could think of. The following day, at the bottom of its front-page story reporting Stravinsky's death, *The Times* printed quotes from three of them – the conductor Colin Davis, the choreographer Sir Frederick Ashton, and the Master of the Queen's Music, Sir Arthur Bliss. And there, right at the bottom of the page, was the all-important credit: 'Reuter.'

I had made it on to the front page of *The Times*, an achievement of such magnitude that it warranted a personal message of congratulations from the editor-in-chief. I walked on air for a week.

One of the traditional tests that news agency reporters were taught to apply to their stories was whether they would be intelligible to a milkman in Kansas City. Why Kansas City? Because it is just about in the geographical centre of the United States and used to be regarded – perhaps it still is – as a perfect symbol for Middle America. So we were taught to use simple English, short words not long words, and explain what needed to be explained to someone who may not have been following the news too closely. (In show business, the question that used to be asked of a new show was 'Will it play in Peoria?', a small town in Illinois that, like Kansas City, was regarded as epitomising the virtues – or otherwise – of Main Street, USA.) They were good lessons to learn, and they have served me well.

Part of my time as a Reuters trainee was spent working on what was then called the World Desk, the hub of the global operation, through which correspondents' dispatches were filtered, rewritten, edited and retransmitted around the world. Teleprinters would chatter around the clock, spewing out miles of paper bearing the news of the moment. The job of the World Desk was to make sure that the copy was fit to be read by that milkman in Kansas.

Sometimes, it also needed to be translated. Reuters stringers (part-time correspondents) in west Africa, for example, sent their dispatches in French, in the form of telegrams. We graduate trainees were expected to turn them into Reuterese and add whatever background material might be required for the benefit of readers in Middle America.

'Fine, you've translated it,' was the irritated response from one senior sub-editor as he glanced over one of my early efforts. 'Now see if you can turn it into a news story.' Graduates were still something of a rarity in Fleet Street, and we were tolerated rather than welcomed by many Reuters lifers. One former trainee described them well as 'dinosaurs, who affected a proletarian loathing of graduate trainees but were actually often quite kind and instructive beneath the veneer of philistinism'.

On the relatively quiet overnight shifts, while Europe and Africa slept, the graduate trainee's most important job was to cross Fleet Street at 3 a.m. to Mick's Café to buy doughnuts. The night editor, known, inevitably, as the Prince of Darkness, would doze with his head resting against the teleprinter, from which incoming news dispatches would periodically be disgorged. It was a foolproof technique, guaranteeing that he would be woken by the sudden whirring and spluttering as the machine sprang to life with a fresh piece of news.

One night, I learned another important lesson: a story that may look like just another routine bit of news may well be life-changing to someone, somewhere. A short dispatch arrived at the World Desk from a stringer in Papua New Guinea. A young British volunteer teacher had been found murdered. Her name was Sandra Smith and she had, briefly, been my girlfriend at Sussex. I subbed the dispatch as best I could, explained the circumstances to the editor, and hoped that her parents had already been told. I could not bear the thought of having to break the news to them myself.

In May 1971, I was shipped overseas to spend the next twelve months learning how to be a proper foreign correspondent in a proper foreign country. Reuters, unlike VSO five years previously, had decided that it might as well make use of my A-level Spanish, so I was posted to Madrid to be the third man in a three-man bureau.

Spain was still ruled by the Fascist dictator Francisco Franco, who had seized power after the 1936–39 civil war. There was no political activity to speak of – Fascist dictators do not tend to encourage a spirit of lively political debate – so most of the work was either sports-related or what is known in the trade as 'soft features', the kind of stuff that gets published on a newspaper's inside pages when there is nothing else around. In my first two weeks, I found myself reporting (mainly on the basis of Spanish news agency reports rather than first-hand) on football, gymnastics, horse-riding, cycling and boxing.

Humdrum it may have been, but it still required at least a smidgeon of journalistic and linguistic skill. Late one night, after filing yet another tedious football report, I received an unusually laconic message from head office. 'Multitks yr soccer. Fyi opps reporting other team won.' (Translation: 'Many thanks for your football report. For your information, the other agencies are reporting a different result.') In the circumstances, I got off lightly: Reuters does not like having to issue corrections, and it is not easy to explain away the idiocy of a correspondent who gets a simple score line wrong.

I was on firmer ground when it came to covering the European Amateur Boxing Championships. Not because I knew anything about boxing – I had never seen a boxing match in my life – but because I was at the ringside with two other news agency reporters from Reuters' two main rivals, Associated Press and United Press International. We sat side by side, each with our own phone, and soon realised that our lives would be much less complicated if we checked with each other before phoning in our reports, just to make sure that we all agreed.

Our bosses would certainly not have approved, and I suspect there will have been several boxers surprised to discover from the following day's papers that they had felled their opponent with, say, a right hook, when they could have sworn it was a left jab. It was not what I had imagined when I had dreamt of being a foreign correspondent: 189 bouts over eight days, 200 words per fight, dictating a report about one fight while simultaneously making notes about the next one. Fleet Street's finest boxing correspondents were there as well, of course, but they could afford to take a more relaxed attitude, knowing that the agencies would hold the fort.

'Well done, chaps,' they said, patting us on the head as they popped out to the bar. 'Keep it up.' I told myself it was all good experience.

My first boss in Madrid, John Organ, was a boisterous, charismatic man who spoke fluent Spanish at the top of his voice with a pronounced English accent. He knew everyone, and everyone knew him – on the phone, he would invariably begin any conversation with the single barked word '¡Oiga!', roughly equivalent to 'Hey!' His habit of wearing a full-length opera cloak when the weather turned chilly guaranteed that he was noticed wherever he went. Our normal arrangement was that he worked more or less regular office hours, while the Number Two man and I would alternate between afternoon and evening shifts.

It was in Madrid that I learned how to operate a telex machine, a skill that is now about as useful as being able to illustrate a biblical text inscribed on vellum. Sending a telex involved typing a message on a keyboard that would punch holes into a paper tape that generated pulses to be transmitted over a special telegraph line. The telex machine in the Reuters Madrid office in 1971 did not have a paper read-out facility, so it became essential to be able to read the tape itself to check for errors.

During office hours, we had a full-time telex operator, Pedro Diez, a short, wiry man with a pencil moustache and only one hand as a result of an accident with a civil war-era grenade that he had picked up as a child. Our less kind colleagues liked to suggest that only a ramshackle operation like Reuters would see fit to employ a one-handed telex operator. Watching Pedro at work, holding one end of the telex tape between his teeth as he threaded the other end through the transmitter mechanism, usually put an end to the jokes.

Many years later, when I was reporting from Lebanon, I had

good reason to be grateful for what Pedro had taught me – being able to hammer out my own telex tapes was a useful skill when hotel telex operators were under pressure from gaggles of sharp-elbowed correspondents.

Reporting from a country under Fascism was not an ideal introduction to the world of the foreign correspondent; in the dying days of Francoism, Spain was somnolent to the point of being comatose. It was hardly an encouraging environment for an impatient young reporter. But after a few months of little but sports results, I began to get my first nibbles at real stories.

> Madrid, Sept 4, Reuter – The embalmed body of Eva Perón – second wife of former Argentine dictator Juan Perón – was returned to the ex-president here last night after a mysterious disappearance lasting 16 years...
>
> Eva Perón – heroine for millions of Argentinians – crossed the French–Spanish frontier early yesterday morning in a blue Italian hearse flanked by Italian and French outriders. This appeared to confirm rumours that her body had been buried in Italy since its mysterious disappearance from a labour union headquarters in Buenos Aires in 1955.

The exiled ex-President Perón, who had been living in Madrid since being ousted in a *coup d'état* in 1955, was a permanent pain in the backside for the Reuters Madrid bureau, because the Argentine media were obsessed with his every move and constantly demanded extensive coverage of his activities. He was known to be playing a key behind-the-scenes role in Argentine politics from his Madrid base, and he eventually returned to power in 1973.

On one occasion when he had been scheduled to make an important speech, we had been instructed to provide full cover for the benefit of Reuters' many clients in Argentina who would be hanging on his every word. My colleague on duty that night decided that, in the event, the speech was far too boring to warrant a dispatch and, towards the end of the evening, the following exchange of messages took place. (A word of explanation: although all Reuters messages were sent either via telex or over dedicated lines, they were still written in cablese, the language that had been developed during the telegram era, when messages were charged by the word.)

PROMADRID EXLDN. BAIRES QUERYING WHEN PROPOSE FILE PERON SPEECH. PLS ADVISE URGENTEST.

PROLDN EXMADRID. UNPROPOSE FILE PERON SPEECH. SERMON ON MOUNT SHORTER AND BETTER. WHAT PROPOSE DO IS DOWNCLOSE. GNITE.

(Translation: 'To Madrid from London. Our office in Buenos Aires is wondering when you intend to file your dispatch on Perón's speech. Please let us know as soon as you can.'

'To London from Madrid. I do not intend to file anything about Perón's speech. The Sermon on the Mount was both shorter and better. What I intend to do is close down the office and go home to bed. Good night.')

Let us just say it was not a career-enhancing move.

The American newspaper columnist Joseph Alsop once defined the job of a foreign correspondent as a cross between an undertaker and a second footman: '... an undertaker because he is always present at scenes of death and destruction; a second footman because he meets the most interesting people under the most humiliating circumstances.'[24] Others have likened reporters to vultures, forever hovering over those in distress in the hope of being able to feed off their demise. A news editor I once worked for used to mutter on distressingly quiet news days: 'What we need now is a damn good hijack.'

It was not a hijack but a particularly gruesome traffic accident that introduced me to the 'undertaker' side of the trade that I had chosen to enter. A late-night phone call from London alerted me to the news that a coach carrying twenty-six Canadian tourists had been hit by a truck about eighty miles south of Madrid. Eighteen people had been killed and the Canadian newspapers were screaming for details. After a three-hour taxi ride, I arrived at the scene to find the badly mangled coach lying on its side in the road, and local police officers who were ghoulishly happy to shine their torches on the human remains still visible in the wreckage.

As dawn broke, having worked through the night, I was allowed to talk to some of the survivors in the local hospital. Most were French-speaking Canadians from Quebec; none had been told that many of their friends had been killed, and I found myself not only having to break the news to them but also acting as interpreter between them and the hard-pressed Spanish hospital staff. It was grim stuff, yet I felt in my element. Even more so when I saw the giant headlines on the Canadian front pages and the magic byline: 'by Robin Lustig, Reuter staff writer'.

In a letter home, I wrote: 'I thoroughly enjoyed covering the story (if you'll pardon the word "enjoy" in this context) but it's really what I went into this business for. At last, he cried, some *real* reporting!'

It sounds callous in the extreme. How could I have enjoyed – how could anyone enjoy? – being witness to such distress and human suffering? How can reporters want to cover wars, to see people being killed and injured, and to witness the worst that human beings can inflict on each other? It is not easy to explain, but in the same way as an undertaker who can take pride in a well-conducted funeral, or a surgeon who can 'enjoy' performing a particularly complex operation, reporters take satisfaction from a job well done, a story well told. It can often look like heartlessness, even callousness, but mostly, or so I hope, it is neither. The high number of war correspondents who suffer from post-traumatic stress, or who turn to drink, is an indication that they, too, are human and react as all humans do to scenes of death and destruction.

Reporters are driven by a belief that people deserve to know what is happening around them. It may be a war, or it may be a traffic accident, but they are entitled to an accurate account of what happened, however distasteful may be the process of acquiring the information. To get at the truth, a reporter has to get close.

But that sometimes posed problems for Reuters, which always insisted on explicit sourcing for its news stories. So when I filed dramatic accounts from Spain of clashes between protesting students and riot police – 'Violence erupted at Madrid's troubled university today when riot police, some of them on horseback, beat men and women students with riot clubs' – I was immediately asked what my source was.

'I was there. I saw it,' I replied.

Back came from the rewritten copy from London: 'A Reuter correspondent saw both men and women students shielding themselves from the blows…' Honour satisfied.

Beneath the surface calm (now there's a good journalistic cliché for you) of 1970s Spain, unrest was bubbling. On a clandestine trip to Barcelona, I was able to meet representatives of the illegal *comisiones obreras*, or underground trades unions; and, in the north, the Basque separatist movement ETA was already active. In December 1970, just a few months before I arrived in Madrid, ETA had kidnapped the German consul in San Sebastián, and in 1973, shortly after I had left, it assassinated the Prime Minister and Franco's designated successor, Admiral Luis Carrero Blanco, having concealed a powerful bomb beneath the street along which his motorcade was driving.

Somehow or other, I managed to find enough interesting material to produce a couple of pieces for the *New Statesman*, now being edited by my mentor, Tony Howard. I had to use a pseudonym (for many years, a mysterious freelance journalist named Francis Roberts seemed to follow me from assignment to assignment: wherever I was, there he was too), because Reuters strictly banned any moonlighting by its correspondents. Another fictional freelance, Bob Lowrey, made an occasional appearance in the *Daily Express* as well, just to ensure that political neutrality was maintained.

On one occasion, when the Fascist regime was growing particularly jittery about a wave of illegal strikes, both the *International Herald Tribune* and the *New Statesman* were banned from Spain because they had published my reports on the unrest. I regarded the government's action – of course – as a medal to be worn with pride.

On the whole, though, my journalistic output from Spain consisted of little more than sports results, student riots and then more sports results. It was all a good experience, and I learned a lot of tricks of the trade, but I was not sorry to return to London at the end of my twelve-month stint to find out what the future had in store for me. And I was still hoping to find a way to break into broadcasting.

That is why, when I saw an advertisement for a reporter to join Yorkshire Television's local news programmes, I immediately sent off an application. 'Come to Leeds for an interview,' they said, so I decided to combine the day trip from London with a call on an old flatmate from my student days who was a trainee on the *Yorkshire Post*.

'Let's meet at Yorkshire TV,' he said. 'I've applied for the same job.'

He got the job; I didn't. Instead, I stayed with Reuters, and six months later they sent me to Paris.

Paris. Then, as now, a plum posting. The cafés, the women, the art, the architecture. All it lacked was news. The French President, Georges Pompidou, was not one of Europe's most dynamic or charismatic leaders, and with the near collapse of the Fifth Republic during the student–worker uprisings of 1968 still fresh in the country's collective memory, there was little appetite for political experiments.

I found myself a tiny studio apartment close to the Arc de Triomphe, at 8 Rue du Dôme, a narrow street at the top of some steps just off the Avenue Victor Hugo in the fashionable 16th *arrondissement*. The location was to die for, but the apartment itself was a hovel. I never again made the mistake of choosing a home by reference to its postcode.

The Reuters bureau was at 36 Rue du Sentier, in a ramshackle building that proudly bore the name of the *Daily Mail* over its front door, a reminder of the days when that paper was rightly famed for its network of foreign correspondents. (The last time I looked, the words were still there.) The Reuters office was reached by means of an ancient clanking lift with steel concertina doors. Working there felt as if I had gone back in time, to the great days of the pre-war foreign correspondents, hard-drinking, chain-smoking, with endless supplies of stories from far-flung places. The bureau chief, Jonathan Fenby, was ferociously bright and attacked typewriters with such energy that, when he was in full creative flow, it sounded as if the bureau was under machine gun attack. He later became Reuters' editor-in-chief before moving to *The Independent* when it launched in 1986, becoming deputy editor of *The Guardian* and then editor of *The Observer*. He later edited the *South China Morning Post* in Hong Kong and wrote several well-received books on both France and China.

My tasks in Paris were not significantly different from what I had become used to in Madrid; the main difference was that there was a lot more sport. Every afternoon, someone in the bureau – usually me – was required to translate the editorial from *Le Monde*, a useful way to brush up one's comprehension of literary French. In continental Europe, unlike in the UK, journalists prided themselves on the use of a language as complex and flowery as possible, a reflection of continental journalism's origins in the literary salons rather than in the seventeenth-century scandal sheets of the UK. *Le Monde*'s editorials were not written for the benefit of milkmen in Kansas City.

I had expected that at least one benefit of having left Madrid would be that I need no longer concern myself with every cough and sneeze of the Argentine ex-President Juan Perón. But I was wrong because, when he returned to Argentina in late 1972, his route from Madrid to Buenos Aires included a refuelling stop in Senegal, west Africa. Reuters clients in Argentina would, of course, expect to be informed when he arrived there and when he left again and, as the Reuters stringer in Senegal was able to transmit his stories only via Paris, I was instructed to make myself available to receive his all-important phone call, expected at around 5 a.m.

When the call failed to materialise, I managed to make my own call to Dakar airport, got through to the control tower and was able to confirm not only that the great man had arrived but also that he had left again. The stringer finally made contact some hours later, presumably having had the benefit, as I had not, of a decent night's sleep. So much nervous energy expended for so little of genuine news value. On the other hand, if I had discovered that the plane had not landed as scheduled, that would have been a big story, at least in Argentina, so the exercise was not an entirely pointless one.

Phoning airport control towers became something of a speciality during my Reuters days. Hijacks were not uncommon and the only reliable way to find out who had hijacked what and why was usually to talk to the man in the airport control tower, who was in direct contact with the hijackers. My technique was simple but effective: on getting through to the airport switchboard, I simply barked, in as authoritative voice as I could manage: '*Ici Paris. Le tour de controlle. Vite.*' It is possible that the switchboard operators assumed that I was an important government official as there was not always time to spell out the fact that I was a reporter. All that mattered was that it worked without me having to tell any lies.

On 1 January 1973, the UK joined what was then still called the European Economic Community, or Common Market. Reuters decided that they needed an extra hand on deck in their Brussels office, and I was the one who drew the short straw. I have never had much affection for grand institutions and, although I consider myself a European to my fingertips (with my background, what else could I be?), I was not thrilled to be sent to a city where every story seemed to be about an acronym: EEC, NATO or WEU (the Western European Union, a singularly useless body that was finally put out of its misery in 2011).

I did, however, learn the art of covering European summit meetings, which involved many long hours of waiting, followed by thirty minutes of crazy activity, usually in the early hours of the morning, to produce a news story that was of very little interest to anyone. During the 1990s, by which time I had joined the BBC, I covered far too many such summits, in many different European capitals, and

I developed a passionate loathing for them. But even I recognised that someone had to report on them, and that the task was bound, sometimes, to fall to me.

The goal of the agency reporter at a summit meeting is to get the story of the summit conclusions before anyone else does. A leaked draft communiqué from a friendly diplomat, even a whisper in a deserted corridor, is all that is needed, but it can make all the difference between plaudits and angry messages from the bosses in London.

The Reuters bureau chief in Brussels in the early 1970s was the hyperactive and supremely well-connected Robert (Bob) Taylor. If anyone in Brussels wanted to know what was going on, Bob was the man they asked. More than once, while waiting for news at a European summit, I would fight my way to the front of a gaggle of reporters being briefed on the latest developments only to find that it was my own boss doing the briefing.

Once, he was already hammering away at a telex machine when I emerged from an official end-of-summit briefing with the official spin on the outcome. Bob had already picked up the main points from his own sources, but the official version that I relayed to him differed in some minor respects from what he had already sent to London. 'Fuck,' he said. 'Watch this story bend.' And, as he continued to type, the later intelligence was seamlessly and elegantly woven into what had gone before. It was so much less confusing for Reuters' clients than having to issue a correction.

Even in 1973, British newspapers were reluctant to take news from Brussels unless they could be persuaded that it might have a direct, preferably harmful, relevance to their readers' everyday lives. 'Want to get your stuff printed in London?' the *Daily Express* correspondent advised me. 'Start every story with the words "British housewives today face…"' *Plus ça change.*

I did not much like Brussels; neither the story, nor the weather (it was February), nor the city itself. So I was perfectly happy to return to Paris after a couple of months and pick up where I had left off. The biggest story in town before I left had been the Vietnamese peace talks between the US National Security Adviser Henry Kissinger and

Le Duc Tho of North Vietnam. An agreement was finally signed in January 1973, and Kissinger and Le Duc Tho were jointly awarded the Nobel Peace Prize. The American singer-songwriter Tom Lehrer was one of many who regarded the award as grotesquely inappropriate, famously remarking that 'political satire became obsolete when Henry Kissinger was awarded the Nobel Peace Prize'.

So what else did Paris have to offer an impatient young foreign correspondent in the early 1970s? An occasional student riot, a bizarre murder case in which a British teacher was accused of having killed his father while on a camping holiday in southern France, and the end of the historic food market at Les Halles, which had fed Parisians for more than a century.

I also had the doubtful privilege of writing one of the first reviews of *La Grande Bouffe*, the official French entry to the 1973 Cannes Film Festival. It was the story of four middle-aged men who decided to commit suicide by eating themselves to death, and it was hugely controversial because, as I reported in the studiedly non-judgemental prose required of all Reuters correspondents:

> It shows the four men gorging themselves over several days in the company of three whores whom they recruit to liven up their last days, and a fat schoolmistress who turns out to be more rapacious than the prostitutes.

I clearly took the view that readers deserved to be given as detailed an account as possible of what the film showed:

> The most controversial sequence shows the death of Michel Piccoli, who expires oozing excrement after the most audible and prolonged breaking of wind ever depicted on a cinema screen.*

One of the greatest joys of the journalist's life is that you never know who you are going to meet next. I did not expect, when I was sent

---

* The Mel Brooks film *Blazing Saddles*, which also featured a famous wind-breaking sequence, was not released until the following year.

to report on a demonstration at the cathedral of Notre Dame by anti-nuclear protesters who had chained themselves to the cathedral's pillars, to bump into an old student friend, Albert Beale, who later went on to become one of Britain's leading pacifist campaigners and a stalwart of *Peace News*. These days, he still describes himself as a 'militant pacifist, born-again atheist, and freelance agitator'. He was, of course, pleased to see me, as it meant their protest might get at least a couple of lines of coverage in the next day's papers.

I also met one of the great legendary figures of post-war European journalism, the former Reuters Paris bureau chief Harold King, who had become the doyen of Europe's foreign press corps due to his extraordinary access to two of the most influential figures of the time: Joseph Stalin and Charles de Gaulle. It was said that, as President, de Gaulle used to begin his news conferences with the words: '*M. King, messieurs…*'

In 1943, while based in Moscow, King had filed a famous Reuters dispatch breaking every rule in the book. It began with the words:

> Premier Joseph Stalin, in a letter to me, said Friday that the winding-up of the Communist International 'puts an end to the lie' that 'Moscow allegedly intends to intervene in the life of other nations and "Bolshevize" them'. The letter was in reply to a series of questions that I had submitted to Mr Stalin.

So much for the Reuters rule that the words 'I' or 'me' must never appear in news copy; on the other hand, it was impossible to argue with the quality of the source. When King died in 1990 at the age of ninety-one, the *New York Times* described him as 'a Reuters reporter whose letters from Stalin helped to shape the West's perception of the Soviet Union'.

By the time I met him, King was a much-diminished figure, a man in his seventies who had failed to find a role once his days as a correspondent were over. The thriller-writer and former Reuters correspondent Frederick Forsyth, author of *The Day of the Jackal* and many other bestsellers, said of him: 'He was regarded by few with liking, by many with fear, and had a reputation for eating young journalists for breakfast and spitting out the pips.'[25] My own bureau chief, Jonathan Fenby, recalled that when he was reporting on the 1965 French presidential election campaign, King ordered that he should not be left alone in the office since he had shown that he had Communist sympathies by reporting a speech by the Socialist François Mitterrand which had been critical of the General.[26]

Together with a friend, Duncan Greenland, I invited King to dinner at a restaurant of his choosing on the right bank of the river Seine, just across from the Île de la Cité. I no longer remember what we ate, but I do remember that we consumed large quantities of *vin rouge* and ended the evening by carefully helping him into a taxi to take him home.

I was always on the lookout for new opportunities, even though I had been with Reuters for less than three years. But when I was offered a new job, I turned it down: the American news magazine *Newsweek* asked if I would like to be their Paris stringer. When I asked what the job entailed, I was told that I would not be expected to write any articles, merely feed New York with the raw material with which they would write the stories. 'Colour, quotes and anecdotes' were what they required from their stringers, which did not sound quite my cup of tea, so I politely declined.

I had been in Paris less than a year when Reuters, in its infinite wisdom, decided that it was time for me to pack my bags again. I was sent to Rome, stopping off in London just long enough to be immersed in an intensive, four-week Italian language course. Every morning, I would buy a copy of *The Times* and try to translate its main stories into Italian, while my tutor provided a copy of the Italian newspaper *Corriere della Sera* which I would be required to translate into English. It was an admirably efficient way of enabling me to master enough of the language to function adequately as a journalist as soon as my feet touched the ground at Fiumicino airport. It also meant that from then on, if I ever tried to speak Spanish, it sounded suspiciously like Italian.

I fell in love with Italy the moment I landed, and I have remained besotted ever since. I am convinced that God intended me to be an Italian and that it was only by an unfortunate accident of geography that I ended up with a British passport. The food. The wine. The art. The music. The scenery. The language. The people. *Che bellezza!*

Rome is a city that excites strong passions. It is overcrowded, often ill-kempt, and its ancient monuments are usually either hidden behind scaffolding or visibly decaying. The traffic is appalling, the drivers are certifiably insane and the corruption is endemic. Yet there is no other city in Italy where I would dream of living; the northern cities of Milan, Turin and Genoa are too Teutonic; the tourist honeypots of Florence and Venice are too pleased with themselves, and the southern cities of Naples, Bari and Palermo are too crumbling and anarchic even for my taste.

Years later, when I was working in the Middle East, I began to understand why northern Italians sometimes call Romans *gli Arabi*, the Arabs. There is an undeniable cultural similarity: the love of bargaining, the delight in finding a semi-legal way through the thickets of official bureaucracy, and the understanding that a no can always become a yes if the price is right.

For a foreign correspondent, Italy is both heaven and hell. The country and its people are full of the most amazing stories, yet only some of them are true and, for the diligent journalist, sorting out the fact from the fable can be well-nigh impossible.

Admittedly, Italy was going through a particularly bad patch when I arrived there in 1973. It was virtually bankrupt and a chronic shortage of small-denomination coins, which the mint could no longer afford to produce, resulted in people using postage stamps, telephone tokens or boiled sweets instead of small change. Banks issued *assegni circolari*, or circular cheques, to take the place of scarce banknotes. The cheques were not legal tender, but they could, in theory, have been cashed at the bank. Of course, no one bothered.

Poor Italy. A country with the richest cultural history in Europe – Michelangelo, Leonardo da Vinci, Titian, Canaletto, Dante, Machiavelli, Verdi, Vivaldi, Puccini, Pavarotti, Christopher Columbus,

Galileo – has also suffered the most inept, venal and corrupt political leaders. Harry Lime was definitely onto something when he said in *The Third Man*: 'In Italy, for thirty years under the Borgias, they had warfare, terror, murder and bloodshed, but they produced Michelangelo, Leonardo da Vinci and the Renaissance. In Switzerland they had brotherly love, they had 500 years of democracy and peace – and what did that produce? The cuckoo clock.'

Italians look back on the 1970s as the *anni di piombo*, or years of lead, a time of terrorism from both the extreme left and the extreme right, when murders and bomb attacks were almost part of everyday life. Within a year of my arrival in Rome, eight people had been killed in a bomb attack on an anti-Fascist demonstration in Brescia; thirty-four people were killed in a Palestinian terrorist attack at Fiumicino airport; two members of the neo-Fascist MSI party had been murdered, allegedly by the extreme-left Red Brigades; there were reports of a planned military coup, backed by the US, to prevent the Italian Communist Party coming to power; and twelve people were killed in a bomb attack on an overnight train between Rome and Munich. The former Prime Minister, Aldo Moro, had disembarked from the train shortly before the bomb exploded. (Moro was kidnapped and murdered by the Red Brigades in 1978.)

I got used to being woken during the night by a phone call from the Italian news agency ANSA, and a voice telling me: '*C'è stato un attentato.*' ('There has been an attack.') Luckily, my flat, right next to the Quirinale presidential palace, with its gorgeous views over the rooftops of Rome's historic centre, was only a minute's walk from the Reuters office, so I could be filing the first dispatches within moments of a tip-off. The difficulty, as so often with terrorist attacks but doubly so in conspiracy-loving Italy, was trying to establish who was responsible for the latest outrage. The newspapers were constantly full of speculation about behind-the-scenes manipulation by foreign powers: right-wingers were convinced that Moscow was pulling the strings – this was, after all, at the height of the Cold War – while the left were equally convinced that Washington was in control.

As it happened, the conspiracy theorists were often more than half justified in their suspicions of dark deeds at the highest levels. It usually took several years for the truth to emerge, which was no use to hard-pressed news agency reporters churning out instant copy. But the arrest of the head of Italy's military intelligence agency, General Vito Miceli, on suspicion of involvement in a plot to launch a military coup was a good indication that something nasty really was going on beneath the surface. (Miceli later became a Member of Parliament for the neo-Fascist MSI party.) In 1976, the *New York Times* reported that, four years earlier, he had been paid $800,000 (equivalent to about $4.5 million now) by the US ambassador in Rome 'to demonstrate to these people our solidarity about what they're doing'. The CIA station chief in Rome had strongly objected to the payments, and complained in a telegram to Washington: 'The ambassador has made clear his intention of not asking for too many details from the recipient of the money and not to impose any condition on the use of the money.'[27]

Phone calls in the middle of the night are an occupational hazard for any reporter, but especially for news agency correspondents, who are expected to be ready to leap into action whatever the hour. In Rome, where the health of the Pope was a constant preoccupation, too many such calls seemed to be based on rumours circulating somewhere in South America.

'Robin, old boy. Sorry to wake you. We've had a message from Buenos Aires asking us to check out the rumours there that the Pope has died. Would you mind checking?'

'Tell them he's fine. If he had died, I would have filed the story. Good night.'

Risky, perhaps, but I trusted our friends at ANSA. They would have let me know if I needed to get up, and I did not fancy my chances of getting a sensible response from the Vatican press office if I had phoned them at 3.30 a.m. In fact, I would not have got any response at all. An institution that regarded a century as a historical blip was not temperamentally suited to a 24-hour news operation.

If I had been starved of excitement in Madrid and Paris, I was soon overdosing in Rome. The Reuters bureau was run by one of the agency's least likely managers you could imagine: Chris Matthews, whose languid manner and long blond hair gave him the look of a man who had stepped straight out of a film by the Italian director Federico Fellini. So perfectly Fellini-esque were his looks that when he was spotted one night in a Rome bar by a Fellini casting agent, he was immediately signed up as an extra in the maestro's next film. I very much doubt that the Reuters bosses ever found out.

Chris's mother, Tanya Matthews, was a redoubtable correspondent in her own right, and for many years she was the BBC's correspondent in Tunisia. She was of Russian origin, and Chris had inherited her striking Russian looks. When the Reuters board of directors turned up in Rome on what could easily have passed for a state visit – they were a crusty medley of elderly newspaper owners and executives, each one more hidebound than the next – their shock at the appearance of their local bureau chief was a joy to behold.

The chairman of the Reuters board at the time was Sir William Barnetson (later Baron Barnetson of Crowborough), chairman of the United Newspapers group, a man of military bearing who gave the impression that he expected Reuters outposts to be run along military lines. He was visibly unimpressed by the soft leather shoulder bag that Chris carried everywhere (man bags were hardly commonplace in the 1970s) and remarked in a voice dripping with sarcasm: 'I like your handbag, laddie.' The following day, Chris bought an identical bag and presented it to Sir William as a gift from the Rome bureau: 'because you said you liked it so much'.

Shortly before the Reuters directors descended on Rome, the bureau had been joined by the company's first ever female graduate trainee. Anne Rubinstein (now the bestselling author Anne Sebba) suffered a treble handicap: not only was she a graduate and a 21-year-old female, but she also had blonde hair. The Reuters general manager, Gerald Long, made it perfectly clear that he regarded her as a guinea pig: 'The standard of your work and behaviour will determine whether or not Reuters hires other women in the future.' Anne suffered even more than the rest of us during the directors' visit to Rome: in an article written many years later, she reported that during a supposedly social gathering one evening: 'I became aware that an elderly gentleman peer

... clearly suffered from a nervous tic as his hand kept wandering onto my knee.'[28] Anne has never publicly named the peer in question, but as he is now long dead, I am able to identify him as the 11th Earl of Drogheda, who was then the managing director of the *Financial Times*.

Not long after my arrival in Rome, one of the telephones in the office was removed. Supposedly, only one person – the Pope's personal doctor – knew the number; the idea was that if the phone rang, we would instantly know that we were about to learn something important. The death of a Pope (Pope Paul VI was seventy-six years old at the time and died the year after I left Rome) was the sort of story that no news agency wants to be beaten on. But because of the vagaries of the Italian telephone network, the phone rang constantly – and it was never the Pope's doctor. It was no good for our nerves and it had to go.

Italian politics were widely seen as a joke during the 1970s; governments lasted on average no more than eight months before the headlines would again scream: '*Crisi di governo!*' I soon learned that the word *crisi* should not be routinely translated as 'crisis' – it meant, in a political context, simply that a coalition administration would need to reshuffle a few ministerial portfolios before reappointing the same men belonging to the same political parties to slightly different jobs. These coalition administrations were known with good reason as 'revolving-door governments', and the whole system, riddled as it was with corruption, came crashing down in the early 1990s, when a series of corruption inquiries uncovered the full scale of the iniquity. At one point, half the country's MPs had been indicted in connection with the '*mani pulite*' (clean hands) investigation; the two main governing parties, the Christian Democrats and the Socialists, both collapsed, and a new force – and new face – emerged as Italy's saviour. His name was Silvio Berlusconi and, whatever else he may have been, he was no saviour.

I was one of a very small and select group of correspondents who took Italian politics seriously, and it was a source of constant frustration to me that Reuters in London, and the international media in general, did not share my belief that something important was going on beneath the surface. Only once, in 1975, when regional elections resulted in huge gains for the Italian Communist Party, did any of the political stuff that I churned out from the Rome bureau make an impact. Was Italy really going Communist? A founder member of the EEC, a fully paid-up member of NATO, a nation sometimes called 'America's Mediterranean aircraft carrier' – in the hands of the Reds? No wonder the Americans were twitchy.

When the government collapsed the following year, I reported:

> The fall of Italy's most fragile government since World War II heralds the start of this crisis-racked nation's most critical period for 30 years.
>
> It could end with the arrival in power of the powerful Communist Party, an event which would have enormous international repercussions and, in the opinion of US Secretary of State Henry Kissinger, could spell the end of the NATO military alliance.

It did not happen. It never did. Hence my frustration, and the rest of the world's lack of interest. But a freely elected Communist government in western Europe at the height of the Cold War would definitely have been of interest. I still believe that it was worth taking seriously: after all, this was a time when, in the UK, rumours were swirling of plots to overthrow the government led by Harold Wilson (some MI5 people were apparently convinced that he was a Soviet agent, or at least a Soviet sympathiser, even though there was never a shred of evidence), and in Washington President Nixon was being forced to resign over the Watergate scandal. For conspiracy theorists the world over, there were rich pickings to be had; but for correspondents trying to stick to what could be proved, it was tough going.

There is good reason to believe that Italy had become NATO's 'red line', and that a decision had been made that, at whatever cost, the Italian Communist Party must not be included in any government coalition. The party had carved out a position that was notably more pluralistic than the official Moscow line (although it later emerged that it was still receiving several million dollars a year from its Soviet sister party) and, for many years, its leader, Enrico Berlinguer, together with the leader of the Spanish Communist Party, Santiago Carrillo, was a leading exponent of 'Euro-communism'. Nevertheless, to Washington, Communists in a NATO government, and with access to NATO's military secrets, would be a step too far.

Euro-communism accepted the principle of multi-party democracy and the possibility of cooperating with other non-Communist parties in government. In Italy, there was constant talk of a *compromesso storico*, a historic compromise between Communists and Christian Democrats to bring together the two dominant political strands in post-Fascist Italy. It is likely that the terrorist attacks of the 1970s were, as many Italian leftists suspected at the time, part of a deliberate 'strategy of tension', designed to frighten voters away from the idea of allowing the Communists to enter a national government. And when Aldo Moro was kidnapped and killed in 1978, it was widely believed that he was on the brink of signing a power-sharing deal with the Communists.

In the highly charged elections of 1976, marked by an extraordinary intervention from Pope Paul, who instructed Italian Catholics not to vote for the Communists, they narrowly failed to overtake the long-dominant Christian Democrats, winning 34.4 per cent of the vote, less than four percentage points behind the Christian Democrats. After months of haggling, the Christian Democrat veteran Giulio Andreotti formed a minority administration that was dependent on Communist abstentions in parliamentary votes. It lasted less than three years, and was the closest the Communists ever got to national power.

I found the byzantine world of Italian political intrigue endlessly fascinating. And I struggled mightily to engage foreign readers in what too often seemed like an alphabet soup of endless political party acronyms. After a young Communist activist was shot dead at a neo-Fascist rally in the town of Sezze Romano, south of Rome, I reported on his very Catholic funeral.

As the sun's last rays bathed the Cathedral square in light, the symbols of Communism and Catholicism overlapped and seemed almost to merge.

The heavy walnut coffin was carried solemnly from the Cathedral and hundreds of red flags dipped in respect. Fists were raised in a Communist salute that seemed to be directed at the small crucifix carried by a priest in front of the coffin.

Perhaps I had been reading too much Hemingway.

After five years in the business, I was beginning to learn the hard way what makes headlines and what does not. Any story containing the words 'spaghetti' or 'Mafia' could be guaranteed to do well because editors rarely like to confuse their readers by offering them material from outside their comfort zone. And even an über-serious agency like Reuters could always find space for another 'funny foreigners' story.

Rome, 20 Feb 1975, Reuter – An enterprising Roman countess has launched a baby-sitting agency with a difference: the baby-sitters are grannies.

I think it was the word 'countess' that made it such a lovely little story.

The kidnap of the American teenage grandson of one of the world's richest oil billionaires, allegedly by the Mafia, certainly made the headlines and, for five months in 1973, the saga of the abduction of J. Paul Getty III was a major international news story, especially in the US.

When his severed ear turned up in the post, together with a note threatening that unless a ransom was paid, he would continue to turn up 'in bits', the headlines got even bigger. Getty's billionaire grandfather was a notorious miser – he had installed a coin-operated telephone in his Surrey mansion for the use of his guests – and was not at all keen to pay the $3 million that the kidnappers were demanding, on the not unreasonable grounds that if he paid up, his fourteen other grandchildren would all instantly become kidnap targets as well.

The Getty kidnap saga – he was eventually released after the ransom was paid – also taught me that luck can play a large part in a journalist's life. I had been due to fly to Turin to attend a media preview of the Turin shroud, a piece of cloth in which Christ's body was said to have been wrapped after he was crucified. The shroud was normally kept under lock and key in Turin's cathedral, but it was due to be shown on Italian television to allow believers a rare glimpse of one of the Church's most venerated relics.* The Vatican had advised everyone to watch the programme but, unfortunately, while waiting to board the plane to Turin, I had dozed off in the departure lounge and missed the boarding announcement. By the time I awoke, I had missed the flight.

All I could do was return to the office and prepare to grovel, but I was still desperately trying to think of ways to explain why Reuters would not be able to report on this major ecclesiastical event when I learned that the Getty ear had turned up. One severed human ear easily outranked a faded piece of ancient cloth of doubtful provenance, so my airport transgression was instantly forgotten.

All reporters dream of getting a scoop, a story of such global importance that their byline will scream from every front page and they will become a household name. Life, of course, is not like that, especially for an agency reporter whose output is likely to be 99.9 per cent mundane. Just occasionally, though, if you are in the right place at the right time, if the wind is in the right direction and the gods are smiling on you, you might get a scoop. I can claim two mini-scoops during my career, both of them dating from my time in Rome.

Scoop Number One: September 1974, when Italy was teetering on the brink of bankruptcy. An emergency summit had been arranged on the banks of Lake Como between the West German Chancellor, Helmut Schmidt, and the Italian Prime Minister, Mariano Rumor. After the assembled reporters had spent several hours hanging around, a deal was finally announced: the Germans had agreed to lend Italy $2 billion to stave off disaster. I rushed to the nearest phones in the lobby of the hotel where the summit meeting had been held. So did

---

* Radio carbon tests in the 1980s established that the cloth dates from the medieval era and is therefore definitely not the shroud in which Christ's body was wrapped.

the correspondent for the German news agency, DPA. But I was much younger than he was, and I got there first. I dictated the news flash – and, the following day, I received a message of congratulations from London informing me that German radio had interrupted its programmes to broadcast my dispatch and attributed it to Reuters.

In the news agency world, it does not ever get better than that.

Scoop Number Two: November 1975, a quiet Sunday morning. The Italian news agency ANSA opened up its service only after lunch on Sundays, even though its journalists were already at work in the morning. The tape machines in the Reuters office were silent. But our bureau was in the ANSA building, and we had built up a good working relationship with some of its journalists. Mid-morning, an ANSA journalist put his head round the door: 'I thought you'd like to know that [the film director] Pier Paolo Pasolini has been found murdered on the beach at Ostia.'

I made a quick phone call to the Ostia police, who confirmed it. It was another Lustig scoop, and it took Reuters' rivals twenty minutes – twenty minutes! – to catch up. More than forty years later, I still glow with pride.

The murder made a major international impact, and not only because of the fame-cum-notoriety of the victim. He was a director who specialised in portrayals of the underbelly of Italian society, and his killing, apparently by a teenage male prostitute, was inevitably seen as somehow mirroring his art. As I wrote later that day, Pasolini was 'an apparent victim of the twilight world his first films depicted and from which his first stars came'.

There was an unfortunate aftermath to the Pasolini story, which involved me being summoned to appear in front of an investigating magistrate to explain exactly how much I knew and when I knew it. Pasolini was a highly controversial figure of outspoken left-wing views, and his death immediately gave rise to suggestions that he had been bumped off on the orders of the state. The Italian journalist Oriana Fallaci reported that a 'secret witness' had told her that two young men had been spotted in the area where Pasolini's body was found, in addition to the male prostitute who had been charged with his murder.

When Fallaci was summoned to name this 'secret witness', she gave the name of a journalist friend of mine called Kay Withers. When Kay was summoned in turn and asked where her information had come from, she named me. In fact, as I told the magistrate, she was mistaken, but he took some persuading and, a few months later, the whole silly tale was recounted in the *New Statesman* as a perfect example of the Italians' love of conspiracies. I had to write a long letter of explanation to my bosses in London, who did not generally take kindly to seeing the hallowed Reuters name in such disreputable company.

The rumours surrounding Pasolini's death persisted, especially in light of the convicted murderer's retraction, thirty years after the event, of the confession that he had given to police after being picked up driving Pasolini's car. To this day, many believe that the full story has not been told. Just another Italian mystery...

There was no mystery, however, about the story that won me a fatter sheaf of newspaper cuttings than any other that I wrote during my four years in Rome. The *International Herald Tribune* even put it on the front page:

Rome, 13 Aug 1975, Reuter – An entire generation of Italian motorists is mourning the loss of its first love – the tiny Fiat 500, first of the world's minicars and symbol of Italian family motoring.

The recent announcement that Fiat has stopped producing the 500 after 18 years marked the end of a key era in this automobile-mad nation's history...

For many thousands of Italian motorists, the noisy, uncomfortable 'cinquecento' was their first car. Lovingly cared for, repaired in the backyard, often repainted and rebuilt, it enabled Italians to graduate from the Vespa or Lambretta scooters, which dominated Italy in the 1950s, to four-wheeled motoring.

It took Fiat only thirty-two years to realise their mistake, and, in 2007, they introduced a new, updated version of the 500 that seems to have become just as popular as the old one was. (My own car in Rome was a red Fiat 124 sport coupé, which I bought second-hand from a fellow correspondent. Much cooler than the 500.)

I suspect, looking back, that, despite all the frustrations, Rome is still the best city on earth in which to be a foreign correspondent. Not only is it crammed full of artistic, cultural and gastronomic delights, it is also very conveniently situated for quick flits to news hot spots in the Middle East, which is why for many years it boasted an international press corps far more numerous than Italy's own news importance would have warranted.

I am not sure what the appropriate collective noun for foreign correspondents is but, during my time in Rome, they included a wonderfully eclectic bunch, many of them larger-than-life characters who could have walked straight off a cinema screen. The leader of the English-speaking hack pack was Peter Nichols of *The Times*. He had arrived in Rome in 1957 and stayed there for more than thirty years until his death, aged only sixty, in 1989. He had twinkling eyes and a ready smile, but was only truly at home in the shadowy corridors of Italian politics and the Vatican. He was close to one of the most sinister of all Italy's post-war politicians, Giulio Andreotti, who was often suspected, but never convicted, of being one of the Mafia's most influential friends in government. Peter was always the first person I turned to when I needed someone to explain the latest convulsions on the political scene.

He was married to a stunningly attractive Italian film star, Paola Rosi, of whose charms he was so proud that there was a giant nude photograph of her hanging on the wall of the living room in their Rome flat. It always made visiting them somewhat tricky, as no visitor would wish to be caught looking more at the photo than at the hostess herself.

The *Daily Express* man was Robin Stafford, known once I arrived on his patch as 'Big Robin' to differentiate him from me, aka 'Little Robin'. He was a correspondent in the great tradition of *Express* correspondents, from the days when the paper was still justifiably proud of its global reach, and he was as much at home reporting on the weddings of celebrities as on the front line during the Six Day War of 1967. There were few places that he had not reported from; he once told me that when he was based in New York, he had to change his listing in the telephone directory because 'Robin' was a popular name for female sex workers in that city, and he was fed up with all the phone calls seeking to engage his services rather than offer him stories.

The ANSA building in which Reuters had its offices was at 94 Via della Dataria, just below the Quirinale palace and only a few steps up from the Trevi fountain. Just along the corridor from the Reuters office was the *Chicago Tribune*, whose correspondent Phil Caputo had been one of the first US marines to land in Vietnam in 1965. He later wrote a much-praised memoir of his experiences there, *A Rumor of War*, as well as several well-received works of fiction. When things were quiet, he and I, joined by Sari Gilbert, who wrote for a variety of US publications, would amuse ourselves by improvising quasi-Shakespearian verses on whatever topical subject took our fancy.

Another Rome-based Vietnam veteran was the Pulitzer Prize-winning William (Bill) Tuohy of the *Los Angeles Times*, a big man with a shock of white hair and an endless fund of stories. He spent nearly thirty years with the *LA Times*, heading their bureaus in Saigon, Beirut, Rome, London and Bonn. He ended his career back in London, where he would sometimes phone me to seek advice about the intricacies of the British political scene. He died in 2009 at the age of eighty-three.

Just outside the Reuters office was Visnews, now Reuters TV, which processed and edited news film from Africa and the Middle East before feeding it into the Eurovision network, which, pre-internet, was the only way international broadcasters could get access to TV pictures from far-flung parts. The Visnews man at the time was Ivor Gaber, who, in his postgraduate days, had taken over my flat in Hove when I left university and who later became one of my closest friends. He and his wife Jane lived near us in London later on, and their three daughters were roughly the same age as our children. After working for several years at ITN and the BBC, Ivor became a leading media academic and Britain's first professor of broadcast journalism.

The *Daily Mirror* was represented by Madelon Dimont, the daughter of the journalist and novelist Penelope Mortimer, and stepdaughter of the barrister and playwright John Mortimer, creator of *Rumpole of the Bailey*. She had been living in Rome since 1960, and in 1973 she married Lee Howard, a twenty-stone mountain of a man and a former editor of the *Mirror*. Madelon hired me on the quiet as her tip-off man and paid me a generous monthly retainer just to be sure that she and the readers of the *Mirror* never missed a story.

I loved spending time with all these people; after all, if you are interested in journalism, the stories that journalists tell cannot fail to be enthralling. And whatever other failings they might have, journalists are almost invariably great storytellers.

We Reuters drones worked a lot harder than many of our colleagues, but there was still time for long lunches and weekends away on beaches or in the mountains. After one particularly long lunch – probably *melanzane alla parmigiana*, followed by pasta and a salad at our local *trattoria*, the *Galleria Sciarra* – I returned to the office well refreshed and in a dangerously irresponsible mood. For some reason, we started discussing the recent visit to the Vatican by the then Prime Minister of Israel, Golda Meir, the first such visit since the establishment of the Israeli state in 1948.

So I sat at my typewriter and wrote a spoof dispatch:

Pope Paul VI today announced his forthcoming marriage to the Israeli Prime Minister, Golda Meir. More…

I tore the paper from the typewriter and handed it to a colleague. 'What do you think?'

'Great story,' he said. Then he swivelled round in his chair and pushed the sheet of paper down the chute that led to the telex room on the floor below from where telex operators transmitted our stories to London. They never read what they typed; they just sent whatever came down that chute.

I was down the stairs in a flash. If I had not stopped the dispatch being transmitted to London, my career would undoubtedly have come to an early and ignominious end. But I got to it in time, and learned my lesson: never mess around with 'joke' stories in a newsroom. (An equivalent rule applies in radio studios: never say things you might regret in front of a microphone, even if you think no one is listening. I wish I had not had to learn that lesson the hard way as well.)

In early 1977, I found myself on a flight to the Libyan capital, Tripoli, having been granted an almost unheard-of journalist's visa by Colonel Muammar Gaddafi. He was not, as a rule, keen on foreign correspondents, but on this occasion he was only too happy to be in the international spotlight because he had acted as mediator to help negotiate the release of a French archaeologist, Françoise Claustre, who had been kidnapped nearly three years previously by rebel fighters across the border in Chad.

Once freed, she was put on display at a news conference in Tripoli, to which I dutifully turned up, along with a hundred or so other representatives of the foreign press. Gaddafi bathed in his moment of glory, but his security police were keen to see the back of us at the earliest opportunity. Every time I left the hotel, I was followed – conspicuously – by a gentleman in dark glasses and leather jacket. So when Reuters suggested that I should stay on in Tripoli for the full seven days permitted by my visa – 'see what else you can pick up while you're there' – I did something that I probably should not admit to even today. I headed for the airport, jumped on a plane back to Rome and, when they asked why I had not stayed as instructed, I told them that the message had never reached me. I am sure that William Boot of *Scoop* would have approved.

I loved living and working in Rome, but after three years I was beginning to feel more and more frustrated. I was also worried that I was putting down roots; I was not yet thirty years old, and I was not quite ready to sink into the easy, indolent life of the British expatriate. I decided it was time to move on, and it was *The Observer* that offered me a way out.

At the suggestion of David Willey, who in the 1970s was not only the BBC's man in Rome but also *The Observer*'s, I had filled in for him during the summer when he went away for a few weeks' break. The mysterious Francis Roberts, who had written occasionally for the *New Statesman* from Madrid, now started popping up in *The Observer* from Rome. (An equally mysterious Oliver Moore made occasional appearances in *The Times* as well.)

David was every foreign correspondent's idea of what the perfect foreign correspondent should be like. A gentleman from head to toe, erudite, charming, superbly well-connected and always ready to help a colleague, he became, and still is, a good friend. I used to watch in amusement as successive BBC reporters would fly out from London, looking for ways to steal his job from him. He saw them all off, and is still there, well into his eighties, still reporting for the BBC.

After a couple of years writing as a summer relief correspondent for *The Observer*, I wrote to the foreign editor, Bill Millinship, to ask if there was any chance of being taken on as a staff reporter based in London. I had applied to *The Observer* once before while I was still a student at Sussex, but on that occasion Millinship had written a polite 'get lost' letter. This time, I struck gold. 'Funny you should ask,' he replied. 'We were just thinking that perhaps we should hire an extra person.' And so Lustig's Golden Rule of Career Advancement was vindicated: never begrudge the cost of a postage stamp. (These days, since the advent of emails, you do not even need to buy a stamp.)

It was a wrench to leave Rome and, as soon as I resigned from Reuters, they told me that they were about to send me to Zambia. I would have liked that – Africa was still in my blood – but it was too late. I had made my decision: after seven years as an agency man, it was time for a change.

CHAPTER 9

THE OBSERVER

What the British public wants first, last, and all the time is News.
SCOOP, EVELYN WAUGH

JOINING *THE OBSERVER* IN 1977 was not a risk-free undertaking. True, it was a newspaper with a glorious past, but its future prospects were exceedingly uncertain and at the time when I leapt aboard, the good ship *Observer* was in a pretty rickety state. I am not by temperament a risk-taker, but with no family to support and no other commitments, I calculated that this was probably the perfect time to take a risk. I had, after all, done the same thing aged eighteen, when I flew off to Uganda, so it was probably right, before I entered my fourth decade, to take one more leap into the unknown.

It was also a gigantic leap when it came to the kind of journalism that I was expected to produce. At Reuters, the emphasis was always on clarity and speed, whereas on a once-a-week Sunday paper with a reputation for stylish writing, I was clearly going to have to make some dramatic adjustments to the way I went about my business. I welcomed the opportunity, although I was unable to change gear overnight. When I handed in my first story on a Wednesday lunch-time, I was told kindly that it would have been perfectly all right if I had taken another couple of days.

The Observer likes to boast that it is the oldest Sunday newspaper in the world. It was founded in 1791 by W. S. Bourne, who borrowed £100 in the confident expectation that the paper would make his fortune. It would be, according to its advertisements, a newspaper 'Unbiased by Prejudice – Uninfluenced by Party ... Whose Principal is Independence'. But instead of making Mr Bourne's fortune, it lost him a fortune, and during the first hundred years of its existence, under a variety of owners, it was at various times (I quote from the official history) 'a scurrilous gossip sheet, government propaganda rag and provocative thorn-in-the-side of the establishment'.

By the time of its hundredth birthday in 1891, *The Observer* was being edited by a remarkable woman called Rachel Beer. She had been born in India and was a member of the Iraqi Jewish Sassoon family, one of the wealthiest dynasties of the nineteenth century. She was also married to *The Observer*'s then owner, Frederick Beer. Two years after taking over as editor, she bought the *Sunday Times*, and somehow managed to edit both papers simultaneously, an arrangement that I doubt would be regarded as acceptable today. It was under her editorship that *The Observer* published the admission by the French army officer Count Ferdinand Esterhazy that he had forged the document that resulted in the conviction for treachery of the Jewish army officer Captain Alfred Dreyfus.

In his memoirs, Esterhazy made no secret of his rabid anti-Semitism, and described his shock when he was first introduced to Rachel Beer to discover that, like Dreyfus, she was also Jewish. He wrote that she resembled a stick 'wrapped in an entirely white dress, decorated with evidently very expensive jewels, but in indisputable bad taste, and on top decked out with an enormous pink hat, the most incredible Jewish Judaic figure that one could see'. He was particularly struck by

> the most fantastic Jewish nose that was ever produced by the twelve tribes; a nose with which it is impossible to turn when you enter an ordinary street; a nose which can only be driven in a cab, and even there, it will disturb the coachman; and over this extraordinary monument, a ruffled mane, not curly but woolly – characteristic of this race, and badly dyed with piss-colour henna.[29]

By the time I arrived on the scene, *The Observer* was a good deal less exotic. It had been edited from 1948 until 1975 by David Astor, the second son of Waldorf and Nancy Astor, and therefore in his own way also the scion of one of Britain's wealthiest dynasties. (The paper had been owned first by his family, and then by a family trust, since 1911.) Under his editorship, it had developed into a powerful voice for liberalism: it supported the independence movements in Britain's colonies, opposed Britain's involvement with France and Israel in the Suez military campaign against Egypt in 1956, and played an important role in the establishment of the human rights group Amnesty International.

In the words of one of the paper's best-known and longest-serving columnists, Katharine Whitehorn, the paper had a well-established reputation for three things:

> It is well-written, often broke and usually on the side of the underdog. Chimney sweepers' boys, slaves, Luddites, the Peterloo protesters, young offenders in adult prisons (as long ago as 1817), females underpaid and over-punished; the poor, those without votes or drains, the downtrodden – *The Observer* has always been the place to read all about them.[30]

Astor had hired an extraordinarily disparate and talented team of writers and journalists, including the historian A. J. P. Taylor, George Orwell, Arthur Koestler, and the critic Kenneth Tynan. To the socialite Lady Pamela Berry, the wife of Lord Hartwell, owner and editor-in-chief of the *Daily Telegraph*, Astor's *Observer* was best characterised as 'a lot of central Europeans writing about a lot of central Africans'. Unfair, not entirely true, but quite astute nonetheless.

With the paper losing sackloads of money, Astor handed over the editorship in 1975 to his deputy, Donald Trelford, and the following year the paper was sold (for £1, plus the promise of a £3 million investment) to what was then one of the world's largest oil companies, Atlantic Richfield. It was a bizarre match, but it saved *The Observer* from the clutches of Rupert Murdoch or Robert Maxwell and, for a time, the new owners were welcomed by the paper's journalists as the least bad on offer. They were wealthy and they were based in California – too far away, it was thought, to be unduly meddlesome.

I met Trelford just once before I joined the paper: I had flown to London from Rome for a job interview with the home news editor, Bob Chesshyre, and the foreign editor, Bill Millinship, before being wheeled in for a courtesy chat with the editor. They wanted to take me on board as a general reporter, based in London, which suited me just fine: at the time, the paper had only one other non-specialist reporter, George Brock, who later joined *The Times*, where he rose to become managing editor and then professor of journalism at City University, London.

George and I were encouraged to do what reporters most love doing: poke our noses wherever the fancy took us and see what we could find. I had had few opportunities while I was working for Reuters to do much real reporting, by which I mean interviewing people with notepad in hand, following up leads and stitching together a story from a variety of sources. It also made a welcome change to be writing about things that readers were actually interested in, rather than bashing my head against a brick wall of indifference to news from foreign places.

Although Astor had handed over both the proprietorial and the editorial reins by the time I arrived, his influence was still everywhere. The paper's values were Astor's values. As Trelford put it after Astor's death: 'If the paper was characterised by humour, idealism, a sense of justice and a wide-ranging curiosity about the world and the vagaries of human nature – which it was – those qualities had their source in David's own complex and elusive personality.'

Many of the people he had hired were still writing when I got there, including such figures as the Commonwealth correspondent Colin Legum, whose book *Africa: A Handbook*[31] had been invaluable to me as a student at Sussex. I was hugely in awe of him, as I was of enigmatic foreign correspondents like John de St Jorre and Mark Frankland, both of whom had backgrounds in MI6. The formidable Terry Kilmartin, the literary editor whom Astor had hired after they served together during the war in the Special Operations Executive (Kilmartin had saved his life when he was wounded being air-dropped into occupied France) ruled over the arts pages.

Perhaps the most formidable figure of them all was a woman who in theory was a mere 'editorial secretary'. German-born Gritta Weil looked and sounded as if she had walked straight out of the pages of a John le Carré novel; she was heavily built, had a smoker's voice and a no-nonsense manner and knew everything about everyone. She had arrived in Britain on the Kindertransport as a fourteen-year-old refugee from the Nazis, and later met the economist E. F. ('Small is Beautiful') Schumacher, who knew Astor and got her a job on *The Observer*. She became an indispensable mother figure to the paper's stable of foreign affairs writers, making all their travel arrangements, looking after their domestic needs and, in the case of one of them, Gavin Young, caring for him devotedly during a long and distressing terminal illness.

After her retirement, she set up and ran an *Observer* alumni organisation that she named *Friends of The Observer*, which held an annual get-together for *Observer* staffers down the years. Bob Chesshyre, in an obituary for *The Independent*, said of her:

> At her appointment, as a refugee from the Nazis, she symbolised the eclectic character of the post-war Observer; by the time of her death 65 years later she was the sheet anchor to all those who worked for the paper under the its [sic] post-war editor David Astor and in the years following his retirement.[32]

There was a strong family spirit at the FOBS gatherings, but the Astor generation were not invariably on exactly the same wavelength as those of us who followed them. When the art historian Anthony Blunt was sensationally unmasked as a Soviet spy in 1979, I was told that Terry Kilmartin knew him well, so I plucked up the courage to ask if he had any idea where Blunt might be hiding.

'Probably at his place in Italy,' he replied.

'Might you have a phone number?'

'Possibly, but I certainly wouldn't let you have it.'

Not everyone from the Astor era was an ascetic analyst of global affairs or man of letters. *The Observer*'s legendary chief sports writer Hugh McIlvanney, for example, was made of more traditional Fleet Street stuff, hard-drinking and professional to his fingertips. He was named Sportswriter of the Year seven times and was the only sports writer ever to be named Journalist of the Year. Most Saturday evenings, after the presses had started to roll, he could be found in the sixteenth-century pub next door, the Cockpit, often till closing time. Occasionally, he would return to the office to spend the night there rather than having to find his way home.

It was not usually a problem but, in May 1980, when a small team of us under the direction of Donald Trelford were commissioned to write an instant book about the dramatic siege at the Iranian embassy in London, we took over the editorial conference room as our base of operations and worked almost round the clock to get the book written within ten days of the end of the siege. That meant we turned up very early on the Sunday morning, not a day when Sunday paper journalists can normally be found in the office, to continue our labours. And there, slumped across the conference table, we found McIlvanney, fast asleep.

'Hugh,' said Trelford gently. 'It's time you went home.'

McIlvanney opened his eyes, took one look at us and groaned.

'Christ almighty. I knew there was a chance I might get woken by a security man – or even by a cleaner. But not the fucking editor!' And, with that, he was gone.

In April 1989, he was at Hillsborough stadium in Sheffield, when a catastrophic policing failure resulted in ninety-six people being crushed to death and more than 700 injured in one of the world's worst ever football disasters. It was a Saturday afternoon, and Hugh phoned in to the news desk to give us the first horrific account of what had happened. I was the news editor and, as the death toll steadily mounted, I grabbed the phone and asked him one of those questions that only an insufferably idiotic deskman would ever ask.

'Hugh, how can you be sure they are all dead?'

In the circumstances, his response was admirably restrained.

'They wouldn't cover their fucking faces if they were alive.'

On the whole, though, the *Observer* newsroom was a model of decorum. A tough-as-old-boots managing editor, Ken Obank, who took charge of the news desk on Saturdays, was known to utter an occasional expletive, and on one occasion was said to have hurled a typewriter out of the window because one of his page layouts had been changed. When I delivered my copy to him, he would usually turn straight to the last page, and, without having read a word, put his pencil through the last paragraph. 'Every reporter always writes at least one paragraph too many,' he would say.

At the other extreme was the section editor who read through a piece I had written and then phoned me from the other side of the office: 'Robin, darling, it's a simply wonderful piece. But, listen, top of page three, second line, are you *terribly* attached to the comma?'

My very first story for *The Observer* was not exactly prize-winning stuff.

> Britain has had its wettest winter for a century … underground water tables are amply replenished after falling to dangerously low levels during the great drought [of 1976].

But I soon got into my stride, and three weeks after joining the paper, I was on the front page with the results of an investigation into the way crooked doctors were ripping off the NHS.

> The National Health Service is paying up to three times more than is necessary for certain drugs because some doctors are prescribing products sold at inflated prices...
>
> An investigation by The Observer has revealed that it is perfectly possible – and legal – for companies to charge whatever price they can get for their goods. And it is the National Health Service which suffers.

I had got hold of the story by the simple expedient of answering the news desk telephone one lunchtime and listening to a furious pharmacist ranting about how the NHS was getting ripped off. It took a few dozen more phone calls – and an independent chemical analysis of the drugs in question – to confirm that the story was both true and, equally important, legally watertight.

There are many definitions of news; I quoted the one from *Scoop* at the beginning of this book. Another one is: 'News is what someone,

somewhere, doesn't want you to print. Everything else is advertising.'
It has been misattributed to many different people over the years,
including George Orwell, but it seems to have its origins in a line
from an American newspaper, the *Harrisburg Independent*, in 1894:

> There are but two classes of people in the world – those who have done
> something and want their names kept out of the paper, and those who
> haven't done anything worth printing and want their names put in.

In a reporter's ideal world, we would write only about the former, but the
sad reality is that the bulk of the stuff you read every morning is about
the latter. During my time in Rome, when my duties included covering every utterance emanating from the Vatican, we developed a rule of
thumb: would we have been surprised if they had said the opposite? 'The
Pope believes in God, the Vatican announced.' Not news. 'The Pope no
longer believes in God, the Vatican announced.' News. Definitely.

The way *The Observer* was produced in the 1970s was not significantly different from the way it had been produced when Rachel
Beer was editing it in the 1890s. We reporters bashed away at our
typewriters, handed our copy to sub-editors, who passed it to linotype
operators, who typed it all out again to create metal lines of type,
from which pages were put together, cast onto rotary presses, printed and – eventually – distributed throughout the nation. The giant
presses were housed below street level at 8 St Andrews Hill, just a
stone's throw from Fleet Street, and the editorial floor would vibrate
alarmingly as they rumbled into action to produce the first edition on
a Saturday night. A sigh of relief would ripple through the newsroom:
another week gone, another paper produced. Time to go to the pub.
By Monday, our words would be lining the cat litter tray but, for a few
brief hours, they represented the totality of our professional abilities.
I was, and am, a hopeless romantic about newspapers, even if, like
everyone else, I now consume my news mainly on the screen of my
smartphone. (I am also a hopeless nostalgic, so *The Observer* is still
delivered to my home every Sunday morning, just as it has been, year
in, year out, ever since I can remember.)

Romantic about the rumble of the presses and the smell of the printers' ink I may have been, but there was nothing at all romantic about the way the printing unions regularly held the paper's management to ransom. If there was something in the paper that they took exception to – even an advertisement – they simply refused to start the presses. Unless the management conceded to their demands, an entire week's edition would be lost.

At *The Times* and *Sunday Times*, it got so bad that in 1978, the papers' then owner, the Canadian media tycoon Ken Thomson, shut down both papers for nearly a year in an attempt to break the unions' power. The tactic failed utterly and cost him an estimated £40 million. In 1981, he bailed out and sold the papers to Rupert Murdoch, who was very much more successful at breaking the unions, even if his overall influence on British journalism has been mixed at best and pernicious at worst.

While the *Sunday Times* was off the streets, sales of *The Observer* rocketed. But as soon as it returned, our sales fell back again, and for most of my time on the paper, we had such an inferiority complex (commercially rather than journalistically) as the *Sunday Times* expanded into a multi-section behemoth that we even ran an advertising campaign with the tagline ' *The Observer*: not as thick as the *Sunday Times*.' It was not exactly the best marketing strategy ever devised. (By 2015, sales of *The Observer* had dropped to around 200,000 copies a week, while the *Sunday Times* was still selling more than 800,000.)

When Murdoch bought Times Newspapers, he shifted the hugely successful editor of the *Sunday Times*, Harold Evans, to edit *The Times*, and I was sent to interview him and write a major profile. This was more than daunting: Evans was probably the most respected editor of his day, and to write something that I knew he would read first thing on the following Sunday morning had me hesitating over every word.

I should not have worried. Uniquely of all the people whom I profiled – and I wrote quite a few profiles at that time – he sent me a friendly note a few days after publication. I had reported that some of his colleagues at the *Sunday Times* had complained that he was sometimes indecisive, which in the circumstances was a risky thing to write, given that *The Observer*'s former editor and owner, David Astor, had been so notorious for his inability to make decisions that the phrase 'the editor's indecision is final' was coined especially for him.

Evans responded with great style on a scribbled postcard:

> Please name the people who think I can be indecisive and I will hound them. I think I will. Perhaps – well, on the other hand…

For a period, I was, in the medieval terminology of the Fleet Street craft unions, father of the National Union of Journalists chapel at *The Observer*, in other words, the elected representative of the editorial staff in all matters relating to pay and conditions. That meant I was entitled to attend joint meetings of all the unions that had members at the paper, the so-called imperial chapel (why did it sound as if we had all enrolled as freemasons?), but on the one occasion when I did so, and dared to say something, I was roundly mocked by my colleagues in the print room for foolishly presuming that the views of the journalists might be of any interest to them. Trade union solidarity was a laudable principle, and I have never to this day crossed a picket line, but the print unions often made it a very hard principle to abide by.

A much more pleasurable encounter was the regular Wednesday morning editorial meeting, at which all the paper's senior journalists would gather to discuss what should go into the following Sunday's paper and, nearly as importantly, how to put the world to rights. As well as the editor and his deputy – first John Cole, who became a nationally known figure when he was appointed the BBC's political editor in 1981, and then my old friend and mentor Tony Howard – there were the best of the Astor old guard, all of them with wisdom and experience by the bucket-load. And when Atlantic Richfield appointed Conor Cruise O'Brien as the paper's editor-in-chief – not an appointment wholeheartedly welcomed by Trelford – there were often fireworks.

O'Brien was another man of significant accomplishment: as an Irish diplomat in the 1960s, he had served as a UN envoy in what is now the Democratic Republic of Congo; he was later appointed vice-chancellor of the University of Ghana, and then entered Irish politics and became a government minister in the early 1970s. By the time he joined *The Observer*, he had become an outspoken opponent of Irish republicanism and an equally outspoken supporter of Israel, both of them positions that were guaranteed to provoke lively debates among the paper's senior editorial staff.

According to his biographer, in the early '70s, Conor had been 'simultaneously the most hated man in Ireland and the most admired outside of it'. In 1977, the *Irish Times* commissioned an opinion poll to establish who voters would least like to see running the country: Conor topped the poll. He was a man who delighted in vigorous debate and who was, at least by the time he joined *The Observer*, not much inclined to see merit in any views other than his own. On the subject of Britain's nuclear deterrent, for example, 'if the conventional wisdom among the British intellectual elite was in favour of unilateral disarmament, then he, virtually automatically, would be marching in the opposite direction'.[33]

His views on Northern Ireland meant that he had little time for *The Observer*'s well-established and highly regarded Ireland correspondent, Mary Holland, who had written with great distinction about the civil rights movement in Northern Ireland and whom Conor regarded as unacceptably sympathetic to Irish nationalism. In 1978, after Holland wrote a piece to mark the tenth anniversary of the start of the Troubles in Northern Ireland, he told her in a memo:

> I deeply regret and feel personally ashamed that this piece should be published in *The Observer* ... I think that it is a serious weakness in your coverage of Irish affairs that you are a very poor judge of Irish Catholics. That gifted and talkative community includes some of the most expert conmen and conwomen in the world and in this case I believe you have been conned.[34]

When Mary's contract expired the following year, it was not renewed. She did, however, return to *The Observer* fold after Conor's departure in 1985.

I had little direct personal contact with Conor during his time at *The Observer*, although I was always an admiring onlooker during his editorial sparring jousts at the Wednesday conferences. On the one occasion when I was able to spend some time alone with him – in a car on our way to catch a plane during the 1979 general election campaign, when he wanted to see Margaret Thatcher in action – I failed to take full advantage of the opportunity. My difficulty was that Conor had a gentle, lilting voice and was generally much better at talking than listening, and I have an unfortunate habit of tending to fall asleep in cars. To nod off while being talked at by the editor-in-chief is not usually a good career move, but if Conor even noticed, he seemed not to mind – and my discourtesy went unremarked.

Trelford managed the awkward relationship with an editor-in-chief who had been appointed over his head with consummate skill. The two men could not have been more different: Conor was bulky and often somewhat dishevelled; Donald was, in the words of *Private Eye*, 'small but perfectly formed', not an intellectual heavyweight but a master of the art of survival. Lord Goodman, chairman of *The Observer* and in his day the best-connected lawyer in London, said of him: 'Donald Trelford is the vicar of Bray. He has a remarkable facility for staying upright in a shipwreck.'[35]

After Conor's departure from *The Observer*, Trelford was asked why he had fired him. His reply spoke volumes: 'I fired Conor because I realised that if I fired him, Conor would survive – and that if I didn't fire Conor, then I would not survive.'[36]

In July 1977, just two months after I had joined the paper, I found myself at the Old Bailey, reporting on a trial that seemed to belong in the Middle Ages rather than in the latter part of the twentieth century. The anti-permissiveness campaigner Mary Whitehouse had brought a private prosecution for criminal blasphemy – the first such case for more than fifty years – against the newspaper *Gay News* and its editor, Denis Lemon. Their crime, she alleged, was to publish a poem imagining the lustful thoughts (and actions) of a gay Roman centurion as the body of Christ was taken from the cross after his crucifixion.

> As they took him from the cross
> I, the centurion, took him in my arms –
> the tough lean body
> of a man no longer young,
> beardless, breathless,
> but well hung.

(When *The Observer* published an extract from the poem, the last two lines of that passage were omitted.)

The trial was a gloriously anachronistic piece of theatre, as it was bound to be with John Mortimer defending Denis Lemon and the then young and upcoming Geoffrey Robertson, now one of Britain's most eminent human rights lawyers, defending *Gay News*. The judge, Alan King-Hamilton, was also a gift to any court reporter, a man with a penchant for making outrageous comments and who made little attempt to conceal his own personal view of the legal proceedings over which he was presiding.

When he died in 2010 at the age of 105, *The Guardian* recalled in its obituary that in one case, 'on hearing that Germaine Greer was to give evidence, he remarked, "Oh, God," and then put his finger to his lips saying to the solitary press representative "Ssshhh"'.[37] During the *Gay News* case, when discussing the merits of a review of a sex manual for gay men that had appeared in the paper, he remarked: 'What I don't understand is why homosexuals need help in this way ... It's all quite beyond me, I'm afraid. Wouldn't you expect that any reader of *Gay News* already knew?' To his credit, the columnist, critic and TV personality Bernard Levin, who was giving evidence on behalf of *Gay News*, explained that gay men needed no more help from sex manuals than straight men, and that there were 'a great number of such manuals available to cater to heterosexuals' needs'.[38]

Perhaps King-Hamilton's most notorious outburst from the bench came in 1979, just before he retired, when the jury in a trial of alleged anarchists decided, to his fury, to acquit them. He ordered the jurors back into court the following day to hear him sentence the one defendant who had pleaded guilty and said: 'Now you know what you have done, I pray to God that none of you will ever have occasion to regret it.' The *Sunday Times* called it 'a disgraceful epitaph to an undistinguished judicial career'.[39]

The jury in the *Gay News* trial were more to his liking: they found both the paper and its editor guilty of criminal blasphemy and he imposed fines of £1,000 on the paper and £500 on Denis Lemon, in addition to a suspended nine-month prison sentence. It was to be the last gasp of a common law offence that had survived for far too long, even though it was not until 2008 that the offence was finally abolished.

One of the many oddities of the *Gay News* case was that no one had attempted to define criminal blasphemy for more than half a century. Judge King-Hamilton was well up to the task and, although he was himself Jewish, he set out his understanding of the law exclusively as an offence against Christianity:

> The offence of blasphemous libel occurs when there has been published anything concerning God, Christ or the Christian religion in terms so scurrilous, abusive or offensive as to outrage the feelings of any member of or sympathiser with the Christian religion so as to tend to lead to a breach of the peace.

He later wrote in his memoirs that his summing-up in the case was 'the best, by far, that I have ever given. I can say this confidently without blushing because, throughout its preparation, and also when delivering it, I was half-conscious of being guided by some divine inspiration.'[40]

Another oddity was that during the six-day trial, I got to know, and like, Mary Whitehouse. We met in the Old Bailey canteen every lunchtime, and although each of us loathed what the other stood for – she regarded *The Observer* as only very marginally better than *Gay News* – we got on extremely well. Not for the last time, I discovered that being a reporter gave me a unique opportunity to meet people whom I would never otherwise have encountered. The *Gay News* case also infected me with a lifelong weakness for courtrooms and the law, although I soon came to realise that not every case contains as much drama as an Old Bailey trial with a cast including John Mortimer, Judge Alan King-Hamilton and Mary Whitehouse.

Some, on the other hand, are even more dramatic – and when I found myself back at the Old Bailey two years later, it was to report on a trial that really could have been labelled, in the words of that tired old tabloid favourite, 'The Trial of the Century'. In the dock of Court Number One was John Jeremy Thorpe, former leader of the Liberal Party and one of the most colourful politicians of his time. The charge: conspiracy and incitement to murder Norman Scott, who claimed to have been his gay lover.

It was one of the most convoluted, bizarre, and frankly unbeliev-able, tales in British political history. But what it boiled down to was a simple story of love and betrayal – Scott believed that Thorpe had loved him and promised to look after him, and over a period of more than fifteen years was obsessed with making people believe his story: that they had been in a relationship, and that Thorpe had behaved extremely badly towards him. Eventually, fearing public exposure (homosexual activity was illegal until 1967), Scott said, Thorpe had ar-ranged for the hiring of a hitman to kill him. The gunman had driven Scott and his dog Rinka onto Exmoor, had shot the dog, turned his gun on Scott, but the gun had jammed.

By the time the case reached the Old Bailey in May 1979, I had been researching and reporting on the life and times of Jeremy Thorpe for nearly two years. I had started when *The Observer* engaged the services of two former BBC journalists, Barrie Penrose and Roger Courtiour, who had interviewed the former Labour Prime Minister Harold Wilson about his suspicion that South Africa had mounted a dirty tricks campaign against anti-apartheid figures in the UK. The trail led them first to Thorpe, who had always been in the forefront of the anti-apartheid campaign, but then to the explosive story of the plot to kill Scott.

The Observer, however, was nervous – so I was dispatched to try to stand up their story by re-interviewing some of the people from whom they had obtained their information. It was a thankless task that resulted in little more than me having several front doors slammed in my face. *The Observer* ran their material nonetheless and, from then on, I was the paper's designated Thorpe reporter.

When the alleged hitman, a former airline pilot called Andrew Newton, emerged from prison in April 1977 after having served a sentence for illegal possession of a firearm and an intent to endanger life, he sold his story to the London *Evening News*, claiming that he had been paid by people acting on behalf of 'a leading Liberal': 'I was hired to kill Scott: gunman tells of incredible plot'. The former Liberal MP Peter Bessell, who was now living in California, was also talking of having been involved in a murder plot to deal with the Scott 'problem'.

Thorpe had responded by holding a press conference at the National Liberal Club.[41] With him were his wife Marion, his lawyer John Montgomerie, and his fellow Liberal MP, the raconteur and broadcaster Clement Freud. There were more than eighty of us crammed into the room, waiting to hear how he would deal with the flood of salacious allegations that were now threatening to engulf him.

First came the prepared statement:

> Anyone expecting sensational revelations is likely to be disappointed … Not a scrap of evidence has been produced to implicate me in any alleged plot to murder Norman Scott … He is neither the only nor the first person I have tried to help, but a close, even affectionate relationship developed from this sympathy. However, no sexual activity of any kind took place.

Then it was time for questions. Keith Graves of the BBC, who later became a neighbour of mine when we were both Middle East correspondents and lived in the same block of flats in Jerusalem, detonated the bomb: 'The whole of this hinges on your private life. It is necessary to ask you if you have ever had a homosexual relationship.'

Marion Thorpe exploded: 'Stand up and say that again.'

Keith, who was not easily intimidated, did so, at which point the lawyer, John Montgomerie, stepped in to say that he would not permit his client to respond.

The police got busy, however, and in August of the following year, Thorpe was arrested and charged, together with three alleged accomplices: his former friend and ex-deputy treasurer of the Liberal Party, David Holmes, who had been best man at his wedding; John Le Mesurier, who was a carpet dealer and business acquaintance of Holmes; and George Deakin, a fruit machine salesman who was alleged to have been brought into the conspiracy because it was thought that he would know where to find a hitman.

The whole story sounded preposterous, but if Andrew 'Gino' Newton's gun had not jammed that night on Exmoor when Rinka the Great Dane lost her life, Norman Scott would also have died. Gay sex, a murder conspiracy and politics is about as combustible a mix as any headline writer could ever hope for – so when Thorpe and his co-defendants appeared for their committal hearing at Minehead Magistrates' Court in Somerset, there were so many reporters that the modest-sized courtroom was bursting at the seams.

The usual practice at committal hearings was that reporting restrictions confined media reports to little more than the name of the defendants, the nature of the charges, and whether or not bail was granted. So we were expecting just to get a good look at Thorpe and write down what few details we were allowed to divulge. We knew there was a theoretical possibility that one or more of the defendants might apply to have the reporting restrictions lifted, but why would they? Thorpe's lawyer, Sir David Napley, had already made it clear that he was most unlikely to make an application, and no one had any reason to suppose that Thorpe's co-defendants would be any keener to see the story given the full Fleet Street treatment.

Day One. Bombshell in court. Deakin's lawyer applies for reporting restrictions to be lifted. Application granted.

Panic on the press benches.

Suddenly, we realised that every word spoken, every salacious piece of evidence presented by the prosecution, could now be reported in all its glory. Thorpe's name could be publicly linked to the alleged murder plot and the details disclosed. For a bunch of 'colour writers' who had expected to produce no more than some finely turned prose on the demeanour of the defendants, this was terrifying. Few of us possessed the shorthand skills necessary for accurate court reporting.

For me, reporting only for a Sunday paper, the problem was not insurmountable. I could still turn in my colour piece as planned, relying, if necessary, on the dailies for any verbatim quotes. I also made sure to sit next to a man from *The Times* who had impeccable shorthand and was very happy to share the essential quotes during a break in the proceedings. Jostling with us for notebook space were such luminaries as the novelist and crime writer Sybille Bedford and the satirist Auberon Waugh, eldest son of Evelyn Waugh, who invited me to dinner one night, together with David May of the *Sunday Times* and Ronnie Payne of the *Sunday Telegraph*, at the Waugh family residence at Combe Florey, about twenty miles away. It was the closest I ever got to meeting my fictional journalist hero, William Boot.

Court reporting for a Sunday newspaper is trickier than it might appear. All the best bits of the evidence have already appeared in the daily papers, so what is left is mainly colour and atmosphere. But even when reporting restrictions have been lifted there are still strict rules about what you can say while a case is under way, because nothing that appears in print must risk being held to interfere with the administration of justice. It would not be a good idea, for example, to say of a witness that he was 'clearly lying through his teeth', or that a defendant 'looked guilty as hell'.

So I edged as close to the limits as I dared. I reported that 'the two Mrs Thorpes, wife and mother, sit stonily side by side'. I revealed that Mrs Deakin, wife of one of Thorpe's co-defendants, 'occasionally tries to relieve her evident boredom by reading a historical romance paperback', and that the chief prosecution witness, Peter Bessell, 'delivers his evidence in the manner of a company executive dictating a note for the record to his personal secretary'. The aim was to give readers a flavour of what it was like to be sitting in that courtroom, without risking that I would end up sitting in a prison cell.

Once the case had been sent for trial at the Old Bailey, I got to work preparing a lengthy background piece on Thorpe, ready to be published once the trial was over. Like most of the reporters who had immersed themselves in the detail of the saga, I was confident that Thorpe would be found guilty, even though some of the prosecution evidence was not exactly rock-solid. I was much influenced by two of my sources who had been his contemporaries at Oxford, the editor of *The Times*, William Rees-Mogg, and the ballet critic Oleg Kerensky, grandson of the Russian Prime Minister Alexander Kerensky, who was overthrown by the Bolsheviks in 1917. When I interviewed each of them about their memories of Thorpe, I was shocked by the depth of their contempt for him. Even as an ambitious student politician, it seemed, he had earned himself a reputation for sharp practice, deceit and double-dealing.

I also interviewed a former Conservative MP, Ian Harvey, who had resigned from Harold Macmillan's government in 1958 after being arrested while having sex with a guardsman in St James's Park and charged with gross indecency. One of the biggest mysteries of the Thorpe saga had been why such a senior politician would take such huge risks in his private life, whatever his sexual orientation but especially if he faced the risk of criminal prosecution. Harvey had no difficulty explaining the mystery: 'The greater the risk, the greater the pleasure.'

The Old Bailey trial opened on 8 May 1979 and it did not take long for Thorpe's QC, George Carman, to blow a gaping hole in the credibility of the prosecution's main witness, Peter Bessell, who had signed a contract with the *Sunday Telegraph* for the publication of his story once the trial was over. Fatally for the prosecution case, the contract specified that his fee would be doubled if Thorpe was found guilty, meaning, as Carman lost no time in pointing out for the benefit of the jury, that he had a clear financial interest in tailoring his evidence to make a conviction more likely.

Carman was another of Thorpe's Oxford contemporaries, and, according to Thorpe's biographer, had helped Thorpe with his law essays in return for support at the Oxford Union. He also, although none of us knew it at the time, was leading as risky a private life as Thorpe had been: after his death in 2001, it emerged from a biography written by his son that he had a serious alcohol problem, was a wife-beater, addicted to gambling and, despite his three marriages, probably bisexual.[42]

One of his main difficulties as Thorpe's defence counsel was dealing with his client's sexual orientation: it was an essential element in the case, given Scott's insistence that they had had a physical relationship, but Thorpe had always categorically denied that he was gay. Carman's solution to the problem was skilful and subtle, the result of a deal agreed with the prosecution to stop them calling a long line of witnesses who were prepared to give evidence about Thorpe's secret sex life.

During his cross-examination of Scott, Carman asked:

You knew Thorpe to be a man of homosexual tendencies in 1961?
    Scott: Yes, sir.
    Carman: He was the most famous and distinguished person you had met at the time?
    Scott: Yes, sir, I think so.
    Carman: You were flattered that for a short time he introduced you into a different social world. I suggest you were annoyed because he did not want to have sexual relations with you.
    Scott: Of course that's ridiculous, because he did.

As Thorpe's biographer pointed out, what Carman had managed to do, almost in passing, was leave the impression in the jury's minds that 'Scott was a predator who had accurately assessed Jeremy's "weakness" at their first meeting and set out to exploit him'.[43]

When it was the turn of the defendants to present their case, only one of them, George Deakin, chose to give evidence; Thorpe, Holmes and Le Mesurier all stayed silent. And when the judge, Mr Justice Cantley, gave his summing-up, before sending the jury out to consider their verdicts, he sounded to many of us on the press benches as if he was leaning heavily in one direction.

The defendants, he said, all had an 'unblemished reputation'. The evidence against Thorpe was 'almost entirely circumstantial', and although he might clearly have had a motive for wanting Scott disposed of, the existence of motive did not constitute proof. Cantley was not, however, conspicuously well-disposed towards Thorpe's co-defendant George Deakin, whom he described as 'probably the sort of man whose taste ran to a cocktail bar in his living-room'. The main prosecution witness, Peter Bessell, was an even lower form of pond life: '[he] told us he was a lay preacher at the same time as being sexually promiscuous. And therefore a humbug.' Norman Scott was 'a hysterical, warped personality, accomplished sponger and very skilful at exciting and exploiting sympathy'. The hitman, Andrew Newton, was 'a highly incompetent performer for all his self-advertisement … capable of inventing an entirely false story … One must look at his evidence with great care.'

The comedian Peter Cook famously parodied the summing-up in one, deadly sentence: 'And now, you are to retire – as indeed should I – to consider your verdict of "Not Guilty."'

On 22 June, after two and a half days of deliberations, the jury duly returned their verdicts: they found all four defendants not guilty. It was a Friday, and their verdict presented me with a serious, immediate problem: much of the background article that I had spent so many months researching and writing was now unpublishable, for the simple reason that what can be said without fear of a libel writ about a man who has just been acquitted of a conspiracy to murder is very different from what can be said about someone who has been convicted. My article had already been set in type, so I sat down with the galley proofs watching a lawyer go through it paragraph by paragraph.

'You can't say that … or that … or that … This bit's all right … but not that … or that…'

It was an excruciatingly painful process. All that work, all those words, wasted. What remained bore little resemblance to what I had originally written.

It was like the slow unpeeling of a mask. Jeremy Thorpe's face, which for most of his trial had been set in an unmovable frown, suddenly came to life … For the first time in 15 years [he] no longer had to worry about Norman Scott. The ordeal was over. For good.[44]

I was not alone in my professional pain. Both the BBC and the commercial TV network LWT had to cancel their planned documentaries, the *Daily Mirror* dropped its plan to publish Norman Scott's autobiography and, irony of ironies, the *Sunday Telegraph* cancelled its ill-advised contract with Peter Bessell.

Within just a few weeks of the end of the trial, a highly unusual insight into the minds of the jurors was published in the *New Statesman*,[45] which obtained an interview with one of them that had been conducted by two *Guardian* journalists, Peter Chippindale and David Leigh. (*The Guardian* had decided not to publish it on the grounds that it would probably lead to an action for contempt of court. Its caution was well-founded: the government did take action against the *New Statesman*, but lost. The Lord Chief Justice, Lord Widgery, ruled that although it was important to uphold the principle that jury room deliberations should remain secret, this particular article 'demonstrated that the jury had approached its task in a sensible and responsible manner'.)

What the interview revealed was that the Bessell contract was a crucial factor in the jury's decision to acquit. Bessell and Holmes were the only two sources who claimed that there had been a conspiracy to murder, but Bessell's evidence was fatally tainted by his contract with the *Sunday Telegraph*, and Holmes chose not to give evidence. The jury were convinced, apparently, that there had been some sort of conspiracy, but they were not satisfied beyond reasonable doubt (the standard required in a criminal court) that it was a conspiracy to murder.

Q: If the charge had been conspiracy to intimidate, or something like that, would you have convicted?
A: Oh, undoubtedly, yeah. We was all certain of that.

In 1981, Parliament passed a new contempt of court act that meant no future such jury interviews could be published. Under section eight it became an offence 'to obtain, disclose or solicit any particulars of statements made, opinions expressed, arguments advanced or votes cast by members of a jury in the course of their deliberations in any legal proceedings'. Four days before the new act came into effect, *The Observer* published my account of two juries that I had sat on, in which I described in some detail – although without identifying the cases – the very different ways in which the two juries had arrived at their verdicts.[46]

As far as I know, it was the last such article ever to appear in the British press.

Fortunately, the Thorpe case now reads like a tragic tale from a very different era. Cabinet ministers and other MPs are now openly gay and a politician's sexuality is no longer regarded as career-defining. Even when the Prime Minister is reported to have done unspeakable things with the head of a dead pig during his student days, the public reaction is one of mirth, perhaps of scorn, but there are no calls for his resignation. Thorpe spent his entire adult life pretending to be someone he was not, and becoming ever more desperate to prevent people from learning the truth. It destroyed his career and blighted the lives of dozens of his friends and political colleagues. So when I hear people lamenting the appalling iniquities of contemporary political life, I remind myself that not everything is worse now than it used to be.

The Thorpe trial had been postponed to make way for an event that was to have a far more lasting effect on British politics than the downfall of the former leader of the Liberal Party: the 1979 general election that brought Margaret Thatcher to power and ushered in eighteen years of unbroken Conservative Party rule. It was a period during which Britain changed more fundamentally than at any time since the immediate post-war years that saw the establishment of the welfare state and the National Health Service. Nationalised industries were sold into private ownership, and a massive process of de-industrialisation was begun, resulting in the collapse of Britain's coal, steel and ship-building industries. Revenues from North Sea oil paid for a programme of tax cuts for the better-off, and Thatcher's supporters exulted that she had 'made Britain great again'. That was not *The Observer*'s view, nor was it mine.

For the three weeks of the 1979 election campaign, I was one of the team of journalists on the Thatcher campaign bus. To be strictly accurate, I was on one of the two campaign buses, because we drove round the country in convoy: the candidate and her team in one bus, with the 'reptiles', as her husband Denis referred to us, following close behind. We got so few chances to interact with her directly that, after a week of steadily mounting frustration, the travelling press wrote her a letter, signed by all of us, begging for a chance to actually talk to her.

> The first week of Thatcher's campaign trail has been a success. Or rather it has achieved what it set out to achieve – plenty of pictures in the papers. So far, Mrs T has refused only two photographers' requests: she does not enjoy kissing babies, and she very sensibly refused to hold a giant pair of scissors near her face...
>
> Smiling at cameras is one thing, talking to reporters is quite another. So far, we scribblers have had scarcely a 'Good morning' to call our own.[47]

One evening, close to midnight, our wish was finally granted, and we were ushered into her hotel suite for an impromptu press conference. The main issue of the day was her party's taxation proposals, a subject on which the *Financial Times*'s political correspondent Elinor Goodman, later of *Channel 4 News*, was both impressively knowledgeable and commendably insistent. Eventually, proceedings were brought to a close after Denis, in an audible whisper, had muttered to an aide: 'Who is that dreadful woman?'

I found Thatcher to be impressive and terrifying in equal measure. Her stamina left the rest us breathless with exhaustion; her certainties were absolute, her belief in victory unshakeable. (To be fair, there was little doubt in anyone's minds that she would win, since the Labour government under Jim Callaghan had very obviously run out of steam.)

'They call me a reactionary,' she would say in every stump speech at town halls up and down the country. 'Well, I am a reactionary, because there's a lot to react against.' And right from the word go, she made no attempt to disguise her approach to government: 'I seek confrontation with no one, but you do not serve the cause of peace and social harmony by shrinking from such challenges.'

As the nation's coal miners were to learn soon enough.

The 1979 Conservative Party campaign was a watershed: adopting techniques imported from the US, Thatcher's handlers understood that what mattered above all was imagery. For the first time in British politics, the interests of the TV cameras were paramount. Hence, Thatcher cuddling a calf, Thatcher in a chocolate factory, Thatcher chatting to shoppers. We take it for granted now, but in 1979, it was a novelty.

It was widely recognised that whichever party won the election would reap the full benefits of the North Sea oil bonanza that was just beginning. Yet there was little discussion of how the oil revenues should best be utilised. Nor, in the years that followed, was there much debate. As Ian Jack wrote in *The Guardian* more than three decades later:

> Oil's failure to intrude into the public debate, particularly in southern Britain, had an important consequence. 'Not fixing the roof while the sun shone', the favourite Tory accusation against the Blair/Brown regime, held true in spades for the way oil receipts were spent in the Thatcher years.[48]

For several years after I joined *The Observer*, I made regular trips back to Italy to report on more bomb attacks, the kidnap of a British businessman, Rolf Schild, and his family (the kidnappers had misheard his name and thought the family were Rothschilds), the uncovering of the shadowy right-wing conspiracy P2, and the trial of a Scottish nanny who was alleged to have been an arsonist and, in the eyes of the excitable Italian press, a witch. Only a year after I joined the paper, Pope Paul VI died, setting in train, as papal deaths always do, a cumbersome and ritual-filled process to choose a successor. The conclave of cardinals who would elect the next pope began their deliberations on a Friday and in the full expectation that they would take a few days to reach a decision – three or four days is the norm – we ran a big double-page feature about some of the most favoured candidates.

Just as the presses were starting to roll on the Saturday evening, a puff of white smoke was seen to emerge from the chimney of the Vatican's Sistine Chapel, where the cardinals were meeting.

Panic. White smoke meant they had chosen a new pope.

But then the smoke turned black, signifying that no new pope had been elected.

Confusion.

Eventually, the senior cardinal in the conclave, Cardinal Pericle Felici, appeared on the balcony of St Peter's Basilica to make the traditional Latin announcement: *Habemus papam*. We have a pope. It was wonderful news for the world's Roman Catholics, but not such good news for the Sunday newspapers.

Donald Trelford appeared at my desk. 'Robin, you used to work in Rome, didn't you? We need to scrap the centre pages and get a profile of the new pope for the next edition. Can you manage 1,000 words in the next twenty minutes?' This was long before Google or Wikipedia, and there was next to nothing about the new man in the cuttings file. I did not quite manage the 1,000 words, so we had to run an extremely large photograph to fill the space.

There was a postscript. A month later, my wife, Ruth, who likes to keep the bedside radio on for most of the night, woke me to tell me that the pope was dead. 'I know,' I replied. 'He died weeks ago.'

'No,' she said. 'The new one is dead.'

I had worked in Rome for four years dreading the moment when the pope would die. Then, within a year of me leaving, two had died in quick succession. I am still not sure whether that means I was unusually lucky or unusually unlucky.

The untimely death of Albino Luciani, known as the 'Smiling

Pope', after just thirty-three days as pontiff, immediately gave rise to all sorts of conspiracy theories. The most popular was that he had been murdered by the Mafia, or someone close to the Mafia, or someone involved in the shady financial dealings that linked the Vatican's bank to organised crime and extreme right-wing political groups. Nothing was ever proved and, having read far more of the conspiracy theories than is good for my health, I remain convinced that he died a perfectly natural death.

In 1981, I was appointed *The Observer*'s news editor, a position that I held until 1985, and then again for a brief period in 1987–88. It was the decade of Thatcherism: deep recession, race riots, the Falklands War and the miners' strike. Not a week went by without the Thatcher name figuring large on the news pages, never more so than when, in early 1984, *The Observer* ran a series of exclusive news reports detailing the shady business activities of the Prime Minister's son, Mark. I had hired David Leigh of *The Guardian*, whom I had first met at Minehead Magistrates' Court during the Thorpe trial, to join *The Observer* to lead an investigations team, modelled on the highly successful Insight team at the *Sunday Times*, but with a fraction of its resources. He was joined by Paul Lashmar, then a junior researcher at the paper, and they soon established themselves as a formidable, award-winning team. (Leigh won a total of seven national press awards during his 45-year career, including Granada TV's investigative journalist of the year and the British press awards campaigning journalist of the year.)

The Mark Thatcher stories, all of which bore the Leigh–Lashmar byline, revealed his involvement with a British construction company called Cementation that was bidding for a multi-million-pound construction project in Oman. On an official visit to the sultanate – the first ever by a British Prime Minister – his mother had lobbied hard on behalf of the company, for which Mark was working as a consultant. It looked like a clear case of corruption at the highest level of government: a Prime Minister lobbying for a contract in which her own son had a direct financial interest.

There were two major problems with the stories: first, we had not a shred of documentary evidence to substantiate them; and second, none of the sources from whom our information came would be prepared to testify in court if Mark Thatcher had chosen to sue us. To his great credit, Donald Trelford agreed to run the stories nonetheless, and I can still hear the high-decibel harangues from Mrs Thatcher's irascible spokesman, Bernard Ingham, who used to phone in to the editor's office on a Saturday night as soon as he had seen the first edition of the following day's paper.

The original tip had come from a Labour MP, who had mentioned in passing to a senior *Observer* executive, Magnus Linklater, recently arrived from the *Sunday Times*, that the then British ambassador in Oman had been shocked and angered at the way the contract negotiations had been handled. Not a whisper of this had been heard publicly, of course, although twenty years later, David Leigh, who by then was back at *The Guardian*, gained access through a Freedom of Information Act request to internal government documents that confirmed the whole story. The ambassador, Ivor Lucas, had even cabled a confidential warning to Whitehall about the Cementation contract: 'I believe Mark Thatcher is ... associated with the firm ... It is a little surprising that this decision should have been taken at such an early stage ... and that Cementation should have scooped the jackpot ... They were by no means the first in the field.'

An official at the Department of Trade and Industry recorded on the ambassador's letter: 'The plot thickens.'[49]

Further confirmation came in 2015, in Charles Moore's authorised biography of Margaret Thatcher, which disclosed that Mark had turned up unexpectedly in Oman, much to the consternation of his mother's officials, 'who feared that he was there to advance his commercial interests via his mother.

'*The Observer* story was not easy to shrug off because it came in part from the ranks of officialdom. Mark's actions had ruffled many a feather in the British embassy in Oman...'[50]

I was surprised – I still am – that the rest of Fleet Street seemed largely uninterested in following up *The Observer*'s disclosures. True, Margaret Thatcher had just won a second election victory after the successful British military campaign to regain possession of the

Falkland Islands after they had been seized by Argentina in 1982. She was riding high politically and the conventional view in Fleet Street was that there was little to be gained in opposing her. It was only much later, when Mark pleaded guilty in a South African court to helping to finance a plot to overthrow the government of Equatorial Guinea in 2004, that the papers turned on him. There was now little room for doubt: Mark Thatcher was a wrong 'un. Perhaps *The Observer* simply suffered the journalistic misfortune of being too quick to spot his failings. (In 2003, after the death of his father, who had been given a highly unusual hereditary peerage in 1990, Mark became Sir Mark Thatcher, 2nd baronet. If ever there was an argument for the abolition of hereditary peerages...)

Some weeks after we had started to reveal what Mark and his mother had been up to in Oman, I received a phone call from a man called David Boddy, whom I had got to know when he was one of Mrs Thatcher's press team during the 1979 election campaign. Let's meet for lunch, he suggested, and catch up. Only over coffee did it become clear why he had got back in touch, five years after the election: he wanted to know what it would take to get *The Observer* to stop publishing its unwelcome stories about Mark. I was left in no doubt – not that Bernard Ingham's phone calls had left any room for doubt – that the Prime Minister was seriously displeased by our continued focus on her son's business activities.

I suggested that a full, on-the-record interview with Mark, in which he fully answered all our questions, might be a good way to clear the air. And, sure enough, he then gave an interview, his first since we had started our investigation, but it was to a rival newspaper, the *Mail on Sunday*, and not to us. In it, he announced that he was cutting his links with Cementation and intended to move to the United States. *The Observer*'s front-page headline summed it all up with admirable clarity: 'Mark quits Cementation, Downing Street – and UK.'[51]

Boddy has since confirmed that Mark was widely regarded by his mother's advisers as a significant political embarrassment, and that his activities were considered to be damaging both to the Prime Minister and to the Conservative Party. But their problem was that *The*

Observer seemed to know more about what Mark was up to than they did. 'Mark was at best evasive with us and whenever a new revelation occurred, and he was challenged by us about it, he would apologise and say he had forgotten ... Everyone thought Mark was a dangerous loose cannon and that the story had to be silenced.'[52] Recalling the time when he had got lost in the Sahara desert for six days during a motor rally in 1982, the Thatcher team used to joke among themselves that perhaps it would have been better for all concerned if he had not been found.

It takes a lot of courage to pursue – and publish – stories like the ones *The Observer* ran about Mark Thatcher. There is a constant threat of being sued for libel, and there is often intense pressure from politicians who will lose no opportunity to fulminate against the supposed iniquities of an 'irresponsible and unaccountable' press and the unfairness of 'trial by newspapers'. Nick Davies of *The Guardian*, who uncovered the *News of the World* phone-hacking scandal in 2011, has graphically described what it can mean to be an investigative reporter faced by a barrage of denials about a story that has been painstakingly, and convincingly, corroborated, often over a period of several months.

> Like a malignant cell, a horrible thought silently formed itself – I had screwed up. I'd got the story wrong – a big story, that had gone round the world, that had had politicians and public figures standing up on their back legs shouting for action. And it was wrong, or maybe it was wrong, or I couldn't be sure, but if it was wrong – on that kind of scale – [*Guardian* editor Alan] Rusbridger and I really were in a deep pit of foul-smelling trouble.[53]

The bravery of war correspondents is regularly recognised and garlanded in awards ceremonies; investigative reporters require just as much courage and strength of character, but without the benefit of body armour. They need to be insanely obsessive, never happier than when delving into shadowy recesses where they are not welcome, and they need to be angry, because without anger at injustice, dishonesty or political chicanery, they will never have the energy to keep digging until the truth emerges.

I would never argue that newspapers are not sometimes guilty of over-stepping the mark, but I do believe that their occasional excesses are the price we need to be prepared to pay for a vigilant and robust media which, in the words of *The Observer*'s founder, are 'unbiased by prejudice and uninfluenced by party'. As the American founding father Thomas Jefferson, principal author of the US Declaration of Independence, put it: 'Were it left to me to decide whether we should have a government without newspapers, or newspapers without a government, I should not hesitate a moment to prefer the latter.'

The 1980s was a decade during which if you heard the words 'terrorist attack', your first thought was always that Irish republicans must have been responsible. The '70s had echoed to the sound of bomb outrages – Aldershot in 1972 (seven people killed), the M62 coach bombing (twelve killed), the Guildford, Woolwich and Birmingham pub bombings (twenty-six killed) in 1974, and the assassination of the leading Conservative MP Airey Neave in 1979. There was no let-up in the decade that followed: Chelsea Barracks (two killed) in 1981, Hyde Park and Regent's Park (eleven killed) in 1982, Harrods (six killed) in 1983, and Deal Barracks (eleven killed) in 1989.

But there were two days in particular during that grim period that entered the history books as moments when the British political establishment was shaken to its core. The first was 27 August 1979, when the IRA killed Lord Mountbatten, a senior member of the royal family and last viceroy of India, while he was out on a boat with his family in the Irish Republic. Also killed were his fourteen-year-old grandson, Nicholas, a fifteen-year-old crew member, Paul Maxwell, and his son-in-law's 83-year-old mother, Lady Brabourne. The attack has since been described as the 'most shocking single political assassination in Irish history'.[54]

In a statement issued some weeks later, Gerry Adams, the vice-president of Sinn Féin, referred to Mountbatten's murder as an 'execution' and said: 'What the IRA did to him is what Mountbatten had been doing all his life to other people; and with his war record I don't think he could have objected to dying in what was clearly a war situation.' A known IRA bomb-maker, Thomas McMahon, who had been arrested two hours before the blast that killed Mountbatten, was later convicted of having planted the bomb. He was sentenced to life imprisonment but released in 1998 under the terms of the Good Friday Agreement that brought to an end the IRA's 'bombs and bullets' campaign. (In 2015, Adams met Prince Charles in Dublin, the first such meeting between a senior Sinn Féin leader and a member of the British royal family, and said: 'Both he and we expressed our regret for what happened from 1968 onwards … He and his family were hurt and suffered great loss by the actions of Irish republicans. I am very conscious of this … and I thank all involved, including Charles, for their forbearance.')

On the same day as the Mountbatten murder, the IRA also blew up a British military convoy at Warrenpoint, on the border between Northern Ireland and the Irish Republic, killing eighteen British soldiers, the deadliest attack on the British army during the entire IRA campaign. It was a bank holiday Monday, but even though it was six days before the next edition of *The Observer* would be published, it was obvious that the attacks would still be a huge story for the following Sunday. I was itching to get to the scene, but neither my fellow reporter George Brock nor I could track down our news editor. Mondays are usually sacrosanct for Sunday newspaper journalists, and bank holiday Mondays count double. So George and I took matters into our own hands: he would get himself to County Sligo, where Mountbatten had been killed, and I would head for Warrenpoint. We would explain what we had done when the news editor surfaced and hope that he would approve of our initiative. Fortunately for us, he did.

By the following weekend, we were able to piece together many of the details of the attacks. From Warrenpoint, I reported that a 500-pound bomb had been concealed in a hay cart parked in a lay-by and detonated by radio signal from across the border as the army convoy passed.

Six soldiers died in the blast; the rest dived for cover behind a stone gatehouse on the opposite side of the road ... It was to prove a costly mistake. As they hurriedly set up what the Army calls an instant control point (ICP) and radioed for help, the terrorists were calmly waiting under cover to detonate their second bomb, which had been placed inside the very gatehouse which the stunned troops were using for shelter. When reinforcements arrived by helicopter, the second bomb went off, a full 25 minutes after the initial blast. Twelve more men were killed.[55]

The other IRA attack that shook the political establishment took place on 12 October 1984, during the Conservative Party conference in Brighton. I was *The Observer*'s news editor by then and, in the small hours of the morning, my wife, Ruth, who was again listening to the BBC World Service, shook me awake.

'There's been a bomb attack in Brighton.'

I am still ashamed of my reaction – but it makes some sense if you understand that for a news editor, even in the middle of the night, all that matters when a story breaks is (i) do I have someone on the spot?, and (ii) if I don't, how soon can I get someone there?

What I mumbled to Ruth was: 'It's OK. We've got someone there.' And I went back to sleep.

It was a Friday morning and by the end of the day, with the help of a team of eight reporters, I was able to start pulling together a lengthy account of how the IRA had somehow managed to hide a bomb in the Grand Hotel and very nearly blow up the entire British Cabinet. We thought we had managed to establish exactly where the bomb had been hidden, and we were confident enough of our information to make it our headline: 'The Secret of Room 628.' Only during the trial of the IRA bomber, Patrick Magee, nearly two years later did we learn that we were one room out: in fact, he had left the bomb under the bath in the adjoining room, Room 629. Journalism, as is often said, is only the first draft of history.

To write that draft, in those far-off pre-computer days, was a matter of literally cutting and pasting the contributions from all the various reporters who had beavered away trying to find as many pieces of the jigsaw as they could. My task was to fit the pieces together so that they formed a recognisable picture, as I had become *The Observer*'s main rewrite man whenever a comprehensive pull-together of the week's biggest story was required for the centre pages.

My usual practice was to ask each reporter to type out all the information they had acquired, in as much detail as possible, stuff it all into my bag and go home late on a Friday evening for an all-night writing session. I would cut up their contributions into single paragraphs, and then roughly stick them together in an order that seemed to make some sort of sense. Only then would I sit at my typewriter and, surrounded by bits of paper of various shapes and sizes, laid out on the floor of my upstairs study, try to create an intelligible narrative. Black coffee helped, and I would try to be done by 4 a.m. I still think of those days – and nights – every time I use the 'cut' and 'paste' buttons on my computer.

Now fast forward to March 1988. It is a Saturday afternoon, and we are putting the final touches to the stories destined for the front page.

'Robin, Mary Holland is on the phone from Belfast. She says it's urgent.'

Mary's voice is shaking and her words make my blood run cold.

'I've just seen a man die in front of me.'

Two off-duty British soldiers had driven by mistake into a crowd of republican mourners. It was a time of huge tension; two weeks earlier, three IRA members had been shot dead in Gibraltar by British army special forces. At their funeral, a loyalist gunman had opened fire and killed three people. It was the funeral procession of one of the cemetery victims into which the two British corporals had stumbled.

I transferred Mary's call to the copy-takers and she dictated her chilling account of what she had just witnessed:

I saw one man with an iron bar jump on top of the car and start to batter it. A man was dragged out and hauled past us. He wore a thick emerald green sweater and his face was covered with blood...

Shots rang out ... The priest was kneeling beside the body of a man who was naked except for his underpants and shoes and socks. His head was covered with blood from gunshot wounds. At this stage he was still breathing.

Father Reid, a priest who was giving him the last rites, asked me if I knew how to do mouth-to-mouth resuscitation, then asked me to try and telephone an ambulance. At this stage, there were just the two of us in the car park – and the dying man. A local bookmaker let me use the phone to call an ambulance. When I came out, there were two bodies and the Army and police had arrived...

As I went towards the first body in the car park, a youth walking away from it said to me: 'Short and sweet, anyway.'[56]

A few days later, Mary wrote an anguished follow-up in the *Irish Times*:

How did we let it happen? He passed within a few feet of myself and dozens of other journalists. He didn't cry out, just looked at us with terrified eyes, as though we were all enemies in a foreign country who wouldn't have understood what language he was speaking if he called out for help.[57]

There was something peculiarly appropriate about the fact that on my last day on the staff of *The Observer*, in October 1989, the paper's news columns were again dominated by an IRA-related story. The Guildford Four – three men and a woman who had been jailed in 1975 for bomb attacks on two pubs in Guildford in which five people were killed – had just been released after spending fifteen years in prison for crimes they had not committed. (Two of them were also falsely convicted of a bomb attack in Woolwich, south London, which killed two people.) Because I had established a close working relationship with their lawyer, Gareth Peirce, I was able to interview one of them, Paul Hill, the day after he was freed. The story was splashed across the top of the front page under the headline: 'Hill's strange taste of freedom'. Inside was my full-page report on the background to the case – one of the worst miscarriage of justice cases in English legal history – and an angry editorial (yes, I wrote that too) which drew attention to the fact that six more people, known as the Birmingham

Six, were still in jail having been convicted of the murders of twenty-one people in two bomb attacks on pubs in Birmingham. As in the case of the Guildford Four, there were ample grounds for suspecting that the evidence against them had been fabricated.

The Observer's editorial was headlined 'A scandal that shakes the very foundations of justice' and its opening paragraph read as follows:

> The story of the Guildford Four is not just a personal tragedy: it is a scandal. How else to describe the wrongful imprisonment of four innocent people for 15 years, not because someone, somewhere made an understandable, if regrettable mistake, but because of a deliberate, organised attempt to pervert the course of justice?

It ended by urging the Home Secretary, Douglas Hurd, to look urgently at the cases of the Birmingham Six.

> The Crown has finally admitted that, on occasion, police officers can lie and fabricate evidence in order to secure a conviction. This is precisely what the Birmingham Six allege. Their case is every bit as deserving as that of the Guildford Four. They must not be forgotten.[58]

After twelve action-packed years on the paper, it felt good to go out with a bang rather than a whimper.

I often think that too many people forget that even before the horrors of jihadi suicide bomb attacks, the world was no stranger to terrorism. Those who argue that Americans and Europeans would all sleep much safer in their beds if there were no Muslims among us are either too young to remember, or have very short memories, or are deliberately scapegoating ethnic and religious minorities. Perhaps I remember better than many others because I reported on so many of the attacks. Whether it was the Italian terrorism of the 1970s or the IRA atrocities of the '70s and '80s, I wrote far too often of the misery caused by political violence.

I also sometimes wonder why so few people in Europe seem to remember that by far the worst atrocity committed on European soil since the end of the Second World War, far worse on the horror scale than any of the jihadi attacks in Madrid (2004), London (2005), Paris (2015) or Brussels (2016), was committed by people calling themselves Christians – and that their victims were Muslims. It happened in Srebrenica, Bosnia, in 1995, when an estimated 8,000 Muslim men and boys were slaughtered by Bosnian Serbs. I was there a year later, and their ghosts were everywhere.

But back to the '80s. In 1984, I reported extensively from India on a campaign by militant Sikhs for an independent Sikh state of Khalistan. In April of that year, I reported from Amritsar, the site of the Sikhs' holiest shrine, the Golden Temple, which armed militants had turned into their base of operations.

> Thousands of colourfully robed Sikhs, all carrying a traditional dagger or sword, flocked to the Golden Temple … where many attended an angry rooftop meeting addressed by the charismatic Sant Jarnail Bhindranwale, a 36-year-old Khomeini-like figure who openly called on his followers to take violent action against their enemies.
>
> With dozens of heavily armed guards surrounding him, the black-bearded leader, with a decorative sword and less decorative Smith and Wesson revolver hanging at his side, urged his congregation to arm themselves with 'guns, machine guns, bombs and grenades…'
>
> The sight of Sikh activists patrolling inside the Golden Temple with rifles and sub-machine guns slung nonchalantly over their shoulders is one which no government would relish. Yet Mrs Gandhi knows that if she sends troops into the temple, she will unleash violence on a scale unprecedented since partition.[59]

Amritsar was on a knife-edge and on one of several visits to the Golden Temple, I was taken firmly by the arm by a Sikh militant and ushered into the presence of one of their leaders. When I emerged an hour later, I learned that two men had been shot dead just a few hundred yards from where I had been sitting; the militants had been determined to ensure that no foreign reporter would witness the murders. As a lone British newspaperman, however, I was relatively inconspicuous, so I was mostly able to wander the streets undisturbed. On the few occasions when someone did notice me scribbling in my notebook, I was asked just two questions: 'Where are you from?' and 'Are you Mark Tully?', a reference to the legendary Delhi-based BBC correspondent, who had become a major public figure throughout the country.

Despite my 'Who knows what will happen next?' forebodings – which were, and are, frankly, more or less standard fare for any visiting foreign correspondents when they lack a decent conclusion for their dispatches from the frontline – I did not expect to be back in India just two months later to report on the aftermath of what had indeed been a bloody attack by Indian troops on the Golden Temple. 'Operation Blue Star' was launched when the Prime Minister, Indira Gandhi, decided it was time to reassert government authority over the Golden Temple. The official death toll was nearly 500 Sikh militants killed and 130 military dead, although the true figures were probably much higher.

I flew to India this time with my Punjabi-speaking *Observer* colleague, Shyam Bhatia, whose father, Prem Bhatia, was one of India's most eminent journalists and diplomats. Shyam was immensely well-connected and, between us, we put together a lengthy account of what had happened and what it might mean.

Major-General Shuhbeg Singh (Indian army, cashiered) died with his walkie-talkie still in his hands. The man who, for the past two years, had been the military mastermind behind Punjab's bloody rebellion by Sikh fundamentalists, was calling the shots right to the end. He died of bullet wounds, in the smoke-filled basement of one of the holiest buildings in the Golden Temple of Amritsar.

And, again, the conclusion was of grim foreboding.

The 1984 Battle of the Golden Temple, like the 1919 Amritsar Massacre, marks the beginning of a new and potentially turbulent chapter

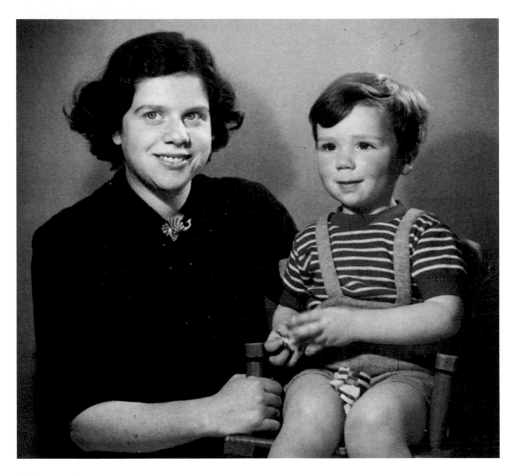

With my mother, 1950

A music teacher in Uganda, 1967

With fellow Reuters trainees (I'm second from the right), 1970

LEFT A reporter at *The Observer*, 1978

BELOW On the front line, Western Sahara, 1978

BOTTOM In Moscow for the end of the USSR, December 1991

With Craig Swan in Bosnia, 1996

In lawless southern Somalia, 1997

Injured in Pakistan, 1997

Broadcasting live from Kosovo (in borrowed carpet slippers), 1999

With Nelson Mandela, Johannesburg, 2001

Commentating at the Queen Mother's funeral, 2002 © BBC

LEFT With President Hugo Chávez of Venezuela, 2005

BELOW In the studio, 2007 © BBC

Three Laptops Lustig,
Istanbul, 2007

Election night in Madrid, 2008

In chilly Birmingham,
Alabama, with sound engineer
Lee Chaundy, January 2009

With sound engineer
Jacques Sweeney and
producer Beth McLeod
in Teotihuacan, Mexico,
July 2009

With producer
Ian Brimacombe
in Chicago (to talk
about global warming!),
November 2009

Crossing the Xingu River
in the Brazilian Amazon
rainforest with Beth McLeod
and Phil Zentner, 2011

ABOVE With Chief Raoni Metuktire of the indigenous Kayapo people, Amazon basin, 2011

LEFT Buying coca leaves on the streets of Tingo María, central Peru, 2012

With the award-winning Nigerian novelist Chimamanda Ngozi Adichie, 2012

in Indian history. The chapter which opened with the 1919 massacre ended with the departure of the British. The new one is only 10 days old, and no one can say how it will end.[60]

There is a good reason why we journalists are so easily tempted to fall back on easy clichés – more often than not, they turn out to be true. I have always tried to resist a tendency to end my reports with what one producer colleague used to call a 'Lustig pompous pay-off', although I hope I never stooped quite so low as to use the standard, all-purpose, one-size-fits-all TV reporter's pay-off:

> As I stand here tonight, with the sun setting on the hills behind me, many questions still remain to be answered. But one thing is certain: things will never be the same again.

The Battle of the Golden Temple led, inexorably, to the events of 31 October 1984, when Indira Gandhi was assassinated by two of her Sikh bodyguards. Again, Shyam and I were dispatched to Delhi – but on this occasion, there was not even time to collect a visa before we left, so when we touched down in the middle of the night, Delhi time, we had no idea whether or not we would be allowed to enter the country.

Fortunately, the frantic long-distance phone calls that we had made during a stop-over in the Gulf had paid off; the visas were waiting for us and our passports were duly stamped. What we soon learned, as we headed into the city along deserted streets, was that anti-Sikh pogroms had already begun as furious Gandhi supporters took a terrible revenge against a community they blamed for her death. About 3,000 people were massacred, most of them in Delhi. (In 2005, a government-appointed commission found that senior members of Mrs Gandhi's Congress party had been involved in instigating the pogroms, and the then Prime Minister, Manmohan Singh, who was himself a Sikh, delivered a formal apology in Parliament for what he called 'the negation of the concept of nationhood enshrined in our Constitution'.)

Shyam and I saw at first hand the results of the killings. An anonymous late-night telephone caller to Shyam's hotel room suggested that if we wanted to see 'dead bodies', we should head for the vegetable market in Old Delhi. It was not exactly a tempting proposition, but we knew we had to investigate. A night-time curfew had been imposed, and there were virtually no taxis to be found (most of Delhi's taxi drivers were Sikhs and they, very sensibly, were staying well out of sight), but we managed to get to the market and we found the bodies.

At first, peering through high metal railings, we saw only what looked like bundles of rags in a courtyard. But then we realised: they were bodies, many of them badly charred, dumped outside a makeshift mortuary because there was nowhere else to put them. But how many were there? It was impossible to estimate, so Shyam, far more enterprising than I was, insisted on clambering over the railings into the courtyard and counting them. He got as far as 119 before I decided that we had been there long enough: the longer we stayed, the greater was the risk of us being arrested.

Just before we left, we spotted what looked like an army truck parked by the side of the road. The back was open, and inside there were yet more charred bodies. No one would ever be able to deny that there had been mass killings – we had seen the evidence for ourselves. That is what reporters do and, no matter how much the technology develops, it is still the only way to be sure.

It was on that reporting trip, however, that I began to realise how technology would eventually force us to rethink some of our cosy assumptions about the supremacy of the printed word. The ceremonial cremation of Mrs Gandhi's body took place on a Saturday, three days after she was killed – *The Observer* would of course want a full report but the timing was going to be tricky. Shyam and I watched it live on Indian television and I phoned the office to let them know that the ceremony was proceeding on schedule.

'We know,' they said. 'We're watching it live as well.'

If TV coverage of an event in India was also being broadcast live in the UK, what was the point in dispatching reporters? The answer was our report about those charred bodies in the makeshift morgue, because there was no TV, live or otherwise, that showed the world what we had seen in that courtyard. Television sees a great deal of what happens in the world around us, especially now that every smartphone can record, and share, video images. But it will never see as much as a sharp-eyed reporter.

There was a deadly aftermath to the events of 1984. In June the following year, two bombs exploded thousands of miles apart – and thousands of miles from India – killing more than 330 people. The first was at Narita airport in Tokyo, where two baggage handlers were killed when a piece of luggage exploded while it was being transferred from a flight from Canada onto an Air India flight destined for Thailand. The second came less than an hour later, when a bomb concealed in an item of luggage in the hold of Air India flight 182 from Canada to India detonated while the plane was over the Atlantic Ocean, killing all three hundred and twenty-nine people on board. Both attacks were blamed on a Sikh militant group called Babbar Khalsa; a Canadian Sikh named Inderjit Singh Reyat was arrested in Britain in 1988, extradited to Canada to face trial and sentenced to ten years in jail after pleading guilty to making both bombs.

One of the great joys of being an *Observer* reporter in the 1980s was that it often involved working with Jane Bown, a genius portrait photographer with a unique style and manner that could charm the most recalcitrant of interviewees. Jane was nearly sixty when we started working together and she had carefully cultivated the look of a little old lady with a shopping bag that just happened to contain a camera. She was not what potentially uncooperative interviewees expected when they were waiting for a Fleet Street photographer to turn up on their doorstep and, more often than not, they simply melted as she bustled around them, frequently rearranging the furniture in their homes to suit her requirements.

Jane worked whenever possible only in black and white and only with natural light. Nearly all her images were taken with the same camera setting: 1/60 sec at f/2.8. Not for her the top-of-the-range light meter or giant reflectors – she would just sit her subject by a window and fire off a couple of dozen shots. 'That's it. Got it.' And it was time to go.

Once we were sent to interview Yitzhak Rabin, then Israel's defence minister, who was on a visit to London and staying in a five-star hotel on Park Lane. When we were ushered into his suite, we found him in the middle of the room, sitting on a sofa, with all the curtains drawn and security men in abundance.

'Oh dear. This won't do,' said Jane. 'Let's get some light in here.' She scuttled over to the windows, threw back the curtains, shoved a chair closer to the light, and told the bewildered Mr Rabin to sit where she could see him. She was deaf to the protests of his bodyguards and, with a resigned shrug, he did as he was told. If I had tried something similar, I would have been thrown out on my ear.

On another occasion, we went to the home of the towering theatrical figure Sir Michael Redgrave, who was already suffering from Parkinson's disease and whose memory was failing. He seemed disorientated and confused when we arrived, and Jane could see that we would have a tough time getting him to focus on the subject of our interview. Then she spotted a hat-stand, festooned with hats. 'Oh, look. How wonderful. Which is your favourite?' His eyes lit up as he chose one.

'Lovely. Put it on and let's go out into the garden.' Her portrait, full of warmth, but with more than a hint of wistfulness, was a Bown classic.

Henri Cartier-Bresson once said that the aim of a portrait photographer should be to 'put your camera between the skin of a person and his shirt'. Jane did that better than almost anyone else. 'Just look at that face,' she would marvel as she peered through the viewfinder of her trusty Olympus camera. 'Isn't it wonderful? Isn't this fun?' I sometimes wondered if she knew that her subject could hear her, because when she got behind that camera, she seemed to be oblivious to everything except the light and the face. Nothing else mattered.

I had to stop working with Jane when I became news editor, because from then on, I was strictly office-bound. I was never as happy sitting at a desk all day as I was out on the road – just as, twenty years later, I was never as happy sitting in a radio studio as I was when flying off to a far-flung place for some real reporting. But helping to shape a news agenda did have some compensations and I was especially proud of the part that *The Observer* played in the campaign to ban lead additives from petrol, spearheaded by the doyen of Fleet Street's environment correspondents, Geoffrey Lean. I also would like to think that our disclosures about Mark Thatcher's distasteful business activities, and his mother's cooperation in them, may also have contributed in a small way to the public good.

A news editor's day is made up of endless telephone calls and endless discussions with reporters and other colleagues about what is or is not a story. Once, a media studies student came to spend a week sitting next to me to observe how the job was done, but after he had asked me for the hundredth time in a day 'Why did you say that?' as I put the phone down, I had to ask him to leave. Editorial decisions are almost always made according to gut instinct: 'Yup, that sounds interesting, go for it,' or 'Nah, don't like the sound of that, see if you can come up with something better.' Ask me to explain why I made the decision that I did and the only answer I could come up with was: 'Because.'

In the days before emails, the telephone was our lifeline. Stories came in by phone, and stories were checked out by phone. Like the phone call from a man who said he was a double glazer and had been hired by MI6 to bug the Soviet trade mission (which in reality was Moscow's spy centre) in north London while replacing their windows. It sounded deeply implausible, but I had a hunch and asked Leigh and Lashmar to check it out. To their surprise, it seemed to stand up, and when Donald Trelford told us that he had received a worried phone call from 'someone in Whitehall', we knew we were onto something.

An MI6 mole infiltrated the Soviet trade delegation in Highgate, north London, and provided valuable information which helped unmask four suspected Soviet spies, expelled from Britain in the past 18 months.

The coup was the first success for Britain's hard-pressed counter-intelligence service since KGB official Oleg Lyalin defected from the Soviet trade delegation more than 10 years ago and provided information which led to the expulsion of 105 alleged Soviet spies.[61]

Five years later, there was a rather odd follow-up to the story, following publication of a book[62] by the double-glazer, who may or may not have been called Bill Graham, and who claimed to have served in the Royal Military Police, the prison service and as a Ministry of Defence security officer.

> The once-profitable career of Mr Bill Graham, an Irish double-glazer who became famous for spying on the Russians as an MI6 agent, seems to have collapsed in bizarre circumstances.
>
> Scotland Yard said last week that an urgent internal investigation was under way into how Mr William Hamilton, a Metropolitan Police Special Branch sergeant, along with Mr Graham and Mr David Murray, a man convicted of IRA offences, came to set themselves up as directors of a private company based in Northern Ireland which rapidly went out of business leaving a trail of unpaid bills.[63]

I tell the story here because it still raises several intriguing questions. Did we ever really know who Bill Graham was? Was his story planted on us by MI6 itself, perhaps as a way of getting some favourable publicity? Assuming that his later book must have been officially sanctioned, what other explanation could there be for his original phone call to the *Observer* news desk? And what was he doing setting up a business with his former Scotland Yard Special Branch handler and a convicted IRA man, unless he was again involved in counter-intelligence activities? In which case, why did their enterprise collapse?

While writing this book, I submitted a Freedom of Information request to Scotland Yard to try to get some answers. I learned that Sergeant Hamilton of the Special Branch was dismissed as a result of the disciplinary hearing for his 'failure to disclose a business interest'. I also learned that guidance to the Scotland Yard press office at the time to help them deal with any inquiries contained the instruction 'NPTD' as the required response to any questions about where Mr Hamilton worked or what his work entailed.

NPTD? Not Prepared To Discuss.

So, thirty years later, I am still none the wiser.

Telephone calls became the bane of my life. One weekend, we were planning a story about a corrupt police officer in Northern Ireland who had been taking bribes. On the Saturday night before publication, he phoned to say that he was sitting in his home with a loaded revolver and would blow his brains out unless I gave him an immediate assurance that the story would not be printed. I had no wish to be responsible for a man's death, but nor did I have any way of knowing whether to believe him, so I asked our Belfast correspondent to rush round to his home and see what was going on.

'There's an empty whiskey bottle on the table and he is very drunk,' our correspondent told me. 'He does have a revolver but I don't think it's loaded.' We decided to go ahead with the story, and the policeman did not shoot himself. But it was a tough decision.

What I had not expected when I took on the news editor job was that I would soon be involved in coverage of Britain's first major military conflict since the Suez crisis. When Margaret Thatcher dispatched a Royal Navy task force to retake the Falkland Islands after they had been seized by Argentina in April 1982, few people expected that Britain would soon be at war. Even so, like all the other papers, *The Observer* had to prepare for all eventualities, so we arranged for a young reporter, Patrick Bishop, to be included among the accompanying press corps who sailed with the task force from Southampton on board SS *Canberra*. He wrote later that one of his editors bade him farewell with the words: 'See you in a week.'[64] It may well have been me.

The only way the reporters could get their copy back to London was by using the military's own communications network. Their dispatches were transmitted direct to the Ministry of Defence in

London, where military censors then combed through them and deleted anything that they deemed sensitive before releasing them for publication. Sometimes what was left was so threadbare as to be almost unpublishable, which posed a huge problem for a Sunday newspaper like *The Observer* which had only one opportunity each week to run the material. For the military, it meant that they had total control over what was reported from the front line. I was reminded of the military's traditional attitude to media relations down the ages: 'Tell 'em nothing till it's over, then tell 'em who won.'

It felt as if the country had slipped a hundred years back in time. Here we were, fighting what seemed like a colonial war over a couple of islands that not one British voter in 10,000 would have been able to find on a map. The Fleet Street papers happily dusted off their uniforms, unfurled their flags and started singing the praises of 'our boys'. Even *The Observer*, no fan of imperial adventures or of Mrs Thatcher, supported her decision to resort to military action. A Fascist dictatorship had seized British territory by force; even the wishiest and washiest of liberals found it difficult to oppose her, and the left-wing leader of the Labour Party, Michael Foot, was among those who backed her decision to go to war.

I photocopied a map of the Falklands and stuck it to the top of my desk. If I had had access to a wall chart and coloured pins, I would have used them too. But I hated the outpouring of jingoism that resulted from the Falklands crisis, which seemed to me to suggest that too many people relished the opportunity to relive the 'glory days' of the Second World War. On the other hand, I was involved in covering a huge story, if only from a desk in London, and no journalist really objects when a big story comes their way, no matter how grim it may be.

Editors were periodically summoned to the Ministry of Defence for off-the-record briefings from senior officials, at one of which, as the task force neared the Falklands after six weeks at sea, we were told categorically that there would be 'no D-Day landings'. The very next day, the British army stormed ashore at San Carlos, exactly as Allied troops had done on the beaches of Normandy in June 1944. So much for 'no D-Day landings'.

'We did not tell a lie, but we did not tell the whole truth,' explained Sir Frank Cooper, the permanent secretary. It was not a 'D-Day landing' because at San Carlos the troops had been unopposed.

His explanation was nonsense. He had lied to us – perhaps in a good cause, but he had lied nonetheless – and then he lied again to a parliamentary committee about not having lied in the first place. I readily accept that in a time of war, the military are not obliged to disclose their advance planning in detail – that would be absurd. But nor do I see the need for lies: why not simply respond to media inquiries: 'We're not going to get into that now'?

For *The Observer*, there was one additional major difficulty while the nation was at war: our defence correspondent, Ian Mather, had been arrested in southern Argentina, together with our photographer Tony Prime and Simon Winchester of the *Sunday Times*. They had hoped to persuade the Argentine air force to fly them to the Malvinas, as Argentina called the Falklands, and get a world scoop by landing there several weeks before the task force was anywhere near. But having been told by the President's press secretary, no less, that they could go wherever they liked, the mood changed when they got to the southern city of Ushuaia, and they were taken into custody with the words 'For you, the war is over' ringing in their ears. They were to spend a total of seventy-seven days in prison, and they never made it to the Malvinas.

CHAPTER 10

TINY VS TINY

It is the unpleasant and unacceptable face of capitalism.
EDWARD HEATH ON LONRHO, WHICH BOUGHT
THE OBSERVER IN 1981

JUST AFTER 6 P.M. on Wednesday 25 February 1981, an ashen-faced Donald Trelford emerged from his office to announce to the handful of journalists, including me, who were still in the newsroom: 'We've been sold.' It was a bolt from the blue, and the start of a tumultuous twelve years in *The Observer*'s history. Atlantic Richfield, who had been welcomed by the staff when they bought the paper in 1976, had sold us down the river, behind the backs of both the board and the editor, to a company that we regarded as irredeemably hostile to everything we stood for. It was as if we had been hurled into a piranha pool. The new owner, the international mining conglomerate Lonrho, and its controversial chief executive, 'Tiny' Rowland, for whom the label 'buccaneer' could have been invented, represented everything *The Observer* most disliked: an unbridled capitalist ethos and a reputation for bribery and corruption in both commerce and at the highest reaches of government, especially in Africa. In 1973, a group of Lonrho directors had tried, and failed, to get rid of Rowland after allegations that he had bribed African leaders and broken international sanctions imposed on what was then southern Rhodesia.

The day after the deal was announced, *The Times* commented in an editorial: 'The secrecy, the complete absence of notice or consultation with the staff of the newspaper, or even with its board of directors, betrays an attitude more appropriate to the conveyance of a property with vacant possession than the purchase of a newspaper. It was a humiliation for the staff.'[65]

But it was a humiliation that the staff decided to suffer, although definitely not in silence, on the grounds that alternative buyers – Sir James Goldsmith, Rupert Murdoch or Robert Maxwell – were unlikely to be any more to our taste, and may well have been even worse than Rowland. Representations were made to the Monopolies and Mergers Commission, which had to give its approval to the sale, and I was part of a delegation of *Observer* journalists who went to a late-night meeting at the Department of Trade and Industry at which we were expected to reach an 'understanding' with our new owners.

What we did not know was that the entire Lonrho board of directors would show up, with Rowland at their head. We were comprehensively outgunned and, after a deeply unsatisfactory meeting, as the Lonrho men in suits left the room, Rowland passed behind my chair and patted me on the head.

'Do you know what your trouble is, Mr Lustig?' he purred. 'You worry too much.'

I had already had some dealings with Rowland, although we had never met face to face. In 1978, I had written a series of articles about the busting of oil sanctions against Rhodesia by British oil companies. The articles were based on confidential documents that were being leaked to *The Observer* by Rowland, and he would phone me at home late at night to check that the documents had reached me, slipped beneath the front door of my flat in a large brown envelope. It was excitingly cloak-and-dagger, but it did not exactly fill me with confidence that he was an appropriate proprietor.

The truth was that once the Astors had sold it, *The Observer*, like any loss-making newspaper, had become the plaything of tycoons, a bauble to be enjoyed, boasted about, shown off to friends and business partners, and then tossed aside. The paper's finances were always in a parlous state, and Atlantic Richfield had got bored with us after discovering that, plaything or not, we had minds of our own. They had not approved of the paper's editorial backing for the Labour Party in 1979 and had been irritated by the refusal of the board of directors to approve their candidate to be vice-chairman of The Observer Trust. The paper had lost something like £8 million in five years and there was little prospect of its commercial position improving. Enough was enough.

Like Murdoch and Maxwell, Rowland was an outsider. He had been born during the First World War in an internment camp in India, to a German father and an Anglo-Dutch mother. His original name was Roland Walter Fuhrhop, and he spent much of his childhood in Germany. In 1934, he and his mother had moved to England, and he briefly became a pupil at a boarding school in Hampshire, where, according to his biographer, some of his contemporaries remembered him expressing Nazi sympathies.[66] After the outbreak of the Second World War, he changed his name to Roland Rowland and enlisted in the British army. In 1940, both his parents were interned on the Isle of Man; he joined them there in 1942 after his discharge from the army ('services no longer required') when he was detained under the notorious Defence Regulation 18B, as a suspected Nazi sympathiser. His mother died on the island in 1944; he and his father were not released until the following year.

Rowland earned the nickname 'Tiny' because of his impressive size: he was well over six feet tall and cut an undeniably imposing figure. The contrast between him and the 'small but perfectly formed' Trelford could not have been starker in physical appearance, although they turned out to be remarkably well matched when it came to survival skills. If Lord Goodman had been right to pay tribute to Trelford's facility for staying upright in a shipwreck, it was not difficult to imagine that Rowland would also stay upright beside him, no matter how severe the storm. Even though Trelford had vigorously, and publicly, opposed the sale of the paper to Lonrho, once the sale went through, the two men somehow managed to work out a form of mutually suspicious co-existence. It was a dangerously fragile base on which to rest an already fragile newspaper, and it was always likely to succumb at some point to the inevitable stresses.

One of the conditions attached to the sale of The Observer to Lonrho was that five independent directors would be appointed to safeguard the paper's editorial independence. A similar condition had been attached to Rupert Murdoch's purchase of *The Times* and *Sunday Times*, but there was never any real confidence that the independent directors would be of much use if push came to shove. Something was better than nothing, however, so they were duly appointed: William Clark, former press secretary to Sir Anthony Eden; Geoffrey Cox, former editor and chief executive of ITN; Derek Mitchell, former Treasury mandarin; Rosemary Murray, former vice-chancellor of Cambridge University; and Lord Windlesham, former member of Edward Heath's government.

Their mettle was soon tested when, in 1984, Trelford directly challenged Rowland's pledges of editorial independence by reporting in detail from Zimbabwe on massacres being perpetrated by President Mugabe's forces in Matabeleland. Lonrho had major interests in Zimbabwe (the company's original name had been London and Rhodesia Mining and Land Company, later abbreviated to Lonrho), but Rowland had been a long-time backer of Mugabe's main rival, Joshua Nkomo. Since Mugabe's election as Prime Minister in 1980, Rowland had been keen to build bridges, and Trelford's reporting seriously threatened Lonrho's commercial interests.

It was not until the Saturday evening before publication that Trelford told Rowland about his story. According to Rowland's biographer, the following conversation then took place:

Rowland: You're trying to destroy my business in Zimbabwe.
Trelford: I have my job to do: to tell the truth as I see it.
Rowland: You have your job and I have mine. You must expect me to protect myself.[67]

The following morning, Rowland issued a statement condemning his editor's actions as 'discourteous, disingenuous and wrong'. He described Trelford as 'an incompetent reporter' and said he would be sacked. Trelford responded by calling Rowland's accusations 'ludicrous, defamatory, and inaccurate', and challenged the independent directors in an editorial to protect the paper from its own proprietor.

I watched the drama unfold from 4,500 miles away, in Amritsar, northern India. I listened to the BBC's reporting of the crisis on my trusty shortwave radio and, when I heard that Rowland had met Robert Maxwell to discuss selling the paper to him, I decided to catch the next flight home. If the paper was going to be sold again, or shut down, I wanted to be there when it happened.

Eventually, 'Tiny' and 'tiny' patched up their differences. Trelford wrote a letter to Rowland praising the 'generous help' that Lonrho had provided to *The Observer* and waved an olive branch: 'Should we not agree to differ on this matter, and respect our right to disagree?' If they could not reach an accommodation, Trelford said, he would resign. Rowland responded by calling their row a 'lovers' tiff', adding: 'I support your editorship and I refuse to accept your resignation.' In reality, he was bowing to the inevitable, because the paper's independent directors had done their stuff and condemned what they called 'improper proprietorial interference in the accurate presentation of news and free expression of opinion'. In other words, Rowland had broken his word and breached the conditions under which the government had allowed the acquisition of the paper. He was shrewd enough to understand that he could afford to lose this battle and still win the war, since Trelford now knew the lengths to which his proprietor would be prepared to go to protect Lonrho's commercial interests.

Trelford was editor from the day I started at the paper until the day I left, and for much of that time he was a great editor to work with. He was a consummate professional, with an instinctive feel for what made a great front page or which stories were worth pursuing. Even though his interests and mine were very different – he was a devoted sportsman, which I have never been, and I was far more interested in foreign affairs than he was – we worked closely together over many years. I doubt that any other editor could have done much better in withstanding the relentless pressures that came from a buccaneer tycoon owner, but as those pressures steadily increased, they inevitably made themselves felt lower down the food chain, and I was no more immune from them than anyone else.

Much to my delight, my old friend and mentor Tony Howard rejoined the paper in 1981 as deputy editor, following the departure of John Cole to the BBC. Like Cole, Howard was steeped in Westminster politics and had excellent political contacts – and Trelford knew that for a paper like *The Observer*, it was essential to be plugged in to the Westminster scene. Howard also had a great knack for spotting talented young writers and while editor of the *New Statesman* he had recruited many who would go on to great success, among them Martin Amis, Julian Barnes, James Fenton and Christopher Hitchens.

Howard was a great gossip and an inveterate schemer, usually over lunch or a glass of red wine, puffing away at an evil-smelling miniature cigar. He was invariably kind to colleagues whom he respected, but could be cuttingly rude about those whom he did not. 'He's got a tin ear' was a favourite put-down for anyone whose prose style did not impress him. I was fortunate to be regarded as part of what less favoured colleagues called 'Tony's A-team', although knowing how he spoke of some of our colleagues behind their backs, I was pleased that I never found out what he said about me when I was out of earshot.

He was oddly old-fashioned in many ways; he attached great importance to good manners – he was always impressed by what he called Tiny Rowland's 'exquisite courtesy', although he never made the mistake of being taken in by it. On one occasion, he described Rowland as 'incredibly good-looking ... like [the film-star] George Sanders ... had beautiful manners – but was thoroughly sinister'.[68]

Howard also had several turns of speech that were uniquely his. Robert Harris, whom Howard recruited to *The Observer* from the BBC to be the paper's political editor, and who went on to become a bestselling novelist, parodied them perfectly in his eulogy at Howard's funeral in 2010. 'I can hear his voice now, as he stands at my shoulder, looking down at what I've written: "Call this a eulogy? You must be off your toot. You clearly haven't done a hand's turn. Even Trelford would have done a better job than this..."'

Howard and Trelford were an odd couple, and Howard never made

much secret of the fact that he was not among Trelford's greatest ad-
mirers. Given his ambition, having edited two weekly magazines (the
New Statesman and *The Listener*), to be the editor of a national newspaper, it was only to be expected that one day he would try to find
a way to take over the top spot at *The Observer*. He made his move
in 1988, while Trelford was on holiday. But Rowland decided that he
wanted to keep Trelford, and the putsch failed.

According to the *Daily Telegraph*, in an account published more
than twenty years later:

> Trelford took [Howard] for lunch and said: 'Tony, you are the most
> political person I know. You must realise, after this, that either I go or
> you go.'
>
> 'And are you going, Donald?' said Howard.
>
> 'No,' said Trelford.
>
> 'Then I'm going?'
>
> 'I'm afraid so.'[69]

When it became known that Howard was leaving the paper, I asked
him if he was considering a return to *The World Tonight* on Radio 4
(the 'puff-puff radio', as he called it), where he had been an occasional
presenter during the 1970s. 'Oh no,' he said. 'I don't believe in going
backwards. But why don't you have a go?'

And so the seed of an idea was planted. I had become increasingly
disillusioned with life at the paper as it became clearer over time that
Lonrho's influence was steadily growing. But, like a frog in a slowly
heated pan of water, by the time I realised how much danger the paper
was in, it was already too late to do much about it. The only option
was to try to jump out of the pan. Others felt much the same way, and
the crunch came just a few months later, first when a bitter row broke
out over stories alleging massive corruption in a multi-billion-pound
arms deal with Saudi Arabia, and then when *The Observer* published
an unprecedented mid-week edition, carrying a leaked government
report into the sale of Harrods department store to Rowland's arch-
rival, Mohamed al-Fayed.

The arms deal stories centred on the Al-Yamamah contract won by British Aerospace (now BAE Systems) that was said to be the most valuable export deal ever signed by a UK company. Tiny Rowland arranged for Trelford to be provided with a sheaf of documents claiming that huge bribes had been paid to win the contract – but several *Observer* reporters declined to touch the story because they knew that the material had come from Lonrho, which was linked commercially to one of British Aerospace's fiercest rivals, the French arms company Dassault.

A number of stories were eventually published, however, leading a Labour MP to accuse Rowland in the House of Commons of causing 'immense damage' to the paper by using its columns to further his own personal commercial interests. Then came the mid-week edition of the paper with its front-page headline 'Exposed: The Phoney Pharaoh,' a reference to Mohamed al-Fayed, who had won a battle against Rowland for ownership of Harrods in 1985 and against whom Rowland had been waging an obsessive vendetta ever since.

The report by the government inspectors into the Fayeds' purchase of Harrods was utterly damning ('the image they created ... of their wealthy Egyptian ancestors was completely bogus'), and a total vindication of Rowland's campaign against them. But that was of little comfort to those of us who had come to hate the way the paper had been turned into what looked increasingly like a Rowland propaganda sheet. We appealed to the independent directors to adjudicate in the row over the Saudi arms deal stories, just as Trelford had done over his Matabeleland massacre story in 1984, but this time, faced with the editor's insistence that he alone had decided to publish the Lonrho-related material, they ruled that they had found 'nothing to substantiate the charge of direct proprietorial interference by Lonrho'.

They did, however, add a rider:

> It is not enough that *The Observer* should be editorially independent. It must also be clearly seen to be so. We have to face the fact that the extensive coverage of Lonrho's conflict with the House of Fraser and in particular the special mid-week issue, the timing of which seemed to

serve Lonrho's interests too well for the peace of mind of many readers and journalists, have tarnished the image of the paper.

My close friend and colleague David Leigh, who had done so much to establish *The Observer*'s reputation as a campaigning paper that carried out important and difficult investigations, immediately resigned.

> I felt ashamed. This was not journalism as I knew it, and it was not the *Observer* I had originally gone to work for. I felt it had become a sick newspaper. How could I write stories exposing conflicts of interest in MPs and businessmen, when no-one seemed sufficiently concerned about potential conflicts of interest in my own newspaper?[70]

I knew that I would soon have to leave as well. I had been profoundly uncomfortable as the rows intensified, in part because by 1989 I had been appointed 'assistant editor', a largely meaningless title but one that entitled the editor to expect my loyalty in the face of mutinies from the ranks. As my sympathy was entirely with the mutineers, I was in an impossible position and, in September 1989, I handed in my notice.

I was not alone: the paper's chief foreign affairs commentator Neal Ascherson and the literary editor and poet Blake Morrison both left at the same time. *The Observer* limped on under Lonrho's ownership until 1993, when it was bought by *The Guardian*, and Donald Trelford stood down as editor after eighteen years in the hot seat.[*]

Tiny Rowland was ousted as chief executive of Lonrho in 1994 and died in 1998, aged eighty.

Looking back, I am surprised that *The Observer* survived as long as it did under Lonrho's ownership, and that I survived as long as I did at *The Observer*. In the early Lonrho years, only the business pages seemed to reflect the interests of the owners and, as I never wrote

---

* In 2014, at the age of seventy-six, he became father to his sixth child, Poppy.

for, nor had any interest in, the business section, I was able to write whatever I wanted to, subject only to the agreement of the editor. But, over time, the brutal reality of media ownership became impossible to ignore: no editor, however skilled, can withstand proprietorial pressure for ever. A newspaper is a business like any other, and ultimate power will always lie in the boardroom, not in the editor's office.

The broadcaster Andrew Marr, who was briefly editor of *The Independent* in the 1990s, wrote:

> The truth is that, except for editors who are highly influential in trusts or companies owning their titles, editors are hirelings. Proprietors regard their editors as talented and interesting servants … Tiny Rowland treated Donald Trelford … with cold brutality whenever his commercial interests were involved … Rowland was exceptionally nasty but Trelford's plight was hardly unique.[71]

As for independent directors, appointed in the forlorn hope that they could turn carnivores like Rupert Murdoch and Tiny Rowland into cuddly pussycats, the protection that they offered turned out, predictably, to be illusory. They never paid the piper, so they never called the tune. Magnus Linklater, who by 1989 had left *The Observer* to become editor first of the *London Daily News* (owned by Robert Maxwell, so the words 'frying pan' and 'fire' inevitably come to mind) and then of *The Scotsman*, wrote after the independent directors' Al-Yamamah adjudication:

> To conclude, as they did, that *The Observer*'s coverage of the House of Fraser saga had 'tarnished the image of the paper' is probably the strongest political statement ever made in public by independent directors on their own newspaper. To have taken the matter any farther would have been to invite a direct confrontation with Mr Rowland, which they would certainly have lost. They might have gone out with guns blazing, but they would have gone out.[72]

To entrust press freedom to the whims of frequently megalomaniac media tycoons is far from satisfactory, but I have never been able to envisage a workable alternative. I am not a fan of statutory press regulation, on the grounds that any political involvement, however indirect, in deciding who publishes what must always be resisted.

There is a case for restricting media ownership to companies that do not already have a significant media presence, but in the rapidly changing world of global digital corporations that also create their own content, like Amazon and Netflix, it may well be that the days of the Rowlands, Murdochs and Maxwells are already drawing to an end. Whether what comes next will be better or worse, well, as that favourite journalists' cliché has it, only time will tell.

As a stand-alone Sunday newspaper, albeit one published by the same group as a six-day-a-week paper, *The Observer* is especially vulnerable. So much of what used to be a Sunday paper's unique offering – the long reads, the arts and books pages, and the colour magazines – are now offered by the daily papers as well, so it is hard to see why a Sunday paper is any different from its Saturday siblings. Even when I left *The Observer* in 1989, it was becoming ever more difficult to argue that we were providing our readers with something that they could not find elsewhere. These days, I spend far longer reading the Saturday papers than the Sunday ones, and I doubt that I am alone in that.

So will there still be an *Observer* in ten years' time, or will it have become a *Guardian on Sunday*? There has never been an *Observer* presence online, as its digital content has always appeared under the *Guardian* brand, so I think it is highly unlikely that it will maintain its print identity for much longer. I shall shed a tear when it goes, for it was, in its time, a great paper. But even great papers sometimes die.

CHAPTER 11

ARE YOU JEWISH?

How odd of God
To choose the Jews.
Not odd of God
Goyim annoy 'im.

WILLIAM NORMAN EWER / LEO ROSTEN (ATTRIB.)

MY WIFE RUTH, WHO is Jewish, likes to tell people that I never knew I was Jewish until I met her. She is not entirely wrong. Even now, I do not really know how to answer the question: 'Are you Jewish?' I usually say yes, because it is easier than 'Well, it depends what you mean by Jewish.' The fact is that I was never asked the question, nor did I ask it of myself, until I was well into my thirties, which probably explains why I have not yet been able to come up with a satisfactory answer.

When we moved to Jerusalem after I was appointed *The Observer*'s Middle East correspondent in 1985, the question came up on virtually a daily basis.

'Hi, I'm Robin Lustig of *The Observer*.'

'Hello. Are you Jewish?'

I exaggerate, but only slightly.

I had always known, of course, that my parents were Jewish, or rather that the Nazis said they were Jewish. But during my childhood, and into my early adulthood, no one ever asked me if I was. I didn't ask, either. If there were other Jewish pupils at my school, I was never aware of them, and the same applied when I went to university. As far as I knew, none of my friends were Jewish. Call it denial if you will – and I know some will – but I was brought up in an environment as religion-free as it is possible to imagine. The first time I entered a synagogue was the day I got married in one.

Ruth came from a much more traditionally observant family. They marked all the major Jewish holidays and fasted on Yom Kippur, the Day of Atonement. It would have broken her father's heart if his only daughter had not been married by a rabbi and, as I did not really mind either way, I was perfectly happy to go along with his wishes. There was a small problem, however: easy-going and progressive as our chosen rabbi was, he still felt the need to satisfy himself that I was, in fact, Jewish.

To do that, all that he required was some kind of documentary evidence that my mother was Jewish. (My father, in this context, was of no importance.) So I asked my mother if she had any piece of paper that said, in terms that would satisfy a rabbi, that she was Jewish. Fortunately, she did, and pulled from the back of a desk drawer an old German passport, issued by the Nazis and stamped with a large, and unmistakable, J.

J for Jew.

It was just what the rabbi needed, so, thanks to that Nazi document, I was able to get married in a synagogue. The first Jewish religious service of any kind that I had attended was my own wedding. I enjoyed both the irony and the inescapable conclusion: my best answer to the question 'Are you Jewish?' would be 'Well, the Nazis said my mother was – does that count?'

The truth is, as I belatedly came to realise, that other people thought of me as Jewish long before I did. Jean-Paul Sartre was probably right when he suggested that the best definition of a Jew is anyone whom other people call a Jew. When I first grew a beard in my late twenties, a colleague remarked that it made me look like a trainee rabbi, which struck me at the time as a very odd thing for him to have said. When I first arrived in Rome, the correspondent for the Israeli newspaper *Ma'ariv*, who was also a prominent member of Rome's Jewish community, asked me if I had any plans for New Year. As it was only early September, I was surprised to be asked so far in advance. Only much later did I realise that she was referring to the Jewish New Year, which falls in September or early October.

I had also been vaguely aware, after my appointment as *The Observer*'s Middle East correspondent had been announced, that there was some whispering behind my back to the effect that it might not be such a good idea for a Jewish correspondent to be sent to cover such a sensitive region. What puzzled me about that reaction was the unspoken assumption that I would automatically be sympathetic to Israel, a country about which I had no strong feelings either way and which I had visited only once before. I was obviously much more Jewish to the people around me than I was to myself.

My Jew-blindness, which is how I think of it, is easily explained. For both my parents, having grown up in Germany under the Nazis, being Jewish brought only danger and unhappiness. Once they escaped to the UK, being German while Britain was at war with Germany was similarly not a good thing to be. So it was much better to say as little as possible about their background and hope to blend in with their surroundings. As neither of them had come from a religious family, there was not a lot of Jewish baggage to leave behind and, to this day, my father always emphasises that the Nazis classed him as 'non-Aryan' rather than 'Jewish'.

All of this obviously rubbed off on me, even though I was blissfully unaware of any of it until I was well into adulthood. I still think that it is to the great credit of my parents that they were able to raise both their sons in such a way that our heritage, problematic or otherwise, was simply never an issue. For better or for worse, we were who we were. When I have to fill out official forms, in the box asking my ethnicity, I write 'white British' and in the box for religion, I write 'none'.

None of this makes me, as some Jews would claim, a 'self-hating Jew', for the very simple reason that I neither hate myself, nor do I hate all Jews, which would be absurd. I judge people on their merits (what Martin Luther King called 'the content of their character'), not on their religious faith or even on the faith of their mother. In my naivety, I cling to the idea that the world might be a better place if others did the same.

My first experience as a journalist working in Israel was not an auspicious one. Ruth and I had flown out a few weeks before I was due to start work there to find somewhere to live. We were later joined by Donald Trelford, who had arranged for us to conduct a joint interview (together with my predecessor as Middle East correspondent, Colin Smith) with the then Israeli Prime Minister Shimon Peres. The arrangement was that we would meet Peres over breakfast at the King David Hotel, the grandest hotel in Jerusalem, record an interview and then publish it verbatim in the following Sunday's paper.

The night before the interview, we all went out to dinner and consumed large quantities of wine. My two colleagues started swapping stories about their National Service exploits in, respectively, the RAF and the army. As I was unable to join in their tales of derring-do, Ruth and I bowed out early and left them to it. It was just as well that we did because the following morning both my colleagues were very much the worse for wear.

The interview went ahead as scheduled, however, and the tape was duly handed over to a commercial transcription agency to be transcribed and sent to Peres's office for approval. Within half an hour, the agency phoned Colin with bad news.

The tape was totally blank.

Someone (not me, obviously) had forgotten to press the record button.

We decided that it would be far too embarrassing to admit this to Peres's office, so we spent the next several hours reconstructing the interview as best we could from memory. We knew that it was a highly risky thing to do, given that what we came up with would be checked by Peres's people line by line, and there was every chance that they would realise that we had not, in fact, recorded anything.

The point of the story is that they cleared it without raising a single query, which was testament not to our superhuman memory, but to the depressing fact that politicians rarely say anything new in a set-piece interview. We had been able to reconstruct Peres's words so accurately because he had said nothing to us that he had not said a thousand times before. The genuine news value of our encounter was precisely zero, but we still published it at length, because an 'exclusive' interview with a Prime Minister is never to be sneezed at.

Ruth and I had hoped that we would be able to find ourselves a beautiful home in an old, stone-built house with an orange tree in the courtyard, but we ended up moving into Colin Smith's flat in a modern apartment block in the part of the city that had been seized by Israel in the 1967 Six Day War, just next to the Hebrew University on Mount Scopus. It was far from ideal, on both aesthetic and political grounds, but we had been unable to find anything else suitable and it did have the benefit of a huge balcony with breathtaking views over the Judean desert towards Jericho and the Dead Sea. On a clear night, we could see the lights of Jordan, and after a thunderstorm, the desert would magically come alive with wild flowers. (Israelis like to claim that they have 'made the desert bloom'; our evidence was that the rain could do it without any human assistance, Israeli or otherwise.)

It had long been my ambition to be a Middle East correspondent, both because I was fascinated by the history of the region and because I very much wanted to spend some time in Jerusalem, a city as historic and as beautiful as Rome. If in one lifetime I could live in both cities, I would have no cause for complaint. Ruth was less keen on the idea, but she agreed to make the move on the condition that it was the only foreign posting I would go for. We already had one young child, and as soon as we arrived in Jerusalem, we discovered that another one was on the way. Raising two small children away from home was not going to be easy, especially as we both knew that I would spend a lot of my time travelling around the region.

The two main stories in the Middle East in the mid-1980s were the civil war in Lebanon, which had begun in 1975 and showed no sign of stopping, and the war between Iran and Iraq, which had begun in 1980 when Saddam Hussein invaded Iran. Israel and the Palestinian territories, by comparison, were relatively quiet: this was before the first Palestinian uprising, or intifada; the PLO was a banned organisation and Yasser Arafat was safely out of harm's way in Tunis, having been expelled from Lebanon after the Israeli invasion in 1982.

Israelis have a reputation for rudeness, so it was good to have my prejudices shattered within days of my arrival. I was searching for an address on the outskirts of Jerusalem and had stopped off at a local shop to ask for directions. After a lively discussion among the shop's customers over which would be the best route for me to take (no one has ever accused Israelis of not having a well-developed talent for arguing), one man put a stop to all the talking. 'Follow me. I'll jump in my car and take you there.' I met plenty of rude Israelis during my time in the region, but I also met plenty of friendly ones as well.

No one can spend more than a few days in Israel without having to confront the legacy of the Holocaust. Without the Holocaust, there would probably be no Israel, and even though most Israelis do not come from families that have had a direct experience of the Nazis – either because they came from Arab nations like Morocco, Yemen and Iraq, or because they are non-Jewish Arab Palestinians, who make up 20 per cent of the country's population – the Holocaust is an inescapable element in the national psyche. Less than a month after I moved to Jerusalem, I met the 49-year-old twins Yitzhak and Idit Bleier, originally from Hungary, who had been among more than a thousand twins used as experiments in Auschwitz by the SS doctor Josef Mengele.

> The children were kept in special barracks, boys in one, girls in another … 'I saw what they were doing there,' said Yitzhak softly. 'I saw the crematoria, I saw everything that happened: the bodies lying on the ground like wooden logs, the people electrified on the fences, the long lines of people being taken to the gas chambers.[73]

A few days later, I reported from a special public hearing into Mengele's crimes that was being held at the Yad Vashem Holocaust Memorial.

> My own abiding memory will be of Zerak Taub, a square-jawed Hungarian who was only 11 when he and his twin brother arrived at Auschwitz. Taub demonstrated how Mengele carried out his famous 'selections', deciding in a fraction of a second which of the new arrivals would live – at least for now – and which would go direct to the gas chamber.

Taub put his right hand in front of his chest, clenched in a fist with the thumb pointing across his body. Then, with a hardly discernible movement, he flicked his wrist and the thumb was pointing the other way. This way, life. That way, death.[74]

But it was Lebanon that made most of the headlines in the mid-'80s. A tiny country about one-twentieth the land mass of the UK (or three-quarters the size of the US state of Connecticut), it was carved out of the remains of the Ottoman Empire at the end of the First World War when France was mandated by the League of Nations to take responsibility for both Lebanon and Syria. Its population is a religious hotch-potch: mainly Muslim (both Sunni and Shia), Christian (both Maronite and Greek Orthodox) and Druze. No one knows for sure how many there are of each religious denomination because there has been no official census since 1932. At that time, the population was 53 per cent Christian, but more recent unofficial estimates suggest that the country is now divided into roughly 60 per cent Muslims and 40 per cent Christians. (There are thought to be no more than a hundred Jews left in Lebanon, from a community that used to number several thousand.)

The numbers are important, because the Lebanese National Pact drawn up in 1943, when the country became independent, provides for the top offices of state to be divided between the main religious dominations: the President must always be a Maronite Christian, the Prime Minister must be Sunni, the parliamentary speaker must be Shia, the Deputy Speaker and Deputy Prime Minister must both be Greek Orthodox, and the army chief of staff must be a Druze. After the fifteen-year civil war (1975–90), no one wants to risk upsetting the apple cart by holding a new census that could well show that changing demographics should dictate a recalibration of the pact.

In 1985, when I first set foot in Lebanon, Israel was beginning to withdraw some of its troops from the south of the country, which it had occupied since it invaded in 1982. I flew to Beirut via Cyprus (the border between Israel and Lebanon has been closed ever since the establishment of Israel in 1948) and met up with *The Observer*'s

Beirut-based stringer, Aernout van Lynden, a handsome half-Dutch aristocrat who had served in the Dutch special forces and later became a distinguished war correspondent for Sky News. I was relieved to be able to latch on to someone who knew something about guns, because in the days before the invention of hostile environment courses, the sum total of my battlefield knowledge was which end of a gun the bullets come out of.

We teamed up with a Swedish radio correspondent, Agneta Ramberg, and headed south towards the Israeli front line in a battered Mercedes taxi. As we threaded our way through the chaotic Beirut traffic, Agneta pulled a packet of Marlboro cigarettes out of her bag and offered one to me. When I declined, on the grounds that I was trying to give up smoking, she said: 'If the reason you're trying to give up is that you're worried about your health, you probably shouldn't be in Lebanon.' I took the cigarette and we have been close friends ever since.

> The shooting started at Teir Dibba, just as we were flagged to a halt at the United Nations post a mile across the valley. It was sporadic, short sharp bursts of semi-automatic gunfire.
>
> The Israeli 'iron fist' was moving on to its next target … 'Don't go too far, be careful,' said the French soldier at the checkpoint. 'They still have two tanks at the far end of the village.'[75]

Crossing the front line into Israeli-held territory proved to be a lot easier than getting out again. At checkpoint after checkpoint as we tried to make our way back to Beirut, we were stopped at gunpoint. One Israeli soldier was particularly suspicious of us in our ancient Lebanese taxi, and he stuck his automatic weapon through the open window to point straight at us. 'That was seriously scary,' said Aernout, after we had calmed the soldier down and driven away from the checkpoint. 'He was very, very frightened, and a frightened soldier with a gun is extremely dangerous.' If Aernout had been scared, I felt a lot better about having been terrified. And it taught me that being frightened when a gun points at you is a healthy reaction. It's when you no longer feel frightened that you are in real trouble.

As night fell, we decided to find somewhere we could spend the night, and we drove into the Phoenician port city of Tyre, famed for its magnificent Roman ruins but not exactly overrun with tourists. We banged on the door of a modest hotel that looked as if it had been closed for several months. They had no food or water but they did have beds. In town, looking for food, we encountered an Englishman who was horrified when we told him where we intended to sleep. 'You will do no such thing. That place was bombed last week and could collapse at any moment. You can sleep at my place.' He said he was an engineer, although what a British engineer was doing behind the front lines in southern Lebanon none of us asked. But we accepted his offer of hospitality, and the following day we found a way back across the Israeli lines and headed north to Beirut.

It was on that same coast road, with its fabulous views out over the Mediterranean, that two years later the American journalist Charles Glass was kidnapped. He and I, with another American correspondent, Mary Curtius, then of the *Christian Science Monitor*, had had dinner together the previous evening in an excellent Japanese restaurant – Beirut was nothing if not surreal, even in the midst of a civil war – and none of us had any reason to doubt that, with 7,000 Syrian troops now very visibly deployed in Lebanon, we no longer faced the daily threat of kidnap that all Westerners had grown used to living with. Glass knew Lebanon a lot better than most of us, having reported from the country for the best part of a decade, but even his experience and depth of knowledge were no protection against being in the wrong place at the wrong time. In a piece I wrote for *The Spectator*, to which he frequently contributed, I said:

> To have been in West Beirut at all was, as we now know, a sad error of judgement … A Lebanese friend told me: 'You should never believe in appearances. After twelve years of war, we Lebanese know better than that. The Syrians may be in the streets, but they do not control them.'[76]

Mary and I left Beirut as soon as we could after Glass was kidnapped, taking the ferry to Cyprus from Jounieh on the Christian side of the city. It seemed a sensible precaution, in the circumstances, and, to my lasting regret, I have never been back.

❦

I would never describe myself as being addicted to fear, yet I loved spending time in Beirut, even though it could justifiably claim for much of the 1980s to be the most dangerous city in the world. Each visit would be preceded by anguished late-night conversations with fellow correspondents in the bar of a hotel in Larnaca, Cyprus: 'Is it safer this time than last time? Who's been there most recently? What are the Syrians up to?'

Then the hair-raising drive into town from the airport – always with a known, trusted driver – and the black comedy check-in formalities at the Commodore Hotel. Always the same, coded question: would Mr Lustig prefer a room on the mortar shell side of the hotel, or the car bomb side?

For those of us who were based in Jerusalem, there were added dangers. If we were to have the misfortune of falling into the hands of a band of kidnappers, it would be essential to ensure that they did not have any reason to suspect that we had any connections to the 'Zionist entity' to the south. So we developed a ritual before leaving Cyprus, meticulously going through all our pockets, purses and wallets to remove any old cinema tickets or credit card receipts that were written in Hebrew, and checking that not a single item of clothing had an Israeli laundry or dry cleaners' tag still attached. We knew that failure to de-Israelify ourselves could easily have been tantamount to a death sentence, because, not without reason, Lebanese militia groups were paranoid about Israeli spies in their midst, and they were not the kind of people to give careless journalists the benefit of the doubt.

Even in the midst of civil war, Lebanon was a stunningly beautiful country. The lush orange groves and fruit orchards, the glistening Mediterranean, the majestic Chouf mountains, all won the country a reputation as the Arab world's favourite holiday destination, before it slid into chaos. I used to have a huge framed poster hanging on the wall of my office, featuring an aerial photograph of an idyllic-looking Beirut beneath a bright blue sky. The caption read: '*Beyrouth: mille fois mort, mille fois revécu.*' ('Beirut: died a thousand times, reborn a thousand times.')

But reporting from Lebanon presented more challenges than simply staying alive. As any war correspondent knows, the first question to be answered in any dispatch from the front line is: 'Who's fighting whom?' And it is closely followed by the second question: 'Who are the good guys and who are the bad guys?' My hero, William Boot, in *Scoop*, was on the button:

> 'Can you tell me who is fighting who in Ishmaelia?'
>   'I think it's the Patriots and the Traitors.'
>   'Yes, but which is which?'
>   'Oh, I don't know about that. That's Policy, you see.'[77]

Lebanon was not a fictional construct of Evelyn Waugh's imagination, but I often felt a close affinity with poor Boot when I was there, and it sometimes showed through in my reporting.

> It is difficult, in the midst of all this carnage, to see any pattern to what has been happening. Yet there is a pattern of sorts, a massive jigsaw of countless pieces, slowly and painfully being forced together to make a picture which once again can be called Lebanon.
>
>   Many of the pieces have to have their edges shot away to make them fit, and some have to be thrown away all together. But at the end of this tortuous process, it is still possible that Lebanon will, against all the odds, be seen to have survived.[78]

Or, as I might have put it, if I had been more honest: 'What's going on? I haven't a clue.' I was reporting on what became known as 'The Battle of the Camps', when a Lebanese Shia militia group called Amal launched an all-out attack on Palestinian refugee camps on the outskirts of Beirut, killing several hundred people.

At the bottom of the page on which that report was published, there was a fact box labelled 'Guide to the fighting factions'. Six different Palestinian groups were listed, followed by four Lebanese Shia groups, and five labelled 'Others'. A total of fifteen armies in a country the size of a postage stamp. No wonder I also quoted the Lebanese poet Kahlil Gibran: 'Pity the nation divided into fragments, each fragment feeling itself a nation.'

We knew terrible things were happening in the camps, but seeing for ourselves was a major challenge. Eventually, a small group of us persuaded local relief workers to allow us to accompany their convoy as they tried to provide medical aid to the besieged Palestinians. It seemed a good idea at the time, but as we approached one of the camps, we immediately found ourselves caught up in the middle of a fierce gun battle between Amal militiamen and armed Palestinian defenders.

We took cover behind a low stone wall, but after a few minutes I was joined by an Amal gunman, who crouched down beside me and started to let off long bursts of automatic fire over the top of the wall. Until that moment, I had had no idea how deafeningly loud sub-machine gun fire is if it is directly next to your ear, and I remember turning to the gunman and saying to him, absurdly, and in English: 'I do wish you'd stop doing that.'

He simply smiled back and offered me his gun.

Did I want to try?

I did not.

A few weeks later, when the fighting had died down, I ventured into Sabra camp, where, in 1982, hundreds of Palestinians had been killed by Lebanese Christian fighters allied to Israel.

As we pick our way gingerly through the rubble of a dynamited house, the young Palestinian in front of us suddenly draws his revolver and flicks off the safety catch. 'It is still dangerous for us here,' he says. 'Amal is outside and we are exposed here.' None of the young men has yet dared to leave the camp for fear of the Shia militiamen still lounging by the entrances.

On our way out of Sabra camp, we understand why. The bulky Amal fighters by the devastated mosque are all wearing identical T-shirts. 'Kill 'em all,' says the inscription across their chests. 'Let God sort them out.'[79]

On 14 June 1985, TWA flight 847 was on its way from Athens to Rome, en route to California, when two armed men burst into the cockpit and forced the pilot to divert to Beirut. On board were eighty-five Americans, twenty-four British citizens, and thirty-eight people of other nationalities. After refuelling in Beirut, the plane took off for Algiers, then returned to Beirut, then headed back to Algiers, and back again to Beirut. About a hundred passengers and female crew members were released, but the rest were taken off the plane and spirited away into the southern suburbs of Beirut, close to the airport and under the control of various Shia militia groups.

The TWA hijack became a huge international story. The US television networks flew in their biggest stars for round-the-clock coverage of the crisis and arranged for specially chartered private jets to shuttle between Beirut and Cyprus to ship news film for onward transmission to New York. On one occasion, when I was in the airport control tower eavesdropping on conversations with the hijackers still on board the plane, I overheard a wonderfully surreal conversation between the air traffic controller and the pilot of one of the chartered Lear jets as it came in to land.

Pilot: 'Attention control tower. Wish to advise there are dogs on runway.'

Tower: 'We can confirm that. Wish to advise there are also hijackers.'

I spent countless hours in that airport control tower and filed thousands of words over the next two weeks, all of them typed out on my battered portable typewriter and then either telexed or dictated over the phone to London.

The man in the Beirut control tower was about the most relaxed participant in the whole drama.

Last Thursday afternoon, Issan Mansour, lounging in front of a dusty panel of dials and switches in his eyrie above the runway, fielded the latest shopping list from the gunmen on board the parked TWA jet. Food, drink, newspapers: even the demands had become routine. That night, by mutual agreement, the control tower was left completely unmanned. Everyone, terrorists included, needed some sleep.[80]

It took two weeks before the hostages were released, after Israel had agreed, despite earlier denials, to release seven hundred Lebanese Shia prisoners being held in Israeli jails. The news of the deal broke early on a Saturday morning, perfect timing for a Sunday newspaper, but not so perfect for a correspondent who had been up far too late in the Commodore bar.

I was woken by a furious hammering on the door of my room. 'Lustig. Get the hell up. We've got a story.' It was David Blundy, my rival on the *Sunday Times*. He could have let me sleep and raced ahead without me, but that was not Blundy's way. We may have been rivals, but we were also friends and colleagues. I like to think I would have done the same for him.

During my three years based in Jerusalem, I reported from every country in the region with the exception of Sudan and Yemen. In Egypt, I watched a full-scale riot by police conscripts and spent a day hidden in a shop selling hijabs to report on the growing Islamisation of Egyptian fashion; in Jordan, I was arrested for trying to interview a local mayor who was regarded as 'too close to the Muslim Brotherhood', and then advised, discreetly, that I would not be welcome back. (I had no problems, however, when I returned to Jordan in 1999 to cover the funeral of King Hussein for the BBC.)

In Iraq, I was an invited guest of Saddam Hussein and nearly gave a heart attack to a young Iraqi journalist who had been sent to spy on visiting foreigners. As we drove past yet another giant portrait of Saddam, I turned to her in mock puzzlement and said: 'Remind me to ask someone who that guy is.' The look of sheer terror on her face as she feared that we could have been overheard told me all I needed to

know about the brutality of his regime. I was among several dozen foreign reporters who had been invited to Iraq, ostensibly to report from
the front line on how well the Iraqi military were doing against Iran.
The truth was that they were not doing well at all, and we never got
anywhere near the front. Instead, we were taken on official tours to
Karbala and Najaf, two of the holiest shrines to Shia Muslims, where
we were expected to be suitably impressed by Saddam's benevolence
towards Iraq's Shia majority. Beautiful as the shrines were, in strictly
news terms they were of far less interest than a visit to the battlefield
would have been.

When I went back to Iraq eighteen years later, after Saddam had
been toppled by the US-led invasion in 2003, it was as if I was visiting
an entirely different country: in the 1980s, no Iraqi would dare to be
seen talking to a foreign reporter, whereas after his demise, they all
wanted to talk, incessantly, about the chaos and violence into which
their country had been plunged.

In Saudi Arabia, I met highly educated and accomplished women
who tried to convince me that wearing a full face veil and not being
allowed to drive a car did not necessarily mean that they were being
discriminated against. And in Kuwait I was told that the only people
who had the right idea about how to deal with the Palestinians were
the Israelis. Being surprised became routine; being depressed became
inevitable. I tried to seek out people who wanted to build bridges
between the region's warring communities, but they were hard to find.
Wherever I went, the men with the guns were in charge, even if they
wore sharp suits and wide smiles whenever they sipped coffee with
Western reporters in opulent five-star hotels.

I was never under any illusion that my brief flits across the region
enabled me to do anything more than provide an instant snapshot of
what I was able to glean in a few days. Sometimes, not even that: on
my first visit to Damascus in March 1986, for example, I was startled
one evening by the sound of a massive explosion, followed by the
sound of emergency vehicles racing through the city. As I had no idea
where the blasts had occurred, I headed for the local offices of Reuters
and the Associated Press ('Is anything happening?') to ask what they

knew. The answer was that they knew nothing and had no intention of trying to find out. The local Syrian stringers knew better than to ask awkward questions: 'We'll wait to see what the official Syrian news agency says, and then we'll report that,' they said. It later emerged that sixty people had been killed in the blast, which the Syrians blamed on Iraq. If I had been able to find out at the time what it was, it would have been a major story – but I failed. Just as I had discovered outside Ealing police station right at the beginning of my career, being in the right place at the right time is not always the same as knowing what is going on.

To be a foreign reporter in Syria – or in Iraq or Libya, or any of the other countries in the region for which the words 'police state' might have been invented – was to understand that I was being spied on every minute of the day. When I went to the Ministry of Information in Damascus to pick up my official accreditation, the man in charge of issuing the required documents greeted me with a file bearing my name placed ostentatiously on his desk. 'Ah, Mr Lustig,' he beamed. 'We know *all* about you…' As I had just arrived from Jerusalem via Cairo, but had claimed to come from London, this was not what I wanted to hear. Nor was I reassured when I got a glimpse of the hotel room plan – I had gone to introduce myself to the telephone switchboard operators – and noticed that the rooms on each side of the one that I had been allocated had been shaded in. Not available for guests, it seemed. Reserved for state security.

Most of my visits to the Gulf were attempts to get close to the 'tanker war' between Iran and Iraq, the two regional superpowers who had been at war since 1980, with incalculable losses on both sides. It was a war of which Henry Kissinger was said to have remarked that it was a shame that there could be only one loser, but after the Iranian Islamist revolution of 1979, most Western sympathies were with Saddam's Iraq. After Iraq invaded Iran, the war quickly got bogged down, and by the mid-'80s, the Iraqis had started bombing tankers in the Gulf carrying Iran's oil exports. Iran retaliated by hitting vessels from Gulf states backing Iraq.

In May 1987, the crew of an Iraqi Mirage F-1 fighter jet mistakenly attacked a US navy frigate, apparently in the erroneous belief that it was a tanker. Thirty-seven Americans were killed, because the frigate's captain had failed to engage the vessel's automatic anti-missile system. The Middle East press corps flocked to Bahrain to report on what looked like a hugely embarrassing US military failure. My report on the news conference held in the Bahraini capital, Manama, by the frigate's unfortunate captain reflected my incredulity.

> To the American servicemen on board the USS *Stark*, the little blip on their radar screens was obviously a friendly aircraft. It had to be, since no one would have any reason to attack them.
>
> 'Perhaps we Americans sometimes see the world a bit differently,' said their commander ruefully. 'We tend to assume that people are not out there to shoot at us.'

A navy review board later recommended that the frigate's captain should face a court martial, but he received a letter of reprimand instead and chose to retire early. It was not the US military's finest hour, but once we had reported on the immediate aftermath of the attack, we reporters decided to take full advantage of the fact that we had a rare opportunity to see what was going on in Bahrain, and we started poking about to see what other stories we could dig up.

That was when the Bahraini authorities decided that they had seen enough of us. An impeccably courteous official from the Ministry of Information summoned us to a news conference at the hotel where we were all staying and made an important announcement. It went something like this:

> I am sorry to inform you that we have just been informed by the hotel management that this hotel has to close with immediate effect so that urgent repairs can be carried out. We have tried to find you alternative accommodation, but without success, so as a courtesy we have arranged for you all to be transported direct to the airport to fly back to your respective homes. For your convenience, buses are waiting outside the hotel and will be departing shortly.

The charm with which the message was delivered may have been impressive, but the bottom line was clear enough: we were being summarily expelled.

᷈

Until my run-in with Jordanian security forces over my encounter with the Muslim Brotherhood mayor, Jordan was the easiest of Israel's neighbours for me to visit, even though the two countries did not sign a formal peace treaty until 1994. The borders with Lebanon and Syria were closed, and to get to Cairo required either a flight or an impossible drive across the Sinai desert.

All that was required to cross into Jordan was a quick taxi ride from Jerusalem down to the Allenby Bridge, which marked the de facto border at the river Jordan (a piddly little trickle rather than a mighty biblical waterway, prompting Henry Kissinger's alleged remark that it is 'proof of what good PR can do'), then through the Israeli checkpoint on foot and another taxi ride into Amman. Total distance: less than forty-five miles.

There were always at least two good reasons for spending a few days in the Jordanian capital, even though it could easily have qualified as the most boring city in the Middle East. First, the journalistic reason: it was where Yasser Arafat's Number Two, Abu Jihad, lived, and he was usually more than happy to entertain visiting reporters to brief them on the latest thinking in the top echelons of the PLO. Remember, this was long before the signing of the Oslo Accords, which gave the PLO a formal status and a formal presence in the Palestinian territories – in the '80s, it was still an imprisonable offence to show a Palestinian flag or to belong openly to the PLO, so Jerusalem-based reporters had either to talk to so-called 'Palestinian notables' who pretended to have no connection to the PLO, or flit across to Amman or Cairo.

Abu Jihad (real name Khalil al-Wazir) was a slight, dapper man who lived with his wife and family in a comfortable home in the Amman suburbs. He was a co-founder of Fatah, the biggest faction in the PLO, and as the commander of its military wing undoubtedly bore personal responsibility for the deaths of many Israelis over the years. In 1988, he was shot dead in an Israeli commando raid in Tunis.

My personal reason for visiting Amman was that it was the home of two American correspondents who were to become very close friends and who later played an important role in my move from print to broadcast journalism: Deb Amos of National Public Radio and Rick Davis of NBC. We would go out for dinner nearly every night to an Italian restaurant, Romero's, and they would fill me in on all the latest Middle East gossip. It was their insights – they had arrived in the Middle East a few years ahead of me – that frequently wove their way into the imperfect tapestries that I created most weekends for *Observer* readers.

Rick was expelled from Jordan in 1988 for 'biased reporting', but he and Deb then transferred to London, so we still saw quite a bit of each other after I joined the BBC. We had lunch together the day before Saddam Hussein invaded Kuwait in 1990 and, Middle East experts that we were, we agreed that although there were already signs of Iraqi military activity close to the Iraq–Kuwait border, Saddam would never be daft enough to start another war so soon after the end of the eight-year bloodbath against Iran. Wrong again…

In the mid-'80s, when I was living in Jerusalem, it was still relatively easy for correspondents to travel to and through the Palestinian territories of the West Bank and Gaza Strip, despite the permanent Israeli military presence. A car with Israeli licence plates would rarely have any difficulty negotiating the Israeli army checkpoints, and the simple expedient of placing a black or red checked keffiyeh, much favoured by Palestinian youths, on the car's dashboard would usually be taken by potentially hostile Palestinians as a sign of at least neutrality, if not outright sympathy. (The so-called 'separation barrier' or 'security fence' that was to form a physical wall between Israel and the West Bank was built only in the mid-'90s as a response to a spate of Palestinian suicide bomb attacks.)

Only rarely – fortunately – do the horrors of conflict impinge directly and personally on the journalists reporting them. For me, the execution of Farzad Bazoft was one such occasion, and the deaths of

David Blundy, John Schofield and Marie Colvin were three others. They were all friends and fellow journalists, so it was not surprising that I was personally affected by their deaths. Natasha Simpson, however, was not a journalist; she was just eleven years old when she died, a victim of an attack at Fiumicino airport in Rome by gunmen belonging to the Palestinian group headed by Sabri Khalil al-Banna, better known as Abu Nidal.

> A little over eleven years ago, I attended the christening of the first-born child of some friends in Rome. She was a noisy infant, and she yelled throughout the ceremony. The vicar, I recall, was on the loquacious side, and I disgraced myself by giggling as he struggled to make himself heard over the lusty bawling of the little girl.
>
> Nine days ago, she died, in a hail of machine-gun fire at Rome airport. Her name was Natasha Simpson.
>
> … Anyone who earns his living, as I do, covering the Middle East is likely to have seen more than his fair share of death and destruction. There is no shortage of tragedy, of pointless waste, or of inhuman brutality. Many children have died over the years, each of them mourned by family and friends. To that extent, there was nothing special about Natasha, other than that she was someone I knew.[81]

Tony Howard told me that he did not much like mawkish sentimentality on his op-ed pages but, on this occasion, he was prepared to make an exception.

Reporting from Israel in the 1980s was like walking on eggshells. It often felt as if every single Jew and Palestinian on earth was born with an unshakeable conviction that the world's media were deeply and implacably biased against them. No reporter escaped unscathed, but the antipathy was especially evident toward the British. Many Jews believe that anti-Semitism is rife among the English upper classes, and that the Foreign Office is stuffed full of public school-educated Arab

sympathisers who harbour fantasies of being the next Lawrence of
Arabia. Palestinians blame the UK for the Balfour Declaration of 1917,
in which the then Foreign Secretary Arthur Balfour told the Zionist
Federation that 'His Majesty's government view with favour the establishment in Palestine of a national home for the Jewish people,
and will use their best endeavours to facilitate the achievement of
this object...'

The remainder of the sentence is much less well known: '... it being
clearly understood that nothing shall be done which may prejudice
the civil and religious rights of existing non-Jewish communities in
Palestine, or the rights and political status enjoyed by Jews in any
other country.'

The Balfour Declaration may have been one of the earliest examples
of what diplomats like to call 'constructive ambiguity', a way of agreeing a text that can mean different things to each party that signs up to
it. What exactly is a 'national home'? Is it the same as a state? Zionists
insist that it is; non-Zionists argue that there was no such implication.
And how do you establish a 'national home' for Jews, while doing
nothing to 'prejudice the civil and religious rights of existing non-Jewish communities'?

As so often in diplomacy, an ingeniously constructed form of words
has led to countless deaths. Another example came after the Six Day
War in 1967. When Israel occupied the West Bank, Gaza Strip and
Golan Heights, UN Security Council Resolution 242 famously called,
among other things, for the 'withdrawal of Israeli armed forces from
territories occupied in recent conflict'. It did not, however, specify
which territories. All of them? Or only some of them? The French
text, however, referred to the 'retrait des forces armées israéliennes
des territoires occupés...' which translates as 'from *the* territories occupied', implying all such territories. Fifty years later, the ambiguity
still remains.

When I first arrived in Jerusalem, I had to apply for accreditation as
a resident foreign correspondent in order to acquire a press card that
would enable me to pass through police and military checkpoints.
Among the forms that I was required to sign was one agreeing to be

bound by military censorship – in other words, that whenever I wrote anything that referred directly to Israel's defence forces, I would have to submit it to the military censors' office before transmitting it to London. As soon as I had signed it, I was handed a document that listed the names and home telephone numbers of every government spokesperson, information that in most other Western democracies would take many months, if not years, to acquire. The contrast between these two pieces of paper – military censorship and laudable government accountability – seemed to sum up so many of Israel's contradictions, and they soon got me into trouble.

In October 1986, two Israel air force officers ejected over Lebanon when they ran into trouble during a bombing mission against PLO targets near Sidon. One was located and rescued, and then flown back to Israel, hanging on to one of the landing skids of a military helicopter as it flew low over southern Lebanon. The other man was not found and was reported to have been captured by Amal militia forces. (He was later handed over to Hizbollah and is believed to have died while in captivity.)

The rescue was a huge story and the BBC World Service phoned me to ask if I could do a short interview about what had happened. Before going on air, when I put in a call to the Israeli military spokesman to get the latest information, I learned that the missing man was the plane's navigator. I duly passed on this nugget to the BBC's global audience, without even thinking of checking with the military censor since the information had come directly from the military's own press office.

Big mistake. As I soon discovered, press officers and censors do not always see eye to eye. I was hauled in for a severe reprimand from the censor and warned that I was at risk of having my accreditation withdrawn.

I had already had a run-in with the military censors less than two weeks previously. The *Sunday Times* had published a huge exclusive story detailing the closely guarded secrets of Israel's nuclear weapons programme, based on the testimony of Mordechai Vanunu, a former technician at the Dimona nuclear facility. Vanunu had disappeared shortly before the story was published – he had been lured to Rome in a classic honey-trap operation by a female agent of the Israeli spy agency

Mossad. He was then drugged and bundled onto an Israeli navy vessel to be taken back to Israel, where he was tried in secret on charges of treason and espionage and sentenced to eighteen years in prison.

For me, as *The Observer*'s Middle East correspondent, the story was a nightmare. There was simply no way I could follow up the *Sunday Times*'s scoop, not only because I had no access to their information but also because Israel was, and still is, neuralgic about anything to do with its nuclear weapons programme. I did what I could, pieced together a story for the following weekend and, in accordance with the rules, submitted it to the military censor. Back it came, with every line deleted except the ones repeating information that had already appeared in the *Sunday Times*. When it was published, it was accompanied by the words: 'The following report was submitted to the Israeli military censor, who ordered four significant deletions.'[82] In the circumstances, it was the best we could do.

One of the oddities of the way the system worked was that anything that had already been published overseas could subsequently be published in Israel, so that enterprising Israel-based correspondents, including some Israeli journalists, would occasionally arrange for information that they had acquired to be published under a London dateline with someone else's byline. Did I ever do that? Next question, please...

June 1987 marked the twentieth anniversary of the Six Day War, during which Israel had won a lightning victory against the combined might of its Arab neighbours. The war had ended with Israel in control of all of Jerusalem, a city that had been divided between Israeli and Jordanian control since Israel's war of independence in 1948, as well as the West Bank, Gaza Strip and Golan Heights. The repercussions of that victory, with Israel still in effective control of the territories it conquered, continue to this day.*

---

* Israel withdrew its troops and civilian settlers from the Gaza Strip in 2005, although with Egypt, it still maintains a blockade of all Gaza's borders.

I chose to mark the anniversary by telling the stories of Israelis and Palestinians who had been born in 1967, the so-called Generation of '67, and to reflect their thoughts two decades after the war.

> Najeh [Palestinian]: The very first Israelis I ever saw were soldiers. They came to my village and entered the school ... When I see any soldiers, I think that those soldiers will be killed some day ... Some day there will be another war, and the Arabs will be successful. We will take back all of Palestine.
>
> Yaacov [Israeli]: You have to understand the Jewish people. We are a small people; our identity in the past was as a persecuted people, a hated people. Young Israelis like me feel that it is about time Israel is not oppressed but a nation that is independent and controls its own destiny.[83]

Being a foreign reporter in Israel in the 1980s was to live a life quite different from those of ordinary Israelis, or indeed of ordinary Palestinians. I might spend a morning talking to militant Israeli settlers in a West Bank outpost, and then the afternoon with equally militant Palestinians in a coffee shop in a refugee camp perhaps only a kilometre away. They inhabited worlds so deeply divided from each other that I sometimes felt like a science fiction space traveller, traversing galaxies that were no more than a couple of miles apart.

Even without leaving Jerusalem, I could walk in less than half an hour from the loud, bustling Mahane Yehuda food market in the west of the city, the heart of Jewish Jerusalem, thronged with shoppers in knitted skull-caps or long black frock coats and wide-brimmed hats, along the Street of the Prophets, where my son was one of the youngest pupils at the Anglican School (we wanted him to learn to read in English, not Hebrew), and end up at Damascus Gate, the heart of Arab Jerusalem, from where battered buses and taxis would take passengers to towns and villages on the West Bank of whose existence Jewish Israelis were hardly aware.

The stories I filed from Jerusalem were a relentless litany of ever more pessimistic analyses of how attempts to begin a 'peace process' between Israelis and Palestinians were going nowhere, and how Israeli politicians were endlessly jockeying for power in a coalition government that was often borderline dysfunctional.

Under the terms of the coalition agreement, the Prime Minister, Shimon Peres, of the left-of-centre Labour Party, and the foreign minister, Yitzhak Shamir, of the right-of-centre Likud, were due to swap jobs halfway through the government's term – but Peres seemed to spend much of his time trying to find a way to back out of the deal. In the event, to everyone's surprise, it stuck, and the job swap duly took place in October 1986.

They were an odd, ill-matched couple from very different Israeli political traditions. Peres came from the country's Labour establishment; he was urbane, smooth and an arch-schemer; he had played a major role in creating Israel's military capacity in the days before it became an independent state and later was a key player in moves to develop Israel as a nuclear power. (The film star Lauren Bacall was his first cousin.) Shamir, by contrast, was a man of little charm and fewer words, a former Mossad official with a reputation as a hard-liner who had refused to back the 1977 Camp David peace agreement between Israel and Egypt.

He had also been a leading member of the pre-independence Jewish paramilitary group known as the Stern Gang, which was responsible for the assassination of the British minister of state in the Middle East Lord Moyne in 1944 and of the Swedish UN Middle East mediator Count Bernadotte in 1948. I asked him once during an interview if he would accept that there was little difference between what he had done in the Stern Gang and the 'terrorism' of which he routinely accused the PLO.

This was his reply: 'There are two important differences between the activities I undertook before independence and the terrorism practised by the PLO. First, our aim was never to destroy a country or a people – it was to fight for an independent state. Second, we never attacked civilians – our objectives were always military.'[84]

Which might have been fine if it were true. But, some years later, I had good reason to recall his words as I stood in the grounds of the

Kfar Shaul mental hospital on the outskirts of Jerusalem. Scattered through the grounds were the remains of an Arab village, Deir Yassin, which had been attacked by Jewish fighters in April 1948. According to one of the most respected books of Israeli history: 'More than 200 Arab men, women and children were slain, their bodies afterward mutilated and thrown into a well.'[85] The killers were members of two Jewish paramilitary groups, one of which was the very same group that Shamir had assured me 'never attacked civilians'. Deir Yassin was not the only such atrocity in the period leading up to Israel's declaration of independence, but it became one of the most notorious and, as news of the massacre spread, thousands of Palestinians fled from their homes to find safety in neighbouring countries. It is their descendants who make up the bulk of the five million Palestinian refugees who are still eligible to receive help from the United Nations, more than one and a half million of them in refugee camps in Jordan, Lebanon, Syria, the West Bank and the Gaza Strip.[86]

I returned to Israel many times after I started working for the BBC, and I watched with sinking spirits as the divide between Israelis and Palestinians deepened with every passing year. The brief moment of optimism after the signing of the Oslo peace accords in September 1993 was followed by the murders of more than twenty Israelis, the massacre of Palestinian worshippers in the West Bank city of Hebron by a Jewish settler in 1994, the assassination of the Israeli Prime Minister Yitzhak Rabin by a Jewish extremist in 1995, suicide bomb attacks on Jerusalem buses in 1996, and then the second Palestinian intifada, or uprising, in 2000.

There have always been too many people on both sides of the Israel–Palestine divide who subscribe to the old Leninist principle of 'the worse, the better'. The theory is that if you can ensure that people believe that the situation is getting worse, the more likely they are to follow your vision of a better future. So, immediately after Oslo, extremists on both sides were determined to blow as big a hole as possible into an admittedly flawed agreement that was so full of compromises that it offered neither side anywhere near what they regarded as their rightful due. (Its most serious failing was that it contained no requirement that Israel should halt its settlement-building programme in occupied Palestinian territory, apparently because the then Israeli Prime Minister, Yitzhak Rabin, feared he would not be able to get the agreement approved by the Knesset if he had agreed to such a provision.) Palestinian attacks on Israelis would inevitably trigger an Israeli military crackdown, thus 'proving' that nothing had changed. Similarly, attacks by Israeli zealots would serve to warn moderate-minded Israeli leaders that they were not carrying their country with them.

When the second intifada erupted in October 2000, I wrote of 'what seems to be a total loss of confidence on both sides in the idea that problems can be solved by negotiation ... The streets are in charge. Vengeance is in the air ... I have never felt so fearful for the future of this blood-soaked region.'[87] As things turned out, my fears were amply justified: over the next four years, an estimated three thousand Palestinians and one thousand Israelis lost their lives.

In 2003, on the tenth anniversary of the signing of the Oslo peace accords, I found two families, one Israeli, the other Palestinian, each with a child who had been born at roughly the time of the famous handshake on the White House lawn in Washington between Yitzhak Rabin and Yasser Arafat.

> Shortly after Simon Griver [Israeli] told his 10-year-old daughter, Sivan, that a man from BBC radio was coming to visit them, he found her playing a game of make-believe with her eight-year-old brother, David. Sivan was pretending to be a radio newsreader. 'Here is the news,' she said. 'We have just heard that there has been another suicide bomb in Jerusalem and David has been killed.' Then she turned to her brother and asked: 'David, what is it like to be dead?'
>
>   ...
>
> Taghreed Kishek [Palestinian] has a 10-year-old daughter too. Her name is Merna and she lives with her mother and younger sister in the West Bank town of Ramallah. They too live in fear – not of suicide bombs – but of Israeli tanks and guns. Last year the Israeli army staged a major incursion into Ramallah ... The memory of those terrifying nights of bombs and missiles has never left them. When I met Taghreed

and her daughters at her parents' home, she told me: 'One night, my daughter became so cold and pale from fright that I really thought she was going to die.'[88]

I tried to arrange for the two families to meet, because they had so much in common. But Israelis were not allowed to cross into the West Bank, and West Bank Palestinians were not allowed to cross into Israel. There was no way to bridge the divide. Ten years later, when Sivan and Merna were both twenty, I got back in touch with their families. Both would have been happy to meet me again, but by then no one was interested any more in the shattered hopes of Oslo. I still hope that if somehow they do get to meet one day, they might become friends.

Having moved to the BBC, I quickly discovered that reporting from Israel–Palestine for the world's best-known public broadcaster was fraught with even more difficulties than I had encountered while writing for *The Observer*. The BBC's output is obsessively monitored by pro-Israel lobby groups, determined to find evidence that the BBC is institutionally biased against Israel and that its reporting is, in consequence, not to be trusted. In the US, where pro-Israel groups are both well-resourced and, often, highly influential, I found myself under attack in ways that would sometimes have been farcical if the underlying issue had not been of such importance.

When I spoke at a fundraising event for one of the BBC's partner stations in Boston, for example, I found protesters brandishing placards that branded me as an 'anti-Semite', which, given my family background, was probably a step too far. On another occasion, a US-based pro-Israel media monitoring group organised a mass email campaign to protest against something that I had said on air, the effectiveness of the protest being somewhat marred by the fact that the emails were all identically worded and referred to me as 'she', thus suggesting that the furious complainants had not actually heard the item to which they took such grave exception.

Trying to steer a steady course through the claims and counterclaims of a decades-long conflict was tricky enough when all I had to worry about was what I said on air. But then some bright spark invented emails and the internet, and suddenly BBC journalists were expected to publish their material in many different ways. Before long, I was writing a weekly email newsletter, and then a blog as well, in addition to making radio news programmes.

The BBC's editorial guidelines for news presenters – a set of rules that should really have been inscribed in stone for Moses to bring down from Mount Sinai – are meant to help presenters negotiate a path between the safe ground of 'news' and the treacherous shoals of 'comment'. They are not, alas, quite as clear cut as 'Thou shalt not kill.'

> Our audiences should not be able to tell from BBC output the personal prejudices of our journalists or news and current affairs presenters on matters of public policy, political or industrial controversy, or on 'controversial subjects' in any other area. They may provide professional judgements, rooted in evidence, but may not express personal views in BBC output, including online.

The fine distinction that separates 'professional judgements' from 'personal views' is the kind of thing that could easily keep you awake at night if you were the worrying kind. And it can equally easily lead you into trouble, especially if you want to comment on highly contentious issues that happen to be dominating the headlines. BBC bosses loved the idea of their senior journalists 'interacting' with viewers and listeners online – but they quaked in fear at the thought that we might occasionally say something mildly controversial. So every word that I wrote online had to be vetted and approved by at least one senior editor; fortunately, I was blessed most of the time with an editor who saw the world very much as I did, and who allowed me as much latitude as between us we felt we could justify.

I faced a particularly delicate challenge in December 2008, when the Israeli military launched an operation in the Gaza Strip that they called Operation Cast Lead. The aim, they said, was to stop rocket attacks from Gaza into Israel and to halt the smuggling of weapons into Gaza from Egypt. During a three-week operation, between a thousand and fifteen hundred Palestinians were killed. Thirteen Israelis also lost their lives. I knew I should write about it, but I also knew that it would be like traipsing through a minefield in hob-nailed boots. The chances of escaping without injury were extremely slim.

Sometimes, it's useful to try to look at the world through someone else's eyes. So here's what I might be writing today if I were a Palestinian living in Gaza.

'You want to know what it's like in Gaza at the moment? It's Hell on earth. But that's nothing new – it's always Hell on earth here. Since the day I was born, I have lived in a stinking, rotten prison, with no freedom and no dignity. I remember my grandfather telling me about the beautiful home he once had, and of the lemon trees and olive groves he tended – I still have the huge metal key to his house, and he told me before he died that one day I would be able to go back and live there again. Yeah, right. I doubt it still exists: it was probably buried under the Tel Aviv ring road years ago…

'Do I support Hamas? Yes, I do – because they stand up for me and they fight for me. I'm not a fundamentalist – I like to drink beer and I don't pray very often – but I don't see anyone else taking on the Israelis, and I can't live my whole life like a snivelling dog, just waiting for the next blow to fall.'

…

And here's what I might write if I were an Israeli:

'You want to know why Israel is attacking Hamas in Gaza? Do you really need to ask? Do you know how many rockets they have fired at us since we left Gaza? How many times they have tried to send suicide bombers into Israel to kill us in our shopping malls and our bus stations? Have you any idea what it feels like when your neighbours are terrorists?

'Am I worried that we're losing friends around the world? Let me tell you something: the Jewish people have learned over hundreds of years that friends don't save you. For hundreds of years, we have been both hated and weak: if it's a choice between that, and being hated and strong, well, I'm sorry, I know which I prefer.

'Look at a map. Look how small Israel is. It's all we've got, and if we lose it, we lose everything. I'm sorry if some Palestinians have lost their homes – but so too have hundreds of thousands of Jews, in Iraq, Yemen, Egypt, and many other places. We remember the Holocaust, even if you don't. We all know what it means to suffer.'[89]

(Old habits die hard: I have just checked that I have quoted roughly the same number of words from each viewpoint.) I knew that the piece would generate a reaction: what I did not anticipate was more than 750 comments – a huge response by usual BBC blog standards – before the in-house moderators called a halt. But I had got through the minefield in one piece, and I emerged unscathed.

One of the laziest clichés available to a Middle East correspondent is to describe Israel as a nation of contradictions. So here goes: Israel is a nation of contradictions. It has a vibrant and diverse culture, and produces some of the world's leading musicians, writers and film-makers. It is in the forefront of global medical, scientific and technological innovation. Its press is free and rumbustious, and its civil society groups are vocal and active.

Israelis also tell good jokes: a driver in Jerusalem, notorious for its appalling traffic, is looking in desperation for somewhere to park. He casts his gaze heavenward and pleads with the Almighty: 'Lord, if you will just find me a parking space, I solemnly swear that I will attend synagogue every day and follow every one of your teachings as set out by the rabbis.' And at that precise instant, a parking space appears directly in front of the driver's eyes.

'Forget it, Lord,' he says. 'I've found one.'

All of this, to a European liberal like me, is highly admirable and makes Israel one of the most exciting places to report from anywhere on earth. It also makes it unique in the Middle East, where liberal democracies are somewhat thin on the ground. But there is another side to Israel, and it is this other side that over recent years has become increasingly dominant.

The Israeli right, as represented in the coalition government headed by Benjamin Netanyahu, has led a campaign of vilification against the liberal left that threatens the country's claim to be a rare beacon of democracy in the region. The Israeli academic Naomi Chazan, a former deputy speaker of the Knesset, wrote in December 2015: 'For far too long, the orchestrated assault on inclusive concepts of Israeli society has been ignored and its consequences sadly neglected. The latest attempts at discrediting democratic voices across the political spectrum have made it abundantly evident that dark winds symptomatic of proto-fascism are sweeping the country.'[90]

With the rise of jihadi extremism in the region, public attitudes in Israel have hardened markedly. According to an opinion poll published in March 2016,[91] nearly half of Jewish Israelis believe that the country's Arab population should be transferred or expelled, and 79 per cent believe that Jewish Israelis should be given preferential treatment over non-Jews. So much for the pledge in Israel's declaration of independence to 'ensure complete equality of social and political rights to all its inhabitants irrespective of religion, race or sex...'

Israelis see themselves as a people under constant threat of annihilation, surrounded by enemies who, if they could, would murder them all. Every time an Israeli is stabbed or shot by a Palestinian, that conviction is reinforced. If outsiders fail to share their perception, the only reason must be that the outsiders are anti-Semites. The writer Linda Grant, whose Israel-based novel *When I Lived in Modern Times* won the 2000 Orange Prize for fiction, put it well: 'Like fairground distorting mirrors, the world looks at the Israelis and sees a giant, a monster, but the Israeli looks and sees a tiny, cowering figure, the puny kid walking to school, tormented by bullies.'[92]

For most Israelis, nothing is more important than to make sure that Jews will never again be weak. As my fictional Israeli wrote in 2009, it is better to be hated and strong than hated and weak. When Golda Meir became the first Israeli Prime Minister to be received at the Vatican, she told Pope Paul VI: 'Your Holiness, do you know what my earliest memory is? A pogrom in Kiev. When we were merciful and when we had no homeland and when we were weak, we were led to the gas chambers.'[93]

If it were possible to put an entire nation on a psychiatrist's couch, it would be tempting to analyse the Israeli psyche as a classic case of an abuse victim turning into an abuser. Every single Israeli Jew, whether from a European or an Arab background, has a family story that is scarred by memories of fear and exile. It should come as no surprise that the last words every Israeli whispers before going to sleep at night are 'Never again.' In 1948, in 1967, and again in 1973, Israel's neighbours joined together to try to destroy the country by military force; on each occasion, against the odds, Israel beat them back. As the saying goes, just because you are paranoid, it does not mean that they are not out to get you.

Throughout the thirty-plus years that I have been reporting from, and about, Israel and Palestine, I have generally tried to avoid answering the question posed by interlocutors on both sides: 'So how do *you* think the conflict should be resolved?' To even suggest a possible solution is the surest recipe I know for becoming instantly dragged into a quagmire from which there is no escape. But perhaps now is the time to be just a little bit braver, so what follows is an attempt to set out, if possible without offending anyone, a few observations born of my experience in the region. I shall aim to be, in the words of the founder of my old newspaper, *The Observer*, 'unbiased by prejudice, uninfluenced by party'.

My starting point – and even as I prepare to write the words, I know how much trouble they will cause – is that the establishment of the state of Israel in 1948 may well have been, in retrospect, a mistake. This does not mean that I think Israel should be wiped off the face of the map, or that the Jews who live there should be expelled. Israel exists, it has eight and a half million citizens, of whom roughly three-quarters are Jews, and they have as much right to live in peace and security as anyone else.

But do I accept Israel's right to exist as a Jewish state? I accept its right to exist, just as I accept the right of any other legitimately established state to exist (for example, I accept Kosovo, which has been recognised as a sovereign state by more than a hundred members of the United Nations, but not Abkhazia or South Ossetia, which have not). But as a non-believer, I have some difficulty in accepting the concept of a state that has a specific religious faith enshrined in its identity. (And, for the avoidance of doubt, I should add that I have as much difficulty accepting the idea of the Islamic republics of Iran, Pakistan or Afghanistan as I have accepting the Jewish state of Israel.)

As I cannot accept religious scripture as a basis for international law, I base my acceptance of Israel's right to exist on a resolution of the United Nations general assembly passed in November 1947 with the support of the two undisputed post-war great powers: the United States and the Soviet Union.* I can well understand the superpowers' reasoning – especially President Truman's wish to 'rescue' those victims of the Nazis who had managed to survive the Holocaust. But I also suspect that at least some of the political leaders who proclaimed themselves to be enthusiastic pro-Zionists did so because it offered them an opportunity to direct some of the quarter of a million Jews displaced by the Second World War away from their own shores. Support for Zionism could easily become a handy disguise for anti-Semitism, just as, confusingly, what these days is called anti-Zionism can sometimes be used in exactly the same way. (Not all anti-Zionists are anti-Semites, even if some anti-Semites choose to disguise themselves as anti-Zionists.)

Much of the furore in 2016 over alleged anti-Semitism in the Labour Party stemmed from this blurring of the distinction between Jews and Zionists. Some people openly and deliberately use the word Zionist (or the abbreviation Zio) as an insult, hoping that by calling someone a Zionist instead of a Jew they can avoid being labelled anti-Semitic. It is an easy elision to make, given that for many Jews, being a Zionist is intrinsic to their sense of identity.

---

* UN Resolution 181 envisaged the establishment of independent Arab and Jewish states and a 'special international regime' for Jerusalem. It was rejected out of hand by all Arab governments.

So if I accept Israel's right to exist, why do I suggest that its establishment might have been a mistake? Because, just as the Jewish anti-Zionists of the early twentieth century had feared it would, I fear that it has turned out to be bad both for Jews and for the rest of the world. Unlike the historian who described the establishment of Israel as a Jewish triumph, an Arab tragedy and a British failure,[94] I am tempted to argue that it was not, in fact, even a Jewish triumph.

Zionism sprang from a belief that Jews could never be safe until they had a homeland of their own. Given the experience of the Tsarist pogroms, the Dreyfus affair in France and then the Nazis' attempt to physically eradicate all of Europe's Jews, it was a perfectly reasonable belief. Many Israelis still believe that no Jew can feel really safe unless they live in Israel. They are, however, in a minority among the world's Jews, since, nearly seventy years after the establishment of the Jewish state, more than half the world's estimated fourteen million Jews still choose to live elsewhere, the vast majority of them in the United States. (There is an old joke that goes: 'What is the definition of an American Zionist? An American Jew who gives money to a second American Jew so that another Jew can go to live in Israel.')

It is at least questionable whether the descendants of the Jews who moved to Israel from Europe in the aftermath of the Second World War are really any safer than they would have been if their forefathers had stayed in Europe, as my paternal grandparents did. My personal experience has been that I feel immeasurably safer living in the UK than I ever did living in Israel. Nowhere except in Israel have I seen shoppers in supermarkets with automatic weapons slung over their shoulders – shoppers, not security guards – and it was in Jerusalem, not London, that I discovered that the father of one of my son's school friends routinely travelled to and from work with a revolver in his briefcase.

So what about the descendants of the half a million or more Jews from Arab countries who fled to Israel in the years following the establishment of the Jewish state? They make up more than half of Israel's Jewish population, but it is perfectly possible to argue that if there had been no Israel, and no war of independence that pitted the nascent

Jewish state against the entire Arab world, the Jews of countries like Morocco, Yemen, Iraq and Libya might well have been able to stay put. Not that a Middle East without Israel would necessarily have been a region of perpetual peace and prosperity, but it is unarguable that the creation of the Jewish state in 1948 introduced a new, highly unstable fault-line into a region that had barely emerged from its Ottoman past and was already undergoing rapid, oil-fuelled economic and social change.

Take Shalom, an Israeli taxi driver I once met. His parents had been Iraqi Jews who fled to Israel in the 1950s, shortly before he was born. They named him Shalom (peace) as a symbol of their hopes for the future, but his son had been killed in Lebanon while serving with the Israeli army, and he was consumed with rage. Just one story of many.

Under Israeli law, any Jew anywhere in the world is automatically entitled to Israeli citizenship and to take up residence in Israel. (An exception is made for those with 'a criminal past, likely to endanger public welfare'.) The law defines a Jew as 'a person who was born of a Jewish mother or has become converted to Judaism and who is not a member of another religion'. The same citizenship rights are also automatically available to 'a child and a grandchild of a Jew, the spouse of a Jew, the spouse of a child of a Jew and the spouse of a grandchild of a Jew, except for a person who has been a Jew and has voluntarily changed his religion'.

So I could become an Israeli citizen tomorrow if I wished, thanks to my mother's Nazi-era passport, as could my children. But my near namesake, the late Roman Catholic Cardinal Jean-Marie Lustiger of Paris, who converted to Catholicism at the age of thirteen and whose Jewish mother was killed in Auschwitz, would have been turned away. So would my father, who became a member of another religion when he was confirmed in a Lutheran church. To the Nazis, his confirmation made not a jot of difference – to them, once a Jew, always a Jew – but Israeli law sees these things differently.

I first realised how problematic is the idea of Jews as a race apart when I visited the Museum of the Diaspora in Tel Aviv. In the main entrance hall was a giant multi-screen video display, showing images of dozens of Jews from all four corners of the globe: white Jews, black Jews, brown Jews, Jews with round eyes and big noses, Jews with slanted eyes and small noses, brown-eyed Jews and blue-eyed Jews, dark-haired Jews and fair-haired Jews. How, I wondered, could anyone argue that they all belonged to the same 'race'?

In the early twentieth century, many eminent Jews angrily rejected the concept of Jews as a separate race and regarded Zionism as a dangerous ideology that would inevitably lead to trouble. They thought the British government was wrong to publish the Balfour Declaration in November 1917, supporting the Zionists' aspiration for the establishment in Palestine of a 'national home for the Jewish people'.

Just three months before the declaration was published, the British Secretary of State for India, Sir Edwin Montagu, who was only the second unconverted Jew* ever to sit in a British Cabinet (his cousin Herbert Samuel was the first), wrote an anguished memorandum to his Cabinet colleagues:

> Zionism has always seemed to me to be a mischievous political creed, untenable by any patriotic citizen of the United Kingdom. If a Jewish Englishman sets his eyes on the Mount of Olives and longs for the day when he will shake British soil from his shoes and go back to agricultural pursuits in Palestine, he has always seemed to me to have acknowledged aims inconsistent with British citizenship and to have admitted that he is unfit for a share in public life in Great Britain, or to be treated as an Englishman … It seems to be inconceivable that Zionism should be officially recognised by the British Government, and that Mr. Balfour should be authorized to say that Palestine was to be reconstituted as the 'national home of the Jewish people'.[95]

---

* Benjamin Disraeli, who was Prime Minister for nine months in 1868 and again from 1874 until 1880, had converted from Judaism to Christianity at the age of twelve.

Imagine the reaction if a leading politician were to say anything re-motely similar today. But the irony is that it was Hitler's discredited theories about race that led directly to the near universal acceptance of the notion that Jews are a race apart – an irony of which I am the living embodiment, as someone whose only officially accepted claim to be Jewish is a document that was issued to my mother by the Nazis.

Some Jews who accept that definitions based on race are deeply problematic nevertheless argue that they are a clearly definable people. They share a culture, a tradition and a language, even if they do not all share a religious faith – therefore, as a people, they have the right to a homeland, a state, in exactly the same way as, for example, the Amer-ican people have the right to a homeland. I have some sympathy with this argument, although it immediately raises an issue of practicality. What do you do if the homeland that you claim is yours by right is also claimed by another people, who claim an equivalent right?

Palestinians may not be a race apart, any more than Jews are, but they can also claim to be a people, albeit a people with a tradition that is a good deal less rooted in history than that claimed by Jews. They share much of their culture, and of course their language, with the rest of the Arab world, but their history, especially since the arrival of the first modern Zionists in the late nineteenth century, is uniquely theirs.

Perhaps these arcane discussions about the precise nature and defin-ition of Jewishness are beside the point. Most Jews who identify them-selves as Jews firmly believe themselves to be a separate and identifi-able racial group, as indeed does English law. According to guidance issued by the Crown Prosecution Service, a House of Lords ruling in 1983[96] that Sikhs should be regarded as a separate racial group and therefore covered by the anti-discrimination provisions of the Race Relations Act should also be regarded as a 'persuasive authority for Jews being included in the definition of a racial group as well as a religious group'.[97]

And, in 2009, a Jewish school in north-west London was found to have broken the Race Relations Act by refusing admission to a boy whose mother's conversion to Judaism was not recognised by the Office of the Chief Rabbi. In the words of the Court of Appeal, 'the requirement that if a pupil is to qualify for admission his mother must be Jewish, whether by descent or by conversion, is a test of ethnicity which contravenes the Race Relations Act'.[98]

Many of the early Zionists were young idealists who saw the building of an entirely new nation as a wonderful opportunity to put their idealism into practice. Many young Jews of my generation leapt at the chance to spend a few months on an Israeli kibbutz, in the days when they were still a vibrant example of communalism in action, in which no property was owned individually and everything was shared according to need. Perhaps if I had realised at the age of eighteen that I was Jewish, I also would have headed off to a kibbutz rather than to Uganda to teach music.

But one of the saddest conversations I ever had in Israel was with David Passow, a wonderful man who, with his wife Aviva, was a neighbour of ours in Jerusalem. (Their three adult children, Judah, Mimi and Sam, all became good friends of ours – Judah is an award-winning photographer with whom I often worked on stories for *The Observer*.) David had been a passionate Zionist all his adult life; he had served as a rabbi in the US navy and had played an active role after the end of the Second World War in encouraging European Jews to emigrate illegally into what was still British-ruled Palestine. But when I visited him in 2001 shortly after Ariel Sharon had become Prime Minister – a man regarded by many, both in Israel and in the Arab world, as a war criminal – he remarked: 'If I had known that this is how we would end up, I would never have started.' For him, the dream of a Jewish homeland, the 'light unto the nations' of the biblical prophecy, had turned into a nightmare.[99]

I stir up this hornet's nest for a reason. It is not because I question Israel's right to exist, nor because I question the deeply felt ties that bind millions of Jews to the Jewish state. My reason is this: all my experience of war suggests to me that a prerequisite for the resolution of any long-lasting conflict is that each party to the dispute must make a serious effort to understand how it feels to be on the other side. In South Africa, for example, a peaceful transition from a brutal system of apartheid that classed the black majority as second-class citizens was made possible only when white leaders came to accept that the system was so unjust that it was simply unsustainable. And an essential element in that transition was what became known as a truth and reconciliation process, during which those who had been responsible for some of the countless injustices of the apartheid era were given an opportunity to speak openly about what they had done and seek immunity from prosecution.

Likewise in Northern Ireland, where a successful peace process bringing together Protestants and Catholics was possible only when leaders of the two communities came together in a mutual recognition of past injustices. All conflicts create victims on both sides, but conflicts that cannot be ended by a decisive victory of one side over the other will end only when each side recognises that the other has suffered as well.

So it seems to me to be self-evident that any resolution of the Israel–Palestine conflict must include a recognition by Israelis that the establishment of their state caused immense harm and trauma to the Palestinian people who were already living there and to their descendants. At the same time, Palestinian and other Arab leaders must acknowledge that their refusal over several decades to accept the reality of the Israeli state, and the continuing attacks by Palestinian groups such as Hamas against Israeli civilians, have also been a strategic error that has caused immense harm and suffering.

It is one of the many tragedies of the Israel–Palestine conflict – but by no means unique to it – that neither side is yet able to acknowledge that they are both victims. If more Israelis could bring themselves to accept that Palestinians have suffered immensely over the past seven decades, and if more Palestinians could accept that Israelis still live, with justification, in fear, then there would at least be a chance of making progress towards a lasting settlement of the conflict.

Israel is by far the strongest state in the Middle East, militarily, economically and, despite the sometimes raucous nature of its political debate, socially and politically as well. As the veteran US negotiator Aaron David Miller has noted: 'By any significant standard – GDP per capita; educational assets; share of Nobel prizes; even the global happiness index – Israel leads the region, and much of the rest of the world, by wide margins.'[100]

This impressive regional supremacy, achieved in part with the assistance of generous long-term financial support from the US, has a dangerous side effect: it can lull Israelis into a false sense of complacency. Why do we need to make peace with the Palestinians, some ask, when we're doing just fine as we are? And when outsiders like me suggest that they may be mistaken, they respond: 'Don't you worry about us. We know how to look after ourselves.'

For the past seventy years, from the drafting of UN Resolution 181 up to the present day, the most obvious solution to the problem caused by two mutually antagonistic groups of people claiming the right to the same patch of land has been to divide the land between the two of them. In 1947, it was called 'partition'; these days it is known more commonly as the 'two-state solution'. But I have reluctantly come to the conclusion that, even if once it might have worked, and even if there was nothing wrong with the idea in principle, it is no solution now.

You could argue that the Palestinians have only themselves to blame. If they and Arab governments had accepted the UN's original partition plan, if they had chosen the Gandhian path of non-violence, or the black South African path of mass civil disobedience, instead of hijacking planes and blowing up buses, who knows what they might have achieved? In the words of the Israeli politician and diplomat Abba Eban, they never missed an opportunity to miss an opportunity.

The reason I no longer believe in the two-state solution is rooted in the five-decade-long Israeli settlement-building programme. From soon after the 1967 Six Day War, Israel started building on the land that they had conquered in the West Bank, the Gaza Strip and east Jerusalem. As of early 2015, there were nearly 400,000 Israelis living on occupied land in the West Bank and another 375,000 in east Jerusalem. What that means is that not only all the land on which the settlements are built, but also the roads linking them to each other, and to 'Israel proper', would need somehow to be protected if they were to fall on the Palestinian side of any new international border between Israel and an independent Palestine. A look at a map of where the settlements have been built will quickly confirm that what the staunchly pro-Israel Jewish Virtual Library says of them must be true: '[The settlements'] purpose was to solidify Israel's hold on territory that was part of biblical and historical Israel and pre-empt the creation of a Palestinian state.'[101]

As a result, any attempt to create an independent Palestinian state would end up looking not so much like a patchwork quilt as like a succession of ink blots left behind by a careless colonial conqueror. Israel will, in any case, be determined to provide security for its citizens living on the Palestinian side of any new border, and has always insisted that it must retain a security presence along the border with Jordan.

Add to that the additional complication that the West Bank and Gaza Strip are inconveniently separated from each other by about seventy miles of Israeli territory, so how could they ever form part of a unitary Palestinian state? Suggestions have ranged from the impractical – an elevated road bridge between the West Bank and Gaza that would be used exclusively by Palestinians – to the frankly insane: a tunnel that would extend beneath Israeli soil to link the two parts of an independent Palestine. Many diplomats now admit in private, although very few in public, that the two-state solution is dead, killed off by Ariel Sharon and others who boasted that the settlement-building programme would 'create new facts on the ground' and thereby make a viable Palestinian state an impossibility.

Interestingly, an idea that was frequently discussed thirty-plus years ago, while I was living in Jerusalem, is now beginning to re-surface: some kind of federation or confederation that could serve as an umbrella state linking Israel, Gaza, the West Bank and perhaps even Jordan. Both the Israeli President Reuven Rivlin and the man who was at the heart of negotiations that led to the Oslo agreement, Yossi Beilin, have revived the idea, although it is hard to see in the current political climate either Israelis or Palestinians being at all keen to envisage a joint national identity. On the other hand, in Northern Ireland, Ian Paisley and Martin McGuinness, once implacable enemies, ended up as colleagues in government, so one should never rule anything out.

Toby Greene, of the Britain–Israel Communications and Research Centre (BICOM), wrote in early 2016[102] that a confederation might offer a solution to at least some of the problems associated with a two-state model. In the first place, Gaza and the West Bank could both belong to the confederation, even if not linked physically, if Israel was part of the same political entity. Second, Israelis living in the West Bank could remain as Israeli citizens but resident in the Palestinian region of a confederal state. (At the same time, it would enable the people currently known as Arab Israelis to become Palestinian citizens resident in the Israeli region of the new state.) And third, the security issue could be addressed if all three regions – Israel, Palestine and Jordan – accepted that Israel and Jordan would assume responsibility for the confederation's external borders.

Most importantly, perhaps, a federal structure would answer the Zionists' biggest dilemma: how can they claim to be democrats while continuing to rule over people with no political rights and whose land they occupy? The Israelis in a tripartite confederation could still argue that they have created a Jewish nation, or homeland, while the Palestinians could also claim to have won their own nation. Their borders would be internal borders, not external ones, and Jerusalem would be a shared capital. (After all, the original UN partition resolution envisaged Jerusalem as a city under international jurisdiction, so the confederal model could be seen as being close to the original vision.)

I know that it all sounds absurdly unrealistic and, in the current climate, it undoubtedly is. But I am not ready to accept that the Israel–Palestine conflict is a war without end. One day, each side will produce new leaders who are capable of bridging the divide, just as Menachem Begin and Anwar Sadat did in the 1970s, and as Yitzhak Rabin and Yasser Arafat did in 1993. The only question is how many more people on both sides will have to die before their leaders take the next step.

CHAPTER 12

AT LAST THE BBC

Get on your toes, keep your wits about you, say goodnight politely when it's over, go home and enjoy your dinner.

SIR TERRY WOGAN, ON THE ART OF BEING A
RADIO BROADCASTER

Dear Margaret Budy, I am writing to ask whether you are considering taking on any new presenters, on either an occasional or regular basis, for The World Tonight … I have extensive radio experience, mainly for the World Service, but also for CBC in Canada, IRN, CBS and, as the enclosed cassette illustrates, US National Public Radio.

THE LETTER IS DATED 5 February 1989, and it is just one in a bulging file of similar letters that still sits at the back of my filing cabinet. I was writing to anyone I could think of to find a way out of *The Observer* and I can now reveal, for the first time, that I also applied to be presenter of *Channel 4 News* (they gave the job to a chap called Jon Snow instead). Tony Howard's throwaway remark when he left *The Observer* ('Why don't you give it a go?') had pushed me over the edge: I was determined to become a broadcaster, just as he had recommended when I asked him for advice as a student nearly twenty years earlier.

I had never met the editor of *The World Tonight*. We had no mutual friends or colleagues, but I had read somewhere that she had recently taken over the programme, so I thought that she might perhaps want to try out a new presenter voice. The line in my letter about my 'extensive radio experience' was a huge exaggeration – true, I had been interviewed a few times as a foreign correspondent, but I was always answering the questions rather than asking them, and I had never presented a live news programme in my life. The demo cassette that I sent in had been put together with the help of my Middle East NPR friend Deb Amos, who was now living in London. I had scripted an imaginary introduction to *The World Tonight*, and we recorded it in her flat. I clearly remember that she insisted that I held an umbrella over my head as we did so – she said it was to get the acoustics right, but I have always suspected that it was to make me look an idiot.*

Of all the editors I wrote to, Margaret was the only one to suggest we had lunch together. We ate in a little Italian restaurant round the corner from Broadcasting House, and we seemed to get on well. 'There's only one way for me to find out if you can do this,' she said, 'and that's to give you a couple of presenting shifts.' There was to be no pilot programme, no voice test, just a great big gamble – for both of us – based entirely on the evidence of my demo tape and my CV. And so it was that a few weeks later, I left *The Observer*'s offices in Battersea just a bit earlier than usual to make my way to Broadcasting House. As I walked from Oxford Circus Tube station north along Regent Street, I suddenly stopped dead in my tracks. For a moment, I was unable to take another step. What was I doing? Why on earth did I think I could do this? I was about to present a live news programme on national network radio, and I had never done anything remotely similar before.

The production team must have been just as nervous as I was, but none of them let on. *The World Tonight* had a team of three regular presenters at the time: Richard Kershaw ('magnetically good-looking and telegenic, [he] developed a dashing on-screen persona reporting from the world's trouble spots' – *Daily Telegraph*), who was best-known as a reporter for BBC television's *Panorama* and as a presenter on *Nationwide*; Alexander MacLeod, a former foreign editor at the *Sunday Times* and diplomatic editor at *The Scotsman*; and, less frequently, David Sells, who like me had started out at Reuters and who had then

---

* I discovered over the years that presenters' colleagues enjoy making them look like idiots. They seem to think that because it is for radio, it doesn't matter.

become one of the BBC's best foreign correspondents. I had met him a few times in the Middle East and admired him enormously.

It is probably fair to say that my arrival was greeted with both suspicion and trepidation. I learned much later that some of the team were not best pleased to discover that a woefully inexperienced radio novice was being entrusted with their programme. Fortunately, they never knew that on my first presenting shift, when I took my seat in the studio, I realised that I had no idea what the red and green lights on the studio desk meant. I was far too embarrassed to ask, but by the end of the programme, I had managed to work it out for myself: when the red light was on, it meant that my microphone was live, and the green one went on to warn me that there were ten seconds left before the end of a recorded item. When it went off again, I was expected to say something.

Margaret had lined me up with three consecutive presenting shifts. The first programme passed off without problem, but the second was somewhat marred by a twelve-second silence – an eternity – when a recorded item failed to materialise on time. The producer responsible later rose to become the controller of Radio 4, thus proving what I have always believed to be true: that although mistakes in the studio are to be avoided whenever possible, they are not life-threatening. Unlike brain surgeons or air traffic controllers, radio producers do not risk causing someone's death if they mess things up. The same goes for presenters. My personal theory is that listeners quite like it when presenters get into trouble on air, as long as it does not happen too often – my former colleague Jim Naughtie's slip of the tongue with the name of Cabinet minister Jeremy Hunt probably endeared him to the nation far more than any number of incisive interviews or beautifully scripted reports from the United States.

The World Tonight is one of four news and analysis programmes broadcast through the day on BBC Radio 4. It follows *Today* at breakfast time, *The World at One* at lunchtime, and *PM* at teatime (or drive time if you prefer). Anecdotal evidence suggests that a significant proportion of *The World Tonight*'s listeners tune in either when they are having a bath or after they have gone to bed. Politicians tend to listen in the car on their way home after a late-night vote at Westminster. It has always covered more foreign news than its stablemates, which suited me just fine, especially when it enabled me to travel to the world's hotspots myself to report from the field.

When I started working for the programme, it had a reputation as a bit of a BBC backwater; fewer people listen to the radio in the evenings than in the mornings, and its emphasis on stories from overseas, to the almost total exclusion of any UK news, made it seem to the grittier kind of BBC news people like an eccentric uncle who insisted on telling the family about faraway places they had never heard of. Its calmer, more considered approach to current events, eschewing the manufactured excitability of its daytime stablemates and their sweaty fascination with entrail-gazing in the Westminster village, appeared to its unkinder critics to exude the musty odour of a home for retired schoolmasters, or perhaps a gentlemen's club inhabited by snoozing ex-diplomats and army officers.

None of that reputation was entirely fair, although it was far from being the liveliest listen on BBC radio and tended to be somewhat worthy and joyless. I slowly became aware that I had been taken on board as a symbol of a new approach: I was younger than the existing stable of presenters (I was forty-one when I started), and had a somewhat less solemn approach to news coverage. I did believe in taking the world seriously, but I also had a regrettable fondness for levity, so my on-air tone was perhaps several degrees lighter than had become the *World Tonight* norm. After all, its revered first ever presenter, Douglas Stuart, who had done so much to establish the programme's early reputation, had been praised by senior BBC executives for his 'statesman-like qualities'[103] (he was in fact a distinguished former foreign correspondent), and I had never aspired to be a statesman.

For a few more months, I struggled on at *The Observer* while leaping at the chance to present occasional further editions of *The World Tonight* whenever there was a gap in the presenters' rota. I was indecently keen to make a mark, and rushed into print with a diary column for *The Listener* magazine in which I admitted my childlike excitement at finally having dipped a toe into the world of broadcasting.

> For me, there's a special pleasure in sitting in a studio opposite news-
> readers like Charlotte Green or Peter Donaldson, whose voices have
> reached me in every room of [my] house ... to be reading the headlines
> while Charlotte Green waits patiently to read the news is as if I were
> trying to tell a joke in front of Woody Allen.[104]

Radio 4 newsreaders were gods (and goddesses). Their impeccably mod-
erated tones contributed to an impression that the words they spoke
had been engraved in stone by some superior being. It was The News.
So it was something of a shock to discover that the voices belonged to
ordinary human beings, made of ordinary flesh and blood, who were
enormous fun to work with, and who, very occasionally, were fallible.

Once, after having eaten supper in the BBC canteen, one of Radio 4's
best loved newsreaders became violently ill just moments before she
was due to read the news at the start of an edition of *The World Tonight*. (No, I am not going to name her; it could have happened to
anyone.) As she rushed out of the studio with a muttered 'Sorry', the
newsroom editor laconically handed a pile of scripts to me and said:
'I think you'd better read this.' Which I did, thankful that my musical
training in sight-reading enabled me to stumble through the news
bulletin relatively unscathed.

At Bush House, a World Service newsreader once simply forgot that
she was due to read a two-minute news summary halfway through
Newshour. As the seconds ticked by, with still no sign of her, I frantically searched for the scripts in a computer file, and – again – ended up
reading them myself. Yes, they are gods, but, just occasionally, with
feet of clay.

With the advent of social media, some newsreaders descended
from Mount Olympus and emerged to frolic among mere mortals on
Twitter. They acquired tens of thousands of followers who discovered
what only we privileged colleagues had previously known: that they
are funny, clever and extremely good company. It was all part of a de-
mystification process that turned broadcasters from remote figures intoning Great Truths from on high into fellow mortals trying as best as
they could to contribute something to the sum of human knowledge.

Foreign correspondents who return home to a job in head office, as I had done, are prone to a usually incurable medical condition known as 'foreign correspondentitis'. The symptoms are chronic ennui, a propensity to moan endlessly about the idiocy of their bosses, and an unshakeable belief that their unique talents are grotesquely under-appreciated. I suffered from a relatively mild form of the disease when I returned from the Middle East, but faced with the deepening problems at *The Observer*, I was more than ready to jump ship.

I had to make a decision: was I prepared to risk being able to scratch a living as a freelance broadcaster with a mortgage and two young children to support? With Margaret Budy's help, I wangled a meeting with the diminutive, but formidable, head of BBC radio news and current affairs, Jenny Abramsky, to test the waters. 'I can't make any promises,' she said, 'but if you do decide to leave *The Observer*, I'm sure you'll be fine.' Just to make sure, I introduced myself to the bosses at the BBC World Service as well, calculating that if I could not get enough work at Radio 4, I might be able to carve out a place for myself at Bush House.

So I made my decision and, on the basis of that non-promise from Jenny Abramsky and a sense that it was time to be reckless, I jumped ship. So confident was I that somehow I would be able to make it as a freelance broadcaster that I turned down an approach from Ian Jack and Sebastian Faulks at the not-yet-launched *Independent on Sunday* to join their new adventure. I liked the idea of living on my wits as a freelance, and had had enough of Sunday journalism. Producing just one paper a week left far too much time for people to sit around complaining.

For the next twenty-three years, I juggled the demands of both Radio 4 and the World Service, never sure which of them would decide to dispense with my services first. I cast my net wide because, as all freelances know, it is the only way to insure against penury. I did occasional presenting stints for such now long-forgotten Radio 4 programmes as *Newstand* and *Stop Press*, and I gained invaluable experience as a radio reporter out in the field by making documentaries for *File on 4*.

(I still remember the words of a *File on 4* producer as we walked through the Gdansk shipyards in Poland, crucible of eastern Europe's anti-Communist uprisings. She stuck a microphone under my nose, pressed the record button on her tape machine and barked: 'Tell me what you can see.' The radio reporter's job boiled down to just six words.)

One of my fellow reporters on *File on 4* was Helen Boaden, who later took over as editor and demonstrated a gimlet-eyed approach to editing her former colleagues' scripts. In the years that followed, she rose steadily up the BBC executive ladder, becoming head of Radio 4, director of news, and then head of all BBC radio. She was often spoken of as a potential candidate to be the BBC's first female director-general, and was a staunch defender of – and listener to – *The World Tonight*, unusually among top BBC executives, almost all of whom tend to regard television news as the only thing that really matters. (I was told on very good authority that most evenings at 10 p.m., she would watch the TV news with the sound muted, while listening to *The World Tonight* at the same time. It struck me, if true, as an admirably even-handed way of meeting the impossible challenge of being responsible for all BBC news output on radio, TV and online.)

In 1989, all of the BBC's radio news programmes were based in Broadcasting House, where the ghost of Lord Reith stalked the long corridors of a building that always looked to me like an uncomfortably beached ocean liner. *The World Tonight's* offices were on the fourth floor: one office for the production team, with a glass-walled internal office in which the presenter was expected to sit, out of harm's way, and another down the corridor, for the editor, deputy editor and reporters. That was the room where, every night, a bottle of whisky would be opened even while the programme was still on air. Quite rightly, the tradition came to an end as Auntie's financial corsets were gradually tightened; these days, you would be lucky to find a potato crisp and a salted peanut at a farewell party.

With the impeccable sense of logic of which only the BBC is capable, the studio from which the programme was actually broadcast was one floor below the offices, entailing much dashing up and down stairs as the transmission time approached. Conducting interviews having just leapt down a flight of stairs is not exactly best practice, but somehow we managed not to break limbs or twist ankles, and – usually – the programmes went on air without mishap.

We were, in truth, a motley crew. Among the programme's reporters was Sally Hardcastle, daughter of Bill Hardcastle, a newsman of the old school who had been editor of the *Daily Mail* and then the first presenter of *The World at One*. Sally was a smoker and a drinker with a voice to match and one of the filthiest laughs I had ever heard. Another of the reporters, Michael Vestey, was cut from very different cloth: tall, languid, almost patrician, with political views several notches to the right of centre. He was on loan from the newsroom, but they seemed to be in no hurry to claim him back and he settled into the nocturnal rhythms of *The World Tonight* with consummate ease. He was one of the many victims of the Birtian revolution that followed John Birt's appointment as director-general of the BBC in 1992, and left to become a spectacularly acerbic radio critic for *The Spectator*. As his fellow *Spectator* columnist Rod Liddle, another former BBC staffer, wrote after his death in 2006: 'He had worked for the corporation for more than a quarter of a century and had come, in an almost affectionate way, to utterly and completely loathe it.'[105]

From my very first day at the BBC, I had decided to give the impression whenever possible that I was utterly confident that I knew what I was doing. My experience as a child from a home without television had trained me well in the dissembling arts, and I came to believe, rightly or wrongly, that my colleagues had no idea how thin was the ice on which I was skating. My twenty years' experience as a journalist helped, admittedly, and I soon worked out that in order to ask intelligent-sounding questions, it is by no means necessary to know the answers. This means that most interviews can be conducted from a starting position of total ignorance by asking just three all-purpose questions.

I may be risking expulsion from the National Union of Broadcast Interviewers by revealing them, but here they are anyway.

Question One: 'How significant do you think this is?'

Question Two: 'Why has it happened?'

Question Three: 'So what do you think will happen next?'

There is a fourth, equally useful, question that was originally for-mulated by my friend and co-presenter Claire Bolderson. It worked especially well on the World Service when news broke in a country that we had never heard of.

'But what is happening in the north?'

I had been in love with radio as a listener ever since my childhood in the days of comedy shows like *The Navy Lark* and *The Men from the Ministry*. Now I fell in love with it as a broadcaster. I discovered that it is the most direct and intimate form of communication avail-able between two human beings: my voice, your ears, and nothing in between.

Radio excels at telling stories. It uses the human voice to create a link between people who have never met and who may live on oppos-ite sides of the planet. It also, of course, enables millions of people to enjoy the music of their choice – and music is perhaps the most potent of all art forms. Thanks to downloads and podcasts, listeners can now enjoy that music wherever and whenever they want. Whenever I travel on the London Underground and I see all my fellow passengers with earpieces attached to their iPhones or their iPads, I find myself wondering: 'What on earth did we use our ears for when we were travelling before the invention of earphones?'

That is another of radio's great strengths – its portability and its flexibility. It is the ideal medium for busy people, perfectly suited to the era of multi-tasking. It is hard to read a book while you are doing something else, and it is never advisable to watch a TV show on your iPad while driving to work. But radio? Radio while you are working, radio while you are cooking, radio while you are out jogging. Radio is the perfect companion for the modern age.

In journalism, as in politics, timing is everything. I had left *The Ob-server* at the end of October 1989 to live on my wits as a freelance writer and broadcaster. Less than two weeks later, on 9 November, the Berlin Wall was breached and the Cold War ended in dramatic fashion. By sheer good luck, I was filling a gap in *The World Tonight* presenter rota that night: history was being made and I was able to play a part in writing the very first draft.

As we went on air, crowds of East Berliners were already surging towards the wall and streaming through to the west, unhindered by border guards, following what we now know was an unintentionally garbled announcement that travel restrictions were being lifted with immediate effect. The pickaxes had not yet appeared as I tapped out a script that I feared might be a touch too purple-prosey for Radio 4.

> Tonight's announcement from East Berlin must surely spell the end of the Berlin Wall. How long, I wonder, before the bulldozers move in to tear down that ugliest of eyesores which has disfigured Berlin for the past twenty-eight years? Perhaps it's all too much to take in – the changes have come so fast that it's hard to keep up with the new realities of an eastern Europe in which a forty-year-old political dam has finally burst.

I remember feeling as I spoke the words that perhaps I was over-egging it a bit – I did not really believe that the bulldozers would soon be moving in and that the wall would be literally torn down. Little did I know...

But the extraordinary scenes in Berlin were only one part of the global drama that was being played out that year. In June, the Chinese army had brutally suppressed pro-democracy protests in Tiananmen Square. In August, eastern Europe's first non-Communist government since the end of the Second World War had taken over in Poland, and in October, the Hungarian Parliament had voted to hold multi-party elections.

Then came the 'Velvet Revolution' in Czechoslovakia, the collapse of the Communist regime in Bulgaria, and the violent end of the Ceauşescu regime in Romania. And although hardly anyone had noticed at the time, in March that year, a British scientist called Tim

Berners-Lee had presented a document to his colleagues in Switzerland called 'Information Management: a Proposal' in which he outlined his thoughts on how documents stored on computers could be searched for and shared via special links known as hypertext links. His proposal became the World Wide Web and it changed the world.

1989 was definitely a good year to become a BBC news broadcaster.

Sitting in studios broadcasting to the masses was all well and good, but I wanted more. At heart, I was still a reporter, and I wanted to be out where the action was. I argued, I hope with some justification, that listeners liked it when news presenters reported from the field occasionally, because it added a sense of drama and a different perspective to the coverage. I understand the objections of those critics who say that flying presenters around the world is an unnecessary expense when there are plenty of perfectly competent correspondents available, but I still believe that there are some occasions when presenters can bring an extra element to the coverage of a major event. I also understand the objections of the correspondents themselves, who too often find themselves being 'big-footed' by London-based colleagues who swan in to mop up all the glory. I did try, whenever I could, to share the glory with resident correspondents, but I know that I was often guilty of exactly the kind of behaviour to which I had objected as a Reuters correspondent many years earlier. And when my conscience got too troublesome, I persuaded myself that I had earned my moment in the sun and that my unhappy colleagues' moment would also come in due course.

My first presenter-in-the-field opportunity was in Berlin in October 1990, the day that Germany was reunified. I was chaperoned by Max Easterman, a highly experienced, German-speaking producer and reporter who had every right to expect that he would be covering the story himself. But if Max resented having to look after me, he hid it well, and he arranged for us to broadcast from the revolving restaurant at the top of the television tower in Alexanderplatz, in what had been East Berlin.

It was a good idea in theory: we would gaze down over the newly reunified city, slowly revolving as we did so, in the company of eminent commentators from both sides of the now non-existent Iron Curtain. But there was just one problem: several hundred Berliners also thought it was the best place to be that day, and the restaurant was so deafeningly noisy that we could barely hear our own voices. I doubt that *World Tonight* listeners heard much either above the excited chatter and clattering crockery, but I have never dared to listen back to a recording. It took several more similar experiences trying to broadcast from restaurants and bars around the world (producers love them because they provide 'atmosphere') before I finally put my foot down, having developed a particular antipathy towards hissing espresso machines.

Although the Berlin programme had not been an unalloyed success, thanks to all those celebrating Berliners, I knew that broadcasting live from unlikely makeshift studios overseas was something that I could easily get a taste for. So, when the Soviet Union started to crumble in 1991, I lost no time in plotting to get myself to Moscow so that I could be on hand as it was consigned to the history books.

The assumption was that the moment of its death would be formally recorded as midnight on 31 December. By another of those strokes of luck on which my broadcasting career seemed to depend, midnight in Moscow that year would be 10 p.m. in London, so *The World Tonight* would be going on air at the precise second that the USSR was declared dead. How could anyone resist the opportunity to be live in Moscow at such a historic moment?

Approval was given, and plans were made. Deputy editor Justin Phillips was put in charge of the project and sound engineer Simon Calder, later to become one of Britain's best-known travel journalists, was given the task of making it work technically. As we flew to Moscow on Boxing Day to prepare for the historic programme, we hoped no one had noticed that the Soviet leader Mikhail Gorbachev had defied expectations and resigned the previous day. To all intents and purposes the Soviet Union was already dead and buried by the time we took off from Heathrow.

It was too late for second thoughts. What had been planned could not be unplanned at such short notice, so we carried on undaunted.

The programme was a triumph, thanks to meticulous planning by Justin Phillips and the technical wizardry of Simon Calder. We installed ourselves in the monstrously ugly, 3,000-room Rossiya Hotel overlooking Red Square (it has since been demolished), erected a giant satellite dish on the balcony of Simon's room, and stripped the beds of their mattresses so that we could line them up against the walls to create something like the sound of a studio.

The BBC's Moscow correspondent Bridget Kendall was stationed among the crowds in Red Square and we were all set. The bells of the Kremlin struck midnight (we had also recorded them the previous night just to make sure) and we were off.

Bang. There was a deafening explosion just as Bridget was describing the scene. Then another one. It was only four months since a group of anti-Gorbachev Communist diehards had tried to launch a coup against him – could this be another last-minute attempt to reverse the tide of history?

Bridget extemporised brilliantly. Perhaps it was the Kremlin cannon firing to mark the New Year? The uncertainty was nerve-racking – until we saw the fireworks. Then the penny dropped, and we were able to breathe again. Not a coup after all. The following day, we were told that the unscheduled firework display had been arranged by the US TV network CNN to liven up their coverage – I never discovered if it was true but it certainly added to the drama of the night. After we came off air – I ended the programme with the word *Dosvedanya*, the Russian for goodbye, and the only Russian word I knew – Justin and Simon told me that for the last ten minutes of the programme they had lost all contact with the studio in London and had no idea whether we were still on air.

In fact, we were, and the programme was later awarded a gold medal at the New York Radio Festival. From then on, there was no stopping me, and over the next twenty years I was to present live news programmes from every continent on the planet with the exception of Antarctica. (If anyone is up for it, I am still keen to fill in that last remaining gap.)

Broadcasting live from overseas in the days before Wi-Fi was not for the faint-hearted. The working assumption always had to be that if something could go wrong, it would – and there is an account of some of my more hair-raising moments in Chapter 15. But, at their best, outside broadcasts deliver a sense of both place and drama: outside party headquarters on an election night for example, or on the streets of Hong Kong as the territory was handed back to China in 1997. News reporting has to be more than a bald recital of facts: it has to engage listeners, arouse their interest, and, just as importantly, keep them listening for more than half a minute.

A news presenter's job is never quite as simple as many people think. The derisive term 'autocutie', as applied to television presenters, displays such deep ignorance of what the job actually entails that it may perhaps be worth spelling out exactly what it does involve.

First, you need to make sure that you are up to date with all the news at home and abroad, so that when a producer suddenly appears at your desk and says, 'We've got the Prime Minister of Crisisland on the line, but we have to do the interview right now', you have some idea what has been happening in Crisisland, and, preferably, the Prime Minister's name as well. (In the pre-internet era, my regular reading encompassed four daily newspapers – the *Daily Mail*, *The Guardian*, the *Daily Telegraph* and the *International Herald Tribune* – plus *The Spectator*, the *New Statesman*, the *New York Review of Books* and *Granta*.)

Second, you have to be ready to absorb huge amounts of complex information at speed, often while running into a studio, and then challenge the person who has just spent five years writing the report from which the information has been taken.

Third, you should be able to write intelligible cues, or introductions, that tell listeners what they need to know about each item in such an enticing fashion that they will feel compelled to keep listening.

And fourth, you have to make it sound as if all you have done is pick up a script that someone else has written for you and read out the words in approximately the right order.

Easy.

All presenters depend on the teams with whom they work: the

researchers who dig up the stories, and the producers who track down the interviewees and write the briefing notes (if there is time) that provide the essential background for the interview. As my producer friend and colleague Craig Swan once put it: 'If an item sounds good, it's because the presenter is brilliant. If it doesn't, it's because the producer is crap.' I think he was joking. Half-joking, anyway.

For my first few years at *The World Tonight*, I lived from month to month, waiting anxiously for the monthly rotas to be published to see how much work was coming my way. Eventually, a pattern was established, and after a few years I was even offered a formal freelance contract, guaranteeing me a minimum number of days' work each year. When the Inland Revenue decided that the BBC's team of freelance presenters were not really freelance after all, since few of us had significant amounts of work elsewhere (if only for the simple fact that the BBC took a dim view of us spreading our wares), it was suggested that we should set up our own companies, through which the BBC would then be able to secure our services.

Fortunately for me, my accountant took a dim view of this proposal and, on his advice, I insisted that if the BBC no longer wanted to hire me as a freelance, it should take me on board as a staff employee. As a result, when the Inland Revenue decided a few years later to make a fuss about all the service companies with whom the BBC had signed contracts, I was in the clear.

In 1993, Margaret Budy, the editor who had hired me on the basis of no more than a hunch and a lunch, was appointed editor of the drive-time *PM* programme. Her successor was Anne Koch, a Canadian of Dutch and Hungarian parentage with whom I had already worked a few times as a relief presenter on *The World This Weekend*. As any freelance presenter knows, a change of editor is a time of great danger, because the most obvious way in which the new boss can make a mark is by changing the presenter line-up. So, obviously, I was apprehensive about what she might be planning.

Anne did make big changes but, to my relief, they worked to my advantage. My two long-standing presenter colleagues, Richard Kershaw and Alexander MacLeod, were both eased out, so, as David Sells had already left to concentrate on his work for *Newsnight*, I suddenly found myself as the programme's main presenter. I have to be honest: I was very pleased.

When Anne moved yet another step up the BBC management ladder to become the head of all Radio 4's news programmes, a move that did not go down at all well with her fellow editors, *The Guardian* reported approvingly of how, during her time at *The World Tonight*, she had overseen 'the transformation of a programme which always sounded as if the anchor had just returned from a claret-lubricated supper at his club to one predominantly presented by women'.[106] This was stunningly inaccurate in so many different ways, not least because I was then presenting the programme at least three nights a week, was not a woman, did not drink claret and did not belong to a club. A correction was duly published.

The first thing I did after Anne arrived at *The World Tonight* was ask if we could get rid of the presenter's glass-walled inner office. I had never felt happy being isolated from the rest of the team: for one thing, it made me feel as if I was regarded as an unusually delicate flower, to be brought out only on special occasions; and, for another, I much preferred to be part of the bustle of the main production office, involved in the decisions that were being made and able, occasionally, to make my own contribution to the planning process.

Within a few months of Anne's arrival, several of the programme's longest-serving producers and reporters also left. There were, shall we say, some personality clashes, and Anne was seen as representing a more Birtian approach than some of the team felt comfortable with. She was later named in *The Independent* as one of the women who might one day be running the country: 'serious, considered, straight-dealing … Koch has successfully purged the programme of its fustiness while still maintaining its pedigree'.[107]

I was happy to have passed the fustiness test, although I think the purging, if that is what it was, probably pre-dated Anne's appointment.

I now realise that my own arrival on the programme was probably part of a broader defustification process, even if I had no idea at the time of the deeper currents that were swirling around me.

Fortunately, the new editor approved of my wish to continue reporting from overseas. In 1994, I was dispatched to South Africa in the run-up to the country's first democratic elections, amid grave fears of an impending bloodbath as white extremists threatened to halt the transition from apartheid to majority rule. I remember meeting an Afrikaner pig farmer, whom we somehow ended up interviewing right next to his pigs. Their honking and snuffling offered a rich and atmospheric audio background to his contribution, but the result was not, perhaps, entirely fair to him. I also remember meeting a black South African who as a child had been forcibly evicted with his family from their land. He took us back to see the remains of the village and told us that he had already bought the bricks with which he intended to rebuild the family home. I have wondered many times whether he ever succeeded.

When Anne Koch took maternity leave, her place was filled temporarily by an ambitious young deputy editor from the *Today* programme. His name was Rod Liddle, and it would be fair to say he introduced a new set of behavioural norms to *The World Tonight*. For one thing, he had unusually long hair (for a man) and wore a single earring, both of which marked him out from other male members of the team.

He also was in the habit of presiding over editorial meetings while lying on the floor, and favoured a vocabulary that included many more words of Anglo-Saxon origin than we were used to. After several years with women editors in charge, we had to adapt to a more macho approach to programme-making. After he sprayed a torrent of computer-delivered editorial instructions at the team on his first day, I received a cryptic message via the internal email system from a colleague elsewhere in the building: 'I see there's a lot of willy waving going on today.'

But hidden beneath that rebellious teenager exterior, there was a secret BBC bureaucrat playing the system. I was struck when I interviewed the then director-general, John Birt, that Rod surreptitiously removed his earring and emerged very nearly as a conventional editor. But he soon went back to his natural ways, phoning in to the studio from a pub where he was listening to the programme and berating the duty editor for a 'fucking boring piece of shit' and instructing him to find something more interesting to broadcast in its place.

Among the freelance reporters whom he hired to contribute to the programme was a certain Rachel Royce, who later became his wife, and then, not long afterwards, his ex-wife. Rod and I had virtually nothing in common but for six months we co-existed well enough, even if I disapproved of his ill-concealed antipathy towards, and undermining of, some members of the production team.

It was not until many years later that Rod revealed he had been given a solemn warning when he took up his temporary position at *The World Tonight*. Apparently, a senior BBC executive had, somewhat embarrassed, conveyed the message that although as a deputy editor, forming close personal liaisons with members of staff was tolerated, as an editor, such transgressions would be taken much more seriously. It was, said Rod, a 'don't shag the staff' warning. All a bit pointless, he added, as 'even back then I'd have drawn the line at Robin Lustig, much though I liked him'.[108]

Rod's eventual departure from the BBC, after he had begun to carve out a niche for himself as a deliberately provocative columnist in *The Guardian*, came as no surprise. He had admitted to me that his ambition was to become a famous controversialist, and there was no better way to kick-start the publicity machine than by engineering his semi-sacking after a spectacularly rude column about members of the pro-fox hunting Countryside Alliance.

Although *The World Tonight* devoted a good deal of its attention to what was happening beyond Britain's borders, it did not ignore the dramatic political, economic and social transformations under way at home. The end of the Cold War had set in train a rapid process of economic globalisation that caused substantial disruption to traditional industries. Margaret Thatcher was dethroned in 1990; Britain crashed out of the European exchange rate mechanism in 1992, and the John Major government then limped like a wounded animal to its inevitable demise at the hands of a resurgent Labour Party under Tony Blair in 1997. These were turbulent times and, political junkie that I was, I adored being in the thick of it.

I also enjoyed going to the party conferences every autumn, staying in a succession of gruesome hotels in seaside resorts whose names began with B. Watching the Conservatives self-destruct in Blackpool beneath the baleful eye of a smouldering Margaret Thatcher was true drama, as was the ruthless re-invention in Brighton of the Labour Party under Tony Blair. At Westminster, the endless late-night debates over the EU and the Maastricht Treaty played perfectly for *The World Tonight*, and the entire production team would sometimes decamp to the BBC's studios at Westminster so that we could be at the heart of the action as knife-edge votes were taken after 10 p.m.

The attraction of the party conferences was that they offered an opportunity to meet, mix and gossip with senior politicians in a way that simply was not possible in the more formal, closely guarded atmosphere of Westminster and Whitehall. They also offered front-row seats at the best political drama available anywhere: John Prescott's wholly unintelligible yet utterly wonderful speech in 1993 in support of John Smith and his 'one member, one vote' reforms to reduce the power of the trade unions in selecting parliamentary candidates; Tony Blair's audacious pledge to abolish the Labour Party's pro-public ownership Clause IV in 1994; and Michael Portillo's ill-fated attempt ('Who Dares, Wins') to grab the Conservative Party leadership in 1995. In their own way, they were all moments of history and, for me, it was as thrilling to be in Blackpool, Brighton or Bournemouth as it had been to be in Berlin on the day of Germany's reunification.

But going on air at 10 p.m. at a party conference had one big disadvantage: it was a time when many of the most interesting people were either at dinner or at the bar, not always entirely sober, and not often prepared to break off from their social engagements to make their way to a dingy studio somewhere in the bowels of a conference centre. (At one time, the temporary BBC studios were erected in an underground car park, which even by BBC standards was less than salubrious.) In

Brighton one year, I was reduced to broadcasting from the pavement outside the Grand Hotel, so that I could conduct live interviews with senior political figures without them even having to put down their champagne glass.

Over the years, there was growing controversy about how many people the BBC sent to party conferences, and as the conferences themselves became more tightly scripted and progressively less newsworthy, it became increasingly difficult to justify sending a separate *World Tonight* team. By the time I left, the habit had been discontinued, and I now suspect that there is little good reason for anyone to bother reporting them. Like the noise of a tree in the forest that crashes to the ground with no one there to hear it, would the conferences even exist in the absence of any reporters?

My weakness for political drama means that I have always had a special love for election nights. Uncertainty, suspense, personal anguish, historic shifts in the political landscape: how can anyone possibly go to bed before the last result is declared? Before the invention of Radio 5 Live in 1994, I anchored several of Radio 4's local election results programmes, which was roughly equivalent to commentating at a football match in what used to be called the Conference League. You knew no one was listening, but it had to be done, and someone had to do it.

One year, we went on air without the designated Labour Party representative in the studio after an angry stand-off over his insistence that he must be allowed to bring his pager in with him so that he could receive all the essential prompts from party headquarters. On another occasion, Charles Kennedy fell asleep in the studio at around 3 a.m. and had to be gently nudged awake. (I shouldn't mock: I fell asleep once while on air – and I was presenting the programme.)

It was also Charles Kennedy who, during a lengthy recitation of the results from Wales, read by a colleague in Cardiff, started madly scribbling on a sheet of paper in front of him. When I raised a quizzical eyebrow to inquire what he was writing, he silently held up the paper to show me. It said: 'Who gives a fuck about Wales?'

Once the BBC had launched Radio 5 Live as its dedicated news and sport station, I was spared any more all-nighters on the local election results. But in 1997, I was asked to anchor the World Service's all-night British general election results programme, the first of four that I presided over, from the 'new dawn' of the Blair triumph of 1997 to the 'no one won' confusion of the coalition-generating poll in 2010.

But the establishment of 5 Live offered me a new opportunity: together with my old friend Ivor Gaber, who was now somehow managing to combine the roles of practising journalist and leading media academic, I set up an independent production company to bid for commissions from the new network. As both Ivor and I lived in the shadow of Alexandra Palace in north London, from which the first BBC TV images had been transmitted in 1936, we called the company Palace Radio Productions. We won a bid to produce a regular Sunday morning programme profiling a major figure from the week's news, brought on board a freelance producer, Jan Haworth, and for the next five years, having briefly regained my Saturday freedom after leaving *The Observer*, I was back to weekend working.

It was Jan who did all the hard work on *Spotlight*, finding people to interview about each week's profile subject, encouraging them to be entertainingly indiscreet in front of a microphone and then editing their contributions so that I could write the script. We soon found that the best interviewees were either family members or former schoolteachers, and I enjoyed the more informal tone that I was allowed by 5 Live.

On Tony Blair, the newly elected leader of the Labour Party:

> Suddenly the smile was everywhere. It was dazzling and it seemed so bright that the world of politics was blinded by the Blair glare … He is one of those instantly likeable people whom some people can't stand … living proof that the dolls Barbie and Ken did have sex: he's plastic, too perfect, too smiley.

On Chancellor of the Exchequer Ken Clarke: 'Whenever things get tough in Parliament, Ken Clarke turns into a serial giggler. It's a most

peculiar sound, halfway between a billy goat and a machine gun.'
(His car salesman younger brother was also deliciously rude about the
Chancellor's taste in motor vehicles.)

And *Hello!* magazine:

> ... probably the worst-written magazine in the English language. It has
> developed a style uniquely its own, in which celebs invariably 'welcome
> us to their lovely home', 'speak frankly about their love', and, most
> dangerously of all, 'celebrate many happy years together', which often
> means that they're on the point of splitting up.

When the brat-Brit artist Damien Hirst hit the headlines with his
exhibition of pickled animal carcasses encased in glass boxes, I began
our profile of him with a line written while visiting the show: 'I am
standing in the middle of a cow.'*

I thought it might attract listeners' attention on a Sunday morning.

Every week, I worried about how the subject of our profile would
react. Once I even got up in the middle of the night to drive back
to Broadcasting House and re-record a sentence that I feared might
bring us a libel writ. But only once did I hear directly from someone
whom I had pilloried on air: it was the very grand Cabinet Secretary
Sir Robin Butler, whom I had described as looking as if he had been
born wearing silk pyjamas. When he phoned me the day after the programme was broadcast to say how much he had enjoyed it, I was both
flattered and annoyed. Obviously, I should have been much ruder.

It was fun working for 5 Live, although *Spotlight* was always something of an anomaly as a recorded, scripted programme on a network
that boasted of being neither. Its more natural home would have been
Radio 4, and after a decent interval following 5 Live's decision to kill
us off, Radio 4 introduced a weekly *Profile* slot that bore an uncanny
resemblance to *Spotlight*. Neither Palace Radio Productions nor I was
involved in its making.

---

*   Hirst had split the carcass of a cow down the middle and encased each half in a
separate box, placed side by side. I stood in the space between the two boxes.

Radio 5 Live had been born out of the Scud FM experiment of 1991. The force of nature that was Jenny Abramsky – the head of radio news who knew exactly what she wanted and how to get it – had overcome fierce internal opposition to the idea of an all-day news network at the beginning of the Gulf War and, following on from its success, had developed and launched 5 Live.

Jenny had joined BBC radio in 1969, when, in her words, it was 'hierarchical, intellectual, pulsating with creative energy and full of people at war with each other'.[109] It was little different when she started her own war against its most senior figures more than twenty years later. In fact, it is a pretty accurate description of the BBC even today, where, like in any large organisation, executives can too easily be side-tracked into defending their own bailiwicks rather than focusing on the only thing that really matters: the programmes.

After Saddam Hussein invaded Kuwait in August 1990, I knew that if a US-led coalition went to war to force him out again, I wanted to be able to play a part in reporting it. After all, the Middle East was the one region of the world where I could claim to have some real knowledge. But, as I was now a presenter, I also knew that I was not going to be sent to the war zone, so as soon as I heard that there was likely to be an all-war radio news network, I was first in line to volunteer. Scud FM went on air three days after the first missiles were fired in January 1991, and it stayed on air, seventeen hours a day, seven days a week, until 2 March. I notched up countless hours in Studio 4A of Broadcasting House during that period, many of them in the company of the writer, historian and broadcaster Christopher Lee, a former BBC defence correspondent who became the perfect 'presenter's friend' – someone to talk to in those long, tedious hours that have to be filled when nothing is happening. On at least one occasion, we found ourselves chatting aimlessly like cricket commentators when rain has stopped play, musing on the delightful cakes that thoughtful listeners had sent in to help us survive our lengthy stints at the Rolling Bollocks coalface.

My diary for that time consists of little more than a series of numbers, indicating when I had been booked to be on air: 1815–2200,

0900–1300, 1400–1700. Sometimes, after I had come off air at the end of *The World Tonight*, I would be asked to stay on to read the midnight news as well, so that the editors could incorporate live interviews with correspondents if there were any new developments. Given the time difference with the US, it was not unusual for announcements to come from Washington when much of Europe was already fast asleep. BBC radio news was determined not to be caught napping, although the tension between the rigidity of the evening schedules and the un-certainties of war was never far from the surface.

That tension burst into the open on the evening of Monday 25 February. A few minutes before the end of *The World Tonight*, it was reported that Baghdad Radio had announced that 'orders have been issued to our armed forces to withdraw [from Kuwait] in an organ-ised manner to positions they held prior to 1 August 1990'. Saddam Hussein was surrendering and, as I read out the news flash in the programme's closing headlines, producers were already begging the Radio 4 bosses to allow us back on air. It took until midnight for all the relevant people to get their respective acts together (no one would dare touch *Book at Bedtime*), but we did take over the midnight news and produced an hour-long special programme.

When it was all over, Gillian Reynolds of the *Daily Telegraph*, the doyenne of Britain's radio critics, led the chorus of approval for what Scud FM had achieved.

> Its tone of voice lacked television's pomposity. The listener became part of a privileged dialogue, a serious, informed, experienced and seasoned discourse upon available information. The counterweight of expert opinion came to balance the increasingly evident management of the news. Listeners learned to differentiate between fact and opinion, ob-jectives and perspectives.[110]

But was all this endless war news what listeners really wanted? The evidence suggested that it was: by the end of the Scud FM experi-ment, more than a million people were listening to it regularly, and more than two-thirds of Radio 4's regular listeners had tried it.[111] It was the dawning of the age of real-time news, a foretaste of things to come. I realised that it was not only news junkies and men with a weakness for war who were tuning in when I picked up my children from school and many of the mothers at the school gates told me that they had heard me on air.

As Jenny Abramsky recalled ten years later:

> The country's forces were at war for the first time in ten years, as part of a large allied army … The BBC, as the public service broadcaster, had a duty to keep the families and friends of the 30,000 British army informed … [and] to keep its licence payers informed, as part of the democratic process.

She, just like Julius Reuter more than a century earlier, understood that people do want to know what is going on in the world, and they want to know as soon as possible. But the emphasis on what became known at the BBC as 'The Now O'Clock News' did create problems: first because speed and accuracy are not always compatible, and second, because the demands of an all-news network can sometimes distort news priorities to the detriment of the rest of the output.

In May 2007, for example, Lebanon was engulfed in the most serious fighting since the end of its civil war in 1990. Several hundred people were killed and there was a series of bomb attacks in Beirut. But the BBC's news operation was focused on a different part of the world entirely: southern Portugal, where a four-year-old British girl called Madeleine McCann had vanished from her family's holiday apartment. No prizes for guessing where TV news anchor Huw Edwards was sent…

For a programme like *The World Tonight*, this prioritising of the needs of TV rolling news could be frustrating. Often, a correspondent who might have been expected to be available to tell our listeners about a new development would instead be feeding the voracious appetite of the TV news channel, even though the viewing figures suggested that it was being watched by barely 1 per cent of the potential TV audience, compared to the 20 per cent of the evening radio audience who were tuned in to *The World Tonight*.

Perhaps this is a good place to say something about news audiences and lay to rest the widespread impression that, worthy as it may be, hardly anyone listens to *The World Tonight*. On the night of the Brussels bomb attacks in March 2016, for example, about 750,000 people were listening to the programme, substantially more than the number who watched *Channel 4 News* (670,000), and a far higher number than those who were watching *Newsnight* on BBC2 at about the same time (470,000). Those figures are not untypical (in 2015, *Newsnight*'s average viewing figure was reported to be around 540,000), but because television, by its very nature, is a much more visible medium than radio, it is often assumed that it must have much bigger audiences.

Radio usually tends to stay below the radar, unless the full might of the BBC's marketing department swings into action. During my time there, the Radio 4 priorities were *Today* and *The Archers*. Nothing else counted, which is why every time a new editor arrived at *The World Tonight* and swore that they would raise its profile, they failed. Two examples: when ITV moved its evening news bulletins away from 10 p.m. (the BBC TV evening news at that time was at 9 p.m.), I suggested to Tony Hall, then head of BBC News, that we should run a marketing campaign along the lines of: 'There is still News at Ten. *The World Tonight* on Radio 4.' He liked the idea, but the marketing department thought differently. There was no campaign.

And when all Radio 4's news programmes moved from Broadcasting House in central London to TV Centre in the wilds of White City, *The World Tonight* was the first of the programmes to head west. I suggested that I could write a diary for *The Guardian*'s media pages about how it all went – but the press office said no. They wanted to wait until the *Today* programme moved and then get one of their presenters to do it.

Did we have a chip on our shoulders? Of course we did. But the former director-general Greg Dyke succinctly explained why radio – and especially late-night radio – seems so often to be the BBC's Cinderella service. When I asked him shortly after he arrived at the BBC why he had said absolutely nothing, either in public or to BBC staff, about its radio output, he replied: 'Radio's not a problem. I don't need to waste my time worrying about it.'

Radio 4's news programmes represent the spine on which the network's other programming depends. Look at a ratings chart and the figures peak for every news programme and then dip immediately afterwards. (The exception, of course, is *The Archers*.) On BBC2, the opposite applies, which is why our *Newsnight* colleagues always found themselves off air over Christmas and the New Year. A former head of Radio 4, Tony Whitby, put it well: 'In the realm of ideas, radio operates with uncluttered lucidity: in the realm of the imagination, it soars where other media limp.'

I have been known to express the same thought but much less elegantly: 'Radio is television for grown-ups.'

After Anne Koch left *The World Tonight*, it was decided that the time was right to try an experiment: two job-sharing editors were appointed who would work three days a week each. (They overlapped on Wednesdays.) Prue Keely joined us from *Channel 4 News*, having never previously worked at the BBC, and Jenni Russell came from Current Affairs. It was a brave experiment, and one met with great suspicion both at *The World Tonight* and beyond. One very well-known Radio 4 presenter made the mistake of sounding off at a BBC reception about the utter idiocy of the idea to Sir Howard Davies, former deputy governor of the Bank of England, not knowing that Sir Howard happened to be married to Prue Keely.

His response was suitably frosty: 'I think you'll find that my wife will be able to cope.'

Prue and Jenni told the team at the outset that they were well aware of the potential dangers. 'Do not think', they warned us, 'that you can behave like children do with their parents and try to play us off against each other.' It was easier said than done, and it would be hard to claim that the experiment was a total success, despite their best efforts to make it work.

For the last ten years of my time at *The World Tonight*, the programme's editor was Alistair Burnett (not to be confused with Alastair
Burnet, who was one of Britain's best-known TV news broadcasters in
the 1970s and 1980s). I already knew Alistair well by the time he took
over – he had worked on the programme before as a young producer and had then been in charge of World Service news programmes
before returning to Radio 4. We were an odd couple: he was Scottish,
shy and intensely serious, whereas I was none of those things. Yet
we worked well together for over a decade, united in an obsessive
curiosity about the global changes under way following the end of
the Cold War and a preference for talking to interesting people with
interesting things to say instead of always chasing a new headline from
the latest politician to be caught in the media headlights (although I
did occasionally enjoy chasing headlines as well).

Alistair tended to be more interested in ideas than in people, and
when he sent me overseas on reporting trips, whether it was to Brazil
to look at its rapid economic growth, or to China to report on its
emergence as a world power, the challenge was always to find someone,
somewhere, who would be able to help us turn the interesting idea
into interesting radio.

When I was in the US in the run-up to the 2012 presidential election, Alistair decided that he wanted a report on America's growing
concerns that it was becoming less innovative and losing ground in
the global competition to stay ahead of the game. Thanks to an invaluable American innovation called Google, my colleague Dan Isaacs
and I stumbled across a specialist innovation research centre at the
Georgia Institute of Technology in Atlanta.

So we phoned them. 'Do you have anything that makes a noise and
that we could record for a piece about US innovation?

'Sure we do. Come on down and we'll show you around.' Which is
how we met a robot called Shimon, which was able to play improvised
jazz on a marimba to match the style of a human jazz pianist. It made
an unusual introduction to our report, and was one of the very rare
occasions when you could hear jazz (even if it was robotic jazz) on *The
World Tonight*.

The secret to a successful reporting trip is a talented and hard-working producer. BBC radio reporters usually travel alone, but presenters, because they tend to be older, more decrepit and can rarely be trusted to find their own way out of the door, are usually accompanied by a producer whose task is to take them by the hand and keep them out of trouble. Some producers have been known to refer to their presenter companion as 'the gob on a stick', which you may think suggests a regrettable lack of respect for wisdom and experience. (You may think that; I couldn't possibly comment.)

Craig Swan was my producer-companion in Bosnia, Kosovo, Afghanistan, Pakistan, Hong Kong, Cambodia and Somalia. He is extremely tall, whereas I am not, so when we stood side by side, we looked like a comedy music hall act. We shared a weakness for what we called 'dusty places', countries where mod cons were not universally available, where danger was never far away, but where there was usually a good story to be told.

When we went to Bosnia in 1996, after the war had ended, we flew first to the Croatian capital Zagreb, where we were to meet up with a Serbo-Croat-speaking colleague from the World Service, Pierre Vicary, who had been based in Zagreb for many years and knew his way around, which we did not. It was only a year after our young colleague John Schofield had been killed in Croatia, so the BBC had equipped us with bulky flak jackets. They had not, however, provided us with bags in which to carry them, and they do not easily fit into a suitcase. The only solution was to wear them as we made our way through Heathrow and boarded the plane. Not surprisingly, a lot of people looked at us very strangely.

I have never forgotten our drive south from Zagreb to Sarajevo. As soon as we crossed the border into Bosnia, we started to pass through village after village, all of them abandoned, many with Cyrillic graffiti scrawled on the walls of the houses where Serb fighters had forced the residents to flee. Many of the houses looked relatively undamaged except for a large hole in the roof. The Serbs' technique had been to place a gas canister on the ground floor of a house and then shoot at it, causing an explosion powerful enough to blow a hole in the roof and render the house uninhabitable. It was a frighteningly simple way to enforce the 'ethnic cleansing' policy that Serbian leaders Slobodan Milošević and Radovan Karadžić hoped would enable them to create a purely Serbian state.

In Sarajevo, we met a former Bosnian fighter who had spent much of the war holed up in a sniper's nest overlooking a bridge across the river Miljacka. His instructions were to shoot anyone who tried to cross, and he took us to see the exact position from which he had gazed out across that bridge, day after day, month after month. The experience had clearly left him deeply traumatised.

'When you come back here now, and you look out at that bridge,' I asked him, 'what goes through your mind?'

He did not speak much English but his reply was eloquent.

'What do I think now? I think, "Who gives a fuck about a bridge?"'

But could we broadcast the word 'fuck' on Radio 4? As it would be transmitted well after 10 p.m., the answer was an unhesitating Yes.

There had been an earlier occasion when we had had to seek advice about graphic language on *The World Tonight*. It was a report from Amsterdam about the red-light district, and it included a recording of a pimp touting the services on offer, in English, outside one of the city's brothels. I remember the words exactly.

'Sucky fucky, licky dicky...'

We did what all BBC people are so good at: we referred up. The verdict was quintessentially Radio 4: 'It's fine – most days we run much worse than that on *Woman's Hour*.'

In June 1997, Craig and I were part of a sizeable BBC contingent dispatched to Hong Kong to report on the historic handover of the territory to China. My responsibilities were to provide live commentary on the World Service of all the formal handover ceremonies, read the Six O'Clock News on Radio 4, and then present *The World Tonight* at 5 a.m. local time. It required careful planning, copious amounts of coffee and a strong bladder.

The ceremonies overran, as ceremonies tend to. There was also a torrential downpour as Prince Charles made his solemn speech to mark the occasion, standing in the open air with the rain falling so noisily onto the peak of his admiral's cap that it almost drowned out his words. With the planned timetable going badly awry and my commentary becoming increasingly incoherent, I ventured to ask via my studio talkback button what was going to happen next.

'How the fuck should I know?' was the reply from a harassed producer. 'No one tells me anything.'

It was not what a presenter needs to hear when floundering badly with no script and no guidance.

Because of the overrun, I began to fret that I might not be able to wrap up the commentary in time to switch hats (and studios) to become a Radio 4 newsreader. We made it with less than five minutes to spare: I was handed a sheaf of news scripts and ushered into an adjoining studio just as Big Ben was preparing to strike 6 p.m.

As far as I know, it is the only time in Radio 4's history that its hallowed Six O'Clock News bulletin has been read in its entirety from an overseas location. I felt the spirit of Peter Donaldson hovering above me – it was my proudest moment on air, and a fraught one. But it passed off successfully.

Having waited just long enough to ensure that the People's Liberation Army was not intending to invade Hong Kong the moment it had passed out of British hands, Craig and I made our way to Cambodia, where there were reports that the former Khmer Rouge leader, Pol Pot, who had been in hiding for eighteen years, had been arrested by some of his former colleagues. We thought that as we were in the neighbourhood, it would be worth having a sniff around.

Kevin Connolly, the BBC man who had been holding the fort in Phnom Penh, just in case Pol Pot turned up, greeted us warmly, assured us that we were on a wild goose chase, and jumped on the next plane to Paris, taking all his equipment with him. Not for the first time, Craig and I found ourselves asking that most useless of reporters' questions: 'Whose idea was this?'

Our fixer-translator was a gentle, kindly man who spoke only rudimentary English, one of the very few Cambodians who knew a foreign language and had survived the horrors of the Khmer Rouge era. We asked him, in some desperation, to take us anywhere where he thought there might be sounds that we could record. A visit to a workshop for men with disabilities was not fruitful: it was closed. Likewise a trip to a military gun club, where we had thought there was a chance we would find army officers perfecting their shooting skills. It was deserted.

While we were there, however, we heard the distant rumble of thunder. 'Not thunder,' said our fixer. 'Artillery. I think we go now.'

We thought so too. Back at the hotel, with many apologies, our fixer explained that he feared bad things were about to happen, that he needed to be with his family to make sure that they were all right, and that he would no longer be able to work with us. It was the only time in my entire time as a journalist that a fixer had walked out on me – and I had every sympathy with him.

He was right about bad things happening. The artillery barrage had been the opening shots in a coup by one of the country's co-Prime Ministers, Hun Sen, against the other, Prince Norodom Ranariddh. Each of them commanded their own section of the national army, and for several days there were violent clashes between the rival factions.

Some of those clashes took place directly outside our hotel. Craig carefully hung a microphone out of his window, pressed the record button and recorded hour after hour of gunfire. Telephone lines were down, we were unable to leave the hotel, and I had succumbed to food poisoning. We were stuck.

It was extremely frustrating. We were the only BBC men in town; we had a great story and no way of communicating with the outside world. Eventually, we ventured out, found our way to a nearby hospital and recorded some more sound. With no translator, our options were severely limited. And then the phone rang in my hotel room: London had managed to get through, even if we could still not call them. I described as best as I could what we believed what was happening and we set in place an agreed schedule of calls for the next few hours.

It was not the ideal way to report a story, but it was the best we could do. I stayed close to the phone – and the bathroom – while Craig made periodic forays into town to see what was going on. Each evening, we transferred the best of his material onto a tape cassette and I wrote an outline script, just in case we found a way of getting it out of the country.

The Royal Thai Air Force came to our rescue. Although Phnom Penh airport was still shut because of the fighting, the Thais flew in a couple of transport planes to evacuate their citizens and fly them back to Bangkok. Our hotel had become a centre for terrified Thais, and we were able to persuade one of them to take our cassette to Bangkok and arrange for a BBC colleague to meet them at the airport and then transmit our material on to London. It was a long shot, but it worked. The technical term was 'pigeoning' the material out, and it took me right back to my days at Reuters, which had, after all, at one time used real pigeons as news carriers.

Having successfully informed the world – or at least listeners of *The World Tonight* and the BBC World Service – of the dramatic events to which we had been witnesses, there remained just one further task: to get ourselves back to London. Word reached us that a private charter flight out of Phnom Penh had been arranged for Western business executives whose employers had expensive insurance policies that covered such emergencies – and we would be allowed to join it provided we could each stump up $1,500, in cash, before take-off.

The BBC can be very resourceful when it needs to be, and when a colleague flew in from Bangkok to relieve us, he had with him enough cash to enable us to make our escape. It was all high drama at the time, even if no one now remembers The Great Cambodian Coup of 1997. (Hun Sen was still Prime Minister at the time this book was written nearly twenty years later.)

For the next few years, BBC trainees were sometimes played our report from Cambodia as an example of how to make something out of nothing. The entire report contained not a single interview: just a lot of dramatic sound and a script, beginning, after a dramatic burst of gunfire recorded from Craig's bedroom window, with the words: 'The sound of an army at war with itself…'

❦

When Craig and I reported from Kosovo in 1999, after NATO had intervened to prevent the expulsion of ethnic Albanians by Serb forces, we based ourselves not in the capital, Pristina, but in Prizren, an ancient city not far from the border with Albania. Craig arrived a few days ahead of me, and I was instructed to fly first to the Albanian capital, Tirana, to pick up an armoured vehicle that the BBC had purchased and take it, with a locally hired driver, into Kosovo for the use of the team of BBC correspondents who were already in place.

The vehicle turned out to be an ancient Ford Granada, formerly owned – or so I was told – by the Turkish ambassador to Albania. A man from the BBC's finance department, accompanied by an armoured car specialist, had also flown out to inspect the vehicle before the sale was completed, and then, if they were satisfied, hand over a substantial wodge of bank notes. I declined to be part of the transaction, which eventually took place in a grubby café in the Tirana suburbs where two men in black leather coats were waiting to trouser the cash. The man from the finance department said he had never been so terrified in his life.

The following day, I was introduced to the driver who had been hired to take the car – and me – into Kosovo. Now it was my turn to be terrified. He looked exactly like the kind of man you would expect Central Casting to come up with if you had asked for someone to play an Albanian mafioso. But he was delighted to discover that I spoke Italian, which, like many Albanians who had been reared on a diet of illegally accessed Italian TV programmes during the tyrannical rule of Enver Hoxha, he also spoke. He assured me that we would soon become the closest of friends.

The road north from Tirana to the border town of Kukës, where we were due to spend the night, was narrow, potholed and mountainous. The driver decided to use the Ford's supposedly automatic gearbox as if it was a manual version, crashing through the gears at every hairpin bend, with just one hand on the steering wheel while regaling me with endless anecdotes in a totally unintelligible Italian accent. To add to the joy of the journey, we very soon discovered that the car's armour-plating had made it so absurdly heavy that its engine could barely cope with the mountain roads. The temperature gauge rose alarmingly, and we ended up pouring vast quantities of expensive mineral water into the radiator to stop the whole thing from blowing up. My BBC colleagues in Kosovo would have to make do without the water.

There was already a BBC advance guard in Prizren; they had found a friendly house owner prepared to let us sleep in his spare room and provide us with food and, as he was a Muslim, with carpet slippers for us to wear after we had removed our shoes when we entered his house. Craig decided to photograph me one night, broadcasting live from the man's balcony, microphone in one hand, notebook in the other, and a fetching pair of tartan slippers on my feet. It made me look alarmingly like Grandpa Lustig and conveyed, so I like to think, an entirely inaccurate impression.

A couple of days after I arrived, a group of BBC colleagues turned up from Pristina, claiming to be desperate refugees from the heart of the war zone. Relations between the various TV news stars who were competing for airtime had apparently deteriorated so badly that their colleagues had decided to make a break for freedom and seek relative safety in Prizren. Apart from anything else, they had heard that we had access to a functioning shower. With hot water.

It is easy to forget in the aftermath of the US-led military interventions in Afghanistan and Iraq that in the late 1990s, Western military interventions in Bosnia and Kosovo were widely welcomed by local people. Tony Blair and the then British Foreign Secretary Robin Cook were local heroes – and as I, like Cook, was called Robin and had a beard, I was occasionally warmly embraced by Kosovo Albanians who on hearing my name mistook me for their saviour.

Craig and I had had a less friendly reception in Pakistan in 1997 when we were reporting on a general election. We had gone to Karachi, then as now a turbulent, unpredictable and violent city, to report on the fortunes of the MQM party, which represents Muhajirs, Urdu-speaking Muslims who had fled to Pakistan from India at the time of partition in 1947. Party officials offered to take us out campaigning with them, and we joined a convoy, escorted by police vehicles, into one of the poorest parts of the city.

It soon became clear that this was not MQM territory. Someone started hurling stones and rocks at the motorcade, and then we heard the sound of Kalashnikovs. We had no way of telling who had opened fire, but when the windows of our car shattered and I suffered a nasty head wound from the flying glass, we ducked down into the foot well behind the front seats and suggested to our driver that he should put his foot down.

It was as we were careering out of the area on squealing tyres that I noticed Craig rummaging in his bag. He extracted a microphone, stuck it in front of my face and gave me a one-word order.

'Talk.'

It made a dramatic bit of radio, but I could have well done without it. Our car, which had been provided for us by our hotel, looked a total wreck when we returned it, as did our poor driver, whose working day normally consisted of no more than driving hotel guests to and from the airport. We told the hotel that the BBC would of course pay to have the car repaired, but they would not hear of it, and instead were full of apologies for our most unfortunate experience. The following day, we received another apology, indirectly, from the group responsible for the ambush. If they had only known that the men from the BBC were in the convoy, they said, they would of course not have attacked. In its way, it was comforting to know.

I found that the best way to get approval for foreign reporting trips was to persuade an enthusiastic producer to put forward a proposal rather than doing it myself. Successive editors seemed to suspect that my ideas were sometimes born of a desire to visit a country that I had not yet travelled to, rather than on strictly journalistic grounds. Their suspicions may – occasionally – have been not entirely ill-founded, but I will always insist that my reporting trips were also wholly justifiable in terms of the material they generated. In fact, because for the whole of my time at the BBC I was working for both Radio 4 and the World Service, I usually ended up reporting for both networks on the same trip. (And in case you are wondering, no, I was not paid separately by each network.)

In 2006, the Himalayan kingdom of Nepal was rocked by protests.

It was five years after the heir to the Nepali throne, Crown Prince Dipendra, had shot dead nine members of his own family, including his parents, the king and queen, before turning his gun on himself. For the previous decade, a Maoist insurrection had resulted in the deaths of at least 13,000 people, and by 2006, the rebels were estimated to control 80 per cent of the country. Nepal was in turmoil and it looked as if the protests could result in the overthrow of the monarchy. To me, it was a fascinating story that *The World Tonight* should certainly take a closer look at.

Craig had left the programme by this time, taking with him another of my travelling producer-companions, Bernadette Duffy. They had decided to get married and relocate to the Scottish Highlands, which left me searching for a new comrade in arms. (Craig and Bernie had kept their relationship secret for more than three years, and although I had travelled extensively with both of them, I had no idea what they were up to behind my back. When I eventually found out, it severely dented my faith in my own powers of observation.)

Enter Catherine Miller. Like Craig, she was a Scot and, like him, she also had a taste for travelling to exotic locations. She agreed with me about Nepal, and not only because her brother was a British diplomat in Kathmandu at the time. (My son Josh was also living there.) We both had good reasons, both personal and professional, to want to go – and Alistair Burnett agreed that it was worth a trip. To make it more cost-effective, we suggested to the World Service that if we also travelled to Bhutan, Nepal's Himalayan neighbour, which was as tranquil and stable as Nepal was turbulent, we could produce a half-hour documentary as well, focusing on Bhutan's unusual government policy of prioritising a growth in gross national happiness instead of gross national product. We were confident that we could offer good value for money to licence fee-payers.

Little did we know that within days of our arrival in Nepal, the Parliament would in effect abolish the monarchy and the Maoist rebels would declare a unilateral ceasefire. Our hunch had paid off, and we were on the spot to report on a major political shift in one of the world's poorest countries.

Bhutan is weird. It is often portrayed as some kind of fabled Nirvana, a land of soaring, snow-covered peaks in which people live simple lives, bolstered by their Buddhist faith and true to their centuries-old traditions. It is also a country to which obscenely wealthy celebrities like to flee to be pampered and pummelled in luxury hotels and spas costing well over a thousand dollars per night. Its citizens are expected to wear national dress whenever they are out in public or visit government premises: the men wear *ghos*, a form of white-cuffed kimono, and the women wear sarongs called *kiras*.

The scenery is undeniably spectacular. Who can argue with the Himalayas? And Article Five of the constitution specifies: 'The government shall ensure that, in order to conserve the country's natural resources and to prevent degradation of the ecosystem, a minimum of 60 per cent of Bhutan's total land shall be maintained under forest cover for all time.' The most overused word in any article about Bhutan is 'pristine', so Catherine and I immediately resolved that we would ban the word in all of our reporting.

If you like Singapore or Switzerland, you will love Bhutan. There is a regimented orderliness to it that gives it a slightly Disney-like air. It protects its reputation jealously, and we were closely chaperoned throughout our visit by the king's British-born foreign media adviser, who had previously been a schoolteacher at the English boarding school to which the king had been sent before he ascended to the throne.

Television was introduced into Bhutan as late as 1999, but when the authorities discovered that the two most popular channels were World Wrestling and The Fashion Channel, they were both quickly taken off air. We knew there must be more to the place than beautiful scenery and beatific Buddhists, so Catherine surreptitiously asked our local guide's young assistant what he and his friends did for fun on Saturday nights.

Duly armed with the addresses of a couple of clubs, we gave our minder the slip and set off to explore the subterranean nightlife of Thimphu, the Bhutanese capital. In the first one we found, and this was in a country where the sale of any tobacco products is punishable by up to three years in prison, everyone seemed to be smoking. They were also drinking copious amounts of beer and the music was deafeningly loud. It was not my kind of place, and Catherine later said she had never seen a grown man look as utterly miserable as I did. But at least we satisfied ourselves that, given half a chance, the people of Bhutan were not all that different from anyone else.

The British media are notoriously selective about the parts of the world that they regard as interesting. Anywhere that used to be coloured red on a map because it was part of the British Empire usually qualifies, as does anywhere favoured by British holidaymakers. So Zimbabwe and southern Spain feature regularly, whereas Mozambique and Bulgaria do not. The US is always interesting, because we watch their movies and listen to their music, but Central and South America rarely make it, unless there has been a military coup, an earthquake or a new spate of drug-related massacres. Given that ever since I had applied to VSO as a schoolboy, I had been waiting for a chance to get to know Latin America, I had high hopes that I would eventually be able to persuade my colleagues at *The World Tonight* that it was a region crying out for our attention.

Alistair Burnett shared my enthusiasm, and when both Brazil and Mexico began to emerge as significant economic powers, we seized our chance. A new young producer had recently joined the programme: Beth McLeod spoke fluent Spanish, had spent a year studying in Mexico, and was as keen as I was to do some reporting from a region that rarely figured in BBC news bulletins. So was our Catalan-born producer Eva Ontiveros – so, for a while, our listeners were unusually well-served with reports from Latin America.

In Mexico, Beth slyly arranged for us to visit a gentlemen's outfitters that specialised in the sale of bulletproof clothing. She had hoped that the owner would demonstrate the efficacy of his products by shooting at me while I was wearing one of his jackets, but fortunately neither he nor I, nor the BBC's health and safety team, thought that this would be a good idea. Beth had to be satisfied with recording the sound from a demonstration video.

On another trip, however, she did manage to get me slipping and sliding down a muddy hillside in the Peruvian Andes, on our way to inspect a clandestine coca plantation. She also insisted that I had to buy a bag of coca leaves on the streets of a town with the delightful name of Tingo María. In fact, Beth became something of a specialist in finding bizarre experiences for her long-suffering presenter colleague, all in the interests, of course, of producing good radio. In Qatar, she found a private museum where we were suddenly faced with a macabre shrine to Saddam Hussein, featuring the clothes he was wearing at the moment of his execution, while in Colombia she persuaded a regional governor to lend us his helicopter to fly into what had been one of the most dangerous towns in the entire country.

The relationship between a presenter and a producer while they are on a foreign reporting trip is always a delicate one. From breakfast till dinner, they are rarely out of each other's sight, harnessed by a length of microphone cable and a shared despair at the inadequacies of their colleagues back in London. (On the next trip, of course, one of those hopeless colleagues may well be the travelling producer, at which point the sentiments remain unchanged even if the individuals have swapped places.)

On one occasion, I had to arrange emergency medical treatment for Bernie Duffy in Japan when she developed an agonising eye infection – fortunately, we were due to visit a US military base, where she was immediately treated in their hospital. (When I phoned the BBC's health department in London to seek advice, they were reassuringly relaxed: 'A US military hospital? She'll get the best treatment available anywhere in the world.')

As the years rolled by, however, I became increasingly conscious that while the producers were getting younger and younger, I was not. On one of my trips to Mexico, it dawned on me that the producer and sound engineer who were travelling with me were exactly the same ages as my son and daughter. And then, on my return to London, a senior executive rubbed it in by asking me: 'So how was your holiday with the kids?'

Usually on an overseas reporting trip, the producer will have done all the preparation: tracking down likely interviewees, drawing up schedules and booking the translators and drivers. They will also have put together a briefing pack for the presenter: why we are going, where we are going, whom we are meeting, and why. The presenter's job is to do what he is told, carry the equipment and buy the drinks.

And make the whole thing work.

At some point, there will be a moment of truth. The producer says: 'Do you think we should start putting this together?' And that is when the hard graft begins. How will our report start? Which bits of which interviews will we use, and in what order? Which snatches of natural sound that we have so painstakingly collected along the way – traffic noise, church bells, factory machinery – will we be able to make use of?

And, most difficult of all, who will make all those decisions? I was lucky: I got on well with all the producers I worked with at *The World Tonight*, and we rarely disagreed about anything. Only once, in my early days making documentaries for *File on 4*, did I have such a fundamental disagreement with a producer that, after a whole day of arguing, I finally decided to go to bed and let her decide on her own how to put the programme together. I then got up at 5 a.m. and wrote a script around the audio clips that she had selected, but it was not the best way to make a radio documentary and we never worked together again.

In the days of magnetic tape, we would always have to carry a portable editing machine with us, on which a producer – or, if we were very lucky, a sound engineer – would cut up the reels of tape into short chunks with a razor blade and splice them together with sticky tape, each chunk separated by a length of yellow tape to mark where one clip ended and the next began. It was slow and cumbersome, and no one complained too much when digital editing on laptop computers was introduced and we could bid farewell both to razor blades and to reels of tape.

Digital audio editing is like using a word processing software package: relatively straightforward until the whole thing goes pear-shaped. Sometimes you cannot save the work you have done; sometimes it disappears without trace into the computer's innards. And sometimes it just freezes. Usually, five minutes before you are due to go on air. On one occasion, we recorded an entire 45-minute programme in Washington, edited it with minutes to spare, and sent it to London just as the pips of the Greenwich Time Signal were playing at 10 p.m. Our computer said the entire data file had been successfully sent. The BBC's computers in London thought differently, and our standby team in the studio suddenly found they had to fill a whole programme with no material at all from us. It is on such occasions that you begin to wonder if there might be a better way to earn a living.

Radio 4 used to have a phone-in programme on Tuesday mornings. It was named, unimaginatively, *Tuesday Call*, until it assumed the name of its presenter and became *Call Nick Ross*. When Nick and the programme parted company in 1997, what to call it became something of a problem; a couple of stand-in presenters were hastily drafted in and the name changed from week to week: one week it was *Call Ed Stourton*, and the next week it would be *Call Robin Lustig*.

I enjoyed the roller-coaster nature of hosting a phone-in, because you never know who your next caller will be or what they will say. But it emerged over time – quite a long time, in fact, as I also presented a similar programme on the World Service for eight years – that it is not what I am best at. If a caller said something that I knew to be untrue, I had an irresistible urge to put them right, which tended to make me sound like an irritated schoolteacher. Radio 4 listeners are not accustomed to being treated like dim students.

This was the time when UK broadcasters were forbidden by law from broadcasting the voices of representatives of various Irish political and paramilitary groups, including Sinn Féin, the political wing of the IRA. Most broadcasters got round the ban by hiring Irish actors to read the words of banned spokesmen, but for phone-in programmes it was a nightmare, and I was under strict instructions to cut off anyone who claimed to be speaking on behalf of a banned organisation.

What no rules can prevent, however, is simple human error. On one programme, dealing with proposed changes to the law on abortion, my studio guest was a representative from an anti-abortion group who had a tendency to try to dominate proceedings to the exclusion of anyone else. The programme's producer felt that I was not being firm enough with her and instructed me through my headphones: 'She's ranting. Stop her.'

Alas. Instead of pressing the button in the control room that enabled him to communicate solely with me, he pressed the button that relayed his voice both to me and to my guest. She did not miss a beat.

'I am not ranting, and I won't stop,' she announced, on air, without pausing for breath.

The producer's apology at the end of the programme was abject.

As all presenters of phone-in programmes know, the best callers are those who have a personal story to tell. I have never forgotten a caller who, during a programme in which we were discussing the ethics of antenatal genetic screening for potential disability, said he had been born with very severe disabilities: 'I wish my mother had been screened, because if she had been, I would never have been born.'

On another programme, my studio guest was the then boss of Radio 4, James Boyle, who had sparked the closest thing Britain had seen to a popular uprising in several centuries by daring to introduce some minor changes to the network's schedule. The furore had reached such intensity – there was even a protest march to Broadcasting House – that he decided to face his critics directly by responding to them on his own network.

One caller spoke for the nation: 'Mr Boyle,' she said, 'I have just one thing I want to say to you – you have ruined my life.' His crime? Moving the start time of *The Archers*.

CHAPTER 13

LAHORE, LAGOS AND LOUISVILLE, KY

Perhaps Britain's greatest gift to the world this century.
UN SECRETARY-GENERAL KOFI ANNAN,
DESCRIBING THE BBC WORLD SERVICE IN 1999

IT WAS DURING MY year living in Uganda in the mid-1960s that I had first dreamt of working for the BBC World Service, so it should have come as no surprise that when I finally made it through the grand doors of Bush House more than twenty years later, I was utterly awestruck. I often used to remind myself of the days when I would fiddle with the dial on my shortwave radio, twisting the aerial in all directions to try to pick up the strains of that oh-so-authoritative voice cutting through the crackle.

'This is London.'

Even today, in the raucous, overcrowded media world of Twitter, Facebook, YouTube and the rest, the words still pack a punch.

Newshour, which became my main World Service home, is an hour-long news programme broadcast twice a day around the world and, for more than two decades, I was one of its team of presenters. Although it is a very different kind of beast from *The World Tonight* – faster, more varied, less structured – the basic task of presenting it was no different: get the facts straight, explain what is going on and interview the people at the centre of the story as well as the experts who can (perhaps) make sense of it all. In my constant quest for cost efficiency, on the days when I presented both *Newshour* at lunchtime and then *The World Tonight* in the evening, I would sometimes stuff a reel of tape into my bag and offer a World Service interview with a foreign potentate to my colleagues at Radio 4. Sometimes, although by no means always, they were suitably grateful.

On a good day, *Newshour* can claim to be the best global news programme on earth. Because the World Service brand is so well known, foreign leaders will often talk to the BBC before they talk to anyone else. To take just one example: when serious political unrest exploded in Thailand in the mid-2000s, I found myself interviewing in quick succession the two men at the centre of the protests, Abhisit Vejjajiva (who despite his name is British-born and Eton-educated) and Thaksin Shinawatra. The then head of the World Service, Peter Horrocks, sent me a note suggesting that it sounded as if I was personally trying to negotiate an end to the crisis.

News events in Thailand, like news events in Sri Lanka or Fiji, always present a special challenge for broadcasters: how to pronounce people's names. The names of the two men named above, for example, are pronounced ah-PEE-siht way-CHAH-chee-wah and TAHK-sihn shih-nah-WHAT. The BBC has a special department staffed by very clever people who specialise in pronunciation advice, but there is not always time to consult them, and my nightmare used to be a late-breaking story involving the leaders of Sri Lanka, Fiji and Thailand.

If Wijeyananda Dahanayake of Sri Lanka had ever met Jona Senilagakali of Fiji and Abhisit Vejjajiva of Thailand, I would have been in real trouble. But the World Service prides itself on getting these things right, and I tried not to let people down. On one occasion, when I was given sufficient advance warning of a planned interview with the then Secretary-General of NATO, Jaap de Hoop Scheffer, who is Dutch, I had time to phone his secretary beforehand to ask for help with the pronunciation of his name. (I was rewarded at the end of the recording when he said: 'By the way, congratulations on getting my name right.' Honour was satisfied.) If you want to try it yourself, it is YARP de HOPE SKHE-ffer (KH as in *loch*).

For obvious reasons, no broadcaster was amused when Mount Eyjafjallajökull erupted in Iceland in 2010 (try saying AY-uh-fyat-luh-YOE-kuutl) and, for similar reasons, the Radio 4 newsreader Neil Sleat basked in the boundless admiration of his colleagues in 2013 when he read, faultlessly, a news item about a woman in Hawaii that included – twice, because the newsroom was in a particularly sadistic mood – her family name: Keihanaikukauakahihuliheekahaunaele.

At least she never tried to climb that volcano in Iceland.

I remember endless anguished discussions at the World Service about the correct pronunciation of awkward names. When Yugoslavia fell apart in the early 1990s, Bosnia-Herzegovina soon started making regular appearances in news stories. But was it *Herze-GOV-ina* or *Herze-gov-EE-na*? The authorities were divided, and when I finally got to Sarajevo in 1996 and asked around, I was told: 'Oh, we use both pronunciations.'

Another problem was the name of the former Argentine foreign minister Guido di Tella, who had been in office during the Falklands War. In Spanish, his first name would be pronounced *Geedo*, but he was of Italian origin (hence the *di* in his family name, rather than the Spanish *de*), and in Italian, his first name would be pronounced *Gweedo*. Did it really matter? I thought it did, on the grounds that the one thing everyone cares about is their own name.

But it was not only names that presented linguistic challenges. The BBC's reluctance to use the word *terrorists* has been widely discussed (and criticised) over many years, although I never had any difficulty in finding acceptable alternatives that carried less of a political value judgement and were equally accurate: *killers, attackers, gunmen, bombers, kidnappers* all worked perfectly well. But I did try to avoid the word *militants* that was favoured by some of my colleagues, as I felt it usually failed to describe adequately the nature of their activities.

Words often carry value judgements even when they are entirely accurate. In Zimbabwe, for example, a spate of attacks by men described as *war veterans* (in itself, a troublesome description, as we had reason to doubt its accuracy in some cases) resulted in the deaths of several farmers. The victims were of European origin, so they were routinely described as *white farmers*, a description that carried the clear implication that they were killed on racial grounds. Some of them, however, were also opposition activists, so it would have been perfectly legitimate to suggest that they were targeted for political, not racial, reasons. We had no way of knowing, but had to make a choice anyway.

The biggest audiences for the World Service's English-language programmes are in Nigeria and the United States. In Nigeria, the listeners
are mainly young, well-educated, and upwardly mobile; in the US
they tend to be middle-aged and liberal. Putting together a news programme that interests, intrigues and informs both those very different
groups of people is no easy task. But there can be no doubting the
programme's popularity, and in both the US and Nigeria I have been
treated like a visiting film star when introduced to people as 'Robin
Lustig of the BBC's *Newshour* programme.' That is why, when I signed
off from *Newshour* for the last time before I left the BBC, I specifically
mentioned listeners in both Lagos and Louisville, Kentucky, two cities
where I had met some of the most devoted BBC loyalists anywhere on
the planet. (I included Lahore simply because it was another city with
a name beginning with L. I have never actually been there.)

The people who work at the World Service are an eclectic bunch
from a bewildering variety of ethnic, national and cultural backgrounds. Many began their BBC careers in one of the language services and then moved across to English programmes to allow us to
make use of their specialist knowledge. On the day of the catastrophic
earthquake in Sichuan, China in 2008, when an estimated 80,000
people were killed, the editor of that day's edition of *Newshour* was
himself Chinese, and was immediately on the phone to his sister, who
lived in the affected region. Long before the news agencies had begun
to reflect the scale of the tragedy, we knew that it was huge.

When Russia and Georgia went to war just a few months later, I
was able to interview the 'foreign minister' of one of the breakaway
Georgian republics with a Russian-born BBC producer at my side
providing a simultaneous translation. So if *Newshour* was able to
report the world to the world from a truly global perspective, which
it was, it was in large part because its producers are themselves global
citizens. I probably learned more about the ways of the world presenting *Newshour* than I would have done studying for any number of
Masters' degrees in international relations.

When I started at the World Service in 1989, it still had the feel of an outpost of empire, devoted to the old ways that had served it so well in the past and suspicious of new-fangled ideas emanating from Broadcasting House less than two miles away across central London. When John Birt was appointed director-general in 1992, he set about bringing the hold-outs of Bush House into line; senior managers were shunted out of the way and replaced with appointees who – shock, horror – had no World Service background. World Service lifers had a deeply ingrained belief in their own superiority: they were the BBC gold standard, holding fast to a tradition of excellence that had, sadly, been abandoned by their colleagues elsewhere. Or so they said. Sometimes they were right; more often, I discovered that they were as fallible and as human as everyone else.

Once, after yet another Birtist diktat had been issued from Broadcasting House, I asked a senior World Service executive what it all meant. 'I haven't a clue,' he replied. 'I feel like a minor provincial official in China at the height of the cultural revolution. I know there is great upheaval far away but I have no idea what it means for me.'

When Mark Byford arrived as the new head of the World Service in 1998, you could hear the sharp intake of breath from the denizens of Bush House. Not only had he never worked at the World Service, his previous job – could you believe it? – had been as director of the BBC's regional broadcasting. He might possibly know where Leeds was (after all, he was a Yorkshireman), but he had almost certainly never been to Lagos or Lahore.

I was, and am, a Byford fan, despite the ordure that was heaped upon him when he left the BBC in 2010 with a reported pay-off of close to a million pounds. He was one of the very few senior BBC executives who retained the curiosity and excitement about events that had propelled them into the business in the first place. When a major news story was breaking, he would turn up in the studio control room to encourage the production team. On one such occasion, after he had bounced in (he is a big man, with a personality to match) while the team were frantically trying to keep up with events, a harassed producer responded to his words of encouragement with a simple, if ill-advised, inquiry.

'Who the fuck are you, anyway?'

I made a similar mistake when my phone rang moments before I was due in the studio at the start of a marathon four-hour programme in the wake of the 9/11 attacks.

'I just wanted to wish you luck, Robin.'

'Sorry, who is this?'

'It's Mark.'

'Mark who?'

After he fell on his sword following the corporate nervous break-down caused by the death of the government biological warfare expert David Kelly and allegations that the BBC had erroneously reported that the government had 'sexed up' a dossier on Iraq's weapons cap-ability, Byford became a byword for all that had gone wrong at the BBC. He had become acting director-general when Greg Dyke quit, and his first appearance in the media spotlight had been a disaster. After his departure, however, it became clear that in his role as the BBC's head of journalism he had been an invaluable trouble-shooter – and there were many BBC journalists who could be heard mutter-ing 'If only Byford was still here' as the corporation succumbed to another nervous collapse in the wake of the Jimmy Savile row and an erroneous report that a senior Conservative, who was later identified elsewhere as Lord McAlpine, had been the subject of allegations of child sex abuse.

Radio is a uniquely intimate medium, and listeners, wherever they are, quickly come to believe that their favourite broadcasters are talk-ing only to them. World Service listeners, especially in some of the world's poorest countries, regard the BBC as their lifeline, a window onto a world they can only imagine, bringing them news and inform-ation about places they can only dream of visiting. Many listeners teach themselves English by listening to the BBC, among them the award-winning, Iraqi-born journalist Ghaith Abdul-Ahad, who, when I presented him with the Orwell Prize for journalism in 2014, said he was especially pleased to receive it from me, as I had taught him English while he was growing up in Baghdad.

During the mid-1990s, *Newshour* had an editor, Nic Newman, who seemed to be obsessed with something called the 'information superhighway'. It was going to change the world, apparently, and he commissioned report after report to explain the potential of this new medium of communication to our global audience. I was deeply sceptical (I probably would have doubted the usefulness of the wheel if I had been around at the time of its invention), but Nic was insistent that what we now call the World Wide Web was definitely worth our attention.

Inevitably, there came a time when he instructed me to ask our listeners to send us something called an email. We received a response within moments of me reading out *Newshour*'s new and exciting email address; it was from Kazakhstan, and I was duly persuaded. Life was never the same again.

Journalism had traditionally consisted of one group of people, journalists, telling another group of people, the listeners, viewers or readers, what they had found out. The digital revolution transformed this one-way communications channel into a two-way street and, for the first time, listeners to the BBC World Service were able to contribute in real time to the network's output, adding their comments, reactions and knowledge to what we were pumping out from Bush House.

(We had always received letters from listeners, but they tended mainly to be from Nigerian 'students' begging for help with paying their school fees. I remember one in particular that came from a 'schoolgirl' who enclosed a topless photograph of herself. I suspect some of the letters were genuine, but it was impossible to distinguish the true from the false, so I always sent a polite reply but no money.)

Emails were one way for listeners to communicate with us while we were still on air ('... and we've just received this email from Jonathan in Nairobi...') but the real revolution came with the launch of Facebook in 2004. Thousands of mainly young listeners sent in comments and information via the BBC's Facebook pages, closing the gap between them and us yet further. For the World Service, it was

another revolution: we could use Facebook to trail ahead to forthcoming programmes and publish photographs of locations from which we
were broadcasting and even photographs of the presenters.

Amina (not her real name) was a young student in Baghdad. She
had grown up under Saddam Hussein, lived through the US-led
invasion of 2003 and was now trying to complete her studies while
her country fell apart. For her, Facebook was truly a window on the
world, a way to find new friends outside Iraq and get to know the
people behind the voices she listened to endlessly on the BBC.

Like my colleagues, I replied to her Facebook messages, and after a
while we started interviewing her on air. She spoke faultless English,
was unusually articulate and gave our listeners an invaluable insight
into what it was like to be a young Iraqi living in fear in the turmoil
of post-Saddam Iraq. When the World Service celebrated its eightieth
anniversary in 2012, we invited Amina to come to London to participate in some of the special programmes that were being planned to
mark the occasion.

She had never been out of Iraq and had never travelled on a bus
or a train, let alone been on an international flight. She accepted our
invitation ('I am scared, worried and excited'), but asked if she could
stay at my home while she was in London instead of in a hotel. (My
then 26-year-old daughter Hannah was almost exactly the same age as
she was.) Of course, I said yes.

Amina was a hijab-wearing Shia, immensely proud of both her
religion and her country. Travelling abroad as an unaccompanied,
unmarried young female was hugely problematic, but she was determined to do it. Even getting an Iraqi passport was a major challenge and
just days before she was due to fly to London, she sent me one last
request: could I find out which direction Mecca was from our home,
so that she could pray while she was with us?

With the help of an iPhone app, I was able to meet her request,
and we were even able to provide a prayer rug that I had brought back
from one of my many forays in the Middle East. I drew an arrow on
a Post-it note and stuck it to the rug, pointing in the right direction.
On the day of her flight, a BBC driver took Amina from her home

to Baghdad airport – it was the first time in her life that she had seen it – and we sent a London-based Egyptian female journalist to meet her in Cairo, where she would have to change planes, and escort her to London and through UK immigration.

It all worked, and Ruth and I were at Heathrow to greet her on her arrival. She stayed with us for a week, was interviewed endlessly on the BBC, got to know London's buses and Tubes (they terrified her) and took a boat ride down the Thames. The highlight, however, was a visit to the Emirates stadium in north London, to see her beloved Arsenal play Tottenham Hotspur. (Arsenal won 5–2.)

The BBC World Service must have changed millions of lives over the years; few, I suspect, were changed as much as Amina's.

As the World Service woke up to the new opportunities offered by the digital revolution, Nic Newman decided to capitalise on the possibilities by developing a new interactive programme that would combine listeners' phone calls with their emails. It would be produced not by the World Service but by the BBC's online team and would be transmitted both on the World Service and online in video. I was its first presenter, and soon it was on BBC World TV as well.

The programme started life as *Newstalk*, was then rebranded as *Talking Point* and ended up as *Have Your Say*. For a while, it competed for airtime with another World Service programme called *World Have Your Say*, which was virtually indistinguishable in both title and content and had been developed as a result of some ludicrous inter-BBC rivalries that ended with *Have Your Say* being killed off. I had bowed out by the time the programme was put out of its misery, but it had for a while been genuinely innovative ('distinctive' in the current jargon) and I was proud to have been a part of it.

Talking Point was the BBC's bastard child. Because it was produced by the online team, there was a deliberate decision to make the point that emails and live online streaming were at the heart of what it was offering, and, despite the enthusiastic support of the World Service's boss, Mark Byford, the programme came to be regarded as an unwelcome cuckoo in the Bush House nest. But it deserves its place in the BBC history books for how it enabled World Service listeners to talk directly to their own leaders and to some of the world's most influential policy-makers and thinkers, in a way that had previously been impossible.

Under the leadership of Vicky Taylor, we netted an impressive bag of guests over the years, including several Presidents – among them Thabo Mbeki of South Africa, Olusegun Obasanjo of Nigeria, Pervez Musharraf of Pakistan, and Hugo Chávez of Venezuela – and such other luminaries as Tony Blair, Kofi Annan and Nelson Mandela. (I was especially impressed when, in 2003, we managed to book the actress and Aids campaigner Gillian Anderson, who gave me a kiss at the end of the programme.)

Important guests – 'big beasts' as we called them – required careful handling. Or, to be strictly accurate, their flunkeys required careful handling. In general, the big beasts themselves were perfectly reasonable, even human, and once they were in the studio, they did everything we asked of them.

The first of our presidential guests was Thabo Mbeki, who was in London on a state visit. We were broadcasting at the time from an ancient studio in a Bush House basement, with two tiny video cameras on flimsy tripods to transmit pictures to the website and a rudimentary backdrop to make it look just a little bit like a television studio. Given that both Mbeki and I were wearing headphones, it ended up looking like a radio studio pretending to be a TV studio, which, after all, is exactly what it was.

Mr Mbeki is a small man, and at first I failed to notice that he had arrived in the studio. All around him was a phalanx of much larger security people, his and the BBC's, and a ridiculous number of flunkeys and protocol people. Fortunately, I eventually spotted him in the middle of the scrum. 'Mr President,' I said as convincingly as I could. 'Welcome to Bush House.' Like me, he had been a student at Sussex University, so I was able to break the ice by making inconsequential small talk about the joys of the Sussex countryside.

Things were a lot less straightforward when we tried to pin down Hugo Chávez. He was on a European tour – but not stopping off in London – so there were several weeks of half-fixed, constantly changing appointments in different European capitals. 'The President may be able to do the interview on Monday in Rome, or perhaps it'll have to be Tuesday in Berlin.' We finally caught up with him on Wednesday in Paris. An early-morning Eurostar to the French capital, a taxi to his hotel and then some hasty rigging of a makeshift studio in one of his suites.

We were all ready to go when the President's security people ordered us out and told us to wait in an adjoining room while they went through all our equipment, including the earpieces, to check for hidden explosives. I had been warned that his regular TV show *Aló Presidente*, which aired every Sunday, frequently lasted six hours, and that at a press conference, he had once taken an hour to answer a single question. Somehow I was going to have find a way to shut him up and, as interrupting heads of state is not generally regarded as good manners, I decided to be frank with him.

'Mr President, I know you sometimes like to give very full answers to interviewers' questions,' I said. 'But we have had more than 3,000 questions sent in by our listeners and our programme lasts only one hour.'

'Three thousand?' he smiled. 'I don't know if we'll manage 3,000. Let's go for 2,500.' He did pretty well; we probably managed fifteen.

In the Nigerian capital, Abuja, where we were due to meet President Obasanjo, one of the very few political leaders who have ruled both as a military dictator and then, twenty years later, as a democratically elected President, we were kept in suspense until the very last minute. He was chairing an important meeting, we were told, but he would break off to meet us and then return to matters of state as soon as we were finished.

I was not confident.

But he kept his promise and, exactly at the agreed time, he breezed into the room where we were waiting, resplendent in flowing white robes and raring to go. The callers were coming in thick and fast

– Nigerians are the New Yorkers of Africa, and they love talking – when I heard the frantic voice of our sound engineer in my earpiece.

'His mic has slipped down inside his robes. You're going to have to do something.'

Do something? Do what? 'Excuse me, Mr President, may I just slip my hand inside your robes to retrieve your microphone?'

But fortune smiled on me. Before I had worked out how to resolve the crisis, the President resolved it for me. Without saying a word, he retrieved the mic himself and clipped it back in its proper place with a smile. I have felt a special affection for him ever since.

Interviewing foreign heads of state is not quite the same as interviewing other political figures. In their own country, they are regarded as a symbol of nationhood, to be treated with the sort of deference and respect that we Brits reserve for the Queen, who, let us not forget, has never consented to be interviewed by anyone, foreign or otherwise. On the other hand, coming from outside, and with a flight back to London already booked, the foreign interviewer is probably able to adopt a slightly tougher approach than a domestic broadcaster would feel comfortable with.

No matter how nervous I was, and no matter how fluttery the butterflies in my innards, I always tried to make it clear, by tone and body language, that interviewees, however grand they were, had come on to my territory and would have to play by our rules. 'This is a BBC programme, I am a BBC broadcaster, and you have agreed to do this. So you are going to do it on our terms.' I would constantly remind myself that the President was just an ordinary human being, acting the part of being a President, just as I was another ordinary human being, pretending to be a broadcaster.

> All the world's a stage,
> And all the men and women merely players;
> They have their exits and their entrances,
> And one man in his time plays many parts…[112]

Being a news broadcaster differs in one highly significant respect from being a print journalist. Nine-tenths of the job is the same, but the remaining one-tenth entails being an actor, pretending to be in control, pretending to know what you are talking about, pretending never to be in a blind panic. The way broadcasters phrase their questions is quite different, as is the tone in which they are delivered.

Interviewee: 'Everyone knows that science has proved that the earth is flat.'

Newspaper reporter, politely: 'Is that really true?'

The broadcaster's response is more likely to be:

Broadcaster, disbelievingly: 'That's simply not true, is it?'

A broadcast interview is more than just a means of conveying information: it is a form of drama, constructed in the same way as a play, complete with changes of pace and texture. The overriding fear of any broadcaster is that they are boring. The aim is to keep the listener listening and the viewer viewing, to stop them hitting the off button, or changing channels, leaving the room or falling asleep.

(My favourite compliment, which I always tried to take in the spirit in which I hoped it was intended, was: 'Oh, you do *The World Tonight*? I usually go to sleep listening to you…')

In 2011, I acted the part of myself in an improvised radio play that carefully aped the sound and structure of a Radio 4 news programme.[113] It bore some resemblance to the 1938 American radio broadcast *War of the Worlds*, with me channelling Orson Welles and intoning, 'We interrupt this broadcast to bring you the following news flash…' One of my colleagues was so startled that she sent me a text message: 'God, you sound convincing. So are you acting on *The World Tonight*?'

I replied: 'Yup, every night. In real life, I'm a shy librarian who hates the sound of his own voice.'

Talking Point was nothing if not ambitious. We even managed to record a programme in China, not with live telephone callers, admittedly, but with emailed questions and a studio audience made up of students at Tsinghua University in Beijing. No one told us that there were any subjects that we would not be allowed to discuss, so we included an email question from Taiwan and another one that raised the issue of corruption ahead of the 2008 Beijing Olympics. Our panel of guests were happy enough to respond, but when I watched the programme being transmitted on BBC World TV the following day, the screen suddenly went blank when those two questions were raised.

Our biggest failure was in Washington. We knew there was no chance that President Bush would ever agree to do a live global phone-in show, but we did try hard to persuade his Secretary of State, Colin Powell.

'Send us some tapes and we'll take a look,' his office said. A few weeks later came their response.

'We've watched the tapes. There's no way we're going to do this.'

We did not talk only to politicians: the mountaineer Chris Bonington, for example, was our guest on the fiftieth anniversary of the first ascent of Mount Everest, and memorably explained why he never claimed to have 'conquered' a mountain.

> The way you climb [a] mountain, the way you survive on that mountain, is actually to understand it – to actually work with it, to actually become part of it … you accept what the mountain is, you understand what the mountain is: maybe it lets you climb it, maybe it doesn't.[114]

The best moments in any phone-in programme come when a listener sparks an unexpected response from a guest. In July 1999, on the thirtieth anniversary of the first moon landing, a sixteen-year-old listener in Poland asked our guest Buzz Aldrin – the second man to walk on the moon, after Neil Armstrong – if it was true that his father had tried to persuade the mission planners that Aldrin should go first. Aldrin gave a careful diplomatic reply, but I detected a continuing sense of grievance, even three decades later, when he said: 'In retrospect, I believe the correct decision was made.'

'You said "In retrospect…" Does that suggest that at the time you thought differently?'

It was then that he snapped.

'Jeez, you guys won't leave that alone, will you?'[115]

Talking Point was probably the most stressful programme with which I was ever involved. International phone lines were of variable quality – the ones from the US were particularly bad – and some of

our callers had only a rudimentary grasp of English. On one early programme, there were virtually no callers at all, and I was left treading
water with an increasingly desperate studio guest for a full hour.

The programme was also my introduction to the terrors of live TV,
which meant that I had to learn how to stop the panic showing in my
eyes when everything was collapsing all around me. I never really took
to it (apart from everything else, I hated wearing makeup), especially
after being told that if I was serious about building up my career in
television, I would have to shave off my beard. I wasn't, and I didn't.
Perhaps some people really do have faces for radio.

On one occasion, the programme's guest was to be Rodrigo de Rato,
a former Spanish economics minister, later arrested for alleged fraud,
embezzlement and money laundering, who had just been appointed
managing director of the International Monetary Fund. He was due
to join us from a studio somewhere in South America but had become
seriously exasperated by technical difficulties before we went on air.
He then took exception to something I said in my introduction, and
– to my horror – could be seen on the studio monitor removing his
earpiece and getting up from his chair to leave. The prospect of having
to fill the next hour with no studio guest, fielding questions about
the IMF, never a subject on which I would claim to be an expert,
was the stuff of nightmares. He left, and I soldiered on. No wonder
broadcasters wake up sweating in the night.

Interviewing Tony Blair in Downing Street was another stressful
experience, although at least he was good enough not to walk out
while we struggled to make the technology work. A producer was still
crawling about under the table swearing at cables when the Prime
Minister was ushered in to the Pillared Room at No. 10, the same
room in which John Logie Baird had demonstrated a miraculous new
piece of technology called a television set to Ramsay MacDonald in
1930.

I had interviewed Blair before, but on this occasion I was able to
watch him close up as he fielded calls from around the world about
every topic under the sun. The main focus (this was in December
2002) was on the imminent invasion of Iraq, which everyone knew

was coming. Re-reading the transcript, I was struck by one line in particular. Asked by a listener in Oman what would happen if UN weapons inspectors found no weapons of mass destruction in Iraq, the Prime Minister said: 'It's been made clear throughout: the purpose is to make sure that any weapons of mass destruction Iraq has, they are disarmed of. If they find no weapons, that is another matter.'[116]

As we now know, history tells a different story.

In the run-up to the Iraq War, I decided to keep a diary, so that I would be able to look back and recall what I thought of it at the time, rather than recreate my views later on with the benefit of hindsight. The first entry is dated 19 February 2003, a month before the start of the invasion:

> I have found a relatively comfortable fence, and I am sitting on it. If I were to fall off, it would probably be on the anti-war side, for the simple reason that if the arguments are as finely balanced as I think they are, I'd rather we didn't kill people. Tony Blair thinks otherwise ... the latest opinion poll shows that although a narrow majority of voters (51%) are now 'anti-war', more than 70% of Labour voters still class themselves as satisfied with the way Blair is doing his job.

On the eve of the war, however, I recorded my deepening misgivings:

> I've finally realised why I'm so unhappy about this war. While I do want to see Saddam Hussein defeated, and Iraq 'liberated', I deeply distrust the motives of this US administration ... I have concluded that the Bush people do have a hidden agenda, and that they do intend to extend their influence and power into areas where until now they have been powerless ... What this means is that the war itself isn't the story; what really matters is what happens next. In Iraq itself, we shall see either a US puppet regime installed, to the fury of the Iraqis themselves, or some kind of UN administration...

The war lasted just twenty-six days. I had virtually taken up residence in Bush House, broadcasting hour after hour of war-related news, and then jumping on the Central Line to get to TV Centre in time for *The World Tonight*. I found it exhausting and depressing. Often, I would talk to correspondents who were travelling with the advancing US and British armies, and often, I realised that they knew less than we did in London. The interviews did not necessarily add a great deal to our understanding of what was happening.

> Correspondent 1: I asked a senior officer for the latest developments, and he started quoting reports that he had heard on the BBC World Service…
>
> Correspondent 2: You know, reporting the war from the front line is like looking through a letter box. I can tell you what is happening right in front of my eyes, but I have no idea what's going on beyond my field of vision.

And then it was over.

> Wednesday morning for me started at Bush House, with word from our colleagues in Baghdad that their government minders had all vanished and there were US tanks in the centre of town. By lunchtime, when I was on air, a crowd of young Iraqis were trying to topple a statue of Saddam, conveniently located just outside the journalists' hotel … I feel no spirit of celebration at all – I think Iraq is going to be a violent, messy, angry place for a long time … I'll probably be talking about Iraq until I retire.

A few days later, I presented an hour-long programme live on both Radio 4 and the World Service. It involved a panel of six of the BBC's finest correspondents discussing 'The World after the War' – Peter Day, Frank Gardner, Allan Little, James Robbins, Stephen Sackur, and Justin Webb. (You will have noticed that there was not a single woman among them.)

When I asked our panel of expert BBC correspondents: 'Is the world now safer or more dangerous than it was?', most said 'safer'. That surprised me, because I don't agree. I see plenty of potential for serious unrest in Iraq over the coming months, and it could well spill over into both Iran and Turkey, possibly Syria and Saudi Arabia as well.

My verdict on Blair, for what it is worth, is that he made a judgement, heavily influenced by his unshakeable conviction that he could make the world a better place by removing a dangerous, evil dictator, and he got it wrong. He ignored the warnings from those who knew better than he did what the risks were, and he pushed the available intelligence beyond what was legitimate. In my view, he should have resigned after the UN weapons inspectors reported that there had been no weapons of mass destruction and apologised to the nation and to the families of all the servicemen and women who were killed and injured in the conflict.

I got my own chance to visit post-Saddam Iraq a year after the invasion, to mark the first anniversary of his overthrow. I drove in with a BBC team from Jordan, across the desert and through Ramadi and Fallujah. We had no armed escort, although we did have an ex-military 'security adviser' with us, whose job was to spot trouble before it spotted us. On the long drive to Baghdad, we were advised to place our flak jackets against the doors of our vehicle, where there was a chance that they might stop any bullets that came flying in our direction. It was not exactly state-of-the-art protection, but it was better than nothing.

The BBC, like many other media organisations, had rented a house to act as its base of operations in Baghdad – the street was closed off by security barriers at each end and the house itself was protected by piles of sandbags on each side of the front door. We slept in a second house on the other side of the street, similarly sandbagged, but with the added amenity of a pool table on the ground floor. The street was lined with what had once been handsome villas, some of them still displaying a six-pointed star of David, indicating that they had at one time been the homes of some of the fifty thousand Jews, a quarter of the city's population, who had been living in Baghdad until the great exodus of the early 1950s.

Before leaving London, I had been sent to the BBC health department for a check-up and briefing. 'Ah, a grown-up,' said the doctor when he saw me. (Most BBC volunteers for trips to war zones tended to be at least a couple of decades younger than I was.) 'You've done this sort of thing before, I suppose?' I told him I was a veteran of the civil war in Lebanon.

'Good,' he replied. 'So you'll know what are the two biggest dangers you're likely to face: a fully armed US soldier and an oncoming lorry.' With my colleague Lucy Williamson, then a young World Service producer, now one of the BBC's star foreign correspondents, I encountered plenty of US soldiers and plenty of oncoming lorries. But we emerged unscathed, and we summed up our conclusions at the end of a week in the Iraqi capital in three short sentences: the people whom we met were pleased that Saddam Hussein had gone; they hoped the Americans would now go as well; and they were terrified about the future. Unlike most conclusions arrived at on the basis of an assignment lasting just a few days, those seem to have stood the test of time.

Steve, our security adviser, did his job well. Every time we got into a car, he checked underneath it to make sure no one had stuck a bomb to its underside, and every time we went to interview someone, he stayed outside with the car for the same reason. On one occasion, when I was interviewing a crowd of unemployed construction workers on a street corner, he suddenly grabbed me by the shoulder and pulled me away.

'Enough,' he said. 'It's time to go.' As we drove off, he explained why: the crowd had grown so large that he was worried he would no longer be able to extricate me if trouble started. The rule of thumb was never to stay in one place for more than twenty minutes, because that was presumed to be how long it would take for news of our presence to reach people who might wish to do us harm. I never discovered who had made that calculation, or how.

Broadcasting live simultaneously on Radio 4 and the World Service is a surprisingly complex undertaking. On Radio 4, programmes that are billed as starting at the top of the hour usually start after a two-minute news summary. On the World Service, on the other hand, they start precisely on the hour, with a sixty-second introduction, followed by a five-minute news bulletin, and then the programme picks up again at six minutes past the hour. So the script for a programme that in theory starts at 8 p.m. on both networks might look something like this.

> 20:00.00: (World Service) Welcome to The Best Programme Ever Broadcast. Over the next hour…
> 20:00.58: stop talking
> 20:02.00: (Radio 4) This is The Best Programme Ever Broadcast. With me in the studio…
> 20:06.02: (Radio 4 and World Service) Just a reminder, you're listening to…

The trick, of course, is to write the script so that no one listening, on either Radio 4 or the World Service, has any idea of the mental and linguistic gymnastics involved. And if all that is not complicated enough, something similar happens at half past the hour, when the World Service pauses for a two-minute news summary but Radio 4 happily carries on. A presenter's life in the studio becomes dominated by the clock; every second matters, especially at the World Service, where re-broadcasters around the world install automated systems to pick up and drop out of World Service programmes at fixed times. If you miss a 'hard post', even by a single second, you will have some very disgruntled customers to deal with.

But clocks, like presenters, are fallible. A typical BBC radio studio has at least three clocks: a digital and an analogue display on the wall opposite the presenter, and another one in the corner of the computer screen on the studio desk. When I started at the BBC, in the pre-computer age, Studio 4A in Broadcasting House also had a clock screwed to the desk. It showed a traditional analogue clock face, with an electronic words display underneath it. When the big hand on the clock pointed to the eleven and the little hand pointed to the ten, the words spelt out 'It is five to ten.' Ten seconds later, they changed to 'It is just after five to ten.' And then 'It is four and a half minutes to ten.'

And still some presenters (Jack de Manio on the *Today* programme was notorious) managed to get it wrong.

More than once, I was confronted with clocks that were in disagreement with each other, and on one particularly terrifying occasion, the wall clocks started going backwards. Trying to remain calm as time appeared to be reversing itself required great mental fortitude.

No wonder I always preferred being out of a studio, reporting from somewhere dusty and far away from the tyranny of the clock. In 2005 and 2006, I made two five-part documentary series for the World Service: the first, *Looking for Democracy*, took me to the US, Cambodia, Uganda, Bahrain and Ukraine to examine different types of democratic government and try to define the essential ingredients of democratic rule. A Ugandan MP put it neatly when I interviewed him sitting on the green leather benches of the Parliament chamber in Kampala: 'An election alone does not make a successful democracy, in the same way as a wedding alone does not make a successful marriage.'

The second series, *Generation Next*, was a look at the experience of growing up into adulthood in different societies around the world. I was instructed to write the programmes highlighting the fact that I was the father of two adult children and had observed the growing-up process at close quarters. In the final episode, my daughter Hannah, then aged twenty-one, was one of my studio guests, and towards the end, I asked her to describe what kind of a world she thought her generation would run. She tried to reassure me.

'Don't worry about it, Dad. We'll look after you.'

For a period in the 1990s and early 2000s, I became the World Service's Man for Big Occasions. From the handover of Hong Kong in 1997 to the first anniversary of the 9/11 attacks and several election night specials from, for example, Abuja, Harare, Jerusalem, Moscow and Tehran, I became adept at sounding as if I knew what was going on while perching precariously in a hotel room with a handheld microphone and a laptop computer balanced on my knees.

I always enjoyed reporting on elections. Whether it was in Iran or Zimbabwe, Nigeria or Pakistan, people always seemed to vote in a spirit of hope: a belief that by placing a simple mark on a ballot paper they might help to make their country a better place. To watch people waiting patiently in line outside polling stations, often in blazing heat, was always a useful reminder of the importance that people the world over attach to the basic right to choose their own government.

The funeral of King Hussein of Jordan in 1999 was particularly challenging. He was a hugely influential figure in the Middle East, one of the region's great survivors and regarded as a staunch ally in both Washington and London, where he was known among diplomats as the PLK ('plucky little king'). During his nearly fifty years on the throne, he had cultivated close relations with virtually every major world leader; among those who flew to Jordan for his state funeral were no fewer than four US Presidents (Bill Clinton, George H. W. Bush, Jimmy Carter and Gerald Ford), the Russian President Boris Yeltsin, Hafez al-Assad of Syria and Benjamin Netanyahu of Israel. My task was to act as commentator during several hours of ceremonial, somewhat hampered by the fact that there was no publicly available timetable or schedule and that I was confined to a hotel room watching the local TV coverage.

Makeshift studios for live outside broadcasts require everyone involved to be prepared to adapt to circumstances. In Amman, our sound engineer installed all the necessary technical equipment in the bathroom and spent the entire broadcast sitting on the toilet (the lid was closed). The producer, who was the only person in the team who was able to communicate directly with London, could pass on their instructions to me only by means of hastily scribbled notes: 'Two more minutes…', or 'Keep going as long as you can…'

One note in particular, scribbled while the news was being read from London, struck me as unnecessarily curt: 'Coming to you shorty.' In his haste – or so he claimed afterwards – he had omitted the letter L from the word 'shortly'.

How often, I used to wonder, do listeners ask themselves exactly how a live outside broadcast is reaching them? What would they think if they knew, for example, that I was presenting a programme from a hotel car park, in the dark, with a laptop computer balanced on the front of the car and a satellite dish on its roof? Or that reporting live for *The World Tonight* from a Commonwealth conference in Australia, I was sitting on a beach at dawn, with the ocean lapping at my feet, just so that they could enjoy hearing the sound of the sea?

In Istanbul, we went to great lengths to find a hotel from which we could broadcast while gazing out across the Bosphorus, just so that I could say – accurately – that I was at the exact point where Europe meets Asia. Did it really matter, given that it was for a radio broadcast and I could have been anywhere? I think it did.

But, despite my preference for dusty places and muddy boots, there were some occasions when a studio in London was exactly where I wanted to be. UK election nights combined drama, uncertainty and complexity; they were occasions when even the World Service became an unapologetically *British* broadcasting service – after all, if you could not get a comprehensive results and analysis service from the BBC, where else would you be able to turn? From 1997, when Labour under Tony Blair swept the Conservatives from power after eighteen years in office, until 2010, when an inconclusive result led to the formation of Britain's first peacetime coalition government since the 1930s, I anchored the World Service all-night election programmes and pretended that my name was Dimbleby. In the days before the internet and 24-hour TV news channels, I was told that every British ambassador in the world would be listening, anxious to discover who their new bosses would be.

I had two pet hates as a BBC news presenter: summit meetings and Budgets. For much of the 1990s, I would travel, once every six months, to a different European city to twiddle my thumbs while EU leaders debated and decided the future of Europe. This was the time when they came up with the bright idea of introducing a single European currency, which I was convinced would never happen. I was wrong about that, although I was right to be deeply sceptical that it would ever work.

Under John Major, the UK loudly championed the cause of the

central and eastern European countries who were clamouring to join: the Foreign Office view was that a 'wider' EU could not also be a 'deeper' EU – and being in a union that had more members was infinitely preferable to being part of a project committed to ever closer political cooperation. I do not recall anyone asking what the ramifications might be for the commitment to freedom of movement throughout the EU, so the whole thing became another perfect example of the Law of Unintended Consequences in action.

Reporting from an EU summit meant hanging around in media centres, waiting for someone – anyone – to emerge from the meetings with a hint or a whisper that might, with difficulty, be fashioned into a news story. As a radio reporter, I had to find people who were prepared to talk into a microphone, and I remember far too many occasions when an interview with, for example, the deputy defence minister of Slovenia could be counted as a major achievement. Far too often, we reporters ended up interviewing each other, mainly because we would think of nothing better to do and could find no one else to talk to.

The media centres were sometimes many miles from where the summits themselves were taking place. And they were not always as fit for purpose as we might have liked. In Berlin – yes, Berlin! – we suffered a major power failure, which knocked out all our computers and all the lights. In the darkness, all that could be heard was the tap-tap-tapping of a manual typewriter, the property of an elderly, and very smug, German correspondent.

In Bucharest, at a NATO summit held in Ceauşescu's preposterous Palace of Parliament, which is said to be the third largest building in the world, I was reduced to scurrying along endless corridors searching desperately for someone to interview. Imagine my delight when I knocked on a door and found the Foreign Secretary, David Miliband, inside. He took pity on *The World Tonight* and agreed to talk.

But nothing compared to the nightmare that was the UN climate summit in Copenhagen in 2009. With the representatives of 192 governments gathered in one place for a conference that had been inadequately prepared, in a conference centre that was woefully ill-suited to the task, the risk of failure was high. Delegates and journalists found themselves standing in line for a whole day to be issued with their accreditation – China complained that one of its ministers had been refused entry three times in as many days.

More importantly, the conference failed to agree on a legally binding strategy to deal with climate change. I summed it up at the time as 'too many people, not enough fresh air, and a vast amount of energy expended to produce not very much'. It definitely did not live up to its advance billing as 'the most important gathering in the history of humankind' which is what the then Environment Secretary Hilary Benn had rashly called it. It was a shambles, and trying to report sensibly on a shambles is no fun at all.

Over the years, I developed a deep loathing for news stories that could be characterised as 'men in suits talking to other men in suits'. They rarely produced news that was of genuine importance and too often involved far too many reporters kicking their heels and creating stories out of thin air. Dozens of reporters gathered in the same place at the same time have a tendency to produce something that can closely resemble what bears produce when left on their own in woods.

I developed a similar dislike for Budgets, those annual parliamentary rituals in which Chancellors of the Exchequer drone on endlessly about how well they are running the UK economy and try to disguise the reality, which is that they have no idea at all what they are doing. I have never understood why British governments cannot simply announce their spending plans – and any changes to taxation – in the same way as they announce any other policy, without all the fake excitement that is generated on Budget Day.

Quite apart from any other considerations, it is an unfortunate fact that most of what the analysts say on the day of the Budget turns out to be either wrong or irrelevant within a matter of days, so we could all be spared a huge amount of unnecessary guff if we simply reported what was in the Budget and waited to see what happened.

I admit, however, that part of my antipathy towards Budgets stems from my irrational dislike of any story that has big numbers in it. Show me anything that contains the word 'billion' and I will rapidly look for something else to read. So when the global banking system teetered on the edge of meltdown in 2007–08, I had to dig deep into my reserves of professionalism to report, night after night, on stuff that I had great difficulty understanding.

I spent ridiculous amounts of time trying to work out what collateralised debt obligations and credit default swaps were, and then had to practise saying 'quantitative easing' without sounding as if I had developed a stutter. Not for the first time, I realised that I really should have known much more than I did about what makes the world go round and, not for the first time, I felt immensely fortunate that I was being paid to get my head around a story that everyone else was struggling to understand in their own time.

The BBC excels at many things: world-class TV drama, innovative entertainment formats (*Doctor Who*, *Top Gear*, *Strictly Come Dancing*, *Bake Off*), wildlife documentaries and much, much more. Its programmes – *Test Match Special*, *BBC Proms*, *The Archers*, *EastEnders* – enrich the nation in a way that no other institution can dream of. In 2012, when the think tank Chatham House commissioned a survey to find out which institutions voters thought best served the UK's national interest, the BBC came second, with just the armed forces ahead of it.[117]

But it is also in a league of its own when it comes to corporate meltdowns, and I had the great misfortune to be granted a ringside seat at far too many of these ghastly displays of managerial incompetence. All institutions get things wrong, but what the BBC wins gold medals in is getting things wrong when it gets something wrong.

Exhibit One: the Hutton Report into the death of the government scientist David Kelly in 2003 after he was named as the source for a BBC report that said the government had 'sexed up' a dossier about Iraq's weapons of mass destruction. Lord Hutton was an appeal court judge and former Lord Chief Justice of Northern Ireland who had been appointed to investigate the circumstances surrounding Dr Kelly's apparent suicide – and he came down spectacularly hard on the BBC while largely exonerating the government.

At seven minutes past six on the morning of 29 May 2003, the *Today* programme had reported that the government was facing more questions over its claims about Iraq's weapons of mass destruction, including a claim in what became known as its 'dodgy dossier' that some of those weapons could be ready for use within forty-five minutes of a deployment order being given. The programme's defence correspondent Andrew Gilligan reported in a live interview with John Humphrys:

> What we've been told by one of the senior officials in charge of drawing up that dossier was that, actually the government probably erm, knew that that forty-five minute figure was wrong, even before it decided to put it in. What this person says, is that a week before the publication date of the dossier, it was actually rather erm, a bland production. It didn't, the, the draft prepared for Mr Blair by the Intelligence Agencies actually didn't say very much more than was public knowledge already and erm, Downing Street, our source says ordered a week before publication, ordered it to be sexed up, to be made more exciting and ordered more facts to be er, to be discovered.[118]

It was, as the programme's editor, Kevin Marsh, later put it in an internal BBC email, a 'good piece of investigative journalism marred by flawed reporting'. The suggestion that the government had published a claim that it 'knew' to be wrong was clearly incendiary, but when Tony Blair's press secretary, Alastair Campbell, complained with the full force of the fury of which he was capable, the BBC did exactly what it should not have done: it robustly defended what Gilligan had said without properly examining whether it really could justify the exact words that he had used.

This is not the place to reopen all the old wounds, but the row that ended with the resignations of both the BBC's chairman, Gavyn Davies, and its director-general, Greg Dyke, as well as the departure of Andrew Gilligan, all within three days of the publication of the Hutton Report, was a dismal time to be a BBC journalist. On the day that the report was published, the World Service decided in its wisdom to broadcast Lord Hutton's announcement of his findings live and in full. I was asked to present the special coverage, and when Hutton had finished what amounted to a full-scale attack on the BBC's editorial standards and practices, I said simply, and with feeling: 'Well, that's very good news for the government, and very bad news for the BBC.'

My conclusion, more than a decade later? When two alpha male elephants (in this case, Alastair Campbell and Greg Dyke) clash in the jungle, a lot of lesser creatures get hurt. Both men were spoiling for a fight – Campbell believed that the BBC's journalists had been consistently hostile to Blair and his support for the US-led invasion of Iraq, and Dyke was determined to show Campbell that the BBC was not prepared to be intimidated. His mistake – and it was a serious one – was to fight the battle on the ground of Gilligan's reporting.

Exhibit Two: Sachsgate, when the actor and comedian Russell Brand and the radio and TV presenter Jonathan Ross lost their senses and broadcast on Radio 2 a series of voicemail messages that they had left for the then 78-year-old actor Andrew Sachs (best known as the Spanish waiter Manuel, in *Fawlty Towers*). On one of the messages, Ross could be heard saying: 'He [Brand] fucked your granddaughter.' Although the programme had been pre-recorded, no one who heard it ahead of transmission thought it presented any problems.

Interestingly, after it was broadcast, there were no immediate complaints. But when, a week later, the *Mail on Sunday* drew attention to what had been said, the complaints came flooding in. Russell Brand resigned, as did the much-respected head of Radio 2, Lesley Douglas, and Ross was suspended without pay for twelve weeks. The BBC went into one of its meltdowns and eventually issued an apology, calling the voicemail messages 'grossly offensive' and a 'serious breach of editorial standards'.

But it all went on much too long. The BBC's response to the furore, artificially fanned though it might have been, was far too late in coming. The Prime Minister, the Leader of the Opposition and the Culture Secretary had all had their say by the time the corporation had got its act together, once again leaving the impression that too many well-paid executives were spending too long trying to duck their responsibilities.

When the director-general, Mark Thompson, agreed to be interviewed on *The World Tonight*, I questioned him as robustly as I would have done had I not been working for him. When it was over, he smiled wanly at me across the studio desk and commented: 'You guys really enjoy this sort of thing, don't you?'

He was wrong. I hated it when the BBC fell short. But what use is a BBC interviewer who is not prepared to ask tough questions of his own bosses?

Exhibit Three: the Savile crisis. Yet again, the BBC went into meltdown after its shambolic decision-making processes proved to be utterly inadequate. There is no need to rake over the sordid details: an investigation by *Newsnight* into allegations that Jimmy Savile was a serial child abuser was halted, apparently because the programme's editor was unconvinced by the available evidence, and then, in the midst of a gruesomely public inquest into his decision, the same programme broadcast similar allegations against another public figure, only for those allegations to turn out to be totally unfounded.

It was a catalogue of ineptitude that would have shamed the most shambolic student newspaper. For an institution that likes to think of itself as the world's most respected broadcaster, it was an unparalleled disaster. What made it particularly toxic was that although *Newsnight*'s Savile investigation was axed, two tribute programmes went ahead after his death, despite misgivings about Savile's 'dark side' having been expressed in internal BBC emails. It still seems to me that the real scandal was that executives who had worked closely with Savile over many years, and who were well aware of the suspicions over his sexual behaviour, authorised the transmission of those programmes.

I find that much harder to excuse than an editorial misjudgement over the strength or otherwise of a complex journalistic investigation. No editor's judgement is infallible, and as I had worked closely with the *Newsnight* editor, Peter Rippon, during his time at the World Service, I was convinced that he had made his decision, rightly or wrongly, in good faith. In a piece that I wrote for *The Guardian* – coincidentally, just one day after my last appearance on air as a BBC presenter – I remarked: 'My former colleagues in BBC News might well feel aggrieved that they are taking the brunt of the criticism while light entertainment gets away almost unscathed.'[119]

Another director-general's head had rolled as a result of the crisis: George Entwistle, who had lasted a mere fifty-four days in the job, resigned after a devastating *Today* interview with John Humphrys. Entwistle had joined the BBC as a trainee at about the same time as I joined as a presenter; he had spent some time on *The World Tonight* in his early days and I had always liked him.

Perhaps I have a weakness for thinking the best of people – except when I am interviewing them, naturally – but after more than two decades at the BBC, I came to the conclusion that with very few exceptions, it is run by good, intelligent people with all the right instincts. Sometimes they are asked to do jobs for which they are ill-suited and sometimes they are simply in the wrong place at the wrong time. Greg Dyke was not temperamentally suited to run a major national institution, and George Entwistle was engulfed by crisis before he had had a chance to find his way around. Both men made mistakes, and they paid the price.

It does not make them villains.

CHAPTER 14

QUITE BIG IN BOSTON

Mr Lustig, even my hair is happy.
MAYA ANGELOU

IT WAS 5 NOVEMBER 2008, the morning after the election of Barack Obama as the first black President of the United States, and I was interviewing the poet and civil rights activist Maya Angelou. She was eloquent and emotional, and she did something no other of my thousands of interviewees, either before or since, had ever done.

She started to sing.

> By and by
> By and by
> I'm going to lay down this heavy load

It was one of America's best-known traditional spirituals, dating back to the days of slavery, and it sent shivers down the spine of everyone who heard it that morning. 'My reaction can be described as "thrilled",' she said. 'I am "thrilling", but in the classic sense of that word. It used to mean having a physical reaction when the whole body responds. Even my hair is happy.' One of the BBC's best-known correspondents sent me a note after the interview was broadcast: 'My wife and I stopped in our tracks and cried.'

Whenever I am asked which is my favourite country to report from, I reply that it is the United States of America. Not because of its obvious importance as a global power, but because of the openness of its people. It is a reporter's paradise, where everyone has something to say and is more than happy to say it. Even better, they can nearly always say it in English.

The scene: a golf course at the US military base at Fort Bragg, North Carolina, one of the biggest military bases in the world, with a resident population of around fifty thousand. A colleague and I approach a couple of golfers who look like army veterans and we shout across the fairway.

'Good morning, we're from the BBC.'

'The BBC? So you're Commies, huh?'

I fell in love with the US on my very first visit in 1968 and I have never tired of going back. But I am not blind to its failings, because one of the great advantages of travelling through a country as a reporter is that you get to meet people and see places that most visitors would never know even exist. Yes, we admire the White House, the Grand Canyon and the Golden Gate Bridge, just like everyone else, but we see the underbelly as well.

In Philadelphia, for example, which has a reputation as one of the most violent cities in the country, with an exceptionally high rate of gun crime, I met an African-American woman whose son had been shot dead in a petty argument over a parking space. I asked her what she would say to her son's killer if she ever had the opportunity to meet him.

'I would ask him where all that anger came from,' she replied. It struck me as a very good question, and applicable to so much more than the country's appalling number of gun crimes. (In 2015, more than 13,000 people were shot dead in the US, more than four times as many as were killed in jihadi attacks worldwide.[120])

According to figures compiled by the United Nations Office on Drugs and Crime, the murder rate in the US is four times as high per head of population as it is in the UK. That would suggest a very large number of very angry people in a society that still likes to boast of offering limitless opportunity to every citizen. One of my aims during nearly fifty years of visiting, observing and reporting from the US has been to find a way to explain the vast gulf that separates the national myth from the reality. American politicians routinely describe their country as the greatest nation on earth, but to millions of its citizens, it feels anything but. That's one of the most important reasons why, in November 2016, they elected Donald Trump as President.

My first opportunity to report from the US for the BBC came in 1993, when Bill Clinton was inaugurated as President. Like me, he was a baby boomer, born just after the Second World War – in the words of one of my American cousins: 'He likes the same kind of music we do.' On inauguration day, as I was walking along Pennsylvania Avenue, I passed the White House just as George H. W. Bush was leaving for the last time as President. As his black limousine swished by, I peered in to see if he was as moist-cheeked as Margaret Thatcher had been when she drove away from Downing Street after being ousted in 1990. As far as I could see, there were no tears.

In most movies about reporters, there comes a moment when a telephone rings early one morning, a half-asleep reporter answers it, and a voice says: 'There's a plane to Los Angeles in an hour. Make sure you're on it.' My phone rang late one Sunday night, and it was *World Tonight* editor Prue Keely's voice at the other end.

'I hope you don't mind, Robin, but I've booked you onto a flight to Washington tomorrow morning. It leaves at 7.30 from Heathrow.' Mind? I could not have been happier; it was the height of the Monica Lewinsky scandal and much of the world was engrossed in the less-than-dignified detail of who did what, with what, and to whom in the Oval Office.

The flight to Washington turned out to be a flight to New York. After we touched down, producer Shaun Waterman and I sprinted through JFK to catch a shuttle to DC, jumped in a cab and made it to the BBC bureau with about thirty minutes to spare before going on air. (We learned later that our frantic arrival at the bureau had been captured by a crew from *Newsnight* who were filming in the street outside just as we were tumbling out of our taxi.)

Our Washington colleagues had thoughtfully prepared everything we needed, including all my scripts, which left me with just one task: to sound as if I knew what was going on and interview a stream of studio guests who had been booked for us while we were cruising across the Atlantic at 35,000 feet.

I remember one of the interviews to this day: it was with a highly respected female White House correspondent on the subject of Clinton's ratings with women as more details emerged of his liaison with Lewinsky.

'Why do you think the President is still so popular among women, given what we now know about his behaviour?'

The pundit paused, looked me in the eye, and sighed.

'Because he's gorgeous.'

Some years later, after Clinton had left office, he addressed the Labour Party conference in Blackpool. My former *Observer* colleague Simon Hoggart memorably described how, after Clinton had spoken ('He raised his head, smiled, and scoped the audience, gazing deeply and fondly into their eyes ... He is the Princess Di of world politics'), a senior minister was spotted having a quick cigarette outside the conference hall.

Hoggart asked him why he had felt the sudden need for nicotine. 'I always like a smoke after being made love to,' the minister replied.[121] (I suspect he used a slightly different form of words, but Hoggart was writing for a respectable family newspaper.) That was the Clinton effect.

If radio listeners in the UK came to associate me with bedtime, because of the time of the evening when I was usually on air, in the US, my voice was more usually associated with breakfast. *Newshour*, the BBC World Service news programme that I presented for more than twenty years, is broadcast on public radio stations in more than 200 cities in the US, and as I worked only on the lunchtime edition (lunchtime in the UK), I was on air early in the morning in the US. Once, when I presented the programme from Durham, North Carolina, where we were helping to inaugurate a new studio complex for the local public radio station, more than five hundred people turned up to watch us in action. I told them that I was astonished to see so many of them so early in the morning, especially since watching a radio show being transmitted is not a great spectator sport. (I think I used the phrase 'like watching paint dry', but perhaps I undersold the sheer novelty of seeing a bunch of Brits running around like headless chickens.)

In Boston, where being British is almost like being an honorary citizen, I was recognised (or rather my voice was recognised) by a waitress in an Italian restaurant. 'Are you Robin Lustig of the BBC?' she asked, after having taken our order. Ruth was with me and, as nothing remotely similar had ever happened in the UK, from then on, whenever people asked her what her husband did for a living, she would reply: 'He works for the BBC. He's quite big in Boston.'

Americans who find mainstream US broadcast news coverage less than adequate often turn to the BBC to fill in the gaps. For them, the attraction of *Newshour* is that it brings them news of places that tend not to make headlines on Fox News or CNN. And anyone who speaks with an English accent sounds to many Americans as if they must be better educated, and therefore more knowledgeable. It is, of course, a woeful perception error, but it inevitably works to the BBC's advantage.

BBC radio shows are broadcast in the US mainly on public radio stations that, unlike the BBC, are largely dependent on advertising and individual and corporate subscriptions, rather than being funded by a licence fee or directly by the government. So, each year, they hold fundraisers, and they broadcast endless appeals to their listeners for financial support to help them stay on air. For several years, many stations asked BBC broadcasters to record these appeals, as they found that they raised more cash if the begging was done in an English accent.

This caused some qualms among senior BBC managers who had misgivings about the BBC's name being used, in effect, to extort cash from listeners. So we arrived at a messy compromise: my colleagues and I would record a message that said something like: 'If you enjoy listening to *Newshour*, you will know that you need [insert name of radio station]. Here's how you can support [insert name of radio station again].' And then another, non-BBC voice would say: 'Call 1-800 xxx now to pledge your support.'

That way, we could argue that we never actually asked for cash and the BBC's saintliness remained unsullied. Or so we liked to think.

There were no qualms, however, when some stations invited BBC presenters to be guests of honour and after-dinner speakers at events that had been organised for some of their most generous donors. We were treated like Hollywood superstars, which was a pleasant change from the total anonymity to which we were accustomed back home. It was also a rare opportunity to meet some of our listeners and hear what they liked – and did not like – about our work.

I was often asked, especially in the run-up to the invasion of Iraq in 2003, why the BBC insisted on interviewing pro-Bush neo-conservatives, as well as the more liberal critics of the administration, given that they were already getting plenty of airtime on mainstream US media. My reply was that the BBC was not the Bush-Bashing Corporation, and that we attached great importance to representing all viewpoints, not only those with which our listeners agreed. But I was left with the very clear impression that many of our listeners would have liked a lot more Bush-bashing.

One station, WBUR in Boston, went further than most in cultivating a close relationship with BBC broadcasters by inviting some of us to host their shows as stand-ins for their regular presenters. In general, I think their listeners liked the change of sound, although one caller did once tell me on air: 'I thought we fought a war of independence so that we didn't have to listen to accents like yours any more.'

I often wish, when the future of the BBC is being discussed, that some of the corporation's UK critics could listen to its supporters in the US. For them, even if they live in the richest country in the world, the BBC represents something that they can only dream of: a broadcaster beholden to no commercial interest and to no government diktat. It is a broadcaster that exists only for the public good – to inform, educate and entertain – and that, as a consequence, produces programmes that are the envy of the world.

So why do the BBC's American devotees not help pay for it? Good question, and one that I suspect will eventually be resolved in the next few years. I am in no doubt that they would be happy to pay – indeed,

I have often been asked, 'Where do I send the cheque?' when I have told Americans about the BBC's ever-tighter financial constraints.

There are, of course, plenty of exceptions. The army veteran whom I met on the Fort Bragg golf course was certainly not among the BBC's greatest fans; nor were the protesters in Boston who greeted chief international correspondent Lyse Doucet and me at a public meeting with banners labelling both of us as anti-Semites.

When I was making my documentary series *Looking for Democracy*, in which we examined different forms of democracy around the world, we started in Orange County, in southern California, where they have more elections than anywhere else on the planet and therefore, arguably, could claim to be the most democratic place in the world. They elect all their local officials, including the man who runs the local water purification and sewage plant, and, in some places, they even vote on town planning applications.

But, as so often in the US, there was a downside: hundreds of thousands of illegal immigrants – 'undocumented workers' – most of them from Mexico, who had no right to vote and played no part in the democratic process. If it was democracy, it was Athenian-style, with an invisible slave class whose voices were unheard and whose views were ignored. But this was America, so they were delighted to talk to the man from the BBC.

One of the many joys of being a foreign correspondent is that sometimes you see things that local reporters either have never noticed or simply take for granted. Reporting for the BBC meant being able to travel beyond the Beltway, to leave behind the Washington hothouse of politicians, lawyers and lobbyists and take to the road to talk to 'real' Americans.

'Middle America' – that vast and varied expanse that lies between Washington DC and New York on the east coast and Los Angeles and Hollywood on the west coast. The America, in other words, that foreigners hardly ever see and where not everyone is a liberal. And where better to take the temperature of Middle America than in Rolla, Missouri, a town of some twenty thousand people that likes to style itself 'the middle of everywhere', on the grounds that exactly the same number of people live to the north and south of it, and to the east and west of it.

Ahead of the 2008 presidential election, Catherine Miller and I set off in a rented car from Chicago to drive 450 miles southwest to Rolla, roughly following the line of the old Route 66 that took the victims of the 1930s rust belt depression to what they hoped would be new opportunities in California. Along the way, we passed close to Peoria, the traditional Middle America of showbiz. We also visited an ethanol plant, stopped off in Hannibal, on the banks of the Mississippi, birthplace of Mark Twain, and went on a tour of the Budweiser brewery in St Louis.

Every time we stopped, we gathered material and recorded interviews to be sent back to London. And, because we were now fully paid-up members of the BBC's brave new multimedia world, I wrote a daily diary for the *World Tonight* website and we published our photographs online. Radio was now so much more than mere sounds and voices, and we had to think constantly of what John Birt had chosen to label 'multi-platform content delivery'. I was never convinced that licence fee-payers appreciated how much more they were getting for their money.

We had decided to broadcast from Missouri because ever since 1904, with just one exception, it had voted for the winning candidate in every presidential election. It was justifiably proud of its bellwether status, but we well and truly jinxed it: in 2008, just weeks after our visit, it narrowly chose John McCain, not Obama, and in 2012, it got it wrong again by choosing Mitt Romney. Perhaps too many Missourians felt like the immigration officer at Chicago's O'Hare airport, who, when I told him why we had come to the US, remarked: 'I ain't never gonna vote for a man with a name like Obama...'

In November 2008, Barack Obama won the election with 53.8 per cent of the popular vote, a bigger share than any winning presidential candidate since Ronald Reagan in 1984, and, as the first black President in US history, he became an instant global celebrity. Significantly, a higher proportion of white voters chose him than had voted either for John Kerry in 2004 or for Al Gore in 2000. Being black, it seemed, was no longer an insuperable obstacle to electoral success in a country still riven by racial tensions. There was much talk, which I tried hard to avoid during my many hours of election night broadcasting, of 'new beginnings' and 'new dawns'. I have always been suspicious of sweeping claims.

With the exception of Alberto Fujimori, the son of Japanese parents who was President of Peru from 1990 until 2000 and who ended up in jail for human rights violations, Obama was the first minority head of state to be democratically elected anywhere by universal franchise. So, at some point on election night, I asked the former French Foreign Minister Bernard Kouchner if he could imagine French voters electing a non-white President.

The long pause before he answered spoke volumes.

I plead guilty to being obsessed by US politics. In mitigation, I argue that who leads the most powerful nation on earth is of no little importance to the rest of the world. I also, as a theatre lover, cannot help but admire the sheer drama of US politics: the larger-than-life characters, the sudden upsets, the tension of the TV debates – it is politics designed for the Age of Sensation. It may not lead to good government, but it certainly generates plenty of excitement. If anyone ever doubted it, 2016 provided more than enough proof.

In 1968, when I was still young and impressionable, I watched the Democrats tear themselves apart in Chicago, when the police used tear gas to break up protests during the party's chaotic convention and a grumpy left-wing outsider called Eugene McCarthy threatened to derail the officially favoured candidate Hubert Humphrey. (In 2016, Bernie Sanders bore more than a passing resemblance.) Lyndon Johnson had chosen not to run for a second term as anti-Vietnam War protests looked like sinking his chances; Robert Kennedy and Martin Luther King were both assassinated. That November, the Republican candidate Richard Nixon beat Humphrey by less than one percentage point of the popular vote. There was never any shortage of excitement – and this was at the height of the Cold War, when we believed that we were just one button-push away from nuclear oblivion.

Four years later, Nixon smashed the Democrats' George McGovern with 60 per cent of the popular vote – and two years after that, facing impeachment over his role in the Watergate scandal, he became the only US President in history to resign. Jimmy Carter, Ronald Reagan, George Bush, Bill Clinton, then another George Bush – there was never a dull moment.

The Boutwell auditorium in Birmingham, Alabama. It was 20 January 2009, the day of Barack Obama's inauguration as President, and I was in Alabama to witness the event from a part of the country where the memories of racial segregation were still more raw than almost anywhere else in the US. In 1956, when Nat King Cole had performed in front of a white audience in that same auditorium, he was attacked on stage by followers of the Ku Klux Klan.

The World Tonight's editor, Alistair Burnett, had thought long and hard about how we could cover the inauguration. Dozens of BBC correspondents would be in Washington, so what could we do that would still be fresh at the end of a day of saturation coverage? The answer was to send Lustig to Alabama to talk to people who had been in the forefront of the equal rights struggle.

And so it was that, a few days before the inauguration, I walked across the Edmund Pettus Bridge in Selma with the Rev. F. D. Reese, who in 1965 had marched across that same bridge hand-in-hand with Martin Luther King.

'I saw blood flowing that day ... But now with a black man as President of these United States of America, I know that all our pain and suffering was worth it.'

I rode a bus in Montgomery with Mary Smith Ware, who in 1955, aged eighteen, had been arrested for refusing to give up her seat to a white person. Six weeks later, another African-American woman, Rosa Parks, did the same thing, also in Montgomery, and became a national symbol of the civil rights movement.

And outside the Sixteenth Street Baptist Church in Birmingham, I met Carolyn McKinstry, who in 1963 had been just feet away from a bomb that had been planted in the church by the Ku Klux Klan. Four of her friends were killed when the bomb exploded.

The people whom I met, and tens of thousands of other African-Americans throughout the Deep South, with their still raw memories of discrimination and violence, could scarcely believe what they were seeing as Barack Obama – 'he looks just like us' – took the oath of office on that bright, cold January morning in front of the US Capitol in Washington. In the words of the preacher at the Sixteenth Street Baptist Church on the Sunday before the inauguration: 'We were in the back of the bus. Now we're in the White House.'

For me, as someone who had been a politically active teenager in the 1960s, watching the civil rights struggle from the other side of the Atlantic, the names Selma, Montgomery and Birmingham all had powerful resonances. And to meet some of the people who had been part of that struggle meant a great deal to me. Sometimes to be re-porter really is a privilege.

Sitting in that Birmingham auditorium, surrounded by thousands of African-Americans as they watched a giant screen showing the in-auguration ceremony in Washington, I witnessed levels of emotion that I had never imagined could be generated beneath a single roof. And when the veteran civil rights activist Rev. Fred L. Shuttlesworth, who had been one of Martin Luther King's key lieutenants, entered the hall in a wheelchair, the crowd rose to their feet with a roar that might well have been heard 750 miles away in Washington. (Birming-ham's airport had been renamed Birmingham–Shuttlesworth in his honour just a few months previously.)

It would have been easy – but wrong – to have been swept along on that tide of emotion. I had looked at the figures, and I knew that Obama had won a smaller percentage of white votes in Alabama than in any other state in the nation. So our coverage that night included not only the voices of exultant African-Americans, who made up only one quarter of the state's total population, but also the voice of a white nationalist activist from a group called the Council of Conservative Citizens. He called Obama a Marxist and said it was essential that the US must remain a 'European' nation.

Even with a black President installed in the White House, the Deep
South remained the Deep South.

The relationship between a presenter and an editor is a delicate one.
The editor is the boss, but things tend to work best when editor and
presenter work as partners. Alistair Burnett and I worked as partners
for a decade, not always with the full approval of our colleagues,
who sometimes complained that our weakness for learned articles in
learned journals (we tended to email them to each other late at night)
did not always translate into riveting radio. Even I sometimes chafed
at Alistair's fondness for linking up with foreign policy think tanks and
broadcasting lengthy discussions on weighty global affairs, although
I recognised that there could be real value in standing back from the
noise of the daily news agenda to look at long-term trends around
the world. In 2010, for example, as China was beginning to make
waves with a more assertive foreign policy, we broadcast an entire programme from Beijing, where we got together with the US-based think
tank the Carnegie Endowment for International Peace and Tsinghua
University. One of our panellists came up with a vividly telling image:

> Think of China as a seventeen-year-old, nearly adult, but not quite
> ready yet to shoulder all of an adult's responsibilities. Whenever things
> go wrong – climate change, for example – the first reaction is along the
> lines of 'Why should I clear up the mess? It's not my fault.'

In May 2010, Alistair was keen to mark the end of a UN gathering
in New York called the nuclear non-proliferation treaty review conference. It was one of those events that I automatically file under the
heading 'important, but boring'. Still, a trip to New York is never to
be sneezed at, and my producer colleague Beth McLeod and I had
already been discussing another story on the same side of the Atlantic
that we thought was worth our attention.

And so a deal was done. We would go to New York and labour

mightily to produce some interesting radio on the subject of nuclear non-proliferation (we did get an interview with Henry Kissinger, who had signed up to a manifesto favouring a world totally free of all nuclear weapons, so it was by no means a wasted trip), and then we would head south to report from the border between Arizona and Mexico on a growing row over illegal immigration.

Why Arizona? Because there were said to be half a million illegal immigrants in the state and 57,000 people had been stopped while trying to cross the border illegally the previous year alone. It was also a major entry point for drugs smugglers: marijuana with an estimated street value of $230 million had been seized in the previous twelve months.

The city of Nogales straddles the border. Or, to be strictly accurate, there are two cities called Nogales, one on each side of the border, separated by a high fence and a frontier post. We stayed on the US side of the border, where we were shown around by a border patrol agent. We also met a leading member of the Minutemen militia, who were mounting their own unofficial patrols of the border to fill in the gaps left by the official agents. Both men were helpful, courteous and articulate, and they were more than happy to spend time with foreign reporters sticking our noses into their business. They were proud of what they did, and they wanted the world to know.

The US is full of people like them, which is why it is such a rewarding place for reporters. We are simple folk at heart: all it takes to make us happy is a good story and someone who is prepared to tell it. Someone like Sarah Blazak, who drove me across the two-tier Brent Spence Bridge over the Ohio River between Cincinnati, Ohio and Covington, Kentucky. The fifty-year-old bridge had been officially declared 'functionally obsolete' and was carrying twice as much traffic as it was designed for, but no one could agree on who should provide the $2.5 billion that it would cost to replace it. Sarah's story of how she had to crawl in snail's pace traffic across the bridge every day on her way to and from work ('Every day when I get across, I breathe a sigh of relief') was a perfect illustration for a report on the nation's crumbling infrastructure crisis.

Or the man at the Chinese-owned solar panels factory in Illinois, who told me in a perfect sound bite why it made excellent sense for the Chinese to buy up US manufacturing companies. 'You know how we market these panels? "Made in America – by Americans."'

I have learned a lot more about what makes America tick by talking to people in Rolla, Missouri, or Chattanooga, Tennessee – or even Dunkirk, Ohio (population: 875) – than over any number of fancy cocktails in Washington. If I had never ventured beyond the Beltway, I would never have understood what Washington and the federal government look like to Mr and Mrs Middle America. Too often, I discovered, Washington looks a very long way away, both geographically and culturally – much further, for example, than Brussels seems from London.

And I would never have understood the power of that famous Ronald Reagan quip about the nine most terrifying words in the English language: 'I'm from the government and I'm here to help.'

Terrifying they may be – unless, of course, you want someone to pay for a new bridge across the Ohio River.

CHAPTER 15

ON BEING WILLIAM BOOT

Why don't you go as a war correspondent? ...
After all, you've been to Patagonia.
SCOOP, EVELYN WAUGH

IN AUGUST 1935, A young reporter by the name of William Deedes was summoned by his editor, H. A. Gwynne of the *Morning Post*, and asked if he would like to be sent to Abyssinia to report on an expected war with Italy. Deedes, who later become editor of the *Daily Telegraph* and one of Britain's best-known journalists, also became immortalised in Evelyn Waugh's novel *Scoop* as William Boot of the *Daily Beast*.

Before Deedes set off, having bought what he imagined would be suitable clothes ('three tropical suits, riding breeches for winter and summer, bush shirts, a sola topi, a double-brimmed sun hat ... and long boots to deter mosquitoes at sundown'), Gwynne sent him a note about how to send his reports back to London:

> We shall be glad to have anything you can send by mail, but we want to be on a level with our competitors in regard to telegrams ... While we do not want to be extravagant, yet we want to be in a position to give as good a picture as any other paper with one correspondent can give.[122]

The technology may have changed a bit since the 1930s, but getting the story out remains a major challenge even in the days of Wi-Fi and communications satellites. William Boot was advised to equip himself with cleft sticks in which to insert his dispatches before entrusting them to his runners – I was never reduced to emulating him, but there were times when it came close.

What has always attracted me to the character of Boot is the way he somehow managed to survive as a journalist, totally ill-suited to the task he had been given but making a go of it and coming out the other end in one piece. I can identify with that, even if I probably pretended far more than Boot ever did that I knew what I was doing.

Army veterans tend not, as a rule, to dine out on tales of the battles they lost. Nor do reporters usually regale their long-suffering friends with stories of the scoops they missed. But it would be wrong of me to give the impression that my career as a newsman has been an un-broken succession of jolly japes and stories that changed the world. So here are some of the ones that are probably best forgotten.

Like the time in Abuja, Nigeria, when we were about to broadcast live from a hotel room while simultaneously caring for a colleague who had succumbed to heatstroke. Just a few seconds after we went on air, the power failed and our computers and satellite dish went dead. Desperate inquiries at the front desk were met with calm assurance: 'Do not worry. The power will be back tomorrow.'

The only words that *World Tonight* listeners heard from Nigeria that night were: 'Here in Abuja…'

Whenever possible when reporting from overseas, we would try to send our recorded material to London ahead of transmission, so that even if disaster struck, they would still have something to broadcast. But if you have booked a live guest to be your main interviewee in an hour-long programme from Brazil, there is not much you can do if he gets to your hotel an hour later than requested. That is why, over the years, I developed a deep suspicion for any plans that involved the word 'live' when broadcasting from abroad.

Sometimes, technical mishaps can derail even the best-laid plans. An interview with Britain's top diplomat in Baghdad, recorded by a senior BBC sound engineer while we were both in the Iraqi capital, fell victim to a corrupted digital memory card in a sound recorder; by the time we realised, the diplomat had left town. The same thing happened a few years later when I was granted a rare joint interview, recorded for both TV and radio, with the Nobel Peace Prize winner Archbishop Desmond Tutu of South Africa and the former Irish

President Mary Robinson. Oh, how I yearned for the days when you could see the reels of magnetic tape gently revolving in a Uher tape recorder.

Once, at a Conservative Party conference, I was left making polite conversation with the then Home Secretary Michael Howard in his hotel room, while a producer dashed off to find a functioning mini-disc recorder. He was gone for a very long time, and I was rapidly running out of small talk when Mrs Howard very politely asked me to leave, as she wished to change for dinner, and I was finally ushered out of the door.

Honesty compels me to admit that many of my most serious foul-ups were entirely of my own making. Like the time I was interviewing the ambassadors of Armenia and Azerbaijan (their two countries were at war at the time) and somehow got them muddled up. Or when I was interviewing a guest from a studio in Oxford and, at the end of the interview, when it was time to thank him, my mind went blank and I could not remember his name. Embarrassing? Very.

Even worse was the time when, having finished another interview with a guest who was in a different studio, I remarked to the producer that it seemed to have gone all right 'even though he [the guest] is a bit of a media tart'. When I got back to my desk, I found an email from the guest: 'Next time you call someone a media tart, I suggest that you make sure that your mic is switched off.'

And then there was the occasion when I found myself having to interview one of the world's most respected economists, Professor Paul Samuelson, who after his death in 2009 was hailed by the *New York Times* as 'the foremost academic economist of the twentieth century'. What my colleagues did not know, and what I certainly did not want Samuelson to guess, was that I had only ever studied one term of economics as an undergraduate and had never even got to the end of his bestselling textbook *Economics: An Introductory Analysis*. Somehow, I stumbled through the interview without being found out – but I still break out in a sweat when I think about it.

Jobsworth bureaucrats are a constant threat: in every country in the world, there are officials whose only pleasure in life comes from saying no. And if they choose to say no at the wrong time, it can sometimes spell near disaster.

One of my last assignments before I left *The Observer* was to work on a TV documentary, produced jointly by the paper's fledgling film division and producer-director Anne Webber of Yorkshire Television. (Anne later founded the Commission for Looted Art in Europe, which tracks down works of art looted by the Nazis and restores them to their rightful owners.)

The film told the story of Soviet Jews who had been allowed to leave the Soviet Union to emigrate to Israel, but whose true ambition was to get to the United States. Tens of thousands of them ended up in Italy, waiting in limbo to be granted refugee status by the US immigration authorities. We called our film *Uncle Sam's Refuseniks*[123] and one of our sequences was to be shot at Fiumicino airport as a family, having finally been granted asylum, boarded a plane to New York.

The day before they were due to leave, we discovered that we needed a special permit to film at the airport and, as I was both an Italian speaker and surplus to requirements, I was sent off to do whatever needed to be done.

Some of the relevant offices were closed. Some of the relevant officials were unhelpful. In the heat of a Rome August, I dashed from one side of the airport to the other, knowing that unless I got hold of that all-important signature on that all-important permit, our film would have a very large hole in it. There was nothing at all glamorous that day about being a documentary film-maker.

But the story has a happy ending. After several frantic hours of begging and pleading, I got the permit and we made our film.

Most embarrassing of all was the time when I, in common with many other journalists who should have known better, was taken in by a hoax website. It was in the early days of the uprising in Syria, when a blog called 'Gay Girl in Damascus' appeared, apparently written by a gay woman, half-Syrian, half-American, who was living in the Syrian capital. It offered a vibrant account of life in Damascus and was widely quoted.

It eventually emerged, however, that the author was neither gay nor a girl, nor in Damascus – the blog was, in fact, the work of an

American postgraduate student at Edinburgh University called Tom MacMaster. (After his hoax was revealed, he wrote: 'I do not believe that I have harmed anyone – I feel that I have created an important voice for issues that I feel strongly about … I have only tried to illuminate them for a western audience.')

There was then a totally surreal twist to the tale: a woman called Paula Brooks, who ran the lesbian news website which first published the 'Gay Girl' blogs, turned out in reality to be a 58-year-old retired male construction worker in Ohio by the name of Bill Graber. He apparently had no idea that the gay woman he thought he was corresponding with in Damascus was in fact a married straight man in Edinburgh, nor did the man in Edinburgh have any inkling that Paula was Bill. It was a valuable lesson: just because something is online does not make it true. I once saw a quotation attributed to Abraham Lincoln: 'Not everything you read on the internet is accurate.'

Leaving aside hoax websites (and bad jokes), however, it is the perils of the outside broadcast that give rise to the highest stress levels. Even if the equipment works perfectly, there is never any shortage of malign elements conspiring to make the broadcaster's life a misery. So, over the years, I developed a set of rules designed to minimise the risks.

Do not set up a live outside broadcast position close to a road junction with traffic lights, unless you have established that they do not emit a loud beeping signal every time the lights indicate that it is safe for pedestrians to cross. Similarly, do not plan to go on air from a hotel car park, even if it is the only place where you can get a decent satellite signal, if there are also refuse bins into which hotel staff will tip dozens of empty bottles from the bar.

If you are in Jerusalem, do not base yourself in an Israeli-owned hotel in the occupied eastern part of the city and then expect a Palestinian official to come to your makeshift studio. Check the weather forecast and make sure you have a Plan B if there is the slightest chance of a tropical storm knocking you off air. And always, always, have twice as many batteries as you think you could possibly need.

Broadcasting after dark presents its own challenges, never more so for me than in June 1994, when I was in Normandy for the fiftieth anniversary of the D-Day landings. The day had not started well: the four guests who had been lined up to take part in our programme all found themselves on the wrong side of a security cordon and were unable to get to us.

Then, as 10 p.m. London time approached, I took up my position, seated on a World War II concrete gun emplacement as close to the edge of the cliffs as I dared. The idea was that listeners would enjoy being able to hear the gentle lapping of the waves far beneath me as I described all the solemn ceremonies that had taken place during the day. In one hand, I held my scripts, in the other I held a fat, furry microphone, designed to minimise the noise of the wind as it howled across the clifftops. Beside me on my concrete perch was a flimsy desk lamp, casting a gentle yellow glow onto my scripts.

At exactly two minutes to ten, the lightbulb blew and I was plunged into total darkness. More alarmingly, so were my scripts. With what I hope was admirable sangfroid, I spoke into the microphone: 'I don't know if anyone can hear me, but I now have no light and I can't read my scripts.'

There then followed a scene that could have come straight from one of the Roadrunner cartoons. A sound engineer emerged from a Portakabin a hundred yards or so inland from my position and sprinted towards me. As he got perilously near to the edge of the cliff, he engaged reverse gear and did one of those emergency stops that the makers of cartoons love so dearly.

But he had a torch, which was all that mattered, and for the next forty-five minutes, he stood over me like a sentinel, shining a light where before there had been none. And from then on, I always carried my own torch.

Unlike William Boot, I was never asked to go to a place that did not exist, although on a reporting trip to China in 2005, I did find myself in a place that seemed to teeter on the edge of reality. The model village of Huaxi, sometimes known as 'Number One Village under the Sky' is about ninety miles northwest of Shanghai and boasts that it is the richest village in China. To me, it looked disturbingly like the original Potemkin village, everything perfect, spotless and fake.

When we asked to see inside a typical home, the local Communist Party official who was showing us around took us to what he claimed was his own home, a show house so sparkling that there was not even a tube of toothpaste in the bathroom, nor any other sign of human habitation. And as we drove away at the end of our visit, I did not dare look behind me, in case I might see party officials hard at work, dismantling the entire village and putting it into storage for the next visit by impressionable foreigners.

The aim of any foreign correspondent is to be in the right place at the right time. On occasion, however, things go slightly awry, as they did in October 2000, when the Serbian leader Slobodan Milošević was finally forced from office. Together with several other BBC news people, I was dispatched to Belgrade to report on the drama. But first we had to stop off in Budapest, where we hoped to be able to pick up our visas.

The embassy was unable to help, due to the political upheavals in Belgrade, which left us in a quandary. Some of the team headed for the border by road, hoping that somehow they would be able to get across without visas. But it was a four-hour drive at the best of times and, with no guarantee that the border would be open, the rest of us decided to try an alternative way in.

We had heard that visas were still being issued in Podgorica, the capital of Montenegro, 500 miles to the south, and that it might be possible, in cooperation with journalists from other news organisations, to charter a special flight to get us there. Arrangements were made, and by midnight we were in Podgorica, handing over our passports to a man in the hotel lobby who promised that they would be returned to us, appropriately stamped, by breakfast.

He was as good as his word, and by the following lunchtime we were in Belgrade. (Our colleagues who had tried to get in by road never made it. The border was closed.) The city was utterly peaceful and displayed no evidence of the political earthquake that had just taken place. Once again, I thought of William Boot: 'All quiet here. Weather fine. Send more money.'

It was not quiet, however, in Israel, where a new outbreak of violence had erupted following a visit to the site of the al-Aqsa mosque in Jerusalem by the then opposition leader Ariel Sharon. A quick look at the flight schedules established that if we could get ourselves back to Budapest by the following day, there was one last flight to Tel Aviv before the start of Yom Kippur, when everything would shut down.

Our hotel managed to find us a driver who was prepared to take us back to Budapest but, when he turned up, he had clearly been drinking. So I did what I usually do when I get into the back of a car: I fell asleep. When we got to Budapest airport at 3 a.m., it was deserted, save for Lindsey Hilsum and a crew from *Channel 4 News*. Like us, they were heading for Tel Aviv.

Belgrade, on that occasion, was the wrong place to be, and I was there at the wrong time. It is also possible to be in the right place but at the wrong time, especially if you are on a death watch assignment that entails being on site for an expected death which will, when it happens, be deemed exceptionally newsworthy.

My days as a correspondent in Rome, where the health of elderly Popes was a daily concern, had taught me always to be ready for bad news. But at least I was based there and knew that when the time came, I would be in the right place. It was different as Nelson Mandela became increasingly frail, and the world's news organisations started planning for what they knew would one day be a huge global news event.

I was on the BBC's 'Mandela list', meaning that I would be one of a limited number of reporters dispatched from London if it looked as if death was approaching. Conscious that there was a risk of unwelcome criticism if too many BBC people were flown out to South Africa to boost the local bureau, a rota was drawn up so that some of us would be part of the first wave, but would then be withdrawn after a few days to make way for a second wave who would cover the state funeral. It was a long way to go for a false alarm, but I did make the long flight to Johannesburg once in the expectation of being needed there, only to learn after a few days of anxious waiting that the great man was rallying and would cheat death yet again.

Mandela died almost exactly a year after I left the BBC. His death was announced at about 9.45 p.m. London time, and I knew that my former colleagues at *The World Tonight*, with just fifteen minutes to go before they went on air, would be severely stretched. I sent a quick text message to the editor – 'I'm at home if you need me' – and by seven minutes past ten, as soon as the news bulletin was over, I was on air, recounting my memories of my one encounter with Mandela more than a decade previously. When I had flown to Johannesburg, I had been in the right place at the wrong time; on the day he died, I was in the wrong place at the right time.

News, by definition, is unpredictable. So it follows logically that when you plan ahead, your plans always risk being upended by real news, the sort that was not in the planning diary. And a news presenter who has been dispatched overseas as part of some carefully thought-out plan risks being left looking like a total prat. Wrong place, wrong time. Never a good look for a reporter.

Gdansk, Poland, 4 June 2009: it is the twentieth anniversary of the elections in Poland that marked the beginning of the end of Communism in Europe. It is also the twentieth anniversary of the Tiananmen Square massacre. I am in Gdansk, the crucible of Poland's anti-Communist movement, to present a special anniversary programme, and we also have a major report planned from China to mark the moment when Communism on two continents took two very different paths. It was the sort of intellectually ambitious programme that *The World Tonight* loved.

At one minute to ten, there was a news flash from Westminster: the Work and Pensions Secretary James Purnell had quit and called for the resignation of the Prime Minister, Gordon Brown. It was a huge political story and had come totally out of the blue. As I tried to make sense of what I was being told from London by a less than coherent producer, I scribbled a new headline with the pips of the Greenwich Time Signal ringing in my headphones. There are six pips, one per second: that's how long we had to rethink the programme. And, in the chaos, I entirely forgot which job Purnell had just resigned from.

If Labour's deputy leader Harriet Harman wondered why I was interviewing her from northern Poland, she was far too polite to ask.

But the programme as broadcast bore little resemblance to what we had so carefully planned. As Harold Macmillan (allegedly) said when asked what a Prime Minister fears most: 'Events, dear boy, events.'

Those same events should be the lifeblood for any self-respecting reporter – events, after all, are what we live for, they are what make our hearts beat faster and the adrenalin flow. Except when we are in the wrong place at the wrong time.

A perennial problem for anyone who has to make radio programmes in hotel rooms is how to find a way to get the acoustics sounding acceptable. So, for the benefit of generations of broadcasters yet to come, here are a few tips.

Close the curtains and turn off the air conditioning. You do not want to sound as if you are reporting from the bathroom, so record your scripts while buried under a duvet or at least with your head wrapped in a couple of pillows. My producer colleague Beth McLeod once made me crouch under a table with a low-hanging tablecloth; it was surprisingly effective. Kneeling on the floor in front of a well-upholstered armchair and speaking directly into the back of the chair will also usually work. Needless to say, none of this should be attempted if anyone other than your producer is in the room. There are limits to the indignities that even presenters can be expected to tolerate.

If you feel that you need to liven things up with a bit of street noise, do not be tempted to broadcast live from the street, where police sirens and clanging shop shutters will drown out everything you say. Far better to stay in your hotel room and dangle a second microphone out of an open window. If it gets too noisy, you can simply adjust the volume control. (Once, I dangled myself out of the open window because we did not have a second mic, but this is not a technique I would recommend.)

If you have to broadcast from the roof of your hotel, because that is the only place from which you can get a signal, make sure that you are nowhere near a lift shaft or an emergency generator. And always take an umbrella. If you are relying on the hotel Wi-Fi, be prepared for it to crash at precisely the wrong moment. In the early days of Wi-Fi, I sometimes looked for a local internet café and asked to plug into their network with an ethernet cable. It even worked in Medellín, Colombia, which used to have a reputation as the murder capital of the world.

If there were no internet cafés available, any café or coffee shop that offered Wi-Fi would sometimes have to do. In Istanbul, where gridlocked traffic had left us on the wrong side of the Bosphorus with no time to get back to our hotel, we ended up in a Wi-Fi-equipped cake shop at closing time, munching cream buns while preparing to go on air.

And, on the subject of food, I always tried to think ahead. My backpack usually contained nuts, dried fruit and a couple of boxes of cereal bars. No BBC correspondent should ever be tempted to rely on the hotel minibar for sustenance unless they are prepared for months of arguments with the BBC finance department. They will refuse to believe that you were munching stale peanuts to stave off starvation rather than swigging back mini-bottles of gin.

At one time, the BBC provided military-style cook-in-a-bag rations along with the flak jackets and helmets. They seemed like a good idea, until Craig Swan and I opened a couple of them outside our tent in eastern Kenya, close to the Somali border, in temperatures approaching forty degrees Celsius, and discovered that our dining options were either Lancashire hotpot or bangers and mash.

When in doubt, order a pizza.

CHAPTER 16

EN ROUTE TO MY ROOTS

Like a hot mug of cocoa and warm bedtime hug rolled into one.

PEOPLE TEND TO SAY nice things when you leave a job that you have been doing for a very long time – it is like being a guest at your own funeral. And if I am going to choose my own epitaph, the comment above, from an anonymous listener after I announced that I would be leaving the BBC at the end of 2012, will serve well enough.

My friend and fellow broadcaster Deb Amos once described what we radio reporters do as 'walking around inside listeners' heads'. It is a perfect description, and it helps to explain why many people feel that they have got to know quite intimately the broadcasters whose voices have become so familiar to them.

I decided to leave the BBC because I was beginning to get bored – and that is fatal for any news person. It was getting ever harder for me to maintain the energy and curiosity levels that I knew were essential to do the job properly and, with money ever tighter at the BBC, the chances of me being sent on the kind of overseas assignments that I most valued were becoming ever slimmer. It would be much better, I thought, to leave at a time of my own choosing than to wait for some embarrassed new editor to call me into their office to tell me that my time was up.

I also thought it was high time that I finally tried to kick my unhealthy addiction to news. I had already had an epiphany in the mid-1990s when the office phoned me while I was on holiday in Italy to ask if I could get to Turkey to cover an earthquake disaster. I said I didn't think I could, and when I put the phone down, Ruth remarked that it was the first time that she had ever heard me say no to the office.

A decade later, the World Service wanted to send me to Baghdad, just as Hannah was about to sit her A-levels. She was deeply unhappy at the prospect of having to deal with both the stress of the exams and worrying about my safety in a warzone, so, after much thought, I told my colleagues that I would rather not go. A friend gave me some good advice: 'If you do go, the BBC will remember for a maximum of three months. Hannah will remember for the rest of her life.' But I was shocked with myself that I found it such a hard decision to make.

I presented my last edition of *The World Tonight* on 13 December 2012. The top story was that the government had agreed to pay nearly £2.25 million to a Libyan dissident, Sami al-Saadi, who claimed that MI6 had been involved in handing him over to the regime of Colonel Gaddafi. At the end of the programme, my colleagues played a montage of some of my reporting over the past two decades, over a musical accompaniment of 'Rockin' Robin'. If they had hoped to embarrass me, they succeeded.

My closing words were borrowed from the World War II American broadcaster Edward R. Murrow: 'Good night, and good luck.'

Five days later, I presented my last *Newshour*, and then it was all over: drinks and hugs all round, and out into the piazza outside Broadcasting House clutching my farewell gifts. A few weeks later, arriving for my formal farewell party in the wood-panelled Council Chamber of Broadcasting House, I was stopped at the door. My electronic pass had been disabled and my name was not on the guest list. 'Terribly sorry, sir, but I can't let you in,' said the security man.

One of my guests kindly came to my rescue, and all was well. If you thought the BBC TV series *W1A* was a comedy, I can assure you that it was nothing of the sort. Like all good satire, it got closer to the truth than the most rigorous of documentaries.

I had wondered how I would feel, after so many years in the grip of the daily news cycle, once I was free. I felt liberated, not only from the tyranny of the headlines, but also from the straitjacket into which BBC presenters are bound by their obligation to be impartial on all matters of public controversy. I had had plenty of opinions since I was old enough to voice them, and to have been prevented from sharing them for nearly twenty-five years had been a bigger strain than I realised at the time. For a quarter of a century, not even my family and friends knew how I voted or what I thought.

So once I was free, I felt as if I could suddenly unlock a prison cell in which all those opinions had been held for so long. They rushed out, gulping the fresh air, yelling at the tops of their voices, channelling Martin Luther King.

'Free at last. Free at last. Thank God almighty, we are free at last.'

My blog, Lustig's Letter, which had tiptoed along carefully impartial paths for so long, burst into opinionated life. Some readers commented – to my delight – that they had never imagined I held such outlandish views. When I wrote a particularly angry piece about the British government's reluctance to help with refugee rescue operations in the Mediterranean, the *Guardian* columnist Zoe Williams commented on Twitter: 'I actually didn't have Robin Lustig down as a leftie particularly, even though I loved his voice.'

It felt like a small victory, and I was relieved that my twenty-three years of trying so hard to say nothing publicly that would even hint at my personal views had not been in vain.

Three months after I left the BBC, my mother died at the age of ninety-one. Her death enabled me to undertake a project that I could not even have contemplated during her lifetime – a journey to her roots: to the Polish city of Wrocław, formerly Breslau, where she had been born and grew up – and to Kaunas in Lithuania, to visit the place where her mother had been shot by a Nazi death squad in one of the first mass executions of 1941. My mother preferred not to dwell on memories from that time and had always been adamant that she had no wish to return to her birthplace. I, on the other hand, was irresistibly curious.

Fortunately, one of my oldest friends, Stu Seidel, who had worked for many years for the US National Public Radio network in Washington DC, was similarly curious to trace his own family's roots, and we devised a joint reporting project that we called *In the Footsteps of Our Families*. Stu's family had its origins in Belarus and Lithuania, so we started there, and then made our way by train through Poland and Germany, ending up in New Jersey and New York, where his grandparents and my uncle had eventually settled.

We started in the small Belarusian town of Pastavy, about 150 miles north of Minsk, from which Stu's grandfather Julius had set off almost exactly a hundred years previously. We created a website[124] on which we posted our photographs and audio interviews, and each of us wrote a diary as we journeyed through our families' histories.

> In my mind's eye, I see [Stu's grandfather] on that day in 1914, just months before the outbreak of the First World War, in his too-long trousers and flat cap, sixteen years old, with a battered suitcase containing all he owns at his feet. He is standing, embarrassed, as his mother, aunts and cousins surround him with love and anxiety, dabbing at their eyes with outsize handkerchiefs.

Our next stop was the Lithuanian capital Vilnius, where Stu's grandmother Sara had been born and where my direct ancestor Joshua Höschel ben Joseph had been born in 1578. According to the *Jewish Encyclopedia*, he was one of the most eminent Talmudic scholars of the age, ending up as the head of a religious school in Krakow, where he died in 1648.

The main reason I wanted to visit Lithuania, however, was that my maternal grandmother, Ilse, had been murdered there by a Nazi death squad in 1941. It was only in the early 2000s that my mother found out what had happened: she knew that her mother had been arrested in November 1941 and deported with thousands of other Jews, but she never made any further inquiries because she was terrified of learning that she had died in a gas chamber.

All she knew was what she had been told in a letter from a non-Jewish aunt who had stayed in Breslau throughout the war and who wrote to her in 1946.

> Your mother was picked up by two Gestapo men on the morning of 21 November. The bell rang, she opened the door, still in her dressing gown, and then she had to get dressed in their presence ... Herr Metzner, the chemist, who had rented your dining room, immediately called on me to tell me the terrible news ... They were told they were going to Kovno [Kaunas] ... We tried to find out what was going to

happen to all these people, and where they were going to be sent, but we couldn't find out anything. Once they had gone, there was never any sign of life from them again. However cruel it was that your mother had to be included in this first transport, at least she and the others with her were unaware that they were being taken to their deaths.

Over the next three years, there were to be sixteen further deportations of Breslau's Jews, most of them to the concentration camp at Theresienstadt, in Czechoslovakia, where they perished. The deportees were told they were to be part of 'resettlement' or 'work duty' programmes; among them was the grandmother of a friend of my father's, the cellist Anita Lasker-Wallfisch, who survived both Auschwitz and Belsen. (Anita and my father had shared the same cello teacher in Berlin, although she was originally from Breslau and had returned there before her grandmother was arrested.)

A Gestapo man sat at a table reading out names, and the people who were called had to walk past the table to the other side of the yard. When he called 'Lasker', my grandmother walked past the table, but not without stopping in front of the Gestapo man. She looked him straight in the face, and said very loudly: 'Frau Lasker to you.' I thought he would hit her there and then, but not a bit of it. He just said simply: 'Frau Lasker'. I was extremely proud of her.[125]

I would love to think that my own grandmother displayed similar fortitude.

The Nazis had invaded Lithuania in June 1941, and over the next six months, they murdered nearly all of the country's 200,000 Jews. In Kaunas, a nineteenth-century fort that had been used as the city's prison became the site of the mass murder of Jews, under the command of a Swiss-born SS colonel, Karl Jäger. (He escaped capture at the end of the war and was arrested only in 1959. He had been living in Germany under an assumed name and committed suicide in jail while awaiting trial.)

The Ninth Fort at Kaunas is now a grim, Soviet-era memorial and museum to the 30,000 people who were killed there. I took with me on my visit some of the last letters that my grandmother had written to my mother in the months before her death. They were all carefully written, probably not only because my grandmother feared that they would be read by Nazi censors but also because she may well have wanted to put on as brave a face as she could when writing to her only child.

March 1941: 'Unfortunately things are not going the way I had hoped. I have to be extremely patient, but I am not losing courage. I am still hoping that one fine day, we shall all meet again.'

June 1941: 'My journey to Uncle Ulle [her brother living in Chicago] seems to be impossible. Everything is upside down at the moment – all the work and all the money that has been spent seems to have been in vain.'

September 1941, shortly after her forty-fourth birthday: 'My mood was below zero. I hope next year I will feel happier.'

It was a glorious summer's day when I visited Kaunas, and it took an immense effort of imagination, as I stood on the edge of a field dotted with wild flowers, to conjure up an image of what it must have been like in November 1941 as thousands of terrified people were herded towards mass graves and shot.

> Journalists get used to reporting atrocities dispassionately, and on my visit to the Ninth Fort, I slip into my journalist's coat of armour all too easily. I compose images in the viewfinder of my camera, I record interviews and make notes. But then I stop and force myself to take off the armour. 'Ilse,' I say, as I stand at the edge of the killing field, 'I was here today. You are not forgotten.'
>
> And on the way back to the car, past the giant Soviet-era memorial to the 30,000 dead, we walk past a small lake with girls swimming and laughing. I am not offended. Life goes on.

How do you mourn a murdered grandmother whom you never knew? I tried hard to conjure up her presence as I stood on the edge of that killing field, but the enormity of what had happened there seemed to overwhelm me. I wished I could have found her name on a list, to link her directly to that terrible place. But there are no lists of names at the Ninth Fort.

Her name does figure, however, on a list maintained by the German government in the federal archive: 'Victims of the Persecution of Jews under the National Socialist Tyranny in Germany 1933–1945'.

Cohn, Ilse Gertrud, born 30 August 1897, Breslau
Date of deportation: 25 November 1941
Date of death: 29 November 1941. Kaunas, Fort IX

From Kaunas, Stu and I took a bus to Warsaw, and from Warsaw we took a train to Wrocław, my mother's hometown. Our guide and translator was Mateusz Kornacki, founder of a tour company called What's Up Wrocław. He had arranged for me to visit the city archives, where they were easily able to trace my grandparents' marriage certificate, my mother's birth certificate and my grandfather's death certificate. Mateusz also took me to the city's two Jewish cemeteries, in the second of which, to my great surprise, I was shown my grandfather's grave, totally hidden by ivy but uncovered by a cemetery worker who had worked out where it must be by consulting the cemetery record book. My grandfather had died of a heart attack, aged fifty, just two weeks before my mother's seventeenth birthday, in April 1938.

My mother had adored her father, but as far as I know she never once visited his grave before leaving her hometown for good just over a year after he died. So it was a special moment for me, having already paid my respects at the site of my grandmother's death, to be able to do the same at my grandfather's graveside.

Once I had retraced my mother's family's footsteps, it was time to do the same for my father's family, and given that he was still in excellent health in his mid-nineties, I decided to use him as my guide. So in Berlin, he showed me where he grew up and where he went to school, and we visited the Weissensee Jewish cemetery, more than a hundred acres containing well over 100,000 graves.

Finding his grandparents' graves there could not have been easier. All we had to do was provide their names and dates of death, and the cemetery computer did the rest. A map was printed out, the relevant spot on the grid was identified, and a dotted line was drawn to indicate the route we should take to the graveside. And of course, still wearing my reporter's armour, I recorded an interview with my father while we were there.

Our final stop was on the Isle of Man, where my father had been interned in the summer of 1940 as a 'friendly enemy alien'. He had been arrested at the school in Derbyshire where he was working as a gardener and part-time cello teacher; with the Nazis having overrun northern Europe, Churchill had panicked and ordered that all men of German and Austrian origin living in the UK, refugees and non-refugees alike, should be rounded up. When Italy joined the war later, another 19,000 Italians were added to the list.

My father was held in a government-requisitioned guesthouse on Marine Parade in Peel, on the western side of the island, facing out towards the ruins of Peel Castle and over the Irish Sea. At each end of the street was a high barbed-wire fence and armed guards. Our return visit, my father's first time back on the island in seventy-four years, marked his first opportunity to look up the side street that leads away from the beach. 'It was on the other side of the fence,' he said. 'So we had no idea what was up there.'

What my journey to my family's roots taught me was that I was still very much a reporter at heart. I wrote a series of dispatches for the *Jewish Chronicle* and produced a report from the Isle of Man for the BBC World Service. Over the months and years that followed, I reported from the Democratic Republic of Congo, Sierra Leone, Myanmar, South Sudan and northern Nigeria. I also walked along the entire length of the river Thames (and produced a series of audio reports for *The World at One* along the way, as well as posting audio slideshows on YouTube)[126] and then walked all the way round London.

Twice.

I also became a voluntary reading helper at a local primary school. Whatever else life after the BBC was, it was not boring.

CHAPTER 17

AND FINALLY...

In newspapers, all see
The doings of the world,
Which lead nowhere:
Better never written.

EMPEROR MEIJI OF JAPAN, 1867–1912

WHEN I STARTED WORKING for Reuters in 1970, the only people who could read what I wrote were the readers of publications who subscribed to the Reuters news service. When I wrote for *The Observer*, the only people who could read my articles were those who bought, or were otherwise able to gain sight of, a copy of the paper. And when I started at the BBC, if you wanted to be able to hear my dulcet tones, you had to be close to a radio and tuned to the right wavelength at the right time.

Compared to the world of information in which we now live, it was like the Middle Ages before the invention of the printing press, when the only people with access to the written word were monks, scribes and courtiers. The digital revolution means that more people have more access to more information, wherever and whenever they want it. This is a Very Good Thing.

It also means that journalists equally have more access to more information, and this is also a Very Good Thing. In the days when we had to rely on reference books – *Whitaker's Almanac* was a favourite – we knew less and were able to check less. At the BBC, we made a phone call to the news information library, told them what we needed to know, and an hour or so later, a messenger would arrive with a large brown envelope full of photocopied newspaper cuttings. We got more wrong and corrected fewer mistakes. Now, the wisdom of crowds means that any journalistic error is spotted within minutes. And, more than ever before, newspapers know that their readers expect them to own up to their mistakes.

Like the one the *New York Times* had to correct in October 2000:

> An article in The Times Magazine last Sunday about Ivana Trump and her spending habits misstated the number of bras she buys. It is two dozen black, two dozen beige and two dozen white, not two thousand of each.

Or the even more embarrassing one that *The* (London) *Times* had to publish in 2015, a mistake that ought to have been checkable even before the days of Google:

> Karol Wojtyla was referred to in Saturday's Credo column as 'the first non-Catholic pope for 450 years'. This should, of course, have read 'non-Italian'.

The eminent American journalist David Broder of the *Washington Post* defined a newspaper as

> [a] partial, hasty, incomplete, inevitably somewhat flawed and inaccurate rendering of some of the things we have heard about in the past twenty-four hours – distorted, despite our best efforts to eliminate gross bias, by the very process of compression that makes it possible for you to lift it from the doorstep and read it in about an hour.

All of which is another way of saying that, even if journalists now know more – and have access to more information – than they ever did before, they still know only a tiny fraction of the truth. They work under pressure, sometimes in great danger and usually at great speed: what always surprises me is not how much they get wrong, but how much they get right.

In the new media environment, however – an environment in

which everyone has access to social media sites that enable them to share their thoughts instantly with the world – a journalist's reason for living ('I know more than you do') is being challenged as never before. If you and I both observe the same event, and I then broadcast a report about it on BBC radio while you do the same via Twitter or Facebook, are we both journalists?

Not according to the American Press Institute:

> Merely engaging in journalistic-like activity – snapping a cell-phone picture at the scene of a fire or creating a blog site for news and comment – does not by itself produce a journalistic product. Though it can and sometimes does, there is a distinction between the act of journalism and the end result.
>
> The journalist places the public good above all else and uses certain methods – the foundation of which is a discipline of verification – to gather and assess what he or she finds.[127]

Ah. The public good. If only we could agree on what that is. The National Security Agency whistle-blower Edward Snowden thought leaking information about clandestine surveillance activities was a public good; the US disagreed and charged him, in his absence, under the Espionage Act. I might argue that publishing information about a government minister's extramarital affairs was a public good ('We deserve to know what kind of people are governing us'); the minister himself, or herself, might disagree.

I worry about the future of journalism, and I worry about the future of the BBC. I do not believe that journalism is threatened because more people have access to both information and the means of communication that used to be the exclusive preserve of the professional journalist. It is threatened because not enough people are prepared to pay for access to that information, and if fewer people pay for information, there will be less money with which to pay the information providers.

In the UK, newspaper sales have dropped by more than 40 per cent over the past fifteen years; in 2015, the communications regulator

Ofcom reported that newspapers had become the least popular medium that people use to keep up to date with news.[128] Thirty-one per cent of people said they got their news from newspapers (down from 41 per cent in 2014); radio came next on 32 per cent; then the internet (41 per cent), and top was television on 67 per cent (down from 75 per cent in 2014).

But TV viewing figures are decreasing year by year by 3 to 4 per cent on average, while online video watching is rising. In mid-2016, around five million people watched BBC television's *News at Ten*, but more than twenty-three million followed @BBCBreaking on Twitter. Like many journalists, I now get nearly all of my news via Twitter, obsessively checking for the latest developments and following links to stories recommended by friends and former colleagues. It is the best way I know to keep abreast of what is happening.

But here is the paradox: the people who are tweeting the news that I am interested in are, almost exclusively, professional journalists working for, and being paid by, established news organisations. And as those organisations' business models come under increasing strain, something will have to give. Will it be their Twitter teams, or will it be their investigative teams? Their online video creators, or their overseas bureaus?

When I was a Fleet Street news editor, we would occasionally commission what were called page traffic surveys, in which a sample of readers would be asked which items of the paper they had read and which they remembered. Health stories always did well, as did photographs of attractive women. Stories about famines overseas inevitably did badly.

These days, editors can track exactly how many people are clicking on each story online, how long they spend reading it, what they were reading before, and what they read afterwards. They also know where their readers shop, what they buy and where they go on holiday. This is all useful information – and it is dangerous.

The pressure to prioritise what generates most reader traffic has always been there, but online it is more intense than ever. More clicks mean higher ad rates, and if advertisers want to be able to embed video advertisements on your news site, then you need to be able to offer them video content to go with their ads. 'In the world being born, video content trumps text, and more mere scribes, of all ages and of all digital skill levels, are finding themselves unwanted. The ad tail is wagging the new digital news dog, at a quickening pace.'[129] We live in the age of clickbait.

In June 2016, News UK, which publishes *The Times*, the *Sunday Times*, *The Sun* and the *Sun on Sunday*, announced that it was to invest millions of pounds on producing a hundred hours of video each month for its websites. The company called it 'a significant moment in the UK news industry – marking the point where video becomes one of our major output formats'. And then came the real reason: 'This is a huge opportunity for brands [in other words, advertisers] to reach our engaged audiences in the context of fantastic, original video content.'

Even more significantly, just a few weeks later, the founder of Facebook, Mark Zuckerberg, a man who not only knows what is going to happen next in the world of digital media but has the power and the money to make it happen, announced that Facebook was moving 'towards a world where video is at the heart of all our services'. It was the clearest possible signal that the Future is Video.

For a wordsmith like me, these developments represent a huge challenge. Storytelling now means using all the available media together – words alone, or with just a couple of tasteful photographs, are no longer enough, and even in radio, words and sounds will need to be accompanied online by videos to help grab and retain the attention of listeners and readers.

In 2011, on a reporting trip to Brazil, producer Beth McLeod, sound engineer/camera operator Phil Zentner and I were among the first BBC teams to dip our toes into this new multimedia world. When we met a woman whose home had been demolished to make way for an Olympics-related highway, we recorded her in sound for my radio reports, took photographs of her for an illustrated story online and recorded a video of her to run alongside my words.[130] It seemed ground-breaking at the time; now it is regarded as standard practice.

According to a survey of 50,000 people in twenty-six different countries in 2016, just over half those questioned said they used social media as a source of news, and more than a quarter of under-25s said social media were their main news source.[131] It is not surprising, therefore, that digital advertisers are flocking to the social media sites rather than to the sites of traditional media organisations to find their target customers. In the words of Emily Bell of Columbia University's Graduate School of Journalism, one of the undisputed gurus of this digital world: 'Social media hasn't just swallowed journalism, it has swallowed everything … The phone in our pocket is our portal to the world.'[132]

More accurately, perhaps, social media sites are a portal to a meticulously curated world in which their algorithms decide what we see and which websites we visit. The content that we see, including the ads that appear on the screens of our phones or our tablets, is skewed to what we are thought to want to see, based on an analysis of our click history. Our online world is a world created in our own image, an echo chamber in which we communicate overwhelmingly with likeminded people. It is not the world as it is, nor is it the world as reflected on the pages of the newspapers.

When I was writing this book, the Twitter account with the most followers in the world was an account in the name of the singer-songwriter Katy Perry, which had more than ninety-one million followers. I was not one of them and, as far as I know, I have never once seen a tweet from Ms Perry. Also among the world's top ten Twitterati were Justin Bieber, Rihanna and Taylor Swift – I did not follow them either, nor, for some reason, did they follow me. It was as if, in the digital world, we were totally blind to each other's existence.

Everything that appears online is targeted – in other words, if an advertiser wants to sell a new line of overpriced trainers, the ads will appear only on sites that are known to attract a high number of users who are likely to be interested in buying new trainers. When political parties want to influence a specific group of voters, the rest of us may well be oblivious to what they are doing, so that if you are a lifelong supporter of the Green Party, you are unlikely to see online ads aimed at persuading you to vote for UKIP. Journalists whose job is to monitor such things will find it increasingly difficult to keep an eye on who is spending how much on what.

The money that in the past advertisers spent to buy space in news-papers is now being spent to embed videos on sites like Facebook, which attracts users – in part – by offering news that has been written by journalists employed by the newspapers in which the advertisers no longer advertise. The unfortunate consequence is that while Face-book's profits have been soaring ever further into the stratosphere – in the second quarter of 2016, advertising revenue was up by two-thirds to $6.24 million and its income from operations more than doubled – many newspapers have been plunging ever further into debt. The *New York Times*, for example, lost half a million dollars in the second quarter of 2016; its revenue from print advertising was down by 14 per cent compared to the previous year, and revenue from digital ads was down by 7 per cent.

So how about this as a parable for our times? The Oscar-winning film *Spotlight* was a paean of praise to investigative journalism and in particular to the *Boston Globe*, which uncovered systemic child abuse by Roman Catholic priests and a cover-up by the Church. A decade before it published the results of its investigation, the paper had been bought for more than $1 billion by the *New York Times*. Two decades later, it was sold for $70 million. A newspaper that had contributed immeasurably to the 'public good' had, in twenty years, lost more than 90 per cent of its value. It is a chilling thought for anyone who values the work that journalists do.

Imagine a world in which no one had uncovered the corruption at the heart of international football, or the sexual abuse of young English footballers by their coaches, or of drug-taking in sport, or of MPs' expenses-fiddling, or of police corruption, or of corporate tax-dodging, or offshore banking malpractice. Not one of these was uncovered by regulators or parliamentary inquiries: they were all un-covered by journalists doing what journalists do – shining some light into dark places and reporting on what they found.

But this kind of journalism is expensive, time-consuming and risky. According to the columnist Simon Jenkins, *The Guardian* spent £500,000 on its investigation into international money-laundering by HSBC, and £2 million on its Wikileaks and Snowden surveillance stories.[133] *The Guardian's* pre-tax losses in 2015/16 were an eye-watering £68.7 million. Its former editor Alan Rusbridger insisted that *The Guardian's* online journalism should be free and that revenues could be found from online advertising. The Facebook phenomenon seems to have blown a gaping hole in his strategy.

Journalists like to think that people buy newspapers because they want to read the articles they publish. It is a delusion: most people buy – or bought – newspapers for the crossword puzzle, the sports results, the cinema listings or the classified ads. As *The Economist* put it in 2009: 'A newspaper is a package of content – politics, sport, share prices, weather and so forth – which exists to attract eyeballs to advertisements.'[134]

Before the dawning of the digital age, if you wanted to buy a second-hand car, or a new home, you bought a newspaper and scoured the classified ads. Now, you simply go online, enter the relevant specification ('E-type Jag, low mileage, soft top, max price £10,000'), and hit Enter. An editor once told me that readers will forgive everything in a newspaper except for one thing: move the crossword puzzle to a different page and their wrath will be terrible to behold. It is even worse than when Radio 4 changes the start time of *The Archers*.

So the 'bundle' that used to drop with a thud on the doormat every morning is now surplus to requirements. Who needs ink on paper when you have a phone in your pocket that is, in Emily Bell's phrase, your portal to the world? More significantly, who in their right mind would prefer to pay for that grubby, inconvenient bundle of newsprint when everything you could possibly want to know is available, free of charge, on the screen of your smartphone?

So will newspapers survive? My hunch is that they will, at least for a few more decades, but not for ever. If I were to be able to pop back in a hundred years' time, I would be very surprised indeed to see bundles of newsprint still on sale in corner shops. Medieval scribes were killed off by the printing press, and I see no reason why the pixel should not inflict the same fate on the printing press.

That is not the same as saying that the power of the pixel will kill journalism. As I have suggested, I believe that journalism will have to adapt to the digital world, but I am confident that it will be up to the task. We humans are curious creatures, and we will always want to know more. From our earliest days sitting round fires in caves, we have listened to storytellers, agog to hear tales from the next valley, the other side of the river or the other side of the world.

And that, incidentally, is also why I am confident about the future of radio. The author and radio critic Kate Chisholm put it well:

> Radio's real power is that it takes us right back into a pre-technological world, to a world of storytelling, of discovery through narrative, not in pictures but as an aural experience. We rediscover in radio the kind of world our ancestors knew, where stories were told and information gathered through human connection. It's this that makes radio so much more potent than TV.[135]

After all, like most animal species, our primary means of communication is through sound. A baby cries, a mother soothes or sings, a dog barks, a cow moos, a bird chirps. Each sound carries a message, and that is precisely what radio does. That is why radio aficionados like to claim that the pictures on radio are so much better than the ones on TV: they are made in the mind of the listener, not in the viewfinder of the camera.

On 18 April 1930, which was Good Friday, a BBC radio newsreader solemnly announced: 'There is no news.' Piano music followed. Happy days!

I have often felt tempted to say something very similar, on days so dull that I could only secretly sympathise with any listener tuning in. All credit, therefore, to the *Battlefords News-Optimist*, a community newspaper in Saskatchewan, Canada, which in January 2016 reported on its front page: 'To be truthful, there isn't really anything happening in the news this week ... It's January, the weather has taken a nasty turn and there just isn't much happening.'

There is, of course, always something happening somewhere. But it may not always be the sort of something that news editors think will be of much interest to their readers, listeners or viewers. If you dish up too much dull stuff, you will soon lose them, so the temptation – always – is to find something, anything, with which to fill the columns or minutes that have been allocated to 'news'. There is little point in producing a newspaper that no one wants to read. Similarly, it is a waste of everyone's energy to put together a radio programme that no one bothers to listen to. So the trick is to find a way to report the news that you believe is important in such a way as to attract readers and listeners. If something is important but happens every day – like the war in Syria, for example – it risks being relegated to the 'no longer news' category. As every rookie reporter is taught: 'dog bites man' is not a story, but 'man bites dog' is. If it happens every day, it is not news.

Take the example of railway accidents. At the end of the nineteenth century, they were so frequent that they usually merited just a few paragraphs in the next day's newspapers. Now, however, railway accidents are so rare that when they do occur, they get banner headline treatment. Perversely, therefore, readers may be left with the impression that rail travel is now *more* dangerous than it was a hundred years ago, whereas the truth is precisely the opposite.[136]

When I give talks about journalism in schools, I sometimes ask students to imagine that they have a choice between two different newspapers: one has a headline saying 'All students at Perfection Academy were well-behaved this term' and the other says 'Record number of students arrested after fight at Imperfection Academy'. Which one would they buy? Another useful experiment is to ask them to imagine that they are the editor of the school newspaper. They have a choice of three stories to put on the front page: 'Head teacher praises students at Perfection Academy'; 'New menus planned for school meals'; or 'Shock rise in muggings outside school gate'. The more copies of the newspaper they sell, the more cash they will raise to give to their favourite charity. So which story do they choose? Invariably, it is the one about the muggings.

This preference for the dramatic, on which all news choices are based, gives rise to some serious problems, especially when dealing with crime. The fact is that in nearly all the world's most developed countries, including the UK, crime rates have been falling for several years. Yet fear of crime has not, because the reporting of crimes becomes more sensational the rarer they are. The reporting of climate change is even more of a problem: immensely complex, and immensely slow as an observable process, without question by far the most important issue of our times, yet you would never think so by looking at the relatively low-key reporting of it.

The prize for the best-known boring headline was claimed many years ago by Claud Cockburn, who in the early 1930s was a sub-editor on *The Times*.

> Someone had invented a game – a competition with a small prize for the winner – to see who could write the dullest headline. It had to be a genuine headline, that is to say one which was actually printed in the next morning's newspaper. I won it only once with a headline which announced: 'Small Earthquake in Chile. Not many dead.'[137]

No one has ever managed to find the headline in the archives, however, and the story is almost certainly apocryphal. But *Times* subs were not alone in trying to find ways to alleviate the boredom of a long night at the news coalface. Once, when Ruth and I were on a walking holiday in Tuscany, our fellow walkers challenged me to insert the word 'Etruscan' into the first programme I presented after I returned to work. To their great surprise, I managed it. I also once wrote an introduction to a recorded report in which the first letter of each sentence spelt out 'happy birthday' in honour of our editor's birthday. Until I pointed it out, of course, he had no idea. With such harmless pleasures can dull evenings be livened up.

The choices that journalists make – what stories to cover, which people to interview – reflect their own biases and their best guesses about what will interest their audience. It is instructive, for example, to compare the coverage given to the deaths of different rock musicians:

those who played an important role in the formative teenage years of news executives will always receive far more generous coverage than those whose greatest success fell either before or after the executives' adolescence.

It is this usually unconscious subjective bias that makes it so important to expand and diversify the journalistic recruitment pool as much as humanly possible. If journalists are white, middle class and have a university degree – which is usually the case – the stories that they choose to cover will inevitably reflect their own background. I worried during my two decades at the BBC that as London property prices rose inexorably and BBC salaries did not, the gene pool from which new generations of journalists were drawn became progressively shallower. Who can afford to live and work in London on a succession of three-month contracts other than comfortably-off graduates whose parents are helping them with the bills? A report on social mobility published in 2012 by the former Labour Cabinet minister Alan Milburn said that journalism had moved 'to a greater degree of social exclusivity than any other profession'. The National Union of Journalists went one step further and called journalism 'the preserve of the privileged'.[138]

The *Guardian* journalist Gary Younge has pointed out that in the US, where he worked for many years, on average seven children or teenagers are shot dead every day.[139] Most of them are African-Americans, living in communities from which very few mainstream journalists are drawn. Most of these deaths receive no more than a few lines of coverage in the local newspaper or on the local TV news station. If the news executives making the choices were their neighbours, the scale of the coverage would be very different.

Journalism does not reflect the world in which we live. What it does reflect is only those events that journalists think are interesting, and likely to be of interest to the people who are their target consumers. And as the business models of news organisations come under increasing strain, journalism is further restricted to those stories that can be covered within ever-narrowing budgetary constraints. Why is there now so little on-the-ground reporting from Iraq? Because it costs a fortune to maintain a reporting presence there, and with relatively few Western troops still deployed, and more than a decade after the US-led invasion, the judgement has been made that it can no longer be regarded as a news priority.

When more than three hundred people were killed in a bomb attack in Baghdad in June 2016, it received only a fraction of the coverage given to similar attacks in Paris (a hundred and thirty dead) and Brussels (thirty-two dead). Why? Because bomb attacks in Baghdad had become commonplace – in other words, much less newsworthy – and also because Paris and Brussels are much closer to London than Baghdad is, and British news consumers are far more likely to have been there.

When immigration levels became a major political issue, the media were accused with some justification of having ignored the concerns of people living in places where a perceived influx of immigrants was causing high levels of resentment. I do not believe that this was a result of a deliberate political decision to pretend it was not happening or to sweep it under the carpet – it was, I think, much more likely to have been a result of the fact that most mainstream media journalists live and work in London, in areas where cosmopolitanism and multiculturalism are far more readily accepted than elsewhere.

Perhaps one of the most significant ways in which the development of digital media outlets has affected our perception of the world is that it has made non-metropolitan views far more visible than they used to be. One of the reasons the shooting of young black males by police officers in the US became a major issue was that the widespread availability of camera phones with video recording capacity enabled witnesses to capture and publish incidents that would otherwise have gone unnoticed except by the people directly affected. The non-professional video footage also, crucially, provided an alternative version of events to that provided by the police, and therefore immediately offered a corrective if the official account was less than truthful.

Given the online media's obsession with video content, anything dramatic – and there is nothing more dramatic than a shooting – will automatically be snapped up and widely shared. The effect is that the decisions about which events gain media coverage are no longer in the hands only of professional journalists: a middle-aged, white news editor sitting in a newspaper office or TV newsroom may not think much of 'yet another shooting', but if someone has uploaded twenty seconds of video, the decision will be taken elsewhere. In general, I welcome this democratisation of media decision-making. But it does have consequences that can have a significant impact on public perceptions of danger, especially when it involves fear of terrorist attacks.

On 11 March 2004, ten bombs exploded within three minutes of each other on four commuter trains in Madrid. A hundred and ninety-two people were killed and another two thousand were injured. It was the highest death toll from any terrorist attack in Europe since the bombing of Pan Am flight 103 over Lockerbie in 1988, when two hundred and seventy people were killed. But in 2004, camera phones and social media sites were still in their infancy (Facebook had been founded just a month before the Madrid bombings), and although the attacks were extensively reported, their impact on public consciousness across Europe was much less than that of the Paris and Brussels attacks in 2015 and 2016. As a result, I strongly suspect that people were far more frightened of terrorist attacks after Paris and Brussels than they were after Madrid.

Television news channels devour what they call 'user-generated content', material that is made available to them by members of the public who happen to be on the spot when a news event occurs. Whether it is floods in Yorkshire, a mass shooting in a Florida disco, or bombs in Brussels, non-professional images increasingly dominate both mainstream media and social media coverage of major news events. Images that twenty years ago would have been regarded as too harrowing to show now make their way from non-curated, non-professional sites onto newspaper front pages and TV news bulletins. The jihadi group Islamic State was quick to understand the power of non-curated material by publishing gruesome images of its butchery online and, in effect, daring the mainstream media not to use them. Fortunately, after some initial uncertainty, editors realised the dangers and stopped using them.

Editors and others also need to develop new skills in evaluating the authenticity and provenance of material that comes from non-traditional sources. Atrocity images are endlessly recycled – what may once have been a distressing image of a dead child in Syria can often reappear months or even years later as a dead child in Yemen, or Gaza, or anywhere else where propagandists have access to Twitter or Facebook.

In May 2013, TV news channels were offered non-professional video footage of one of the men who killed Lee Rigby of the Royal Regiment of Fusiliers on a street in south London. The killer's hands were covered in the soldier's blood and he was carrying a knife and a meat cleaver as he explained why they had killed him. No one who saw the footage will ever forget it, and there were hundreds of complaints from viewers who thought it should never have been broadcast. Once again, the horror of such an attack, up close and personal, was beamed into citizens' living rooms in a way that would have been impossible before the arrival of camera phones.

Should it have been broadcast? My own view is that it should have been, appropriately edited, on the grounds that it offered a vivid insight into the killers' motives and was, therefore, in the public interest. There is a danger, I think, that when people are exposed to material that makes them feel uncomfortable – or even sickened – they are tempted to blame the messenger rather than think about the message. Should the media not cover the effects of famine on starving people? Or tell the stories of children who have been sexually abused? Or report from the front lines of conflicts in which thousands of civilians are killed?

There is an important difference of principle between broadcasting propaganda produced by a party to a conflict and disseminating material that has been obtained from a bystander or eyewitness. One line, however, that I would never cross is to broadcast the actual killing of a human being. Basic human decency applies even to journalism.

It comes back to the basic task of all journalism: to tell people things that they need to know in order to make informed decisions about how they wish to be governed and by whom. Walter Lippmann, sometimes called the greatest American journalist of his age, defined the job like this:

If the country is to be governed with the consent of the governed, then
the governed must arrive at opinions about what their governors want
them to consent to ... We correspondents perform an essential service
... We make it our business to find out what is going on under the
surface and beyond the horizon, to infer, to deduce, to imagine, and to
guess what is going on inside, what this meant yesterday, and what it
could mean tomorrow.[140]

Put like that, journalism sounds like the noblest calling on earth.
Sometimes – often – it is. But sometimes it is the polar opposite. I
doubt that phone-hacking, celebrity-baiting and migrant-bashing are
what Lippmann had in mind when he spoke of the 'essential service'
performed by journalists. The Chinese journalist and author Yang
Jisheng put it well when he received the 2016 Louis M. Lyons Award
for Conscience and Integrity in Journalism:

This is a despicable profession that can confuse right and wrong, reverse black and white, manufacture monstrous falsehoods and dupe an
audience of millions. This is a noble profession that can point out the
ills of our times, uncover the darkness, castigate evil, advocate for the
people and take on the responsibility of social conscience.[141]

'Manufacture monstrous falsehoods'. In the six months leading up
to the UK's EU referendum in June 2016, the country's two leading
mid-market newspapers, the *Daily Mail* and the *Daily Express*, which
between them sell more than 2 million copies a day, each published
thirty-four front-page stories about immigrants and immigration. (In
the same period, *The Guardian* and *The Times* each published just six
stories on the same subject.)[142]

Daily Mail: 'Migrant's Channel stroll to asylum in Britain'; '1m more
migrants are on their way'; 'Surrender on illegal migrants'; 'Deadly cost
of our open borders'; 'Record number of jobless EU migrants in Britain'.

Daily Express: 'Britain faces migrant chaos'; 'EU opens door to 79m
from Turkey'; 'EU migrants soar yet again'; '2m EU migrants grab our
jobs'; 'You pay benefits for EU's jobless'.

According to one analysis of EU referendum coverage,[143] weighted to take account of both the content of articles and the circulation of the newspapers in which they appeared, pro-Leave material had an 82 per cent circulation advantage over pro-Remain articles. And of course that coverage was reinforced by the twice-daily press reviews that appeared on broadcast media, when headlines are shown and read out but rarely put into context or challenged.

Within hours of the result of the EU referendum becoming known, the editor of *The Sun*, Tony Gallagher, remarked: 'So much for the waning power of the print media.'[144] But, in my view, that reaction is almost certainly far too glib, as there is no conclusive evidence that newspapers do have a significant direct impact on voting behaviour. On the other hand, a relentless drumbeat on a single subject will inevitably seep into the national consciousness, and when voters express fears about illegal immigration, or about millions of potential Turkish migrants flooding into the UK, even in areas of the country where there are relatively few immigrants, it is not unreasonable to deduce that those fears are based at least in part on what they have read or heard in the media.

Editors have learned from experience over many decades that feeding on fear has always been a highly profitable commercial activity. Their traditional defence is that they do not stoke their readers' fears but merely reflect and report the fears that already exist. It is an argument that comes perilously close to the chicken–egg debate, but it seems unarguable that when a significant section of the print media speak as one on a single subject – and when their coverage is then reflected in the broadcast media – it must have some impact on the way people vote.

Nevertheless, I am not a believer in a tougher, state-backed regulatory regime to teach the press the error of their ways. While I acknowledge that newspapers could, and should, be much better than they are at accurately reflecting the reality of the world around us, I have an instinctive suspicion of anyone who wants to 'crack down' on media misbehaviour. It is no coincidence that the first step that any authoritarian government takes, whether left-wing or right-wing, is to curtail press freedom, and I have no desire to live in a country in which newspapers risk being put out of business for the sin of causing offence or getting something wrong.

I do not seek to minimise the very real distress caused to people who, through no fault of their own, find themselves pilloried or worse in the full glare of the media spotlight. Christopher Jefferies, for example, who had the misfortune to have rented a flat to Joanna Yeates, who was murdered in Bristol in 2010, was disgracefully labelled as her suspected murderer after police had arrested him and leaked highly damaging speculation about him before releasing him without charge two days later. He had every reason to feel aggrieved at the way he was treated, but the proper target of his anger should have been the police, not the press. I have rather less sympathy for show business celebrities whose agents assiduously court publicity when they have something to sell but then cry foul when their clients are caught, sometimes literally, with their pants down.

What the Leveson Inquiry into press behaviour revealed was that far too often, police leak damaging tittle-tattle to reporters when their investigations are at a very early stage. It is unrealistic to expect reporters not to seek to obtain as much information as they can, but it is not unrealistic to expect police officers to act professionally and in accordance with their own code of conduct. When a newspaper reports that 'police believe…' something, it is guilty of nothing more than doing its job, which is why I have always believed that the focus of the Leveson exercise should have been far more on those who talk to newspapers than on those who publish the information they provide.

I do not, however, believe that the identities of people who have been arrested should be kept out of the public domain unless and until they are formally charged. The disappearance of people after they have been dragged from their homes by police in a dawn raid is something that should happen only in a dictatorship – who has been arrested, and where they are being held, is information that must be made public, if only for their own protection. Police gossip about what they may or may not have done is a very different matter.

For an individual who is wrongly arrested, and then released

without charge but after having been publicly identified – especially
if the arrest relates to sexual offences – the price of press freedom can
be very high. But, harsh as it may sound, I do believe that the price
we would pay if the police could drag people into custody without
revealing who they have arrested and why would be even higher.

For me, the bottom line is that the press cannot be half free. Journalists are, of course, obliged to obey the law just like anyone else, and
that includes the laws of libel, contempt and incitement to hatred or
violence. But, in my view, the best way to combat inaccurate reporting is to contest it, not ban it. Social media provide an ideal platform
from which to do so.

The former owner and editor of *The Guardian* (or *Manchester Guardian* as it then was), C. P. Scott, famously wrote: 'Comment is free, but
facts are sacred.' So he would be mightily perplexed by the world in
which the media now operate, a world sometimes called a 'post-facts'
or 'post-truth' world. More than a decade ago, the American journalist
Ron Suskind quoted an aide to George W. Bush as decrying what
he called 'the reality-based community ... people who believe that
solutions emerge from [a] judicious study of discernible reality'. That's
not the way the world really works any more, the aide said. 'We're an
empire now, and when we act, we create our own reality.'[145]

The multi-millionaire Arron Banks, who gave £5.6 million to the
UKIP-backed Leave campaign ahead of the EU referendum, made
a similar point. Quoting the approach adopted by the campaign's
American advisers, he said: 'What they said early on was "facts don't
work" and that's it. The Remain campaign featured fact, fact, fact,
fact, fact. It just doesn't work. You have got to connect with people
emotionally.'[146]

So we have moved on from 'facts are sacred' to 'facts don't work'.
And, for journalists like me, that creates real problems. Because if facts
no longer matter, what is the point of us burrowing away day after
day, week after week, to discover the facts that someone wants to keep
hidden? If newspapers can print lies and still make money, where does
that leave the papers that prefer to stick to the truth?

The digital revolution makes the question even more pressing,

with the pressure on content providers to maximise clicks in order
to maximise revenue. Neetzan Zimmerman, who used to work for
the celebrity gossip website Gawker, said in 2014: 'Nowadays it's
not important if a story's real. The only thing that really matters is
whether people click on it.' In 2015, the US-based online entertainment magazine Slant offered to pay its writers a basic $100 a month
for three articles a week, plus $5 for every 500 clicks.

What price facts when clickbait is where the money is? 'Fake news'
suddenly became a serious global issue after the 2016 US presidential election campaign, during which deliberately faked material was
widely shared over social media. If I write a story claiming that Elvis
Presley has been found alive and well and living on the moon, and
if enough people click on it and share it, I will make money from it.
Who cares if it's total tosh?

Perhaps one reason newspaper sales are falling is that readers do
in fact care about the difference between truth and lies, and they no
longer want to buy papers they don't trust. According to a survey
carried out by the European Commission in 2015, only 22 per cent
of respondents in the UK said they 'tend to trust' what they read in
their newspapers, the lowest percentage in any of the EU's twenty-
eight member states.[147] By comparison, when respondents were asked
in a survey commissioned by the BBC which one source of news they
most trusted, 57 per cent replied the BBC, followed by ITV (11 per
cent), Sky News (9 per cent) and Channel 4 (3 per cent).[148] The highest
scoring newspaper was *The Guardian* on 2 per cent.

So why does the BBC face such constant criticism for the quality
of its news coverage, especially of contentious political issues, if so
many news consumers regard it as trustworthy? The answer is in the
question: it is precisely because so many people trust the BBC that
those who believe their own viewpoint is not being fairly represented
complain so vociferously. In addition, because of the way the BBC is
funded, by means of a compulsory licence fee, everyone feels that they
own the BBC and that it should, therefore, reflect their interests and
their views.

My own experience, having worked at the BBC news coalface for more than twenty years, is that its journalists do try as hard as humanly possible to be fair, accurate and impartial. But that is not the same as saying that they always get things right, or that they are as ready as they should be to admit to their errors.

The first major problem faced by the BBC's journalists is who they are: just like their counterparts in other media organisations, they are overwhelmingly university-educated, overwhelmingly London-based, overwhelmingly young, and overwhelmingly middle class. It is not a problem that is unique to the BBC, but BBC journalists do tend to share a common background, and often they share a common outlook. The key agenda-setters on the *Today* programme on Radio 4 or *Newsnight* on BBC2 are producers in their thirties who think up the story ideas and book the contributors for their programmes. Jeremy Paxman was unforgivably rude but only half exaggerating when, shortly after he left the BBC, he described *Newsnight* as a programme 'made by thirteen-year-olds ... It's perfectly normal when you're young that you want to change the world.'

When Helen Boaden was head of BBC news, she once asked me to give a talk to a group of young news producers. 'You should listen to him,' she told them, 'because the people you're making programmes for are much closer to his age than they are to yours.' She might have made me sound like a dinosaur on display in a museum, but I understood her point. The average Radio 4 listener is in their mid-fifties; the average BBC1 viewer is nudging sixty.

The BBC has a legal obligation to be impartial in its news coverage. According to its editorial guidelines, it is obliged

> to do all we can to ensure controversial subjects are treated with due impartiality in our news and other output dealing with matters of public policy or political or industrial controversy ... The term 'due' means that the impartiality must be adequate and appropriate to the output, taking account of the subject and nature of the content ... Due impartiality is often more than a simple matter of 'balance' between opposing viewpoints. Equally, it does not require absolute neutrality on every issue or detachment from fundamental democratic principles.[149]

You can always tell when the BBC is struggling to be impartial – you hear an interviewer telling an interviewee: 'But some people say…' It is an unmistakable signal that someone, somewhere is doing their damnedest to abide by the guidelines.

Interviewee: 'It took Phileas Fogg eighty days to travel round the world, you know…'

BBC interviewer: 'But of course, some people say the world is flat…'

Absurd? Clearly, but where should the line be drawn? Whether it is the discredited theory of a causal connection between autism and the triple vaccine against measles, mumps and rubella, or the influence of human activity on climate change, or the claim that the UK sent £350 million a week to Brussels, at what point does accuracy take over from impartiality?

These issues are far more difficult to resolve than the BBC's critics often claim but, in my view, the BBC does itself no favours by appearing too often to be uncertain about what it should be doing. The default posture of most BBC interviewers – and I was as guilty of this as anyone else – is to challenge whatever their interviewee says. It stems from a belief that by challenging them and putting the opposing viewpoint, no matter how outlandish, listeners or viewers are given an opportunity to decide for themselves how convincing they find the interviewee's claims. This default mindset is sometimes called 'bothsidesism', because it subscribes to the principle that both sides of an argument always deserve a hearing.

I nearly called this book 'But surely…', as those are the words with which I began so many hundreds of interview questions.

Interviewee: 'Tomorrow will be Thursday…'

Lustig: 'But surely, some people will argue that it could equally be Friday…'

On the eve of the EU referendum in June 2016, more than a thousand business leaders signed a letter to *The Times* backing the UK's continued membership of the European Union. The BBC headline reporting this fact 'balanced' it with another fact: that the vacuum cleaner tycoon Sir James Dyson took the opposite view. As the leading media analyst Professor Ivor Gaber of Sussex University has pointed out, this was hardly news, given that it had already been reported two weeks earlier. It was an entirely spurious attempt to inject balance where there was no need.[150]

One way of approaching the impartiality conundrum is to try to find a way to assess the credibility of the people on each side of a contentious issue. But who assesses credibility? If three hundred professors of economics say the country is heading for disaster, and one hundred professors say the opposite – but they come from more 'prestigious' academic institutions – where does that leave the hapless BBC interviewer? It places a heavy responsibility on the BBC's senior specialists: the economics editor, the science editor, or whoever, to whom non-specialists will turn for advice. It also means that in the constant search for fresh voices and fresh viewpoints, journalists need to balance their craving for novelty with their duty to check the credentials of the author of a new theory about, for example, a cure for cancer.

Too often, the BBC has seemed to confuse 'balance' with 'impartiality'. There is no obligation on the BBC to balance truth with falsehood, nor to include an opposing view every time a contributor suggests that genocide is evil or that rape can never be justified. As the BBC's own guidelines point out, impartiality 'does not require absolute neutrality on every issue or detachment from fundamental democratic principles'. The BBC should never give the impression that it is impartial between good and evil, or between freedom and servitude – but it can sometimes be extremely difficult to steer a proper path.

The BBC as an institution is constantly aware that it is paid for, compulsorily, by people of very different political opinions. It needs to try to satisfy licence-payers who vote UKIP and those who vote for the Green Party. So what do its journalists do if a UKIP candidate makes false claims about, for example, immigration levels, or the cost to the UK of belonging to the European Union? Should the BBC refuse to broadcast them, and risk being accused of censorship, or broadcast them but then also broadcast an immediate rebuttal and risk being accused of partiality?

The issue came to a head during the EU referendum campaign,

when the Remain side complained bitterly that the BBC had failed to challenge sufficiently robustly false claims by Leave campaigners. The BBC's response, as so often when it comes under attack, was to point to explanatory material that ran on its website or on Radio 4, putting rival claims into context and dispassionately examining the available evidence.

But the BBC's vast output can often work to its disadvantage: no viewer or listener can possibly access everything it transmits, which means that complaints usually focus on the most viewed, or most listened to, programmes. It is no good the BBC replying to complaints about skewed coverage on the *Ten O'Clock News* or the *Today* programme by pointing to a much better item on the website or on the Radio 4 statistical analysis programme *More or Less*.

It would have been far better if it had embedded its excellent online Reality Check material in its mainstream broadcast output, even at the cost of generating more complaints from campaigners whose definition of impartiality is coverage that favours their own viewpoint. The problem, as I see it, is that the BBC hates generating complaints – it is, by its nature, a cautious, almost timid, creature, craving love and affection and terrified of causing offence. Its former chairman Michael Grade once told me that the BBC's default posture was a 'pre-emptive cringe', which is totally inappropriate for any self-respecting journalistic organisation.

It needs to be accepted, however, that much of the time, when people demand 'facts', what they are really searching for are judgements with which they agree. I lost count of the number of times during the EU referendum campaign when people said to me: 'I just want the facts about what will happen if we leave the EU,' not realising that there are never 'facts' about potential future consequences of a particular course of action outside the realm of pure science.

And even in science, facts are sometimes less conclusive than many people would like to think. In the 1990s, the media were full of stories about how eating beef from animals suffering from Bovine Spongiform Encephalopathy ('mad cow disease') could risk causing a fatal neurological condition called Creutzfeldt–Jakob disease. How serious was the risk? No one could say for certain, and for a time ministers seemed unsure how seriously they should take the warnings. The scare stories were so prevalent that one government minister, John Gummer, arranged to be photographed trying to feed a beef burger to his four-year-old daughter in an attempt to reassure people that it was still safe to eat beef. (She refused, so he was forced to eat it himself.)

I have a theory about why journalists find it so difficult to evaluate risk accurately. They are hard-wired to try to make their stories as dramatic as they can: they want to be on the front page of the newspaper, or at the top of the news bulletin. So rather than asking a scientist: 'Tell us what you think the risk is…', they would much rather ask: 'Worst case scenario, how serious could this risk be?' The headline then becomes not 'Scientists say eating beef might carry some risk in certain circumstances', but 'Scientists warn hundreds of thousands could die'. Note the word 'could': it is the journalistic equivalent of those Sales signs in shop windows: 'Up to 80 per cent off'. The key words are 'up to'.

After a natural disaster – an earthquake, or flash floods – the first question on a journalist's lips is 'How many dead?' The higher the number, the bigger the story. So if the response is: 'Well, we don't know yet, but it could be in four figures', the headline becomes: 'Thousands feared dead…' And because journalists always want to be first with the news, they will press for answers long before officials are ready to give them.

Why did the plane fall out of the sky? 'It's too early to say' is never good enough. Much better to find someone to say 'We can't rule anything out' and make the headline 'Terrorist bomb fear after plane disaster'.

In my perfect world, every schoolchild would take a compulsory course in journalese. They would learn that in journalese, 'row' means 'difference of opinion'; 'gaffe' means 'honest answer'; and any headline that ends with a question mark should automatically be answered with the word No. They would also learn that the reason headline writers will always go for short, punchy words – 'row', 'crisis', 'killer' – is that they fit across the top of a tabloid-size front page. No one ever called Margaret Thatcher 'Maggie' in real life – they would never have dared – but 'Margaret' is far too long for a front-page headline and 'Thatcher' is not much better. Never underestimate the tyranny of the layout man.

Two of the biggest dangers for journalists are succumbing to the temptation to feed their readers' or listeners' fears, and grasping hungrily at any new angle on a long-running story. Ask a provocative question and no one can accuse you of making stuff up. Search online for a *Daily Mail* random headline generator, and you will soon see where this can lead: 'Has the internet turned property prices gay?', 'Are the Germans giving British people cancer?', 'Have the Poles had sex with taxpayers?', 'Could the unions give the royal family cancer?'

It would be funnier if it was not also so contagious. Journalists feed off each other shamelessly, and what may have started out as a desperate attempt to fill a page on a quiet Tuesday in mid-August can easily end up as a ten-minute discussion on the *Today* programme. I remember a BBC producer once suggesting that we follow up a story in *The Times* about how climate change was enabling British farmers to start growing tropical fruit. I thought I had heard the story before and, when I checked, I discovered that exactly the same story had appeared the previous year, based on the same quotes from the same single farmer. It was not news; it was a press release.

The award-winning investigative reporter Nick Davies of *The Guardian* calls this 'churnalism', the process by which reporters churn out press releases or news agency stories with little or no original work of their own.[151] Real news is expensive to gather and can now often be obtained from non-newspaper providers. The spread of online and social media – and the resulting collapse in advertising revenue for traditional print media – has vastly increased the pressure on traditional news providers to reduce the number of journalists they employ and, at the same time, find something more than just 'facts' to offer to their customers. If news events can be covered in real time, readers have little incentive to spend money on a newspaper a day later that simply tells them what they have already learned from the phone in their pocket. If, on the other hand, it offers a slant on the news that confirms their world view and reassures them that they are not alone in blaming foreigners/Tories/bankers/socialists for all that is wrong with the world, then they might still be prepared to pay for that comfort. Hence the plethora of columnists, commentators and controversialists, who are much cheaper to hire and fire.

When I started writing my post-BBC blog, I soon discovered that the angrier I sounded, the more widely read my blogposts were. People tend not to share with their friends a calmly considered, dispassionate analysis of the latest events in central Asia, but the 'Have you seen this?' messages will flood the digisphere as soon as you launch a furious attack on a politician or public figure. The temptations are obvious: if you want to be noticed in this increasingly raucous multimedia world, you have to shout ever louder. Long gone are the days when the advice to aspiring young journalists was: 'Be angry, but don't shout.'

Tony Blair's former press secretary Alastair Campbell has written of 'a post-factual, post-reason age ... born in the fusion of news and comment in most newspapers as they adapted to TV, developed in the sound and fury of 24/7 TV news, and ventilated by the howling rage of social media'.[157] In the US, where broadcasters are not bound by notions of impartiality, the rabidly right-wing – and often post-factual – Fox News quickly overtook CNN by offering more strident, opinionated coverage that found a ready market among viewers who felt that no one else was reflecting their views. It offers a salutary lesson to those in the UK who argue for less impartiality in British broadcasting.

So where does all this leave the poor old BBC? Is it now an anachronism that needs to be put out of its misery in our brave new digital world? How can the same organisation be responsible for both the triumph of the London Olympics coverage, *Doctor Who*, *Wolf Hall*, *EastEnders*, *Strictly Come Dancing*, *Countryfile* and *The Great British Bake Off* and also the appalling mishandling of the Jimmy Savile sex abuse scandal and what used to be the grotesquely inflated salaries of its top executives? How can it possibly defend levying a compulsory tax on every TV owner, regardless of whether they ever watch a BBC programme?

My answer is simply that it works. For barely forty pence a day, British TV owners are still provided with a uniquely rich mix of output, ranging from Chris Evans, Ken Bruce and Jeremy Vine on Radio 2 to newly commissioned contemporary music on Radio 3 and subtitled Scandinavian police dramas on BBC4. In 2015/16, 96 per cent of UK adults used a BBC service on radio, TV or online each week, and a record 320 million people accessed the BBC's global news services.[153]

By any standards, this makes the BBC one of the most successful institutions in the world. It is also extraordinarily good value for money. Nevertheless, as long as the licence fee is set by government, and after several years of remorseless squeezing, it is difficult to see how the BBC can survive indefinitely in a digital, multimedia age if it is almost entirely dependent on the licence fee for its income. The reality is that it no longer has to compete only with fellow broadcasters like ITV or Channel 4, but also with global digital giants such as Amazon, Apple, Google and Netflix. (Amazon's annual net revenue is more than $100 billion; the BBC's gross revenue is about $6 billion). Far from being a Goliath in the contemporary media world, the BBC is now a minnow.

The conclusion is inescapable: if the BBC is to survive, it needs more money, not less. It needs to be able to invest in new technologies, so that it can deliver content to mobile phones and tablets as smoothly as to TV sets and car radios. It also needs to be able to compete with Amazon and Apple for star names and star formats, as well as for major sports events that generate so much revenue for commercial media organisations. In just one year, it lost *Top Gear* to Amazon, *Bake Off* to Channel 4, and it was Netflix, not the BBC, that bought the drama serial *The Crown*.

Just as newspapers have had to do, I think the BBC will soon have to start charging subscribers for access to premium products. I believe that the licence fee should stay, as a means of funding BBC core output – news and current affairs, light entertainment and some documentaries – but that, over the next decade or so, it will have to be supplemented by additional charges for additional content. I envisage a hybrid funding model that would combine the licence fee with paid-for, add-on packages, much as cable providers like Sky and Virgin Media currently offer different content packages at different prices.

I also think that in developed markets overseas, the BBC should be able to start charging for some of its content. World Service radio output must remain free in poorer countries, but in the US, mainland Europe and parts of Asia, there must surely be substantial revenue opportunities from television viewers who would happily pay to watch David Attenborough wildlife documentaries and endless re-runs of *Mr Bean* and *Fawlty Towers*.

I know from having met many hundreds of BBC World Service devotees in the US over the years that they would happily pay a monthly charge for access to BBC output, over and above what they already pay to support their local public radio station or their cable TV provider. I understand the BBC's fear: that if it starts charging for its content, UK governments will reduce still further the value of the licence fee and argue that the BBC should make up any shortfall by increasing its commercial revenues. It is a justified fear, but I see only one, unpalatable alternative.

The BBC could simply stop doing some of the things that it currently does.

No more local radio, competing head-to-head with local commercial stations.

No more mass-appeal light entertainment shows like *Strictly Come Dancing* or *Bake Off*.

Slash its funding to the arts: no more Proms, shut down Radio 3, sell off its orchestras.

Cut back its online presence to just a slimline news service with links to broadcast output.

It would save many millions of pounds, but it would leave the country incalculably poorer. I cannot believe that an institution that is so widely loved and admired would ever be left to wither away, no matter how revolutionary the changes in the media environment.

Like journalism, the BBC will survive. It will have to change, but it will not die.

❦

'If he grows up to be an asker of questions, he will be, indeed, one of the rare men who may find an answer here and there. Let him be an asker-of-questions.'

My uncle's words, written just days after my birth, still echo in my head. I did grow up to be an asker of questions, but did I find any answers?

Not many, perhaps, but enough to make it worth the effort.

I learned that people the world over are remarkably similar: whether they are destitute villagers in South Sudan, or upwardly mobile city-dwellers in China, or unemployed blue-collar workers in the American rust belt, they want exactly the same things for themselves and their families.

A roof over their head. A job that pays enough to support their family. Access to affordable health care. And an education for their children.

And I learned that most conflicts stem from fear. Fear that your land is about to be taken from you. Fear that you are about to be killed. Fear that you and your family will starve.

When I left the BBC, I tried to draw up a tally of all the changes that I had observed and reported on over the course of more than two decades as a broadcaster. The end of the Cold War, the violent disintegration of Yugoslavia, the Rwandan genocide, the 9/11 attacks, followed by the invasions of Afghanistan and Iraq. The rise of Vladimir Putin, the financial crisis of 2007–08, the quickening process of climate change, the bloody upheavals in much of the Arab world and then the civil wars in Libya, Yemen and Syria. So much death, so much misery.

But there was another side of the picture. The Good Friday Agreement that brought peace to Northern Ireland, the stunning economic advances in China and India, the communications revolution that brought mobile telephones and the internet to hundreds of millions of people. And the health advances: fewer women dying in childbirth than ever before, and fewer children dying before the age of five.

Between 1999 and 2005, thanks to the spread of vaccinations, the number of children who died annually from measles dropped by 60 per cent. The proportion of the world's infants vaccinated against diphtheria, whooping cough and tetanus climbed from less than half to more than 80 per cent between 1985 and 2008.

So, despite all the wars, famines and natural disasters, I concluded that for most of its human inhabitants, the world was a far better place in 2012 than it had been two decades earlier.

These observations are neither particularly profound nor particularly new. I am, after all, a journalist, not a philosopher or a historian. But they are the best I can come up with, and they help me to explain to myself why the world we live in is the way it is. Perhaps they have also helped me to explain it to a few others as well.

EPILOGUE

AT THE END OF *Scoop*, William Boot returns from the war in Ishmaelia to the tranquillity of his country home, where he resumes writing his rural notes for the *Daily Beast*. 'The waggons lumber in the lane under their golden glory of harvested sheaves; maternal rodents pilot their furry brood through the stubble…'

During my forty-plus years as a journalist, I don't think I have ever written about rodents, maternal or otherwise.

It is time I did.

ENDNOTES

1   *The Guardian*, 3 February 2014.
2   http://news.bbc.co.uk/1/hi/world/middle_east/3996733.stm
3   https://audioboom.com/boos/717909-is-fiction-the-process-of-turning-fact-into-truth
4   *Growing Up on The Times* by Louis Heren (Hamish Hamilton, 1978).
5   *The Last Paragraph: The Journalism of David Blundy* (Heinemann, 1990).
6   *The Observer*, 18 May 2003.
7   *The Guardian*, 22 February 2012.
8   https://www.channel4.com/news/my-friend-marie-colvin
9   A. A. Milne, *Winnie-the-Pooh* (Methuen, 1926).
10 *The Observer*, 20 January 1980.
11 Evelyn Waugh, *Scoop* (Chapman & Hall, 1938).
12 *The Observer*, 1 April 1984.
13 https://www.youtube.com/watch?v=YsZqN-uEgQU
14 Observer Foreign News Service, 26 February 1987.
15 *Looking for Democracy*, BBC World Service, September 2005.
16 Archipelago, 53 Cleveland Street, London W1T 4JJ.
17 Susan Lustig, *Born under a Lucky Star*, unpublished memoir.
18 Lustig, ibid.
19 Lustig, op. cit.
20 See Helen Fry, *The M Room: Secret Listeners Who Bugged the Nazis* (Thistle Publishing, 2012), and Sönke Neitzel, *Tapping Hitler's Generals* (Frontline Books, 2013).
21 UPI report, 21 February 1968.
22 Harold Evans, *Good Times, Bad Times* (Weidenfeld & Nicolson, 1983).
23 National Archives, Cabinet document ref. 15/22, 12 September 1970.
24 Quoted in Douglas Stuart, *A Very Sheltered Life* (Collins, 1970).
25 Frederick Forsyth, *The Outsider: My Life in Intrigue* (Bantam Press, 2015).
26 Jonathan Fenby, *The General, Charles de Gaulle and the France He Saved* (Simon & Schuster, 2010).
27 *New York Times*, 30 January 1976.
28 Anne Sebba, *British Journalism Review*, June 2001.
29 Quoted in Eilat Negev and Yehuda Koren, *The First Lady of Fleet Street* (Biteback, 2012)

30 http://www.theguardian.com/media/2002/jun/09/theobserver.pressandpublishing

31 Blond, 1961.

32 *The Independent*, 28 October 2009

33 Donald Harman Akenson, *Conor: A Biography of Conor Cruise O'Brien, Vol. 1, Narrative* (McGill-Queen's University Press, 1994), p. 452.

34 Akenson, ibid., p. 448.

35 Akenson, ibid., p. 441.

36 Akenson, ibid., p. 456.

37 *The Guardian*, 25 March 2010.

38 *The Observer*, 10 July 1977.

39 *Daily Telegraph*, 24 March 2010.

40 Alan King-Hamilton, *And Nothing But the Truth* (Weidenfeld & Nicolson, 1982).

41 Although I was present at the event, I no longer have my notes, so this account is taken mainly from Michael Bloch's invaluable biography of Thorpe, published immediately after his death: *Jeremy Thorpe* (Little, Brown & Co., 2014).

42 Dominic Carman, *No Ordinary Life: A Life of George Carman* (Hodder & Stoughton, 2002).

43 Bloch, op. cit.

44 *The Observer*, 24 June 1979.

45 *New Statesman*, 27 July 1979.

46 *The Observer*, 23 August 1981.

47 *The Observer*, 22 April 1979.

48 *The Guardian*, 19 April 2013.

49 *The Guardian*, 20 September 2005.

50 Charles Moore, *Margaret Thatcher, The Authorised Biography: Volume 2* (Allen Lane, 2015), p. 290.

51 *The Observer*, 1 April 1984.

52 Email to author.

53 Nick Davies, *Hack Attack* (Chatto & Windus, 2014).

54 Tim Pat Coogan, *The IRA* (Harper Collins, revised, 1994).

55 *The Observer*, 2 September 1979.

56 *The Observer*, 20 March 1988.

57 *Irish Times*, 23 March 1988.

58 *The Observer*, 22 October 1989. The convictions of the Birmingham Six were finally quashed in March 1991. All six were freed and received compensation payments of up to £1.2 million for wrongful imprisonment.

59 *The Observer*, 15 April 1984.

60 *The Observer*, 17 June 1984.

61 *The Observer*, 20 February 1983.

62 Bill Graham, *Break-In* (Bodley Head, 1987).

63 *The Observer*, 17 July 1988.

64 Patrick Bishop and John Witherow, *The Winter War: The Falklands* (Quartet Books, 1982).

65 *The Times*, 26 February 1981.

66 Tom Bower, *Tiny Rowland: A Rebel Tycoon* (Heinemann, 1993).

67 Bower, ibid.

68 http://www.webofstories.com/play/anthony.howard/16

69 *Daily Telegraph*, 20 December 2010.

70 *The Guardian*, 3 July 1989.

71 Andrew Marr, *My Trade: A Short History of Journalism* (Macmillan, 2004).

72 *The Guardian*, 3 July 1989.

73 *The Observer*, 3 February 1985.

74 Observer Foreign News Service, 7 February 1985.

75 *The Observer*, 24 February 1985.

76 *The Spectator*, 27 June 1987.

77 Waugh, op. cit., p. 43.

78 *The Observer*, 26 May 1985.

79 *The Observer*, 30 June 1985.

80 *The Observer*, 23 June 1985.

81 *The Observer*, 5 January 1986.

82 Observer Foreign News Service, 7 October 1986.

83 *The Observer*, 31 May 1987.

84 *The Observer*, 2 June 1985.

85 Howard M. Sachar, *A History of Israel* (Knopf, 1976).

86 Figures from the United Nations Relief and Works Agency for Palestine Refugees (UNRWA).

87 http://news.bbc.co.uk/1/hi/world/middle_east/969442.stm

88 http://news.bbc.co.uk/1/hi/world/middle_east/3210533.stm

89 http://www.bbc.co.uk/blogs/worldtonight/2009/01/gaza_points_of_view.html

90 http://blogs.timesofisrael.com/speak-truth-to-power/

91 Pew Research Center, *Israel's religiously divided society*, March 2016.

92 *The Guardian*, 24 October 2000.

93 http://www.nytimes.com/learning/general/onthisday/bday/0503.html

94 Quoted in Roger Hardy, *The Poisoned Well* (Hurst, 2016).

95 http://www.jewishvirtuallibrary.org/jsource/History/Montagumemo.html

96 Mandla *v* Dowell-Lee.

97 http://www.cps.gov.uk/legal/p_to_r/racist_and_religious_crime/#a01

98 *Daily Telegraph*, 25 June 2009. The ruling was later upheld by the Supreme Court.

99 In 2008, Judah Passow called his book of photographs from Israel and Palestine *Shattered Dreams* (Halban, 2008).

100 http://www.realclearworld.stfi.re/blog/2016/04/will_israel_reach_age_100_111810.html?sf=rvvayb

101 http://www.jewishvirtuallibrary.org/jsource/Peace/settlements.html

102 http://fathomjournal.org/two-state-solution-2-0-new-israeli-thinking-on-the-israeli-palestinian-conflict/

103 David Hendy, *Life on Air: A History of Radio 4* (OUP, 2007).

104 *The Listener*, 29 June 1989.

105 *The Spectator*, 30 August 2006.

106 *The Guardian*, 13 April 1998.

107 *The Independent*, 26 September 1995.

108 *Sunday Times*, 3 October 2010.

109 Lecture given at Green College, Oxford University, 30 January 2002.

110 *British Journalism Review*, Vol. 2, No. 3, Spring 1991.

111 Hendy, op. cit., p. 348.

112 William Shakespeare, *As You Like It*.

113 *A Time to Dance* by Julian Simpson, BBC Radio 4, first broadcast 10 October 2011.

114 http://news.bbc.co.uk/1/hi/talking_point/2932072.stm

115 http://www.bbc.co.uk/programmes/p03bh4zn

116 http://news.bbc.co.uk/1/hi/talking_point/2512151.stm#1

117 *Hard Choices Ahead: The Chatham House–YouGov Survey 2012*, Chatham House, July 2012.

118 Transcript taken from Hutton Inquiry Report (HM Stationery Office), 2004, p. 12.

119 *The Guardian*, 20 December 2012.

120 http://www.gunviolencearchive.org/past-tolls

121 *The Guardian*, 3 October 2002.

122 W. F. Deedes, *At War with Waugh* (Macmillan, 2003).

123 Broadcast on 5 December 1989.

124 www.wanderingscribes.com

125 Anita Lasker-Wallfisch, *Inherit the Truth* (Giles de la Mare, 1996).

126 https://www.youtube.com/channel/UCF4ktupD-WtuY8f7b-rdqkQ

127 American Press Institute, 'What does a journalist do?'.

128 Ofcom, 'News consumption in the UK – 2015 report'.

129 http://www.niemanlab.org/2016/04/newsonomics-with-new-roadblocks-for-digital-news-sites-what-happens-next/

130 http://www.bbc.co.uk/news/world-latin-america-13957096

131 Reuters Institute Digital News Report 2016, pub. by Reuters Institute for the Study of Journalism.

132 http://www.cjr.org/analysis/facebook_and_media.php

133 *The Guardian*, 6 April 2016.

134 *The Economist*, 16 May 2009.

135 *The Spectator*, 12 December 2015.

136 See Roger Harrabin, *British Journalism Review*, Vol. 9, No. 3, September 1998.

137 Claud Cockburn, *In Time of Trouble* (Rupert Hart-Davis, 1957).

138 *The Guardian*, 4 August 2016.

139 Gary Younge, James Cameron Memorial Lecture, City University, London, 22 February 2016.

140 Ronald Steel, *Walter Lippmann and the American Century* (Little, Brown & Co., 1980).

141 http://nieman.harvard.edu/awards/louis-lyons-award/yang-jish-eng-speech-transcript/

142 http://www.sub-scribe.co.uk/2016/06/regulation-regulation-regulation.html
143 Loughborough University Centre for Research in Communication and Culture, https://blog.lboro.ac.uk/crcc/eu-referendum/sun-no-longer-hedging-bets-brexit/
144 *The Guardian*, 24 June 2016.
145 *New York Times Magazine*, 17 October 2004.
146 *The Guardian*, 29 June 2016.
147 Public Opinion in the European Union (European Commission, December 2015).
148 Public perceptions of the impartiality and trustworthiness of the BBC (BBC, June 2015).
149 http://www.bbc.co.uk/editorialguidelines/guidelines/impartiality
150 'Bending over backwards: the BBC and the Brexit campaign', www.referendumanalysis.eu
151 Nick Davies, *Flat Earth News* (Chatto & Windus, 2008).
152 http://www.alastaircampbell.org/blog/2016/07/06/many-mistakes-yes-but-no-lies-no-deceit-no-secret-deals-no-sexing-up-and-ultimately-a-matter-of-leadership-and-judgement/
153 BBC Annual Report 2015/16.

INDEX